ONE HEALTH

Zoonotic diseases – pathogens transmitted from animals to people – offer particularly challenging problems for global health institutions and actors, given the complex social-ecological dynamics at play. New forms of risk caused by unprecedented global connectivity and rapid social and environmental change demand new approaches. 'One Health' highlights the need for collaboration across sectors and disciplines to tackle zoonotic diseases. However, there has been little exploration of how social, political and economic contexts influence efforts to 'do' One Health.

This book fills this gap by offering a much needed political economy analysis of zoonosis research and policy. Through ethnographic, qualitative and quantitative data, the book draws together a diverse number of case studies. These include chapters exploring global narratives about One Health operationalization and prevailing institutional bottlenecks; the evolution of research networks over time; and the histories and politics behind conflicting disease control approaches. The themes from these chapters are further contextualized and expanded upon through country-specific case studies – from Kenya, Zambia, Nigeria, Ghana and Sierra Leone – exploring the translation of One Health research and policy into the African context.

This book is a valuable resource for academic researchers, students and policy practitioners in the areas of global health, agriculture and development.

Kevin Bardosh is a Research Fellow at the Division of Infection and Pathway Medicine, University of Edinburgh, UK.

PATHWAYS TO SUSTAINABILITY SERIES

This book series addresses core challenges around linking science and technology and environmental sustainability with poverty reduction and social justice. It is based on the work of the Social, Technological and Environmental Pathways to Sustainability (STEPS) Centre, a major investment of the UK Economic and Social Research Council (ESRC). The STEPS Centre brings together researchers at the Institute of Development Studies (IDS) and SPRU (Science and Technology Policy Research) at the University of Sussex with a set of partner institutions in Africa, Asia and Latin America.

Series Editors:
Ian Scoones and Andy Stirling
STEPS Centre at the University of Sussex

Editorial Advisory Board:
Steve Bass, Wiebe E. Bijker, Victor Galaz, Wenzel Geissler, Katherine Home-wood, Sheila Jasanoff, Melissa Leach, Colin McInnes, Suman Sahai, Andrew Scott

Titles in this series include:
Dynamic Sustainabilities
Technology, environment, social justice
Melissa Leach, Ian Scoones and Andy Stirling

Avian Influenza
Science, policy and politics
Edited by Ian Scoones

Rice Biofortification
Lessons for global science and development
Sally Brooks

'In principle, One Health champions an ecological agenda that counterbalances a top heavy and well-funded biosecurity agenda driven by fear. One Health is directed toward gaining the trust of populations whose livelihood depends on the health of their animals, creating partnerships, and winning the peace as distinct from preparing for wars against (re)emerging diseases. This book is timely and evocative. The authors move beyond One Health rhetoric and call for a critical and realistic assessment of what One Health can become given the complex world of biopolitics, special interest groups, funding flows, professional hierarchies, power relations and the politics of governance.'

Mark Nichter, *University of Arizona, USA*

'This book makes a significant contribution to the One Health movement by showing the added value of the social sciences in advancing closer cooperation between human and animal health in Africa. It nicely shows the need to understand both zoonoses and health as an outcome of complex social-ecological systems, and the importance of political analysis for lasting solutions.'

Jakob Zinsstag, *Human and Animal Health Research Unit, Swiss TPH, Switzerland*

'In this insightful critique, Bardosh and colleagues show how politics, economics, and rhetoric intersect in the 'One Health' movement. They argue powerfully that socio-political forces have shaped research and policy on zoonoses, and that acknowledging this reality will inspire more effective, respectful, and lasting solutions in Africa and beyond.'

Tony L. Goldberg, *University of Wisconsin-Madison, USA*

'In a captivating narrative, Bardosh and others broaden the horizon of One Health by exploring the political economy of emerging and endemic zoonotic disease research and policy development, and by bridging bio- and social science realms. A must-read for all present and future One Health practitioners!'

Katinka de Balogh, *Food and Agriculture Organization of the United Nations, Italy*

'This book on One Health examines how power and politics are interwoven into science and policy. It reveals how One Health – if grounded in an understanding of the complex social relationships that pervade our world – can build resilient and effective systems that sustain healthier people, animals, and ecologies into the future. The case studies give practical advice on how to break down institutional and disciplinary silos in building a more resilient global society. It is social and political analysis at its best!'

Paul Gibbs, *University of Florida, USA*

'Policy direction is at the heart of many disease problems in Africa. This book provides a thorough and honest analysis of the issues in using a One Health approach to harmonize different policy direction in solving health problems. It helps bridge the gap between biomedical and social scientists, and provides conceptual light on how to advance better control or eradication program implementation.'

Charles Waiswa, *Makerere University, Uganda*

'Alongside compelling case studies, this book provides conceptual and practical evidence on the need to understand the interplay between political, social and environmental determinants for zoonotic disease. As the authors make clear, doing so can help us overcome the challenges of effective research and policy implementation, while placing health equity, sustainability and the needs of the poor at the heart of global health.'

Johannes Sommerfeld, *Special Programme for Research and Training in Tropical Diseases (TDR), Switzerland*

ONE HEALTH

Science, politics and zoonotic disease in Africa

Edited by Kevin Bardosh

LONDON AND NEW YORK

from Routledge

First published 2016
by Routledge
2 Park Square, Milton Park, Abingdon, Oxon OX14 4RN

and by Routledge
711 Third Avenue, New York, NY 10017

Routledge is an imprint of the Taylor & Francis Group, an informa business

British Library Cataloguing-in-Publication Data
A catalogue record for this book is available from the British Library

Library of Congress Cataloging-in-Publication Data
A catalog record for this book has been requested

ISBN: 978-1-138-96148-7 (hbk)
ISBN: 978-1-138-96149-4 (pbk)
ISBN: 978-1-315-65974-9 (ebk)

Typeset in Bembo
by Wearset Ltd, Boldon, Tyne and Wear

CONTENTS

FIGURES

TABLES

CONTRIBUTORS

Editor biography

Kevin Bardosh (PhD, African Studies) is an interdisciplinary social scientist with a background in development studies, anthropology and public health. He has acted as an academic researcher and consultant on a number of large, collaborative zoonotic disease research and control projects in Africa and Asia. He is currently a Research Fellow at the Division of Infection and Pathway Medicine, University of Edinburgh, as well as the Emerging Pathogens Institute, University of Florida. He has published in key public health and social science journals.

Author biographies

Neil Anderson is a committed veterinarian. He obtained a PhD in wildlife epidemiology from the Centre for Tropical Veterinary Medicine, University of Edinburgh, in 2009 for his thesis on the ecology of trypanosomiasis in wildlife in the Luangwa valley, Zambia. His research interests centre on the spatial ecology of wildlife disease, with a particular focus on trypanosomiasis. He is employed as a lecturer on the Conservation Medicine and One Health programmes at the University of Edinburgh and as a postdoctoral scientist on the ESPA-funded Dynamic Drivers of Disease in Africa Consortium.

Marie Ducrotoy is a trained veterinarian with a PhD in epidemiology. She has worked on a range of zoonotic diseases as part of the Integrated Control of Neglected Zoonoses in Africa project, including with nomadic pastoralists in Nigeria and Morocco. She is currently pursuing research on brucellosis as a postdoctoral fellow at the University of Edinburgh.

Audrey Gadzekpo, PhD, is an associate professor at the School of Communication Studies, University of Ghana. She has more than 20 years' experience in teaching, research and advocacy on media, gender and governance, and more than 25 years' practical experience as a journalist. She earned her BA from the University of Ghana, MA from Brigham Young University, USA and PhD from the University of Birmingham, UK. In 2005 she was a visiting scholar at the Program of African Studies, Northwestern University and in 2012 a Guest Researcher at the Nordic Africa Institute. She has published extensively on the media.

Victor Galaz is an associate professor and senior lecturer in political science at the Stockholm Resilience Centre (Sweden). He is one of the researchers in the Dynamic Drivers of Disease in Africa Consortium, and author of *Global Environmental Governance, Technology and Politics: The Anthropocene Gap* (2014).

Catherine Grant is a research officer for the Dynamic Drivers of Disease in Africa Consortium, based at the Institute of Development Studies. Her current research is mainly on zoonotic diseases and more generally health and education issues. Before this, she conducted research for, and had management roles in, several international development organizations and universities. She also managed an NHS research department and monitored clinical trials. Catherine has worked in Sierra Leone, Ghana, Ethiopia, Kenya, Mexico, Zambia, Côte D'Ivoire and South Africa.

Melissa Leach is a social anthropologist and director of the Institute of Development Studies, University of Sussex. She founded and directed the ESRC STEPS Centre (2006–2014) and leads the ESPA-funded Dynamic Drivers of Disease in Africa Consortium. She has researched and published extensively on social and political dimensions of environment, health and their interlinkages in Africa, including the books *Vaccine Anxieties* (Routledge, 2007) and *Epidemics: Science, Governance and Social Justice* (Earthscan, 2010). In 2014–2015 she worked closely at the science-policy interface of the Ebola crisis, including co-founding the Ebola Response Anthropology Platform (www.ebola-anthropology.net).

Hayley MacGregor trained as a medical doctor before completing a PhD in social anthropology. She is a research fellow at the Institute of Development Studies where, among other work, she is engaged in interdisciplinary research on disease–environment interactions in the context of zoonotic disease emergence.

Noreen Machila is a veterinarian with experience working with livestock and their rural owners in Africa. She obtained a PhD in animal healthcare and extension from the Centre for Tropical Veterinary Medicine, University of Edinburgh, in 2005 for her thesis on primary animal healthcare and communication for livestock keepers in western and coastal Kenya. Her research interests centre on the social and socio-economical impact of animal diseases and control, particularly focusing on trypanosomiasis. Her publications include studies on the perceptions of livestock owners of trypanosomiasis and its control. She is employed as a part-time lecturer of veterinary extension at the University of Zambia.

Erik Millstone is a professor of science policy at the University of Sussex. Since 1974 he has been researching the causes, consequences and regulation of technological change in the agricultural, food and chemical industries. His research focus has extended over food additives, pesticides and veterinary medicines, as well as BSE, GM foods and obesity. Since 1988 he has been researching the role of scientific experts, evidence and advice in public policy-making. Much of his current research forms part of the STEPs (or Social and Technological Pathways to Sustainability) programme. Relevant publications include: *BSE: Risk, Science and Governance* (with P. van Zwanenberg, 2005), *The Atlas of Food: Who Eats What, Where and Why* (with T. Lang, 2008) and 'Science, risk and governance: Radical rhetorics and the realities of reform', *Research Policy* (2009).

Hannington Odame is a founding member and the executive director of Kenya-based Centre for African Bio-Entrepreneurship (CABE), where he manages initiatives on capacity-building of smallholder farmers and youth agro-entrepreneurs and facilitates their linkages to markets and policy on tree, crop and livestock value chains. He is also part-time regional coordinator of the Future Agricultures Consortium, East African Hub, and its co-convener of Science, Technology and Innovation (STI) theme. Hannington has undertaken policy research, capacity building and evaluation assignments for international and local agencies on innovation systems of agriculture and livestock sub-systems.

Anna Okello is a trained veterinarian with a PhD in Health Policy from the University of Edinburgh. She has ten years' experience in international development, more recently applying integrated 'One Health' approaches to the control of neglected tropical and zoonotic diseases in Africa and Asia. She has just finished managing an ACIAR pig zoonoses project in Lao PDR.

Oscar Okumu is a veterinary doctor and works for the Centre for African Bio-entrepreneurship as a veterinary project officer and research associate. He manages livestock projects, provides capacity-building services in livestock value chains, and is an advisor on animal health and production problems.

Ian Scoones is a professorial fellow at the Institute of Development Studies, and the director of the ESRC STEPS Centre at Sussex. He is an agricultural ecologist by original training, and works on the interface between science and environmental, health and agricultural policy, mostly in Africa. His recent books include: *Sustainable Livelihoods and Rural Development*, *Carbon Conflicts and Forest Landscapes in Africa* and *The Politics of Green Transformations*.

Christian Stein is an independent consultant and research associate at the Stock-holm Environment Institute (SEI) at the University of York. His interdisciplinary research explores the role social networks play for the governance of natural resources and how to harness such understanding to address sustainability chal-lenges. He is applying network research approaches in diverse areas including water resources management, agriculture systems and rural development. He has con-tributed to various research for development projects working mainly in sub-Saharan Africa in the last six years. He lives and works in Berlin, Germany.

Sophie Valeix is a trained veterinarian and a doctoral researcher with the STEPS Centre at the Institute of Development Studies, UK. She has two Master degrees in Epidemiology and in Science and Technology Policy. She has worked on socio-anthropological dimensions to zoonotic diseases in Sri-Lanka, Thailand, France and more recently Ghana.

Linda Waldman is a research fellow in the Health and Nutrition Cluster at the Institute of Development Studies, University of Sussex. As a social anthropologist, her research has focused on diverse dimensions of poverty, and the related issues of gender, civil society, and identity. Her recent research focuses on asbestos-related diseases; peri-urban ecosystems and sustainability; zoonotic disease; and ICTs and health systems.

Susan Welburn is director of the Global Health Academy and professor of medical and veterinary molecular epidemiology at the Centre for Infectious Diseases (CID), University of Edinburgh. She is also leader of the sleeping sickness research group. Her research concentrates on the design and use of molecular diagnostic tools for the study and management of sleeping sickness and animal trypanosomiasis, as well as other neglected zoonotic diseases.

Annie Wilkinson is a health systems researcher at the Institute of Development Studies. She has a background in anthropology but her work is interdisciplinary, specializing in: zoonotic disease, especially viral haemorrhagic fevers; strategies for epidemic preparedness and control; health system change in complex, plural set-tings; and science, technology and innovation for global health, with a focus on diagnostics. In 2014–2015 she was involved in setting up the Ebola Response Anthropology Platform (www.ebola-anthropology.net) and worked at the science–policy interface of the Ebola epidemic both in the UK and Sierra Leone.

ACKNOWLEDGEMENTS

This book is largely the product of research and reflection from the Dynamic Drivers of Disease in Africa consortium (DDDAC), a three-and-a-half year project bringing together natural and social scientists to understand the relationships between ecosystems, zoonoses, health and wellbeing in Africa (http://steps-centre. org/project/drivers_of_disease). DDDAC was funded by the Ecosystem Services for Poverty Alleviation (ESPA) programme, and supported by the United Kingdom's Department for International Development (DFID), the Natural Environment Research Council (NERC) and the Economic and Social Research Council (ESRC). Many of the chapters in this book originally appeared as working papers under the STEPS Centre (Social, Technological and Environmental Pathways to Sustainability), an interdisciplinary global research and policy engagement hub that unites development with science and technologies studies, at the Institute of Development Studies, University of Sussex. Research for Chapter 10 was supported by the Integrated Control of Neglected Zoonoses (ICONZ) in Africa project, funded by the EU's Seventh Framework programme and coordinated by the University of Edinburgh (www.iconzafrica.org).

I would like to thank Ian Scoones and Melissa Leach at the Institute of Development Studies for encouraging me to take on the role of editor for this volume. Ian provided editorial comments on early drafts of the introduction and conclusion, for which I am very grateful. Sue Welburn, coordinator of the ICONZ project at the University of Edinburgh, also provided important support and encouragement for this book project. Lastly, I would like to thank Naomi Vernon at the Institute of Development Studies for help with the copy-editing of the final manuscript and Margaret Farrelly at Routledge-Earthscan.

ABBREVIATIONS

AAT	animal African trypanosomiasis
APEIR	Asia Partnership on Emerging Infectious Diseases Research
AU	African Union
AVMA	American Veterinary Medicine Association
BMGF	Bill & Melinda Gates Foundation
BSE	bovine spongiform encephalopathy
BSL-4	BioSafety Level 4
BTB	bovine tuberculosis
CAHW	community animal health worker
CBEP	Cooperative Biological Engagement Program
CBS	community-based surveillance
CCCs	Community Care Centres
CDC	(US) Centers for Disease Control and Prevention
CGIAR	Consultative Group on International Agricultural Research
COPs	Communities of Practice
CSIRO	Commonwealth Scientific and Industrial Research Organisation
DALY	disability-adjusted-life-year
DERC	District Ebola Response Commands
DFID	Department for International Development
DOD	(US) Department of Defense
DoD GEIS	(US) Department of Defense Global Emerging Infections Surveillance and Response System
DTRA	(US) Defense Threat Reduction Agency
DVO	district veterinary officer
DVS	Department of Veterinary Services
EIAs	environmental impact assessments
ELISAs	enzyme linked immunosorbent assays

ESHIA	environmental, social, and health impact assessment
ETUs	Ebola Treatment Centers
EU	European Union
FAO	Food and Agriculture Organization of the United Nations
GFATM	Global Fund to Fight AIDS, Tuberculosis and Malaria
GHI	global health initiative
GLEWS	Global Early Warning System
GMA	game management area
GNA	Ghana News Agency
GOARN	Global Outbreak and Response Network
HAT	human African trypanosomiasis
HICs	high-income countries
HIV/AIDs	human immunodeficiency virus infection/acquired immune deficiency syndrome
HPAI	highly pathogenic avian influenza
IAEA	International Atomic Energy Authority
ICDDR, B	International Centre for Diarrhoeal Disease Research, Bangladesh
ICIPE	International Centre on Insect Physiology and Ecology
ICONZ	Integrated Control of Neglected Zoonoses
IDRC	International Development Research Center
IDSR	Integrated Disease Surveillance and Response
IFRI	Français des relations internationals
IHRs	International Health Regulations
ILCA	International Livestock Centre for Africa
ILRAD	International Laboratory for Research on Animal Diseases
ILRI	International Livestock Research Institute
IMF	International Monetary Fund
IPC	infection and prevention control
IUCN	International Union for Conservation of Nature
KAP	'knowledge', 'attitude' and 'practice' (surveys)
KCCR	Kumasi Centre for Collaborative Research in Tropical Research
KEMRI	Kenya Medical Research Institute
KGH	Kenema Government Hospital
KGR	Kachia Grazing Reserve
LASV	Lassa virus
LICs	low-income countries
LSHTM	London School of Hygiene and Tropical Medicine
MERS	Middle East respiratory syndrome
MICs	middle-income countries
MLD	(Kenya) Ministry of Livestock Development
MMD	Movement for Multiparty Democracy
MOHS	Ministry of Health and Sanitation
MoPH	Ministry of Public Health
MRU-LFN	Mano River Union Lassa Fever Network

MSF	Medecins Sans Frontieres
NADMO	National Disaster Management Organisation
NAMRU	United States Naval Medical Research Unit
NDVI	Normalized Difference Vegetation Index
NGO	non-governmental organization
NIH	(US) National Institute of Health
NTDs	neglected tropical diseases
NYD	Not Yet Diagnosed
NZDs	neglected zoonotic diseases
OFDA	Office of United States Foreign Disaster Assistance
OIE	World Organisation for Animal Health
PATTEC	Pan African Tsetse and Trypanosomiasis Eradication Campaign
PCR	polymerase chain reaction
PHEIC	Public Health Emergency of International Concern
PPP	public–private partnership
RBT	Rose Bengal Test
RCT	randomized control trial
RNA	ribonucleic acid
RTTCP	Regional Tsetse and Trypanosomiasis Control Programme
RVC	Royal Veterinary College
RVF	Rift Valley fever
RVF CP	*RVF Contingency Plan*
SARS	Severe Acute Respiratory Syndrome
SIT	Sterile Insect Technique
SLIEPA	Sierra Leone Investment and Export Promotion Agency
SNA	social network analysis
TB	tuberculosis
UN	United Nations
UNMEER	United Nations Mission for Ebola Emergency Response
UNSIC	UN System Influenza Coordination Office
USAID	United States Agency for International Development
VHF	viral haemorrhagic fever
VHFC	Viral Haemorrhagic Fever Consortium
VSDF	Veterinary Services Development Fund
WAHID	World Animal Health Information Database
WCS	World Conservation Society
WHO	World Health Organization
ZDU	Zoonotic Disease Unit
ZELS	Zoonoses and Emerging Livestock Systems

1

UNPACKING THE POLITICS OF ZOONOSIS RESEARCH AND POLICY

Kevin Bardosh

Prologue: a tale of two zoonotic disease outbreaks

On 20 August 2014, one of West Africa's largest slums awoke to a cordon sanitaire. Bordering the Atlantic Ocean, West Point remains a visible symbol of Liberia's slow post-war recovery: dirty, crowded and lacking government services. Tens-of-thousands of residents were effectively cut off from greater Monrovia, with limited food and other supplies. Days before, residents had driven out dozens of Ebola patients from a local isolation centre, taking blood-stained mattresses and other material with them, which likely spread the virus and precipitated the quarantine.[1] During the next ten days, the maxim 'Ebola is not real' was a common sentiment in West Point, and indeed throughout West Africa, as rumours continued to circulate about the 'true origins' of the outbreak being a government or foreign conspiracy.[2]

With previous outbreaks confined to remote villages in Central and East Africa, Ebola had never been found in West Africa before. Being a zoonotic disease, the virus is thought to originate in bats from where it spreads to primates and other animals; albeit many aspects of the science remains poorly understood (Saéz *et al.*, 2015). Before the West African outbreak, the virus had actually killed many more chimpanzees and gorillas than people; Ebola is a major conservation threat to dwindling numbers of primates, together with poaching and habitat loss (Ryan and Walsh, 2011).

But for a time, media coverage of the epidemic in Guinea, Sierra Leone and Liberia – which has killed over 11,000 people – made it seem as though it was going to encircle the globe, and kill millions. In the USA and Europe, fears invariably turned to the 'what-ifs' of viral mutation and a more virulent, even airborne, viral hybrid quickly spreading through the modern aviation network (Gire *et al.*, 2014). Sales of protective infection gear spiked and 'Ebola for dummies' guides proliferated. When West Point was quarantined, more than 500 cases had been reported in Liberia alone, and the idea that the killer virus was going to establish itself in an urban slum conjured up images of 'state failure' to the media and international community.

This concern drove President Ellen Johnson Sirleaf to order the military, police and coastguard to surround West Point. But such a draconian measure, done in the middle of the night and without adequate supplies, was sure to elicit resistance from an already suspicious population. As the privileged family of a local politician was escorted out by armed guards, local residents had had enough, became angry and rioted.[3] Like the civil war before, the sense was of a government that was not willing, or able, to look after the interests of its people. Stones were pelted at security forces and residents tried to make an escape. Soldiers responded by beating people and firing live rounds into the crowd, killing a teenager.[4] By the time the lock-down was called off, criticism of the government had reached new heights, and Ebola continued to spread throughout Monrovia. A belated international response then hit the ground, but it took nearly a year for Liberia to be declared Ebola-free.

Now fast-forward to 10 June 2015, and a different bat-associated zoonotic disease, and another quarantined town, are in the international headlines. But this time it is in South Korea, one of the world's most technologically developed nations. The small hamlet of Jangdeok, about 150 miles from Seoul, is being quarantined after a single case of Middle East Respiratory Syndrome (MERS) was detected.[5] With 122 confirmed cases and ten deaths, South Korea was in the midst of an unprecedented MERS outbreak second in size only to Saudi Arabia, where the virus was originally discovered in 2012.[6]

MERS is a corona virus thought to originate in Egyptian tomb bats, and is transmitted to people through physical contact with dromedary camels and the consumption of raw camel milk. In the family of Severe Acute Respiratory Syndrome (SARS) that sparked a global outbreak in 2003, as well as the common cold, MERS also continues to spark pandemic fear, although it is far less deadly than Ebola (Azhar et al., 2014). Most debate is centred on the possibility of sustained human-to-human transmission during the Hajj – the mass gathering of two million Muslim pilgrims in Mecca each year. Repeated health messages to camel owners and keepers to wear protective gear and avoid drinking milk have often gone unheeded.[7] The scope of animal surveillance has also been lacking – due to, as a World Health Organization (WHO) team leader stated, 'cultural barriers' in Saudi Arabia.[8] And MERS has since been found in Nigerian, Tunisian and Ethiopian camels, raising new scientific questions and global concerns (Reusken et al., 2014).

As the MERS caseload grew in South Korea, commentators emphasized how the virus had 'traumatized the country' and the media went into a frenzy.[9] But compared to Ebola in Liberia, epidemic response went very differently in Jangdeok and South Korea as a whole. MERS had not been on the surveillance radar and had clearly embarrassed the government when the initial 'index case' (who travelled from the Arabian Peninsula) visited four major hospitals in nine days, where they spread the virus; but the response effort quickly picked up after initial public criticism. In a matter of days, President Park Geun-hye cancelled a trip to Washington. Antiseptic solution started to be sprayed in the Seoul subway. Hospitals established triage and isolation units. Medical teams monitored thousands of potential contacts. And although inconvenienced (perhaps unnecessarily, as some commentators emphasized), the village of Jangdeok had a cadre of health officials in antiviral protection suits taking temperatures, providing food and making special provisions for the elderly. Unlike in Liberia, the outbreak was over in a matter of weeks.

Introduction

Outbreaks of zoonotic disease, like Ebola in Liberia and MERS in South Korea, are biological, social and political events. They reveal some very complicated and multi-layered interactions between science and politics and our relationship with other species and the environment. That invisible ribonucleic acid (RNA) strains originating in fruit bats and dromedary camels have the capacity to disrupt our established social, economic and political *status quo* attest to our deep interconnectedness to nature, and yet how unknown and unpredictable much of it remains to us. Such diseases provoke panic and anxiety primarily because their origins and behaviour appear so mysterious and alien. The dramatic consequences of past historic pandemics remain very much alive in our collective memory and concerns. These tend to provoke doomsday scenarios; as Laurie Garrett (1994, p620) said in her book *The Coming Plague*: '[Pathogens] are our predators and they will be victorious if we, *Homo sapiens*, do not learn how to live in a rational global village that affords the microbes few opportunities.'

The stark contrast between the quarantines in West Point and Jangdeok, and the wider epidemic response systems, reveal a very visible maxim: infectious disease is intimately connected with wider political economies (Dry and Leach, 2010; Scoones, 2010). In this sense, they act as metaphors for social and ecological pathologies (Craddock and Hinchliffe, 2015; Singer, 2015). That many millions of people die each year from infectious diseases that are, for the most part, completely preventable – like HIV/AIDS, malaria, tuberculosis and various neglected tropical diseases and diarrheal illnesses – reminds us of just how divided our 'global village' remains.[10] Epidemics reveal hidden social orders where science and politics become hard to separate, and the underlying resilience of social and political systems, as much as biology and disease ecology, come to define the limits and characteristics of contagion (Herring and Swedlund, 2010; Bogich et al., 2012). In this sense, globalization opens up a new Pandora's box, where inequalities and inequities have come to increase our collective sense of disease risk (Farmer, 2004a). Microbes are, in effect, critics of our modernity (Barrett and Armelagos, 2013).

Among the variety of microorganisms that can make us sick and kill us, zoonotic pathogens have a particular tendency to cut across different divides, to fascinate and to generate concern. They offer a unique vantage point to inspect relationships between species, the environment and wider political, economic and socio-cultural forces (Nading, 2013). Historical outbreaks of the Black Plague, the influenza pandemic of 1918/1919 and the ongoing HIV/AIDS pandemic have shown just how significant zoonotic diseases can be. Such examples serve as rhetorical devices to justify the need and importance of investing in biosecurity, strengthening global detection, surveillance and response systems (IOM and NRC, 2009; Elbe, 2010a). But they also reveal the need to engage wider issues of poverty, environmental degradation and economic development in the prevention and control of zoonotic infections, both endemic and emerging (Chivian and Bernstein, 2008; Maudlin *et al.*, 2009; Dakubo, 2010; FAO, 2013a).

As complex problems, zoonotic diseases have led to increased recognition of a need to integrate perspectives and actions from human, animal and ecosystem health (Zinsstag *et al.*, 2015a). This has become known as a 'One Health' approach, a concept that was catalysed into the global policy limelight with the avian influenza crisis of the 2000s (Scoones, 2010). One Health has quickly moved from a concept to a global movement, with innumerable publications, projects, initiatives and platforms proliferating across the globe (Gibbs, 2014; Vandersmissen and Welburn, 2014). At its core, One Health stresses the need to work across disciplinary divides through a cross-sectoral, collaborative and integrated approach to zoonotic diseases, as well as other health problems that cut across the human–animal–ecosystem interface. In this sense, One Health is related to a number of parallel movements in public health that promote trans-disciplinarity and systems thinking, such as the EcoHealth movement (Zinsstag, 2012) or the more recent field of 'planetary health' (Whitmee *et al.*, 2015). Although the One Health concept is certainly timely and important, many scholars and practitioners have increasingly highlighted the real-world challenges in moving from the rhetoric to concrete policies, research and disease control programmes in different contexts (Scoones, 2010; FAO, 2013b; Bardosh *et al.*, 2014a; Craddock and Hinchliffe, 2015).

This book offers a fresh perspective on these debates by exploring the political economy of zoonosis research and policy. It focuses on Africa, where zoonotic diseases continue to have a disproportionate effect on human wellbeing and health (Grace *et al.*, 2012a), but where the institutional and organizational capacities, structures and policies to address them – across the fields of conservation, public health, agricultural development and veterinary sciences – remain, in many cases, fragmentary and inadequate, intertwined in complex ways with wider questions about governance and poverty alleviation (Leonard, 2000; Keeley and Scoones, 2003; FAO, 2013a; Okello *et al.*, 2014a).

The book unpacks the rhetoric of One Health and situates it in an uncertain, real world. Such an approach demands attention to the interconnectivities between politics, science, ecology and zoonotic pathogens. Hence a central premise is that zoonotic disease research and policy processes are deeply influenced by social, cultural, economic and political contexts. They are produced by specific sets of actors, interests and networks that configure relationships in specific ways (Keeley and Scoones, 2003). These have profound effects on the ways in which global institutions, governments, scientific research and local worlds are related, made known and manifested. By situating these contexts, and the drive for greater One Health collaboration and coordination, in differences of power, knowledge, values and norms, we seek to raise important, if at times uncomfortable, questions about current priorities, approaches and perspectives to zoonotic diseases in Africa. This allows us to challenge some of the current orthodoxies surrounding One Health, and showcase the value of a political economy approach in charting out how current zoonosis policy and practice landscapes can be made more sustainable, resilient and equitable.

Zoonoses: conundrums and connectivities

As a biological category, scientists have sought to catalogue just how many zoonotic diseases exist. Woolhouse and Gowtage-Sequeria (2005) examined 1407 viruses, bacteria, protozoa, fungi and helminth organisms that can be transmitted via air, bodily fluids, food, vegetation and insect vectors, among other routes. They found that 58 per cent were zoonotic. In a parallel study, Jones *et al.* (2008) mapped emerging disease events between 1940 and 2004, and found that 60 per cent were zoonotic and that most originated from wildlife. As with Ebola and MERS, economists stress the huge economic costs of zoonotic disease epidemics since they affect human health, conservation and the livestock sector. A World Bank study, for example, estimated that six major outbreaks between 1997 and 2009 – Nipah virus, West Nile, SARS, highly pathogenic avian influenza (HPAI), bovine spongiform encephalopathy (BSE), and Rift Valley fever (RVF) – cost the global economy some US$80 billion (World Bank, 2012).

What the science tells us is that the frequency of pathogenic 'spillover' events from animals, particularly wildlife, is increasing due to a host of unprecedented social and ecological changes occurring globally (Daszak *et al.*, 2001). In the Anthropocene era,[11] technological advances, changing socio-demographics, economic developments and a failure of governance are seen as putting undue pressure on agricultural and forested land, as well as livestock and wildlife populations that, together with the effects from global warming, are predicted to significantly shift human–pathogen relationships (FAO, 2013a). This includes global trends in deforestation, soil erosion, insect infestations, desertification, wetland degradation, and species extinctions (Chivian and Bernstein, 2008).[12] Shifting demographics and land-use patterns are also predicted to drive the intensification of livestock industries in developing countries – known as the 'livestock revolution' – through increased demand for meat, especially for poultry and pigs (Tomley and Shirley, 2009; FAO, 2013b).[13] In this sense, biodiversity serves as an important disease *regulator* – by reducing biodiversity we are actually putting ourselves at greater risk from zoonotic infections, which will also have other related consequences for food security and conservation (Chivian and Bernstein, 2008).

While a narrative of rapid socio-environmental change has become implicated with shifting zoonosis dynamics, it is hard to discern how these changes will affect disease ecologies with much certainty, although patterns are clearly emerging

(Ostfeld, 2009). The proliferation of logging and mining roads can open up new 'contact points' between hunters and primates, for example (Wolfe *et al.*, 2005). Close contact with animals and livestock intensification can increase the rate by which viral mutations occur. Increases in vector populations can accompany the expansion of irrigated rice fields as well as rapid urbanization (Jones *et al.*, 2013). Forest fragmentation offers new interfaces for human–wildlife viral exposure, genetic diversification and species adaptation (Paige *et al.*, 2015). Understanding relationships between changes in land use, biodiversity, livelihoods and disease ecology are all essential to mapping present and future zoonotic disease trends (Vinetz *et al.*, 2005; Wood *et al.*, 2012). However, the mechanisms of emergence, from the molecular-level (Pulliam, 2008) to the global circuits of capital that dictate ecosystem changes (Wallace *et al.*, 2015), remain poorly understood and unclear.

This growing concern about emerging diseases, and the associated fear of a future pandemic, have led to a proliferation of new global detection, surveillance and response apparatuses that are considered to be urgently needed to understand and address these new risks (IOM and NRC, 2009). A major focus has been on wildlife-based surveillance systems, high-risk species like bats, rodents and primates and RNA viruses due to their ability to rapidly mutate (Wolfe, 2011). In these surveillance landscapes, animal and human blood samples and viral particles in remote biodiversity hotspots are connected to the high-tech laboratories and global public health institutions that can analyse, regulate, prioritize and respond to them. New scientific knowledge and technologies, such as genomic sequencing, are used to assess these risks. A whole industry of 'viral hunting' (Wolfe, 2011), linked to detection-and-response frameworks, expert and decision systems, and global policy platforms and initiatives has emerged, involving private companies, NGOs, universities, public research agencies and global institutions, such as the WHO, the Food and Agricultural Organization of the UN (FAO) and the World Organization for Animal Health (OIE) (Vandersmissen and Welburn, 2014). These tend to frame their activities to the global pandemic outbreak narrative that so motivates governments and global agencies (Wald, 2008).

A new global governance of risk has followed, where uncertainty and precaution to 'pre-pandemic viruses' and impending global catastrophe is promoted. This questions fundamental notions of state sovereignty; for example, through new global regulatory tools for disease notification such as the International Health Regulations (IHR) and the Terrestrial Animal Health Code (Figuié, 2014), overseen by the WHO and OIE, respectively. Response has tended to occur in a rather top-down and technocratic fashion, with an overemphasis on rapid response, at-source control, and the building of high-tech surveillance and preparedness systems (Lakoff, 2010). The involvement of the military and departments of 'homeland security', especially in the USA, takes the framing beyond one associated with 'global public health' to national security and geopolitical concerns (Elbe, 2010a). This has become big research business; the US government in 2013 spent over US$6 billion on direct biosecurity research and capacity building (Sell and Watson, 2013). Policy and funding thrives on a number of inherent uncertainties and scientific ambiguities around disease emergence, which facilitate the biosecurity policy narrative (Collier *et al.*, 2004). This over-prioritizes the concerns and interests of wealthier nations in protecting their borders and economies at the expense of the priorities and needs of developing countries.

But not all zoonotic infections are prone to global outbreaks with biosecurity threats, nor wrapped up in narratives about rapid environmental change. Many do not spillover to humans very easily, nor do they threaten the shores of wealthier countries and are, therefore, not candidates for major funding from the Global North. Most are, in fact, endemic or 'neglected' (Zinsstag *et al.*, 2015a). Such animal-borne infections create a large 'dual burden', mostly on poor livestock keepers across the world, especially in Africa, Asia and Latin America. They cluster in mixed agro-livestock communities, among pastoralists and in peri-urban slums. Many have non-specific symptoms and are hugely underreported due to a lack of diagnostics and local veterinary and medical capacity (Maudlin *et al.*, 2009). They also receive minimal policy attention because they 'fall in-between' the cracks of the veterinary, public health and wildlife sectors, where existing capacities are low and inadequate (Leonard, 2000). Their locale-specific micro-ecologies mean that they are masked in global and national-level statistics that are fed into decision-making processes (Fèvre *et al.*, 2008). Existing methodologies that orientate global funding mechanisms, such as the disability-adjusted-life-year (DALY), do not necessarily reflect the full societal burden of such infections (Narrod *et al.*, 2012). But they are nonetheless considered major causes of ill health; a recent estimate of the combined burden of 13 major endemic zoonoses – including the pork-tape worm *Taenia solium*, rabies and brucellosis – claimed that they cause some 2.4 billion cases of human illness and 2.2 million human deaths each year (Grace *et al.*, 2012a).[14]

Human–animal interdependencies produce both risks and benefits. Poor people are in close daily contact with their livestock (including wildlife for many), which they rely on for draught power, income and nutrition, as well as for transport, fertilizer, hides and as symbols of cultural exchange, such as dowry payments (Smith *et al.*, 2013). These benefits make animals an integral part to many rural and peri-urban livelihoods in Africa. But animals also present a major risk when zoonotic microbes spread between humans, livestock and wildlife – in un-boiled milk, when people assist with the birth of a new calf, when they eat raw or undercooked meat or when vectors, such as sandflies, tsetse, mosquitoes and ticks, move between them. A case in point is bushmeat hunting. The physical act of butchering and eating forest animals, especially primates, is seen as a major risk for microbes to jump the species barrier (Wolfe, 2005). At the same time, bushmeat accounts for nearly 80 per cent of all animal-based protein consumed in Central Africa, and as much as 50 per cent of the daily protein intake for rural and urban families.[15] In such a context, simply telling people to 'not eat bushmeat' will likely go unheeded, while coercively implementing hunting bans will have unintended consequences on food security for the poor.

Many of the control tools required to prevent zoonotic diseases (whether endemic or emerging) requires engaging with broader social determinants of health, like sanitation, hygiene, food consumption habits, housing, the use of natural resources and livestock management practices. These do not always conform to prevailing notions of simple, standardized and inexpensive control strategies – such as drugs, vaccines and rapid diagnostic tests – that are promoted to gain policy traction (Kim *et al.*, 2005), nor do they sit easily with dominant narratives that surround the biosecurity agenda. Even where vaccines and sophisticated diagnostics do exist, applying these in resource-poor local contexts can prove very difficult (Frost and Reich, 2008). In fact, current zoonosis research and policy efforts tend to drive narrowly conceived and decontextualized community engagement interventions (Bardosh *et al.*, 2014a, 2014b). These overemphasize focusing on dominant risk factor messaging, without seeking to address the root cause of risky practices, or the multifaceted and systemic barriers to behaviour and structural change among local communities (Farmer, 1997; Scoones, 2010; FAO, 2013b; Bardosh *et al.*, 2014a). In this sense, attention to the priorities, capacities and needs of local populations and health systems in resource-poor contexts are neglected and side-lined (Calain, 2007a; Halliday *et al.*, 2012).

Zoonotic infections connect seemingly disparate domains, from the social, cultural, economic, political, biological and ecological in complex and non-linear ways. Their deep interconnectivities create particular conundrums for research and control. These are sites where cutting-edge science meets poverty and development, where livelihood benefits meet livelihood risks, and where global biosecurity narratives, endemic diseases and local realities intersect. Hence, while substantial investments from donors and governments are being made to address zoonotic infections, the appropriateness and consequences of these efforts, both for citizens of the Global North and South, remain unclear.

One Health: buzzword or paradigm shift?

Zoonoses, therefore, are 'wicked problems' that cut across human health, animal health, conservation and food security.[16] Each pathogen, its animal reservoirs and wider social and ecological contexts are deeply interlaced with a series of systemic challenges that pervade the contemporary world, and hence require new perspectives and approaches to address them.

In response, the One Health concept has quickly become a buzzword in global health. As a unifying concept, it is often portrayed through three overlapping circles and connecting arrows to illustrate the interconnectivity between human, animal and ecosystem health. This call to unity and inclusiveness, implicit in the originally used term 'One World, One Health' coined by the World Conservation Society (WCS), has great intuitive and emotive power. It challenges us to think holistically, act collaboratively and plan integrated responses. Overarching principles were first outlined in the 12-point 'Manhattan Principles' organized by WCS in 2003, but have since bifurcated into many others.[17] For example, the American Veterinary Medicine Association (AVMA) defines One Health as:

the integrative effort of multiple disciplines working locally, nationally, and globally to attain optimal health for people, animals, and the environment. Together, the three make up the One Health triad, and the health of each is inextricably connected to the others in the triad. Understanding and addressing the health issues created at this intersection is the foundation for the concept of One Health.[18]

Although One Health has some historical precursors as well as similarities with other contemporary movements in public health, the environmental movement and in sustainable development (see Dakubo (2010) for a discussion about the related EcoHealth movement and Whitmee *et al.*'s (2015) outline of 'planetary health'), the concept's projection onto the international stage was borne out of the avian influenza (HPAI and H5N1) crises in the mid-2000s (see Galaz, Leach and Scoones, this book; Scoones, 2010). This challenged the 'siloed' and bulky bureaucracies, governance and working norms of key international agencies (e.g. WHO for public health; FAO for food safety; and OIE for animal health) where conflicts in priorities and funding are historically rooted (Staples, 2006). To keep pace with the unfolding realities of the virus, the One Health concept provided sufficient breadth to reach across institutional domains and expert networks while still being flexible enough to allow for multiple interpretations where different interests could be accommodated (Chien, 2013). The acceptance of One Health by the FAO–WHO–OIE tripartite, as the collaboration between these agencies became known, effectively moved One Health from the academic fringe to mainstream global policy networks.

A series of inter-ministerial conferences then took place in Bamako, New Delhi, Sharm El-Sheikh, Hanoi and elsewhere to drum up support and hash-out what a One Health approach to avian influenza, or other zoonotic diseases, would look like. A series of goals were established: the need to go beyond the silos of scientific disciplines; promote wide-ranging institutional collaboration at the international and national-level; address the root causes of zoonotic disease; improve surveillance and governance of veterinary and medical systems; strengthen emergency response networks; move from a focus on pandemics to existing diseases of the poor; and develop new research-action strategies that facilitate the translation of targeted disease control programmes (FAO *et al.*, 2008, p18). The concept, and its accompanying movement, has widely been hailed as a significant 'paradigm shift' (Atlas and Maloy, 2014; Zinsstag *et al.*, 2015a). It has also influenced global governance systems for other challenges that cut across the human–animal–ecosystem divide, like food security, food safety, antibiotic resistance and climate change (FAO *et al.*, 2010).

One Health has quickly become a global construct guiding policy rhetoric about zoonotic diseases (Gibbs, 2014). At its core is a notion of shifting key conceptual and operational foundations in global health, agricultural development, conservation and economic development. The adaptation from a 'simple' response to H5N1 to a more internationally coordinated and long-term response to H1N1 was certainly unprecedented.[19] But since the immediate threat of an avian influenza pandemic has receded (together with the biosecurity funding attached to it), One Health has had to adapt and change. A range of policy efforts, partnerships, platforms and research initiatives have since come into existence, which range from the national, transnational and global, and focus on both endemic and emerging diseases (Vandersmissen and Welburn, 2014). In this way, the One Health concept proposes new institutional, material and symbolic configurations.

Recent literature calls for the need for 'validated' socio-economic studies that showcase the 'added-value' of the One Health approach. Constructing the evidence-base is considered paramount in order to convince policy-makers that animal-based interventions, like rabies and brucellosis vaccination in places like Mali and Mongolia, should be prioritized and invested in (Zinsstag et al., 2015a). Although few would disagree with the timeliness of One Health, many commentators have emphasized the significant political, institutional, economic and technical hurdles needed to put it into practice in different national and local contexts, and across different scales (Lee and Brumme, 2013). The movement itself is evolving and grappling with what the concept means in practice.

While One Health proposes a new politics of thinking and doing health, as a political-scientific movement it has, for the most part, evaded social science analysis and engagement (Craddock and Hinchliffe, 2015). For all the discussion about multidisciplinary approaches, there has been a significant lack of priority given to the social, cultural, political and economic dimensions that influence zoonoses research and policy. Yet in this book, we argue that questioning some of the normative One Health assumptions and rhetoric currently at play is an important task, and something that demands contextualized knowledge only possible by detailed analysis of particular cases; something that the chapters that follow offer.

Whose world? Whose health? Perspectives on political economy

This book, therefore, is concerned with unpacking how zoonotic disease ecologies and human wellbeing and health are interconnected with wider social, cultural, economic and political dynamics. Situated within a small but burgeoning social science literature on interspecies relationships, animal health and zoonotic infections (Scoones, 2010; Beinart and Brown, 2013; Dingwall et al., 2013; Nading, 2013; Craddock and Hinchliffe, 2015; Singer, 2015), it takes a political economy approach. Broadly speaking, this involves understanding how socio-political relationships are influenced by dynamics of power, knowledge construction, economic inequalities, norms and values. At its core, we are concerned with deconstructing the homogenizing notion of 'One World, One Health' and replacing it with the plurality of conflicting 'worlds' and 'healths' that play out in the real world. By doing so, we aim to reveal how scientific research and policy pathways are contingent on embedded priorities and perspectives, and shaped by power and politics. This is hugely important. In Africa, resources are greatly limited and the stakes for translating zoonoses research and policy into healthier lives and landscapes are high.

Conceptually, the book engages with a number of prevailing debates about the nature of global health and development. These are discussed in the next sections, and include: the interactions between global domains and local realities; the processes involved in moving policy into practice; relationships between technological and participatory approaches; and how different epistemological perspectives define the nature of knowledge, expertise and research and policy priorities. Each of these represents different domains where political economies influence context and process for zoonotic diseases; hence they provide us with some important conceptual building blocks to think critically about One Health in the real world.

From the global into the local

In their book, *Global Health Policy, Local Realities: The Fallacy of the Level Playing Field*, Whiteford and Manderson (2000) repeat a common maxim among social scientists involved in public health research when they state that 'health policies that are conceived as "global" too often fail because they do not account for local specificities'. One Health seeks to bridge the divide between different spatial worlds but invariably these *interactions* are between people and institutions that have very different knowledge and interests. The global is itself manufactured and constituted within local settings; in real organizations and communities of actors through chains of connections and disconnections (Burawoy, 2001). Powerful discourses are used to shape and regulate how these interactions take place (Briggs and Mantini-Briggs, 2003).

This problematizes the very notion of collaboration and partnership: what are the power dynamics between different partners? Who calls the shots? And what does this mean for local people? There are different interests at play within different sectors, different priorities and variable forms of knowledge. Understanding these dynamics, first and foremost, requires appreciating how the architecture of global health, development, agriculture, veterinary medicine and conservation play out in different local contexts. This is a Herculean task not least because these fields and sectors are continuously on the move. The last 20 years, for example, has seen foreign development assistance directed towards global health programmes increase from some US$5.7 billion in 1990 to US$28.1 billion in 2012 (Institute for Health Metrics and Evaluation, 2012). It has since become commonplace to speak about the 'complex architecture' of global health, with its 'new actors' and their associated logics: international NGOs, the Bill & Melinda Gates Foundation (BMGF), public–private partnerships (PPPs) and large global health initiatives (GHIs) (Buse and Harmer, 2007). The same can be said for other sectors.

Despite this proliferation of donor funds and global attention, there is often little direct accountability for how such major programmes trickle down to their 'local' settings (Lee *et al.*, 2003). In their analysis of trypanosomiasis policy and practice in Uganda, Smith *et al.* (2015) argued that the global assemblage of One Health is 'throttled by a collective, cumulative concern with avoiding the ... developing country state [despite it having] permanency, legitimacy, coordinating authority, and memory'. There is a politics of place and positionality directing these global resources. Differences between wealth, class, education, language, resources, history and geography across policy actors and policy subjects maintain social difference and distance.

Policy into practice

This brings us to the relationship between policy and practice. Policy pathways are typically formed around dominant narratives – storylines with beginnings, middles and ends – that frame the problem and solution (Roe, 1991). By virtue of being intertwined with specific forms of logic, interests and agendas, these tend to reduce uncertainty in order to gather, and maintain, financial and political support. The policy narrative determines what is included and excluded, and in this way defines the limits of action, the value of different types of expertise, which forms of evidence and data are relevant and how plans are to be implemented and examined. Narratives influence the terms by which resources and relevance are negotiated, and invariably leave out and marginalize contradictory, hidden, uncomfortable or inaccessible information and perspectives. Scoones (2010), for example, discusses how biosecurity narratives around avian influenza selectively de-emphasized the important role of the large-scale poultry industry, while locating the blame for viral contagion on narrowly conceived perspectives of backyard poultry practices. But limited analysis and closed-down policy debate can all be very counterproductive when dealing with complex global problems like zoonotic diseases, environmental degradation, poverty and the need for lasting institutional change.

Focusing on officialdom and policy documents hides the much more messy world of policy implementation, and it is therefore necessary to adopt a contextualized understanding of the policy process. This recognizes the disjuncture between the role of policy as a means of mobilizing resources and the actual ways in which policies move into different field situations and local contexts (Mosse, 2005). The actual day-to-day strategies used may differ fundamentally from those promoted, and outcomes and effects may be highly diverse, unknown and difficult to assess.

Health, veterinary and conservation sectors in Africa remain deeply inadequate, fragmented and caught in policy gaps (Leonard, 2000). Jones (2009, p165) describes the ephemeral nature of the state in rural Uganda as 'islands of development' (project villages, district capitals and donor-clinics) in a 'sea of neglect'; Geissler (2014, p252) speaks about public health in Africa being an 'archipelago' restricted to 'well-resourced interiors and impoverished and comparatively uncontrolled exteriors'. Veterinary departments are, for the most part, strapped for cash and under-capacity. A nexus of patronage, fiscal scarcity, weak reward systems, high transaction costs and arbitrary and non-response policy actions characterize the human, animal and wildlife health sectors in Africa (Leonard, 2000).

This context shapes how health and veterinary staff, outreach workers and communities broker and mediate global policy domains based on their own local interests, priorities and perspectives (Lewis and Mosse, 2006). This includes, for example, the ways in which vector control officers reshape control (Nading, 2014); how private veterinary drug shops reorient veterinary public health efforts (Bardosh, 2015); and how surveillance systems become distorted due to prevailing logics of expectations and inadequate resources (Justice, 1986). In this sense, local populations are not passive recipients of scientific knowledge, but active participants who challenge dominant knowledge claims through strategies like resistance, non-compliance and strategic accommodation (Scott, 1990).

Magic bullets and participatory approaches

The third tension, discussed at length in this book, relates to the ways in which decisions about zoonoses surveillance, prevention and control are mediated between contrasting emphasis on technologies and community involvement. The historical dichotomization between horizontal and vertical approaches to public health – between technological 'magic bullets' and 'people-centric' primary healthcare – has come to typify divergent opinions (Biehl and Petryna, 2013). Technocratic solutions are prioritized due to their clear utilitarian and public health value, but also because of their defined metrics, a deep faith in science and technology and the ease by which they frame cause-and-effect relationships (Leach and Scoones, 2006). This all too often includes a neglect of local people's knowledge and understandings that prove, in hindsight, to be vastly important in disease control.

Critics contend that over-prioritizing 'magic bullet' approaches leave little room for building infrastructure, community participation, prevention, and addressing problems of equity, sustainability and social determinants, including confronting powerful industry and political interests (e.g. Calain, 2007a; Scoones, 2010; Biehl and Petryna, 2013). The WHO's Commission on the Social Determinants of Health, a landmark initiative for the agency, has been an important pivotal moment helping to advocate for 'improving daily living conditions' and 'tackling the inequitable distribution of wealth, resources and power at the global, national and local scale' as the foundations for securing a healthier future (Marmot et al., 2008).

But there is also a need to locate how technologies travel, and become translated and used, in different local contexts. Of particular relevance here is Collier and Ong's (2005) notion of the 'global assemblage', which describes how global forms of expertise, techno-science and economics come to configure local worlds, and how they are adopted, used or resisted. This reveals the ways in which technologies themselves shape social relationships – what is often termed the 'social lives' or 'biographies' of things (Appadurai, 1986; Latour, 2000). In this sense, not only is science a socially and politically determined activity, but it is also one that is intimately bound by the availability and characteristics of technologies.

The emphasis on community participation also highlights the need to appreciate the variability of local settings. Communities are heterogeneous and have many hidden power dynamics. Rural populations in Africa often have little or no connection to their political leaders, where decision-making is most often controlled by political clientelism, involving traditional authorities and governments but also new global forms such as INGOs (Leonard *et al.*, 2010). Heterogeneity is also revealed in how disease ecologies are influenced by specific environmental and social changes that occur over different spatial and temporal planes (Giles-Vernick *et al.*, 2015).

Epistemologies: evidence and expertise

The final theme focuses on the arena of data, evidence and epistemology. Broadly speaking, different epistemological perspectives come to determine what forms of knowledge and expertise are valued, and to what effect (Hacking, 2000). Given the centrality of the biosciences in global public health, veterinary science and conservation debates, quantitative, statistical and generalizable data have come to occupy higher ground than social and situated knowledge and expertise. But such knowledge forms are by no means 'neutral' and 'objective' – they are also socially constructed. The biases towards 'hard data' make possible the audit and accountability systems that prevail in global health and development (Nichter, 2008). Scientists, governments, donors and other actors have their own expected norms and values, bureaucracies, and operational logics that invariably shape research designs and the generation and use of data (Crane, 2013; Justice, 1986).

Data are, therefore, linked to their social and political milieu, despite the illusion that, as artefacts, they are freely formed and independent of external influence (Erikson, 2012; Lorway and Khan, 2014). Adams (2013), for example, discusses at length how prevailing values for 'evidence-based medicine' and the 'gold standard' of randomized control trials (RCTs) generate knowledge forms that are narrow and contrived, since they are abstracted from the social contexts and relationships that they depend on. In this sense, the logics of inquiry and the incentive structures that determine them can facilitate the over-looking of local conditions. Scientific research, therefore, can involve much more than 'objective' inquiry and data, but is also about maintaining cognitive, bureaucratic and political orders and interests (Leach and Scoones, 2013).

Research designs and available expertise tend to produce specific types of research results and interpretations. Where the social sciences have remained marginal, social data have themselves all too often been equated with the goal of uncovering individual risk factors or 'exotic' cultural practices; for example in relation to human–animal relations (Craddock and Hinchliffe, 2015). This is most clearly revealed in the popularity of 'knowledge', 'attitude' and 'practice' (KAP) surveys, which tend to be reductionist in nature and narrowly conceived (see Launiala, 2009). The straightjacket of the KAP survey helps facilitate a narrowing of the social world, while also legitimizing it, and so invariably shapes the design of research activities, interventions and policy recommendations.

In this sense, epistemological priorities have come to shape policy cultures. This includes the permeating discourse of cost-effectiveness, and the reigning logic of the DALY and the cost-per-DALY averted approaches (Kim *et al.*, 2005). While this has undoubtedly helped provide a framework for decision-makers, there are important limitations that need to be considered. As Scott (1999) argues in relation to the modernist state, global health and development planning as a process of administrative manipulation aims to order, standardize and simplify society to make it amenable to interventions. This requires rendering local human, animal and ecological worlds intelligible – into 'living laboratories' (Tilley, 2011) – in ways that are inherently selective.

One Health research and policy as *understanding*, therefore, needs to problematize how scientific knowledge and expertise are being constructed, and how this is linked to prevailing social relationships and political interests (Biruk, 2012). But what types of new methodologies and methods are required to realize the lofty goals of One Health? Much of the discussion thus far has centred on the need for new metrics – an adaptation of the DALY or the design of the RCT, for example – and training and degree courses on the new 'discipline' of One Health (Narrod *et al.*, 2012; Zinsstag *et al.*, 2015a). However, what is likely much more important are radically different epistemological perspectives and methods, prompted by the requirement to address complexity, uncertainty and interconnectedness. In this sense, generating a cross-disciplinary conversation – focused on learning, adaptation, and tracking complex system change instead of singular metrics aimed at disease control – requires a genuinely new way of doing science, policy and practice.

A comparative approach

In these four ways, zoonosis research and policy are deeply influenced by political economy. This book seeks to untangle these contextually situated relationships as they play out in different contexts in Africa, from international boardrooms, district offices, among field outreach teams and in the pastures, forests and peri-urban spaces of local people. It shows the ways in which neglecting these contested socio-political spaces is deeply counterproductive for the surveillance, control and prevention of zoonotic infections, whether endemic or emerging. By understanding how power and politics are interwoven into science, policy and practice, our goal is to reveal how a One Health approach that is better grounded in the complex social relationships that pervade our world can ultimately build more resilient and effective global and local systems that sustain healthier people, animals and ecologies into the future.

Without considering complex political economies, and their place-specific enactments, the important ambitions of One Health, both as a conceptual movement and as a set of interlaced zoonotic disease interventions and research agendas, will ultimately fail to live up to its potential and expectations. To avoid such failure, this book offers one contribution to rethinking what a One Health approach should mean in practice.[20] It takes a comparative approach, and is composed of nine empirical case study chapters. These are based on ethnographic, qualitative and quantitative methodologies, and draw on a range of different African contexts, zoonotic diseases and thematic areas, which are briefly summarized below.

Building on the arguments discussed in this introduction, Chapter 2 further lays the foundation for the other case studies by tracing the multiple policy narratives that have grown-up around One Health at the global-level. Galaz, Leach and Scoones identify four narratives that pervade current zoonoses research and policy worlds, with different implications: the 'integration' narrative; the 'risk and surveillance' narrative; the 'cost–benefit' narrative; and the much less emphasized 'local context' narrative. Using a wide range of key informant interviews and policy documents, they argue that moving from One Health rhetoric to implementation is entangled in deeply structural power relations – professional hierarchies; institutional interests; questions of personnel capacity, education and training; the influence of funding flows; and convenient articulations with biosecuritization. Despite the broadening of the concept, this shows that in practice One Health continues to be prone to top-down and technocratic approaches that threaten to place it into a disciplinary silo of its own, and that an opening-up to more locally grounded perspectives and plural forms of knowledge and expertise are urgently needed.

Chapter 3 then further elucidates the contours of the global One Health architecture by exploring the characteristics of current zoonoses research networks. Using social network analysis, Valeix, Stein and Bardosh unpack notions of research collaboration across sectors and disciplines. First, the chapter explores the characteristics of the peer-reviewed One Health literature, and reveals the continued dominance of veterinary sciences, pandemic threats and Northern institutions. The chapter then turns to focus on the characteristics and evolution of research networks linked to Nipah virus – a newly emergent disease from Malaysia – over time (1998–2011). While the analysis reveals a number of positive trends taking place, these are tempered by several important negative patterns. Perhaps the most important is the significant lack of power-broker positions occupied by southern institutions, where the risks from zoonoses are often the greatest. The chapter argues that more attention to fostering trust and localized communities of practice are pivotal to generating a more inclusive One Health scientific network.

In the next chapter, Scoones continues with a global perspective by turning to the ways in which scientific zoonoses networks form and sustain 'techno-fix' narratives. He explores the history and contested research and control landscapes of African trypanosomiasis – a classic One Health disease involving flies, animals, people and environments in rural Africa. The chapter investigates multiple science-policy controversies among this small epistemic community, including the use of chemicals, traps, drugs, biotechnology and nuclear sterilization techniques. The chapter locates the conflicting perspectives and aims of different scientists within broader systems of funding, prestige, authority, institutional politics and development goals. These have provided little scope for collaboration and systems thinking of the ecological and social dynamics at play, and instead tend to compartmentalize the problem. The chapter raises important questions about the feasibility of scientific collaboration on complex zoonoses problems, and about the relationships between research, control and local livelihood contexts.

Chapter 5 turns away from research to focus on the ways in which deep-seated inequalities and exclusions influence rapid response systems to zoonotic 'spillover' events. When the Ebola virus suddenly emerged in West Africa without warning in December 2013, it quickly revealed the fissures of our global public health system. But beneath the surface of the sluggish response, weak health systems and 'resistant' communities, the virus revealed a far more complex, and troubling, reality about how fractured political economies perpetuate epidemics. Bardosh, Leach and Wilkinson locate the origins of the Ebola epidemic in longstanding and overlapping crises of development and politics in West Africa that effectively acted as 'vectors' for Ebola. These underpin different legacies of mistrust, dysfunction and dispossession that drove the virus on its path of devastation. The chapter argues that the outbreak revealed the need to move beyond the principles of collaboration and multi-disciplinarity in epidemic response to focus on re-configuring existing power relationships and notions of expertise to address inequalities and their corollaries.

Chapters 6–8 further unpack the political economies of zoonoses preparedness and response within different institutional, ecological and social topographies. Chapter 6 explores RVF – a vector-borne infection that causes devastating, but intermittent and still poorly understood, epidemics among pastoralists in East Africa. RVF is also a trans-boundary disease interconnected to regional flows of cash and livestock, where it has killed hundreds of people in Kenya and led to massive livestock trading bans from the Horn of Africa to the Arabian Peninsula. Millstone, Odame, Okumu and Bardosh explore the nexus of policy development in Kenya and how knowledge claims have been articulated and defended by different actors. Despite the preparedness plans in place, long inter-epidemic periods generate political complacency. Gaps in current science, surveillance and vaccine technologies coalesce with a lack of investment in systems and infrastructures. Moving beyond this requires, first and foremost, a more inclusive policy process that incorporates different interests and capabilities, especially those of district teams and of pastoralists themselves.

Chapter 7 builds on this analysis by locating the shifting policy narratives and socio-technical processes for another hemorrhagic disease: Lassa fever. A rodent-borne zoonosis, Lassa is endemic to Sierra Leone, where it has quickly moved from a neglected infection to one of great international importance and cutting-edge science. Wilkinson explores the ways in which this mix of biosecurity and public health play out in and around the Kenema research laboratory – a long-term treatment and research hub. While US 'biodefence dollars' have helped to develop new diagnostics and therapeutics, they have privileged certain types of 'laboratory' evidence and investments over other important forms of knowledge and public health priorities. As the disease ecology of Lassa proves to be much more complex than originally thought, and the disease becomes increasingly framed as a national public health threat in Sierra Leone, the importance of untangling the configuration of Lassa in field contexts becomes all the more apparent. This includes efforts to generate new forms of locally grounded ecological and social knowledge in order to inform methods of community outreach, rodent control and understandings of the influence of land-use changes.

As the cases of Lassa and RVF show, zoonoses science-policy debates are frequently characterized by epidemiological uncertainties about changing transmission dynamics, which make improving animal-based surveillance an important One Health priority. Chapter 8 offers a window into how the politics of risk influences wildlife-based surveillance efforts in Ghana for bat-associated pathogens. Waldman, MacGregor and Gadzekpo unpack a range of policy framings around bats, the environment and disease from different sectoral perspectives. They argue that, where human disease risks are ambiguous and not yet established and where resources are limited and different understandings of risk predominate, wildlife-based surveillance falls victim to a 'politics of precaution'. But the emphasis on evidence also makes the control of knowledge a sensitive issue across institutional and disciplinary affiliations. The chapter raises important questions about how policy is constructed and organized around unknown threats, challenging global narratives of 'big system' surveillance for pandemic detection and mitigation.

The following chapter, Chapter 9, presents a more socio-ecological perspective. Grant, Machila and Anderson explore the multiple social-ecological controversies that have surrounded trypanosomiasis in Zambia. They locate four divergent narratives that have shaped the science-policy debates, and discuss the ways in which these reflect incompatible priorities between people, land, animals, economy and the environment. The chapter then goes on to discuss the relevance of these divergent, and contested, policy spaces with a specific focus on the consequences of social and environmental change taking place in the Luangwa Valley, Eastern Zambia. They argue that while 'bringing together' different stakeholders is certainly important, without understanding the ways in which local disease ecologies are interwoven into larger structural dynamics – like cotton growing, urban charcoal markets, human migration and tourism – there are important limitations to how far the rhetoric of One Health can really go.

The last empirical chapter, Chapter 10, switches methodological gear, and offers an 'insider' account of 'doing' One Health in Northern Nigeria as part of a large multi-partner European–African consortium, known as the ICONZ project.[21] Ducrotoy, Okello, Welburn and Bardosh explore the politics of designing and implementing a One Health research project to explore the economic burden and control of brucellosis among Fulani communities in the Kachia Grazing Reserve. They reveal how researcher interests, partner expertise and deeply embedded stigmatization of the Fulani – including a 'politics of blame' surrounding brucellosis – generated unanticipated problems with community access, and in the generation and analysis of scientific data. The chapter provides insights into just how difficult 'One Health' research can be in practice, and raises important questions about the relationships between scientific knowledge, local politics and community concerns.

The concluding chapter reflects on the major crosscutting themes of the nine preceding case studies, and what the implications are for a One Health approach to zoonotic disease in Africa. It does so by mapping out some new conceptual territory, focused on four key issues: conceptual boundaries, systems of action, forms of knowledge and governance regimes. Through these issues, the chapter provides theoretical and practical suggestions for how current programmes and policies can be improved by paying attention to power and politics, and what types of methodological innovations are needed to advance this agenda.

Notes

1 www.telegraph.co.uk/news/worldnews/ebola/11295271/Ebola-inside-Liberias-West-Point-slum.html, accessed 27 July 2015.
2 www.nytimes.com/2014/08/30/world/africa/quarantine-for-ebola-lifted-in-liberia-slum.html?_r=0, accessed 27 July 2015.
3 www.washingtonpost.com/news/morning-mix/wp/2014/08/21/the-nightmare-of-containing-ebola-in-liberias-worst-slum, accessed 27 July 2015.
4 www.nytimes.com/2014/08/21/world/africa/ebola-outbreak-liberia-quarantine.html, accessed 27 July 2015.
5 www.nytimes.com/2015/06/11/world/asia/south-korean-hamlet-under-mers-quarantine-symbolizes-weaknesses-in-system.html, accessed 27 July 2015.
6 MERS causes severe pneumonia and organ failure, but mostly in people with preexisting conditions. As of June 2015, there had been 1329 reported cases of MERS since 2012 with a combined fatality rate of 36 per cent (see: www.who.int/emergencies/mers-cov/en, accessed 27 July 2015).
7 www.bbc.com/news/world-middle-east-29147727, accessed 27 July 2015.
8 http://america.aljazeera.com/opinions/2014/6/mers-saudi-arabiaresearchpatent.html, accessed 27 July 2015.
9 www.nytimes.com/2015/06/09/world/asia/mers-viruss-path-one-man-many-south-korean-hospitals.html, accessed 27 July 2015.
10 To bring the point home, I will quote directly from the WHO:

> In low-income countries, nearly 4 in every 10 deaths are among children under 15 years, and only 2 in every 10 deaths are among people aged 70 years and older. People predominantly die of infectious diseases: lower respiratory infections, HIV/AIDS, diarrhoeal diseases, malaria and tuberculosis collectively account for almost one third of all deaths in these countries.

See: www.who.int/mediacentre/factsheets/fs310/en/index2.html.
11 The 'Anthropocene' is a proposed new geological era characterized by the influence of human activity on the Earth's ecosystem. It is a widely used scientific term, and has been the subject of considerable debate in scientific circles (see Whitmee *et al.*, 2015).
12 For example, Thomas *et al.* (2004) estimated that upwards of one in ten animals and plants on the Earth would be extinct by 2050, mostly due to human activity; Hansen *et al.* (2013) estimated that over 2.3 million square kilometres of primary forest have been cut down across the globe since 2000.
13 Some authors have questioned the mechanisms and consequences of these changes on human–animal relations (see Pica-Ciamarra and Otte, 2011).
14 This included: zoonotic gastrointestinal disease; leptospirosis; cysticercosis; zoonotic tuberculosis; rabies; leishmaniasis; brucellosis; echinococcosis; toxoplasmosis; Q fever; zoonotic trypanosomosis, hepatitis E; and anthrax.
15 See: www.4apes.com/working-groups/bushmeat.
16 The idea of a 'wicked problem' was first used in social planning by the systems thinker and philosopher West Churchman in 1967. It refers to problems that are difficult, or even impossible, to solve because of shifting and incomplete knowledge and conditions.
17 See: www.cdc.gov/onehealth/pdf/manhattan/twelve_manhattan_principles.pdf, accessed 27 July 2015.

18 www.avma.org/KB/Resources/Reference/Pages/One-Health.aspx, accessed 27 July 2015.

19 For example, between 2005 and 2009, some US$4.3 billion were pledged for HPAI and H5N1. In the case of H5N1 there were only 630 human cases and 375 deaths reported in a ten-year period from 2003 to 2013 (Vandersmissen and Welburn, 2014).

20 Readers will no doubt note the absence of a few important dimensions to the zoonosis field that did not find their way into this book: foodborne zoonoses and sanitation, live-stock industries and the increasing urban and peri-urban environment all being the most glaring omissions. Paradoxically, the book is also largely 'siloed' in the social sciences and does not represent a 'trans-disciplinary approach' in the fullest sense of the word. In this regard, it helps set the stage for future work to incorporate a political economy approach into the actual research, policy and practice process, through integrated field studies, interventions and policy development.

21 See: www.iconzafrica.org, accessed 27 July 2015.

2

GLOBAL NARRATIVES

The political economy of One Health

Victor Galaz, Melissa Leach and Ian Scoones

Introduction

One Health has emerged over the last decade as a key concept guiding international research and policy in the field of zoonoses. In its simplest form, One Health refers to integrated approaches as a means to improve human, animal and environmental health. Integrated in this context means multidisciplinary, cross-sectoral and multi-level approaches designed to reduce and address health risks (Zinsstag *et al.*, 2006, 2012). For this reason, One Health is a broad and at times ambiguous 'umbrella' concept. In the world of global health and development aid, where fads and fashions quickly come and go, it risks becoming something of a buzzword for Global Health in the early twenty-first century.

But despite its spread and increased popularity, it has also come under repeated criticism from a diverse set of actors. These criticisms come in different forms, but are related, in one way or another, to the concept's malleability as well as the limited number of concrete examples of effective implementation (Chien, 2013; Lee and Brumme, 2013; Gibbs, 2014). Although a few studies are now beginning to emerge, there is a lack of systematic analysis of One Health as a phenomenon with strong political-economic dimensions. There is clearly a gap in our understanding of how the concept has diffused among scientific and policy communities over time; the key drivers to this rapid expansion; what resource flows and power relations have influenced this process; which actors dominate the concept's international knowledge production and dissemination; and the tangible institutional and policy implications of increased One Health rhetoric.

Based on the analysis of an extensive number of key informant interviews[1] as well as key policy documents,[2] this chapter examines these issues. It explores the concept's emergence, and the political economy of knowledge and practice that has accompanied it. By this we mean the ways in which different interest groups ally or compete with different versions of the concept, and how these interactions are influenced by institutional arrangements and resource flows. This analysis raises fundamental questions about 'whose world, whose health?', and about the interactions between science and policy.

We argue that One Health indeed has multiple interpretations, and is a contested term associated with different policy narratives – storylines that define the problem and solution in different ways (Roe, 1991). Different definitions are at play, based on different discursive assumptions and consequences. We identify four such narratives driving One Health research and policy at the global level: the 'integration' narrative; the 'risk and surveillance' narrative; the 'economic benefit' narrative; and, to a much lesser degree, the 'local context' narrative. While not necessarily mutually exclusive, these play to very different institutional logics and power dynamics that enact the flow of resources and define the limits of activities. This is especially the case with the first three dominant narratives, which all in different ways tend to simplify complex and uncertain dynamics, conforming the agenda to issues that can be easily defined and measured in ways that synchronize with established models of resource mobilization and interests.

The chapter goes on to explore these diverse perspectives on the utility of the 'One Health' approach, asking why, given the emerging consensus around it, One Health is gaining relatively little policy and institutional traction. A wide variety of interviews with key players in international public health and veterinary debates are used to contextualize this debate. Reasons include power-laden professional hierarchies, institutional lock-in around single-sector approaches, questions of personnel capacity, education and training, the influence of funding flows, and convenient articulations with securitization agendas in global health. These institutional bottlenecks combine both to limit One Health implementation in practice, and to reinforce a top-down control and surveillance oriented approach that privileges a particular rendition of One Health, all the time overlooking other 'worlds' and other 'healths'. It therefore often ignores, we argue, perspectives grounded in the knowledge and practices of poorer people in diverse southern contexts, and the political economies that shape the conditions for disease emergence, persistence and spread. The consequences of this selectivity are important and potentially far-reaching, threatening to place One Health itself into a disciplinary silo that compartmentalizes the concept's reach, influence and ultimately its relevance for people's health and wellbeing around the world.

Emerging paradigm, multiple narratives

The idea of an integrated approach to human, animal and environmental health is, of course, not new (Woods and Bresalier, 2014; Murray et al., 2014). The modern One Health movement traces its lineage to a number of parallel concepts, including the term 'One Medicine' coined by American veterinarian Calvin W. Schwabe in the 1970s and often invoked as One Health's direct precursor (Zinsstag et al., 2012; Gibbs, 2014).[3] However, numerous historical antecedents precluded a formal process of labelling, evident in the practice of field-based health practitioners before professionalized, institutional and sectoral silos took hold: Edward Jenner's use of cowpox variolation in late-eighteenth-century England; John Snow and the spread of cholera in London; the pioneering social medicine of Rudolf Virchow; the social and ecological perspective of John Ford (1971) around trypanosomiasis in Africa; and the giant of twentieth century human pathology, Dr William Osler's work on veterinary medicine, to name only a few. Harking back to this tradition, the formal 'One World, One Health' label emerged as the World Conservation Society's copyrighted slogan in 2004, following the Manhattan Principles (Cook *et al.*, 2004), bringing together interests in conservation and health.

But it was only with the outbreak of avian influenza in the first half of the 2000s, and the development of an international response (led by international organizations, notably the World Health Organization (WHO), the Food and Agriculture Organization (FAO) and the World Organisation for Animal Health (OIE), with oversight from the UN System Influenza Coordination Office (UNSIC)) that the term 'One Health' gained international currency (Scoones, 2010). As crises tend to do, dominant models were challenged by the stark realization that new modes of institutional cooperation and integrated approaches were needed to handle a zoonotic outbreak of such potential significance.

In China, Egypt, India and Vietnam, high-level policy meetings were tasked with entrenching a One Health vision across major global and national agencies. These were used as vehicles for raising funds for the avian influenza response, and promised major institutional reforms.[4] Further attempts were made to bring groups together under the auspices of the Institute of Medicine and National Academies' Stone Mountain Dialogue (Rubin *et al.*, 2013). Other major meetings followed with a One Health tag. Public Health Canada, for example, hosted a significant meeting in Winnipeg in the wake of the avian influenza outbreak and the first One Health Congress was held in Australia in 2010.[5] More recent efforts have also been undertaken in Africa.[6] Numerous networks, consortia, initiatives and commissions have been formed with a One Health brief, and there has been a veritable explosion of activity associated with the term.[7] All these efforts have extended and consolidated the One Health approach in a variety of quarters. In terms of policy debates, as well as research funding streams and scientific outputs, One Health has quickly monopolized the field of zoonoses while also making forays, albeit more slowly, into other health-related disciplines.

This varied genesis has meant that the label is malleable but ambiguous, and can be appropriated and used by a wide range of actors and organizations to address a huge range of different issues. This includes the control of dengue (Kittayapong *et al.*, 2012), tuberculosis (Kaneene *et al.*, 2014), leishmaniasis (Palatnik de Sousa and Day, 2011), malaria (Franco *et al.*, 2014), brucellosis (Godfroid *et al.*, 2013), tick-borne diseases (Dantas-Torres *et al.*, 2012), rabies (Häsler *et al.*, 2014) and trypanosomiasis (Ndeledje *et al.*, 2013), among many other infectious disease examples. In terms of the fields of health and medicine, the concept is being applied to parasitology (Thompson, 2013), clinical microbiology (Miller and Griffin, 2012), companion animal vectors (Day, 2011) and vaccine development (Middleton *et al.*, 2014), as well as broad zoonosis prevention and control (Okello *et al.*, 2011) and ecosystem health (Rabinowitz and Conti, 2013). And it has taken root in diverse locations from Australia (Adamson *et al.*, 2011) to North America (Leung *et al.*, 2012) to Europe (Frazzoli *et al.*, 2014) to Africa (Rweyemamu *et al.*, 2013) and Asia (Nguyen-Viet *et al.*, 2014).

Despite the appeal of One Health as a holistic, integrative, cross-sector, interdisciplinary and coordinating approach, there is far from a uniform view of what One Health is or should be. Promoting diversity and inclusiveness has meant the proliferations of multiple definitions and interpretations of what often comes across as a 'common sense' idea. We aimed to locate these divergences, and looked for narrative structures – storylines with beginnings, middles and ends – during an analysis of 28 policy documents concerned with One Health issues from 2004 to 2013. The titles of these policy documents included a range of emphasis, including: 'A New Professional Imperative'; 'Sharing Responsibilities and Coordinating Global Activities'; 'A Strategic Framework for Reducing Risks of Infectious Diseases'; 'Strengthening Veterinary Services for Effective One Health Collaboration'; and 'Building Interdisciplinary Bridges'.[8] These documents reveal that different interpretations of One Health are associated with different assumptions of the nature of problems and solutions, supported by specific institutional, professional and personal interests among the actors concerned, which in turn relate to competition for prestige and funding.

Informed by previous work on policy narratives in this field (Scoones, 2010; Dry and Leach, 2010), we identified three recurrent and dominant narratives that define a One Health position, one much more marginalized narrative and many variations in between (see Table 2.1). The first narrative offers a broad argument for a holistic, integrated approach, necessary to deal with complex interactions between ecology, animals, people and disease. Such issues, the narrative argues, cannot be dealt with by one discipline or one sectoral agency alone. This has been the rallying call in general for cooperation, institutional reform, funding approaches and the redefinition of training approaches. Examples of this framing include FAO *et al.* (2010), WHO (2008) and World Bank (2010). This argument is reflected in the academic literature too, with a number of review articles in key journals making the case for an integrative One Health approach; for example by Zinsstag *et al.* (2007, 2012); Okello *et al.* (2011); Coker *et al.* (2011); Kahn *et al.* (2009); Conraths *et al.* (2011); Rabinowitz and Conti (2013); Hueston *et al.* (2013); and many others. Other related literatures have advocated for the need to address organizational and governance challenges (Leboeuf, 2011; Anholt *et al.*, 2012; Lee and Brumme, 2013; Conrad *et al.*, 2013).

A second narrative focuses on the risks of emergence and spread, and the challenge of surveillance. In this version, One Health is defined as a way to prevent risk and respond to crises in a more efficient and rational way. For example, WHO (2008) 'Applying the One Health Concept' explores the role of One Health as a means to control disease spread through improved diagnosis and surveillance, and

TABLE 2.1 Four One Health narratives

One Health narratives	Framing of the problem	Major preoccupations and emphasis
The 'integration' narrative	We need an integrated approach to deal with complex interactions between ecology, animals, people and disease.	Promoting cooperation, institutional reform, funding approaches and the redefinition of training approaches.
The risk and surveillance 'outbreak' narrative	Control zoonotic disease spread through improved diagnosis and surveillance, and prevention and control activities focused on bringing vets and medics together.	Cooperation in surveillance, including early identification of emerging disease, through 'virus hunting' and identifying hotspots, and contingency planning and coordinated emergency responses.
The 'economic benefits' narrative	We need to show that One Health is cost-effective for it to be accepted by policy-makers.	Promoting econometric analysis as a policy and lobbying tool for support and expansion of the approach.
The 'local context' narrative	Integrated surveillance and response must be built on local contexts and understandings.	Promotion of social and ecological research, as well as inclusive and participatory methodologies that remain cognizant of socio-political contexts.

prevention and control activities (see also CDC, 2011a). This then requires cooperation in surveillance, including early identification of emerging disease, through 'virus hunting' and identifying hotspots, and contingency planning and coordinated emergency responses. This is firmly located within a broader 'outbreak narrative' (Wald, 2008) that highlights the risks of new diseases emerging in far-flung localities, and spreading rapidly through global travel and trade to affect populations and economies in the wealthy Global North (Dry and Leach, 2010). It also aligns with broader narratives around global health security and biosecurity (Elbe, 2010a), and has induced the rapid increase of transboundary epidemic response and alert networks (Galaz, 2014).

The third narrative focuses on the potential economic benefits of implementing One Health approaches. For example, based on economic estimates from six major outbreaks of highly fatal zoonoses between 1997 and 2009, the World Bank has argued that the global benefits of adopting a One Health approach amount to US$6.7 billion per year (World Bank, 2012). Other published literature picks up on this narrative. Grace (2014), for example, offers 'the business case for One Health', while Rushton et al. (2012) and Häsler et al. (2013) present the array of economic rationales for an integrative approach. Zinsstag *et al.* (2006) show the economic benefits of combining human and animal health interventions. Meanwhile Narrod *et al.* (2012) estimate the costs of zoonotic diseases on society, and so justify expenditures on a One Health approach.

Reflecting on the analysis of this recent policy literature, as well as our large number of interviews with key actors in the policy field, we note the marginalization of an alternative fourth narrative rooted more in local ecological and disease contexts, and voiced by people living with, and responding to, disease (Dry and Leach, 2010; Scoones, 2010; Bardosh *et al.*, 2014a, 2014b). This perspective argues that integrated surveillance and response must be built on local contexts and understandings, and can benefit from inclusive and participatory methodologies. Some of these also point to the political-economic contexts in which zoonoses develop and are driven, including structures of production, urbanization and global capitalist relationships and their impacts on disease emergence and spread locally (Hinchliffe, 2007; Forster, 2012). This approach is highlighted in emerging work by social scientists working with field practitioners, and an increasingly better recognized tradition of participatory ecohealth and epidemiology approaches (Waltner-Toews, 2001; Grace *et al.*, 2012b, 2012c; Charron, 2012a).

These four narratives are not necessarily mutually exclusive, and a number of major figures in the One Health movement move between them, at least discursively, with relative ease. However, they play to very different institutional logics and power dynamics that enact the flow of resources and define the limits of activities. The remainder of this chapter expands on these observations, using our interviews with key policy informants to explain the patterns we observed in the policy narratives. Moving from the 'what' to the 'why' and 'how' of One Health, we identify three recurrent themes that help explain why particular versions of One Health have become dominant, and why rhetorical acceptance of the idea, as associated with certain narratives, is often not matched in practice. Ultimately, we argue that the more expansive One Health agenda, and the benefits that are discursively associated with its adoption and diffusion, has not readily come to fruition. Reasons for this are discussed below, and located in organizational mandates and funding flows, disciplinary silos and interpretations of 'integration'.

Organizational mandates and funding flows

As shown by our narrative analysis, One Health advocacy has focused extensively on promoting 'collaboration' and 'integration' across previously disparate fields and organizations. While there were precedents, avian flu provided the defining crisis that catalysed One Health rhetoric onto the global stage, legitimizing it to organizations that had barely collaborated in the past. As a senior United Nations (UN) official put it: 'without avian influenza we would have no One Health. It brought lots of money, and people were brought together.' Avian influenza fit the contours of a global outbreak narrative very closely, threatened to spread to the rest of the world with devastating consequences for the global economy and wealthier Northern populations (Scoones, 2010). Such crises demanded a swift mobilization of funds and new modes of inter-sectoral networking between the major animal and health organizations.

Key individuals were important in this process, not least David Nabarro, a UK medical doctor, who became the UN Secretary General's 'flu tsar' and is now, with the West African Ebola epidemic, the United Nations Mission for Ebola Emergency Response's (UNMEER) special representative. As an aid agency official commented: 'David was a great factor in raising the funds. He is very effective at loosening the purse strings ... David's tub thumping speeches helped raise the profile [of One Health].' New institutional networks were established, notably between the WHO, FAO and OIE, with the UNSIC playing a coordination role. Under the banner One World, One Health, UNSIC was created in 2005 as a means to improve coordination between UN organizations and governments, bringing together diverse groups and raising considerable funds. An aid agency official observed that: 'Avian influenza has seen some of the most effective coordination between international agencies I have ever encountered.... All the FAO has to do right now [in 2008] is shout "avian flu", and people will shower them with money!'

Some informants observed that a new form of organizational networking emerged from the avian influenza crisis, facilitated by UNSIC: 'A movement has been created ... UNSIC is small, flexible, light. It is a model of a new UN ... a solution for big, complex issues.' This reflects a general trend in global health that is concerned with reforming what are perceived to be byzantine, donor-led bureaucracies (Buse and Harmer, 2007). A senior UN official reflected:

> We need to better understand how we can use this model in the future for coordination ... it is a coordination function and also an energising function ... the benefits are extremely significant, but it requires a mandate.... It wasn't enough to say here is something for the global public good, we first had to build relationships.

As a result of the avian influenza experience, significant shifts have occurred. As an OIE official put it: 'These days at the global level there is no longer partition. You can move freely. Before everyone was in their own compartments. There is now free movement of personnel and information. This is an important achievement.'

However, this optimistic view was tempered by other perspectives. Some suggested that, while interactions improved, these rested very much on the dramatic outbreak form of influenza, and its associated politics; 'the turf needs to be political for the seed to grow. It needs a strong political platform [that you only find in an outbreak scenario]', as one interviewee put it. While avian influenza (and subsequently swine flu) established the political and funding momentum for One Health, these new organizational mechanisms need to be extended to endemic diseases and situations that do not threaten Northern populations. But galvanizing the international community is clearly more difficult. As a former US State Department official observed, the One Health agenda does not, seem to be getting the same high-visibility traction and funding from governments and others as many of us would think was warranted because once that immediate scare from H5N1 seemed to have receded ... we've lost some of that high-level political impetus for it.

Political impetus, and so funding, has in both the Global North and South been associated with and supported by risk-based approaches to One Health, particularly the global 'emergence' or 'outbreak' narrative. This has provided the justifications for organizational change, particularly in terms of enacting new coordination mechanisms in times of crisis to reduce costs and improve efficiency of rapid response systems. Thus while the overarching 'integration' narrative is widely deployed at a rhetorical level, it has had less traction when supporting long-term organizational and institutional change, as competition for funds, profile and leadership remain. Moving organizational configurations from ones established in the post-war period around sectoral responsibilities has proved very difficult (Chien, 2013; Lee and Brumme, 2013; Okello *et al.*, 2014a), despite moves towards light-touch coordination and facilitation. In this context, the general arguments for coordination often overlie real competition for funds between sectors and organizations, particularly as the flood of initial avian influenza money has subsided. In this regard, avian influenza was a

> brand ... that could make a number of things happen. It allowed us to focus on something that was a tangible threat and source significant amounts of money from contingency funds. Talking about generic threats at the human–animal interface – zoonoses – is less arresting and makes it harder to draw funds down.

Although the all-inclusive rhetoric of One Health may have helped to reduce traditional organizational conflicts and tensions, and facilitate new forms of collaboration and institutional reach (Chien, 2013), the eventual disbanding of the initial 'outbreak' focus on avian influenza was preceded by a scramble for disciplinary attention and funds. Most investments have emphasized human health impacts rather than long-term, unknown, potential emergence of disease. The reason seems to be that funding flows have prioritized interventions with easily definable metrics, thereby marginalizing more complex drivers of disease such as ecosystem change and socio-political dynamics. Funding flows have instead followed the standard approach of technological solutions and emergency response. However, there has also been a growing emphasis on research and action geared to understanding the drivers of disease emergence, placing greater emphasis on ecosystems and other endemic and neglected diseases.[9] These are relatively marginal in terms of funding and organizational support, and are at an early stage, but they offer the potential for more lasting forms of organizational change that move beyond an epidemic, outbreak focus.

Much of the organizational innovation has occurred between veterinary and human health agencies. However, as a former WHO official commented: 'This paradigm shift requires that animal health and human health and many other sectors such as trade and commerce work together in One Health.' Integration may happen when other organizations have an incentive to collaborate, as happened with avian influenza. 'All agencies now want to be involved – tourism, migration, civil aviation, etc. Everyone wants to be involved in global health issues.' The challenge is in finding concrete incentive pathways for this to take place in ways that preclude major crisis situations.

But there is a tension between an informal, networked 'movement' and more formalized organizational change. As one informant commented, 'There is a need to be flexible, so that people can pull institutions with them. Not very much has been formalised. It is an interesting moment ... we are inventing the future.' Galvanizing people must go beyond the rhetoric. In our interviews, One Health has been variously referred to as a badge, a slogan, a brand and an 'idea too popular for its own good'. There appears to be perennial and systemic barriers to moving the rhetoric into reality; as one researcher observed, 'People sound pseudo-religious about it, but it doesn't penetrate very deeply.'

Professional and disciplinary expertise

The core of the One Health approach is integrating different forms of expertise and professions, especially across human, animal and ecosystem health. However, the idea of harmonious, equal integration has proved more difficult to realize in practice, exposing professional hierarchies, disciplinary biases and difficulties of communication and translation, driven by the legacy of each profession's embedded histories (Lélé and Norgaard, 2005).

Some of our interviewees saw the key push for One Health as coming from the veterinary profession. In the context of declining public funds and long-term institutional and funding neglect in the global animal health field, it represents a new, internationally high-profile policy window to reinvent and deploy veterinary expertise. One Health was seen as 'a push by the vets in the organization', driven by a small epistemic community of 'open-minded vets and a[n] [even smaller] disparate community of ecologists'. However, practising a One Health approach has presented major challenges to veterinarians. As a researcher put it bluntly, 'Today we need system vets who can see the bigger picture, and relate to these wider policy concerns. But most think that vet medicine is just sticking your hand up a cow's arse.' Challenges continue in translating expertise into policy:

> One of the problems is that within veterinary advice systems, the core advisors are nearly all lab vets, not epidemiologists for example. These are the chief technical advisers in governments and agencies.... This [provides] a limited view when the disease is in a population – and the population exists in a social context ... we haven't got enough disease control experts who understand these wider issues. Those who exist don't stick around for long, and don't necessarily get into the international system.

Even more significant challenges have involved integrating veterinary and medical expertise. Some argue that there has been little interest in One Health from the medical profession. As a senior researcher observed: 'engagement of the medical sector is rare … I've never seen a One Health session in a medical conference [except in Africa]'. Vet advocates have faced difficulties in some organizational settings – 'It's mostly medics, and they don't see One Health as a priority', commented someone from the Centers for Disease Control and Prevention (CDC). These challenges reflect a more recent separation:

> When I originally worked in Uganda as a researcher, vets and medics would meet. Discuss over coffee each morning. It was One Health in a way. But sometimes it's a challenge. Medics don't need to be told anything by anyone.

As this quote suggests, professional hierarchies remain strongly entrenched. This was frequently commented on: 'There is mistrust between the two castes – the doctors and the vets. It has prevented lots of collaboration. There is a slight complex of inferiority among the vets. And there is a big complex of superiority among the medics.' In the eyes of many, this makes medical doctors still 'far higher status than vets', so that 'if the medics are in charge they will resist. They want their disease focus.... The medics are in charge these days. Livelihoods and integrated thinking is out.'

Hierarchies notwithstanding, bringing the expertise and 'mindsets' of medics and vets together has also proved difficult. As a veterinarian working in a human health organization commented: 'the thinking between vets and medics is really, really separate. It's challenging.... The minds are still that way, even if they are working on something like avian influenza.' Ways of thinking are situated in institutional histories, training and field experiences. Thus, as one informant put it of avian influenza: 'We've got David Nabarro drawing a picture of a spectre that is going to engulf the world, and you've got vets saying, you can say anything you like but it is [all] about [the] chickens.' Translation and communication problems persist: 'they don't necessarily all speak the same language and therefore that's one of the challenges with the One Health agenda, because it means different things to different people'. Different framings of problems and solutions exist even within the medical profession. As a medical doctor commented: 'as clinicians we take the individual perspective but actually taking this broader perspective of One Health [is challenging]'. While such 'big picture' thinking is more the remit of epidemiologists and others with a population-level perspective, these actors are seen as having less of an influence in directing funding flows and professional change.

Meanwhile, a focus on drugs and vaccines as the technological solution is seen as dominant, in turn reinforcing outbreak narratives. As one informant observed, 'the medical and defence establishments think in very similar ways. Doctors and nurses are the new army and vaccines the new weapons. This is a very different view of health security [compared to the more integrative One Health perspective].'

Thus while One Health acts as a boundary term drawing people together, it is a fuzzy boundary across which differences of understanding, meaning and narrative persist.

A number of interviewees commented on what it would take to strengthen collaboration across professions and forms of expertise so that a truly integrative One Health approach could be realized in practice. This emphasized the need for bottom-up, field-level collaboration. For instance,

> it will certainly take a long time to change the thinking if it comes from above. But if people get involved with each other at a technical level – if they interact – it will come up from below and things will happen.

Hence, integrated activities were identified as key avenues for organizational change. Several highlighted the importance of joint training, 'for example if vet and medical schools have zoonoses classes together, joint seminars', as has happened at universities in Maryland, UC Davis, Cambridge, and the London School of Hygiene and Tropical Medicine (LSHTM)/Royal Veterinary College (RVC) at the University of London (Conrad *et al.*, 2009; Courtenay *et al.*, 2014; Gargano *et al.*, 2013; Winer *et al.*, 2015). However, the longer-term impacts, and the extension of these to southern settings, have yet to be felt, other than in a few noteworthy networks (Rweyemamu *et al.*, 2013; Okello *et al.*, 2015). Beyond training, there needs to be professional incentives for collaboration. But interviewees stressed the lack of support for cross-disciplinary work in conventional academic research and publishing. As noted by one international researcher, 'At university-level you need an incentive to work together as you're measured by publications – if working on a One Health project you have to ensure that there's enough incentives for each partner.'

But One Health is more than integrating vets, medics and ecologists. Some emphasized the importance of drawing social scientists in. This has been highlighted in some research programmes,[10] although overall the visibility of social science, outside some economic inputs, is miniscule. One role for social science envisaged in some commentaries is in connecting better with local perspectives and community-level forms of expertise. One informant argued: 'it's also trying to get the community involved in [a] kind of participatory epidemiology and getting people to be thinking cross-disciplinarily as well as thinking in terms of how to involve the community'. This extends the already formidable challenges of linking scientific disciplines by moving beyond technical integration to appreciating local people's knowledge and everyday, experiential expertise. As the same informant put it: 'it is also going to take cultural brokering between different groups of people who haven't worked together before'. Although urgent and essential to realizing a truly integrative One Health agenda, it is important to ask why this more expansive perspective of One Health has gained little traction.

Making the case for One Health: whose knowledge, whose interests?

How, then, is the case for One Health made, and how does this reflect the different knowledges and interests we see represented, as well as the exclusions we have noted? Earlier we identified four narratives. Across the policy documents and interviews, we have observed the widespread deployment of the 'integration' narrative, although with multiple meanings and interpretations, and with sometimes limited effects in practice. We have also noted the importance of the risk and surveillance outbreak narrative, particularly as it came to prominence through avian influenza as a key means to mobilize political interest and funds.

Sustaining interest in, and implementing, a One Health approach, given other institutional priorities and the absence of fundamental organizational and institutional reforms, has proved an uphill struggle. Demonstrating impact and favourable cost–benefit ratios has become a central theme, supporting a burgeoning 'evidence-base' for cost–benefit interventions to pitch to reluctant and sceptical policy-makers (Häsler *et al.*, 2013). The economic costs narrative emphasizes, so Grace *et al.* (2012b, S71) argued, that 'what cannot be measured, cannot be managed'. Even if this is not strictly true, it is certainly the case that economic measures have a large influence on decision-making. As one senior World Bank advisor put it: 'it's [One Health] economically extremely valuable and a very important thing to do in economic terms. The investments are very small related to the benefits.' Another interviewee reflected:

> what will decision-makers listen to? It's money. So let's not worry too much about all the intangible benefits.... If we can make the case for One Health through the things we can measure. Show the added value [that is what is important].

At a more local level, particularly in the contexts of the developing world, the added value and therefore cost savings of combining human and veterinary health field operations, such as vaccination campaigns, have been highlighted. For example, Zinsstag *et al.* (2007) showed significant benefits for human public health from livestock interventions, with examples of rabies vaccination in Chad and brucellosis vaccination in Mongolia (see also Roth *et al.*, 2003). Joint vaccination campaigns also result in cost savings and net benefits (Schelling *et al.*, 2005, 2007; Zinsstag *et al.*, 2006). In this respect: 'working together is not just a nice way of putting it, but effectively brings us to win–win situations which makes us better address the potential threats, and also of course work more efficiently'. Hence the economic costs and benefits narrative provides operational justification for investment.

While such arguments may be convincing in relation to existing disease challenges, including bringing those previously neglected further up the policy agenda, such cost–benefit metrics cannot be applied when uncertainty and ignorance about future disease emergence and impacts prevail. As one researcher put it: 'The trouble is when not dealing with outbreaks, but more anticipation, early warning, standard measures of cost and benefit are not useful as the events have not yet happened.'

Others pointed to the often-narrow focus of One Health on disease and its control, and on narrow impacts, whether on human or animal health. The coordinator of the One Health Global Network argued for a broadening of the case: 'It's currently only human and animal health, and focused on disease. That's far too narrow. Donors want to hear about development more generally – about poverty, food security, water access and so on, not just about diseases.' This alludes to a wider variety of system-level impacts, many of which are difficult to quantify. An easy response to the challenge of bringing such a diversity of factors into an economic narrative around health has been to limit the focus to the more easily measurable indicators.

Others suggest that the One Health paradigm needs to embrace the wider system factors that contribute to disease emergence. This points to underlying structural conditions and local ecological disease contexts that have largely been ignored in the three dominant narratives, but are, as some commentators suggest, critical to prevention as well as locally attuned responses (e.g. Waltner-Toews, 2001; Charron, 2012a). As a leading figure in the global public health community observed:

> the real solution is going back even further to the determinants, to what's causing those infections in animals and preventing them occurring.... So moving the paradigm, or shifting it from the present rapid detection of response back to prevention hopefully can decrease or even prevent some of these emergences from occurring.

As we suggested earlier, such dimensions can be seen as part of an alternative, though marginalized, fourth One Health narrative. The reasons for marginalization relate partly to questions of organizational mandates and funding and professional expertise. However, political-economic factors work against the more structural and social changes required. They suggest an undermining of response-focused solutions based on drugs and vaccines that serve important commercial interests and have become embedded in standard government responses. As a US State Department official pointed out: 'a lot of health ministries, and health ministers, are focused on a pharmaceutical solution, where the biggest solution might be a social one'. A senior official of the European CDC wondered about whether versions of One Health that suggested shifts in industrial agriculture and food production would ever take hold:

> I believe in One Health, but I'm a little bit cynical as to whether you do get changes in animal husbandry, and particularly surveillance in animal husbandry, if it potentially affects the production of industrial food products. It's a very, very valid approach, an essential approach; I'm just questioning whether people will be prepared to see it through.

In essence, the challenge is around confronting powerful interests and entrenched political-economic relations.

An alternative One Health narrative that takes local contexts seriously also requires the empowerment of alternative voices. This was summed up by one informant:

> One Health could deliver if it's afforded the opportunity of giving people and the community the sense that this agenda is going to service local needs and not just international needs having to do with security and commerce on a grand scale.

Local agendas suggest that there is not One World, One Health, but in fact multiple ways of understanding and producing healthy animals, bodies and ecologies, involving an array of localized practices situated within wider sets of structural drivers (Wallace *et al.*, 2015) and fundamentally requiring a social science perspective that integrates fully with community knowledge and priorities (Parkes *et al.*, 2005; Craddock and Hinchliffe, 2015; Lapinski *et al.*, 2014; Bardosh, 2014). Yet such a view contrasts sharply with the three narratives dominating global discussions of One Health, which all in different ways tend to simplify complex and uncertain dynamics, conforming the One Health agenda to issues that can be easily defined and measured in ways that synchronize with established models of resource mobilization and interests.

Conclusions

One Health has risen up the policy agenda in a dramatic way in the past decade. It has generated much research and policy debate, and a whole series of meetings, workshops, statements, networks, consortia, initiatives and funding flows. In many respects an integrated approach to responding to disease threats through combining animal, human and ecosystem health is simple common sense. It is also not new, as there is a long history of practical, integrated approaches with different labels, such as Ecohealth (Zinsstag, 2012), and none. What is significant about the past decade has been the level of interest in the approach, and the degree of policy attention and resource mobilization associated with it.

Here we have traced the emergence of One Health as a concept. Through an analysis of policy documents and an analysis of key informant interviews carried out since 2008, we have identified three dominant One Health narratives, each suggesting a set of policy responses, and associated justifications. These were 'integration', 'risk and surveillance outbreak' and 'cost–benefit economics'. None of these focused, however, on what we identified as a fourth, somewhat hidden narrative, that offers a rather different framing, and questions the universalized globalism of the core policy narratives. This focused on local understandings, structural drivers, and the diverse framings of health emerging from local settings.

As we argued, One Health was projected to the centre of the policy stage in the context of several avian influenza outbreaks in the early 2000s and large-scale global disease threats with pandemic potential have continued to dominate the research and policy debate. This has driven funding flows for policy initiatives and scientific research, with zoonoses (avian and swine influenza and more recently Ebola) attracting significant interest and associated funding. But a lagging question remains: if One Health is obviously such a good idea (perhaps just common sense), then why is it not more widely practised and institutionalized outside this emergency model? With all the funds, events, publications and initiatives, why has it not had more of an impact? It is of course difficult to assess 'impact', as there are so many variables and attribution is difficult. Meanwhile some remarkable headway has been made, as many of our informants noted. However, as our discussion shows, despite the claims that One Health is central to a global challenge of emerging infectious disease, especially from zoonotic origin (as well as, as discussed above, many other disease challenges without the headline-grabbing policy attention), there are some real constraints to making One Health happen in practice.

Many of these limitations are created by remaining barriers between human and veterinary medicine, as well as lack of human and economic resources and institutional capacities and support, especially in the Global South (Smith *et al.*, 2015; Okello *et al.*, 2014a; Bardosh *et al.*, 2014a, 2014b). In this chapter, however, we elaborate three additional recurrent limitations. These are: organizational and funding modalities, disciplinary and professional silos, and conflicting interpretations of the meaning of integration. All are deeply structural, embedded in particular types of legitimated knowledge, certain institutions and professions, and all wrapped up in complex power relations. They are all at root political economy explanations, of knowledge, organization and interests. This means that existing arrangements, current practices and incumbent, powerful institutions are all difficult to shift. And this despite the cacophony of (common sense) rhetoric, and the increasingly well-articulated justifications, offered in different registers, from economic value to moral imperative, and a whole array of fora.

One of the issues is that it is often not clear what a move to One Health would actually entail in practical terms. Beyond the rhetoric, the substance is often remarkably thin, and remarkably few examples exist on the ground by way of illustration. As we have noted, cynics, with some justification, see it as a last-gasp attempt by veterinarians to claim a slice of the funding pie as well as improved social standing, while others recognize the value in theoretical terms and see more coordination and integration simply as an escalation of transactions costs without any evidence of real tangible benefits. Others see One Health as a threat to professional, disciplinary and institutional specializations that they hold dear. With decreasing public funds for a whole array of activities, others fear the prospect of sharing this more widely, especially to those not traditionally party to such funding sources, such as social scientists and ecologists. So without a clear 'business case' (Grace, 2014) or 'proof of concept' (Bonfoh *et al.*, 2011), too easily the default is the status quo.

These discussions are occurring within a mainstream One Health community, with all the geographical, disciplinary and institutional biases we have identified, and so reflect a particular set of turf wars, particularly between vets and medics. Another, perhaps more fundamental, challenge comes from outside these networks, questioning some of the more fundamental tenets of One Health framing, asking, 'whose world, whose health?' is being talked about by the One Health research and policy communities. This comes from a social science critique that argues that an unquestioning globalism hides politics and disciplines in practice and policy, constraining alternative knowledge and framings about what matters for whom (Dry and Leach, 2010; Scoones, 2010; Hinchliffe, 2014). There are multiple worlds and multiple healths that emerge in context, and tensions manifest between them.

This more political argument does not chime easily with the institutional politics of One Health that is attempting to bring together large, monolithic organizations that have traditionally competed (Chien, 2013). It problematizes the notion of integration and simplistic holism, as this will always involve negotiation of what we mean by 'health' and for whom, and whose knowledge counts – an intensely political process. And it sits uneasily with the classic internationalism of One Health that often elides with a Northern domination of institutions and geopolitics, including in health (Elbe, 2010a; Davies et al., 2014). It questions how health inequalities, and forms of 'structural violence' (Farmer, 2004b) emerge in a highly unequal world, and how this influences how diseases emerge and who gets sick.

Unfortunately, as our analysis has shown, such alternative framings sit outside mainstream One Health networks that, except for a scattering of economists, largely exclude social scientists as well as the broader social determinants of health.

If One Health is to have genuine purchase and real impact, and so become rooted in new ways of thinking and working that genuinely challenge current practice then, we argue, there will need to be a more radical overhaul of current research and policy networks to allow such alternative framings to have a space. The rise of One Health thinking has created in practice quite a narrow set of networks, associated with a core group of people and organizations and set of framings that regularly exclude key aspects of debate. Contrary to the claims, One Health runs the danger of getting siloed and institutionalized with new forms of funding and power, and so becoming subject to precisely the problem it has sought to challenge. We hope that a critical reflection on the political economy of One Health – its origins, narratives, research-policy networks and its future – as offered in this chapter will provide some challenges to the One Health approach as it has emerged, encouraging it to broaden out framings and open up to more diverse knowledges and practices than it has to date, and thus become more easily implemented in practice in the real, diverse, uncertain world.

Notes

1 Interview data is derived from 83 key informant interviews carried out at various points between 2008 and 2013. These were transcribed and analysed by the authors. Interviews came from work carried out for the IDS/SPRU STEPS Centre multidisciplinary epidemics project with Paul Forster, mostly during 2008 (Scoones, 2010); video interviews

at the STEPS Centre/Centre for Global Health Policy workshop on Pandemic Flu Controversies carried out by Naomi Marks (IDS, Sussex, January 2013); Skype and phone interviews carried out for the project on the political economy of trypanosomiasis by Ian Scoones; interviews and discussions at the LCIRAH workshop 2012 (LSHTM, London, 2–3 July 2012), carried out by Ian Scoones; and interviews/informal discussions at the Africa Ecohealth conference (Abidjan, July 2013), carried out by Naomi Marks and Victor Galaz. A total of 28 interviews are quoted in the chapter. These are all anonymized, with additional information provided in a previous working paper: http://steps-centre.org/wp-content/uploads/One-Health-wp3.pdf. Interviewees include senior policy advisors and officials mainly from prominent international organizations, and researchers from various disciplines from all over the world, all working on issues related to 'One Health'. By focusing on active participants in the debate, our aim was to gain insights into the politics of policy processes from insiders' perspectives. Through this multi-pronged methodology, following Keeley and Scoones (2003), we were therefore able to investigate narratives, interests, actors and networks operating in the world of policy and practice, as well as academic research, and so examine the interrelationships between them.

2 In addition to our interviews, we also analysed 28 policy documents published between 2004 and 2013, all frequently cited in discussions of One Health policy, to identify definitions and associated narratives. Documents were selected purposively based on levels of citation, internal cross-referencing and mention by interviewees. These included policy documents from key One Health organizations, including from the AVMA, CDC, OIE, FAO, WHO, WCS, WB, Public Health Agency of Canada, ILRI and Institute of Medicine (for a full list, see: http://steps-centre.org/wp-content/uploads/One-Health-wp3.pdf). These documents were chosen from a purposive search via Google/Google scholar, as well as our own knowledge of these debates, of those that had been widely used (as reflected in Google citations) and also to gain a range of cases across different organizations. While the sample is far from comprehensive, it covers the range of mainstream policy positions as reflected in the grey policy literature.

3 The term ecohealth, which emerged in the 1980s as environmental issues and sustainability became more prominent in public debate (Waltner-Toews, 2001; Charron, 2012), is highly complementary but with different emphases (Zinsstag, 2012). We have chosen One Health as our focus for analysis because of its contemporary policy prominence and its influence on policy framing, research prioritization and funding flows.

4 www.cdc.gov/onehealth/resources/recent-meetings.html#one, accessed 8 July 2015.

5 http://globalhealthvet.com/2011/02/20/one-health-congress-report-14-16-feb-2011-melbourne-australia, accessed 8 July 2015.

6 www.sacids.org/kms/frontend/?m=101, accessed 8 July 2015.

7 See: www.onehealthglobal.net; www.onehealthinitiative.com; www.onehealthcommission.org, among others; accessed 8 July 2015.

8 See endnote above.

9 Examples are: Emerging Pandemic Threats programme funded by USAID (www.usaid.gov/news-information/fact-sheets/emerging-pandemic-threats-program, accessed 8 July 2015); Bill & Melinda Gates Foundation (BMGF) One Health challenge call; UK Government Zoonoses and Emerging Livestock Systems (ZELS) Programme (see www.bbsrc.ac.uk/funding/opportunities/2012/zoonoses-emerging-livestock-systems, accessed 8 July 2015); and the EU-funded Integrated Control of Neglected Zoonoses (ICONZ) project (www.iconzafrica.org, accessed 8 July 2015), to name a few.

10 Recent calls in the UK have explicitly involved social science funding, such as the Zoonoses and Emerging Livestock Systems programme (ZELS). Equally, funding for the Dynamic Drivers of Diseases in Africa Consortium, from which this chapter emerges, also encourages cross-disciplinary working between social and ecosystem sciences (www.espa.ac.uk, accessed 8 July 2015). The UK Department for International Development (DFID) plays an important role in this context as a major funder.

3

KNOWLEDGE FLOWS IN ONE HEALTH

The evolution of scientific collaboration networks

Sophie Valeix, Christian Stein and Kevin Bardosh

Introduction

In this chapter we unpack contemporary patterns of research collaboration currently dominating scientific knowledge production around One Health. Based on an analysis of co-authorship networks and using methods from social network analysis (SNA), we identify key actors, disciplines and geographic regions dominating the scientific discourse relevant to One Health. This allows us to explore: who is doing what, with whom and where?

Understanding co-authorship patterns and the associated flow of scientific knowledge offers an opportunity to track the degree to which notions of integration between disciplines and regions, as promoted by One Health, have actually taken place in different global and national domains. Collaboration in research networks is an important mechanism for the integration of public health issues (Axelsson and Axelsson, 2006). Scientific knowledge guides the ways in which policy-makers, practitioners and others perceive societal problems and design solutions, offering credibility and justification to policy concepts such as One Health. The characteristics of existing research networks represent the latent capacity of individuals, organizations and regions of the world to understand and respond to emerging and endemic zoonoses; hence they act as an important proxy for the resilience of current disease preparedness and response systems.

Such scientific collaboration networks, however, are not neutral but are borne of particular social contexts; their characteristics influence knowledge production and flows between geographies and disciplines. They represent complex interplays between different cognitive, material and socio-cultural structures that shape knowledge production, its dissemination and synthesis. These networks are shaped by the social and political structures of research funding, as well as the cultural values and normative assumptions that guide scientific communities, and their interactions, as they engage in theoretical and practical issues. The notion of 'organizational cultures' is central to understanding the various social and bureaucratic barriers involved in effective research collaboration and the promotion of inter-disciplinary science (Jerolmack, 2013). At the institutional level, major challenges still remain in fostering effective One Health research collaboration; these surround issues of prioritization, mandates, jurisdictions, silos and funding streams, for example. Understanding existing networks can contribute to our understanding of One Health operationalization, and its challenges.

This chapter first tracks the geographic location, disciplines and relationships of key One Health organizations through the analysis of co-authorship networks related to One Health research in the peer-reviewed literature. We then explore one particular zoonosis, Nipah virus, as a case study to map out scientific research networks and their evolution over time. Nipah virus, an RNA virus transmitted from fruit bats to pigs to people, emerged in Malaysia in 1998 and has generated significant research and policy interest due to its potential to cause a future global pandemic. Recent interest in Nipah has also focused on Africa. The chapter maps out the characteristics and evolution of international scientific collaboration for Nipah between 1999 and 2011, and its relevance to our understanding of research networks in regard to the One Health movement and principles.

The network studies presented in this chapter highlight tensions in patterns of global collaboration and their politics, revealing that One Health networks are, despite the inclusive rhetoric, largely dominated by key players from the Global North. In this way, the chapter maps out some of the limits to the current rhetoric of integration and collaboration between disciplines and between regional research communities, and reflects on some of the social and political issues at play mediating these dynamics, as well as possible future directions to address them.

Theorizing One Health research networks

Understanding the evolving system of scientific research in the field of One Health allows us to explore the degree and characteristics of contemporary research collaborations and interdisciplinary science. While international flows of knowledge are impossible to determine with precision,[1] SNA has become an increasingly popular methodology to understand research networks based on co-authorship and citation relationships found in the peer-reviewed scientific literature (Hislop, 2013).[2] Bibliometric data offer a chance to explore networks of researchers who share professional interests. Online databases, such as Scopus or Web of Science, provide information on who is publishing with whom, from what geographic regions and about which topics. Using this information to analyse and visualize networks of scientific collaboration allows the exploration of knowledge flows, identification of cohesive subgroups as well as key players within these networks.

Interdisciplinary One Health collaboration, after all, is a deeply social process and good professional linkages, developed formally and informally during professional meetings and conferences, are significant drivers to developing strong personal relationships based on trust and respect (Anholt *et al.*, 2012). The act of co-publishing is a representation of this social process. It manifests and represents knowledge sharing between researchers (Wagner and Leydesdorff, 2005). Co-publishing includes a bilateral selection process, where both sides are interested in being partners (Schmoch and Schubert, 2008). Adams *et al.* (2005) describe scientific collaboration as being a 'channel of knowledge flows between scientists'. Hence the social study of scientific networks is a powerful tool to analyse and visualize repeated exchanges between social agents, but understanding these dynamics also requires appreciating some important theoretical concepts and complementary methodological approaches.[3]

Sociologists over the past few decades have spent a lot of time trying to understand how social networks form and how they function. A central network theory is the notion of social capital, which represents the latent resources generated by social relationships. The definition of social capital varies in the literature, emphasizing different elements, but the core idea is that relationships provide access to resources. Nahapiet and Ghoshal (1998, p243) define social capital as 'the sum of the actual and potential resources embedded within, available through, and derived from the network of relationships possessed by an individual or social unit'.

Social capital helps the maintenance and growth of a community as the benefits of social relationships go beyond individual actors to strengthen the larger community by creating positive externalities that can, for example, improve information flow, increase the speed of knowledge generation and provide greater capabilities for action (Nahapiet and Ghoshal, 1998). Network theorists also emphasize the role of 'knowledge brokers', who occupy a strategic position in networks and thereby influence network dynamics. Brokers find themselves participating in the knowledge flows but also controlling them since they constitute privileged intermediaries between groups of people (Burt, 2001).

A related concept is the notion of Communities of Practice (COPs) found in the organizational management literature. COPs can be defined as 'groups of people who share a concern or a passion for something they do and learn how to do it better as they interact regularly' (Wenger, 2000). By engaging in the practice of a common activity, they voluntarily share knowledge and establish shared identity and values (Wenger, 2000). Studies on research-based COPs have tended to show that higher individual research performance (e.g. more publications by an individual author) are based on developing long-lasting connections with different types of collaborators. This suggests that key organizations or individuals could serve as unique bonds between different communities (thus acting as knowledge brokers), who hold very different norms and values.

Fostering social capital, COPs and knowledge brokers in zoonoses research networks can be central components of making collaboration and interdisciplinary science happen. But building social capital and encouraging the establishment of COPs bonded through specific knowledge brokers is not necessarily sufficient to operationalize One Health. Their specific characteristics also matter tremendously. Nahapiet and Ghoshal showed that for an organization to learn and innovate, social capital needs to be transformed into what they called 'intellectual capital', which they defined as 'the knowledge and knowing capability of a social collectivity, such as an organization, intellectual community, or professional practice' (Nahapiet and Ghoshal, 1998, p245). The key point here is that individuals and organizations do not exist in a vacuum, but are embedded in relationships that have implications for their ability to access, produce and share resources, including scientific knowledge. An analysis of the patterns of collaboration among researchers and their networks can help to shed light on how zoonosis and One Health scientific discourses have evolved over time, and what this means for addressing health risks at the human–animal–ecosystem interface.

The global One Health research network

This chapter includes two separate co-authorship network studies based on bibliometric data related to One Health. The first study involved assessing the growth and characteristics of the One Health movement through tracking peer-reviewed research publications on the general theme of 'One Health' from 2007 to early 2014, which was extracted from the Web of Science database.[4] The second study focuses on the specific case of Nipah virus and explores in detail the evolution of international scientific collaboration about this emergent zoonotic agent.

With regards to the co-authorship network on One Health, we found a rise of One Health in titles and abstracts of published articles over time, and a particular increase in 2009 when articles on swine flu, as well as broader reflections post-avian influenza, were being published (see Figure 3.1). This reveals the dominant link of

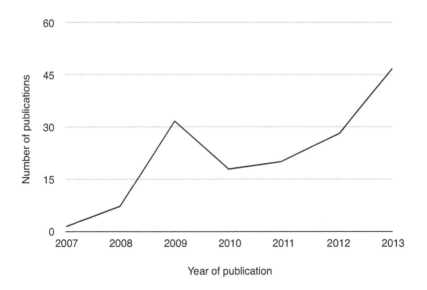

FIGURE 3.1 Annual output of One Health articles in peer-reviewed literature[5]

One Health research to policy concerns about global pandemics. Figure 3.2 shows the co-authorship network of organizations that published together in the field of One Health, based on the 157 articles in the Web of Science database between 2007 and early 2014, and selected post-screening.[6] In this network, a relationship between two organizations is defined by the joint publication of one or more peer-reviewed articles on One Health. As the network map shows, there is a dominance in published outputs by actors from the Global North, who are at the centre of a number of clusters (highlighted by the dense connections within the map). This is despite repeated calls for more integration and representation from the Global South, and the rhetoric about global public goods and 'One World, One Health'. This is reinforced by the data in Figure 3.3, which show that 80 per cent of author-ship was by scientists affiliated with an institution from the Global North.[7]

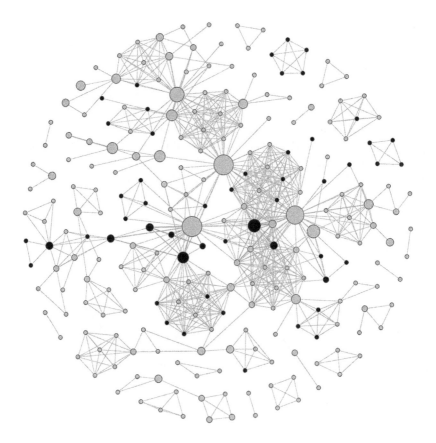

FIGURE 3.2 Co-authorship network of institutions that have published on One Health.

Institutions are colour-coded by geographic representation from Global North (grey nodes) and Global South (black nodes). The node size is based on the number of pub-lications the institution has co-authored

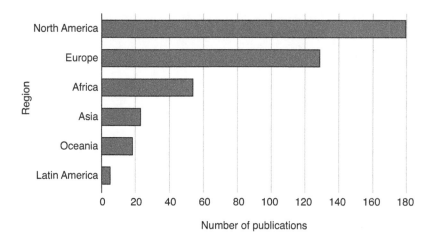

FIGURE 3.3 Publication record, based on regional affiliation of authors

The major clusters within the overall One Health network map shown in Figure 3.2 are shown in more detail in Figure 3.4. This network map highlights organizations that have many co-authorship relationships. While some clusters contain organizations from the Global South, others are exclusively Northern. The network mapping brings to light some of the key actors that connect otherwise disconnected clusters within the overall network (so-called knowledge brokers). These include some of the most prominent One Health research collaborations centred on Switzerland (Swiss Tropical Institute), London (London School of Hygiene and Tropical Medicine; Royal Veterinary College) and the United States (UC Davis), and to a lesser extent the US Department of Agriculture (USDA). These institutions, and their associated individuals, often occupy key positions in the network, thereby bridging otherwise disconnected clusters.[8] These players also appear to act as brokers between scientific and policy worlds (Pielke, 2007). This makes the few science-policy brokers, and their associated institutions (in the USA and Europe), essential for linking the worlds of academic publishing and policy engagement, a separation that appears quite distinct even in this most policy-relevant area of research (see also Galaz *et al.*, this book).

Table 3.1 highlights the disciplinary foci of publications related to One Health, using Web of Science journal information as a proxy for disciplines.[9] It shows the strong representation of veterinary sciences. Medical sciences were also important, making 11 per cent of publications, while there were few articles covering ecological and social sciences. Most publications have appeared in journals associated with veterinary sciences, suggesting that veterinarians are currently driving and dominating the scientific discussion on One Health. However, it proved difficult to associate a certain discipline with some articles; hence the large category of ambiguous disciplinary associations. Some papers were also linked to a range of 'other' sciences, while a few were categorized by the Web of Science as 'multidisciplinary science'.

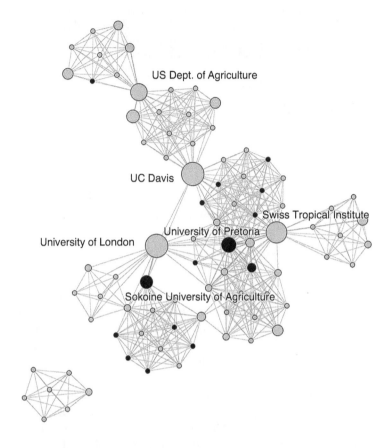

FIGURE 3.4 Network diagram of co-publishing patterns between organizations that have six or more co-authorship relationships.

Nodes are colour-coded by geographic representation from Global North (grey nodes) and Global South (black nodes)

TABLE 3.1 Disciplines associated with articles published on One Health over the period 2007–2014 based on Web of Science categories

Disciplines associated with publications	Percentage
Veterinary	61
Ambiguous	13
Medical	11
Ecology/environment	5
Other	4
Multidisciplinary sciences	3
Social sciences	3

This short co-authorship network analysis does have some acknowledged limitations that need to be accounted for; however, the revealed patterns of scientific collaboration highlight some noteworthy trends in the One Health global research network.[10] The results show that the relative growth of One Health research is largely associated with a relative few key actors and their tightly linked networks, mostly centred in Europe and the USA and involving veterinary science organizations. While southern collaboration is sought, such authors are generally not at the centre of such networks. Two exceptions to this seem to be the University of Pretoria (South Africa) and Sokoine University of Agriculture (Tanzania) (or individuals within these institutions), both of which have significant publication outputs on One Health. In the next section, we focus on the case of Nipah virus, and explore in greater depth the characteristics of zoonoses scientific networks, how they evolve over time and what these network dynamics tell us about One Health.

The case of Nipah virus: exploring network evolution

As noted above, our global research network analysis identified Nipah virus as a major zoonotic disease focus for One Health research. Nipah offers an interesting window into how One Health scientific networks oriented around emerging zoonotic diseases are formed and change over time, and how principles of collaboration, inter-disciplinarity and integration play out in practice.

Among the range of zoonotic pathogens, ribonucleic acid (RNA)[11] viruses attract great attention because of their high rate of mutation and ability to cross species barriers (Jones *et al.*, 2008). In fact, RNA viruses have long been the favourite class of microbial candidates for the next global pandemic, and include Ebola, Severe Acute Respiratory Syndrome (SARS), influenza, polio, measles and West Nile virus. Nipah virus, a more recent addition, was first documented in 1999 in Malaysia, when found in people in close contact with sick pigs presenting severe febrile encephalitis. Scientists found that the likely source of contamination to pigs were four species of fruit bats, the wild reservoir of Nipah, roosting near large pig farms and contaminating fruits with saliva and urine that would then be eaten by pigs (Chua, 2003). The same year, the outbreak spread to several Malaysian states and to Singapore through the importation of pigs from infected areas. The outbreak resulted in 109 human deaths and only stopped after the culling of over one million pigs and the ban of pig exports (Luby, 2013). In Bangladesh, Nipah virus has been found to be transmissible from humans to humans through direct contact; multiple outbreaks have been reported in the country, and occasionally in India, since 2001 (Gurley *et al.*, 2007b; Luby, 2013).

Figuié (2014) coined the term 'anticipated catastrophes' to characterize the uncertain and dynamic risks of emerging diseases. While scientists have debated the likelihood of Nipah causing a deadly global pandemic through sustained nosocomial transmission, there is far from a consensus. The virus strains identified in Bangladesh present greater genetic variability than the initial strains found in Malaysia, which are possibly associated with a greater propensity for human-to-human transmission (Luby, 2013). However, so far the characteristics of the known virus strains are not compatible with a pandemic. As with other RNA viruses, Nipah does have a great ability for mutations, which suggests that these characteristics could change over time. Given these uncertainties, and the relatively small number of human cases to date, it is unclear how much time and money should be devoted to a disease that has so far 'only' caused small-scale outbreaks in Asia.

Nonetheless, significant amounts of research have been conducted on the virus since 1999 for several reasons. First, it is a virus of bats. Bats have been found to be wild reservoirs for many emerging pathogens, especially of Paramyxoviridae family viruses, which includes Nipah but also mumps, measles and rinderpest. Second, Hendra virus (belonging to the same genus as Nipah)[12] has received much attention in Australia, where it has caused infections in humans and horses; research carried out on Nipah stimulates research on Hendra, and vice versa. Third, Nipah has recently been identified in bat blood samples in Ghana and Madagascar (Peel et al., 2012). This has stimulated an active search for the virus in other African countries, with the idea that Nipah's geographic distribution may follow the natural distribution of Old World fruit bats and that the virus might even have originated from the African continent (Hayman et al., 2012). With a distinct and complex disease ecology, possible growing geographic scope and the potential for human-to-human transmission, the pandemic potential of Nipah virus clearly contributes to a relatively visible research portfolio in the world of zoonoses.

It was for these reasons that we undertook a detailed social network analysis of co-publishing trends in Nipah virus research between 1999 and 2011, which allowed us to track changes in the research network of this emerging zoonotic disease from the point of first discovery. We aimed to use this to provide insights into current One Health network dynamics, specifically the structure and characteristics of existing research networks, and what they tell us about scientific collaboration on zoonotic disease. In this regard, we established a few hypotheses about how the research network, if following the One Health policy rhetoric of collaboration and multidisciplinary research, should evolve and change over time. These are summarized in Table 3.2. In general, we assumed that the network would become progressively more collaborative, more interdisciplinary and more integrated as acceptance of One Health principles became more widely disseminated and as the network itself consolidated knowledge and expertise. This would include a growth of cooperation between different types of organizations in the field, greater social and intellectual capital generated through networking and capacity-building efforts, as well as an expansion of research nodes associated with southern researchers.

Nodes and knowledge brokers

Concerned primarily with the strengths and characteristics of collaboration, our analysis of Nipah virus research networks solely involved so-called 'collaborative

TABLE 3.2 Expected network features consistent or inconsistent with One Health collaboration principles

Consistent with One Health	Inconsistent with One Health	Study measurement
• Organizations increasingly linked to others • Increase in number of knowledge brokers	• Organizations remain isolated • Few or decreasing number of knowledge brokers	This includes two SNA techniques: (1) the degree centrality calculus (which corresponds to the number of links each organization has on average during one period), and (2) the count of knowledge brokers based on the betweenness centrality measure (BC).★
• Increases in collaboration between fields and disciplines of research • Increasing rate of interdisciplinary publications	• One or more field(s) still weakly involved in cooperation • Steady or decreasing rate of interdisciplinary publications	Greater involvement of interdisciplinary organizations and a greater cooperation between organizations belonging to different fields. This can be analysed by looking at changes in the shape of networks over time.
• Increases in collaboration between types of organizations	• One or several types of organizations prevails	Greater cooperation between organizations was tested by observing changes in the shape of polarized networks, and by exploring the different types of organizations involved in the network over time.
• Increasing involvement of countries worldwide • Increases in collaboration between different countries (internationalization) and countries of different economic statuses • Sustained involvement of countries where diseases emerge, or outbreaks occur, and collaboration between these high-risk countries (mainly South–South collaboration)	• Progressive exclusion of a group or category of countries in the network • Same countries remain involved over time • Communities of practice are predominately linked by wealthier countries, who control the passage of knowledge by acting as knowledge brokers • Little South–South collaboration.	Number of countries publishing, and observation of their position in the networks over time. This also includes exploring the types of brokers' positions in the network, especially those coming from developing countries.

Note
★ This number corresponds to the 'number of times an actor connects pairs of other actors, who otherwise would not be able to reach one another' (Safahieh *et al.*, 2012).

networks' – where authors co-publish with authors from other organizations.[13] We decided to exclude isolated nodes, which represent organizations publishing by themselves (40 per cent during the first period (46/114 nodes), 62 per cent (133/235) in the second and 22 per cent (60/272) in the third). The resulting 'collaborative network' is presented in Figure 3.5. Organizations having more collaborators are represented as bigger nodes (proportionally to the number of collaborators they have). These network structures show significant change over time.

The early network (1999–2002) showed a clear distinction between the centre and the periphery (see Figure 3.5). The organizations that collaborated the most,

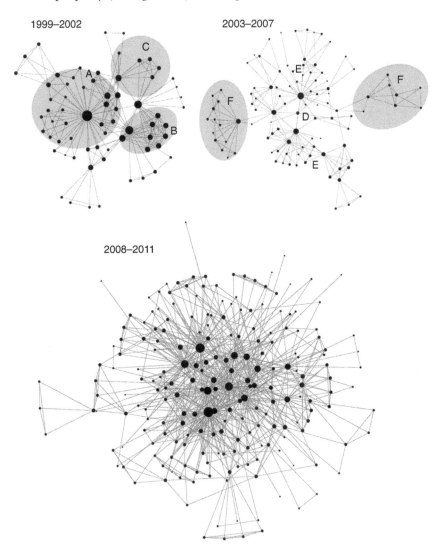

FIGURE 3.5 Networks of collaborative organizations publishing on Nipah across three periods from 1999–2011

and hence had the largest nodes in the network, were the Centres for Disease Control and Prevention (CDC) (with 40 collaborators), the University of Malaya ($n=24$) and the Australian Animal Health Laboratory ($n=19$). We could identify three groups of organizations that were highly collaborating with each other (nodes of a relatively large size). These are groups of organizations actually located mostly in the same geographic regions (see disks A, B and C in Figure 3.5). The first group (disk A) is composed of the CDC (Atlanta, USA) and most of the Malaysian organizations. This is also the most central community in the network. The second one (Disk B) is made up of Australian organizations[14] intensely connected with each other, and also with the University of Malaysia (Malaysia). The University of Malaysia and the Australian Commonwealth Scientific and Industrial Research Organisation (CSIRO) make the link between groups (disks) A and B. The third group (disk C) consists of Singaporean organizations only. Contrary to the 'Australian group' (B), the Singaporean group (C) has no intermediary or knowledge broker. Most of these Singaporean organizations (disk C) are also directly connected to an organization from the central network (disk A). It is worth noticing the central position of the CDC, which seems to have occupied a strategic position of coordinator for the whole network, especially with actors from low- and middle-income countries.

During the second publication period, 2003–2007, the network underwent some significant changes. There was no longer a separation between organizations in the centre and in the periphery; instead, the network was divided into three different levels (see Figure 3.5). The first level was at the centre, or core, of the network (D), and contained the most important collaborators (large nodes). Again, this was the CDC (23 collaborators) and the Australian Animal Health Laboratory ($n=31$) and a new third organization that was not a major node during the first period of analysis: the Pasteur Institute, with 15 partners. The second level (E) included the University of Malaya, present in the earlier network, and a new important actor: the International Centre for Diarrhoeal Disease Research, in Dhaka, Bangladesh (ICDDR, B). At that time, all these foreign (non-Malaysian) organizations were (and still are) recognized as high-quality research centres for transboundary infectious diseases with multiple branches or partners internationally. The third level (F) included two communities of actors at the margins of the network, linked to the core (D) by only one or two nodes. They encompass organizations mainly from high-income countries (with an important presence in the USA) linked with the core of the network by important knowledge brokers: organizations that ensure the link between 'external' groups and the core by having a moderate to high number of connections. Compared to the first period, the network architecture appears to have shifted; in the second period, the network included a greater diversity of countries and continents, which is a sign of increased collaboration between disparate geographic and socio-cultural research groups.

Looking at the last period (2008–2011), there was a substantial increase in the size of the collaboration network, which involved a greater number of organizations (Figure 3.5). In addition to getting larger, the network became less dense over time.[15] These results are not surprising. In a network with a greater number of nodes, the probability that actors will link with one another is lower, and large networks usually appear to be less dense. Moreover, there is no longer a separation between central nodes and the periphery of the network. Instead, the network appears as a dense web of organizations with a core composed of highly collaborative organizations (large nodes) surrounded by a cloud of less and less collaborative nodes (when moving away from the centre).

When exploring network dynamics, it is important to consider the degree of centrality. This reflects the average number of organizational partners each organization has within this main network.[16] As with the total number of nodes in the collaborative network, the number of collaborators also decreased in the second period and then increased in the third. This is consistent with the observed presence of small, isolated networks during the second wave (not shown here because we only looked at the main collaborative network). Indeed, there was a trend towards isolated relationships in the second period. By contrast, in the last period, scientists favoured collaboration with well-connected individuals.

As the number of organizations involved in the network increased, we also saw an increase in the number of organizations that linked otherwise non-connected groups of organizations (knowledge brokers). These organizations appear as visible nodes in Figure 3.6, with a size proportional to the importance of their broker role. The proportion of knowledge brokers[17] increased from 19 per cent in the first period, to 27 per cent in the second and 34 per cent in the third. This indicates greater links between groups within the collaboration network over time. Few organizations have occupied a very central position in all the three periods. For example, besides being connected with a lot of organizations, the CDC also acted as a major knowledge broker. These two characteristics mean that the CDC was collaborating with many partners to produce knowledge while also linking together groups that would not otherwise be linked. These two functions appear to be essential components in the development of strong One Health networks. But as knowledge brokers became more abundant over time, the individual importance of each broker (e.g. CDC) reduced as the power of each broker became sub-divided. This makes the network less dependent on a few organizations to facilitate brokerage functions, which is generally considered a sign of a 'healthy' network that is more likely to sustain itself.

However, the Nipah research architecture simultaneously showed a reduction in the number of actors from low-income countries (LICs) and middle-income countries (MICs) in knowledge broker positions (Figure 3.6).[18] Because of the emergence of Nipah virus in Malaysia, Malaysian universities and government agencies were acting as knowledge brokers during the first period of publication. From 2003, however, fewer organizations from LICs and MICs maintained such positions in the network. The proportion of developing countries involved in knowledge brokerage decreased over time: from 13 per cent in 1999–2002, 4 per cent in 2003–2007 and 6 per cent in 2008–2011. Note that the ICCDR, B was one of the last organizations from a low- or middle-income country that remained as an important knowledge broker during the last publication period, certainly because of the recurrent outbreaks in Bangladesh from 2001 onwards.

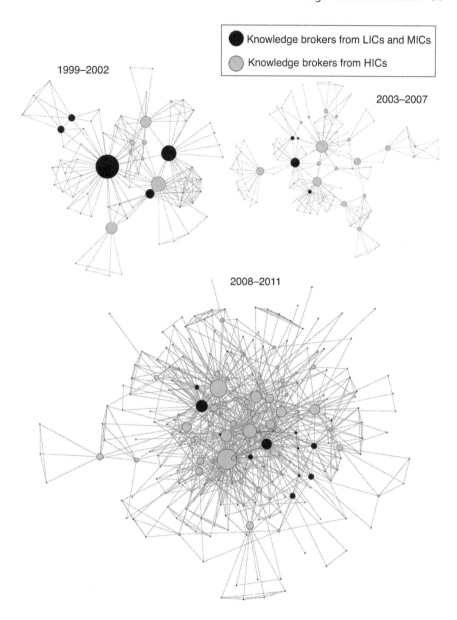

FIGURE 3.6 Visualization of knowledge brokers in the collaboration networks of the three periods studied

Network composition

Our analysis also explored the network composition of Nipah virus research, which included the geographical and disciplinary characteristics of the organizations involved and their relationships. These dynamics are important in tracing the degree of trans- and interdisciplinary science, as well as the inclusion of low and medium-income country researchers, in the One Health community.

We found an increase over time in the level of collaboration between medical, veterinary and environmental health researchers, but this was compounded by a general increase in each of the research disciplines during the second and third periods (Figure 3.7). There was a limited change in the proportions of organizations engaged in Nipah research by field category, with the medical field remaining dominant during all 13 years. The large number of human medical organizations and a corresponding decrease of veterinarians can be attributed to the fact that Bangladesh faced human cases involving person-to-person transmission starting in 2001 (Luby, 2013). This is somewhat unique, since our global One Health network analysis showed a predominance of veterinary sciences. In fact, most authors see physicians as fundamentally less motivated than veterinarians and ecologists in cooperating with other disciplines, due to their tendency to attract greater funding and a latent sense of superiority (Leboeuf, 2011). Our study did show an increase of environmental health research over time, and greater links between the medical and environmental health sectors, which were initially weak but grew progressively stronger. However, the search for the virus outside Asia (e.g. Africa) and in wild species (especially bats) likely contributed to this growth. Interdisciplinary research grew in parallel with the growth of other fields and in parallel with the recruitment

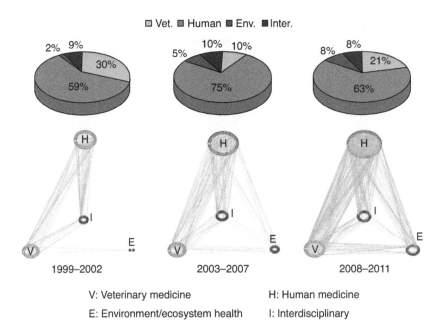

V: Veterinary medicine   H: Human medicine

E: Environment/ecosystem health   I: Interdisciplinary

FIGURE 3.7 Publication periods separated by disciplinary focus. The percentages correspond to the proportions of research organizations involved in one field of research or several (interdisciplinary)[19]

of new organizations. Important interdisciplinary organizations included: the Eco-Health Alliance (USA), the Queensland Centre for Emerging Infectious Diseases (Australia) and the Research Group for Emerging Zoonoses (Germany). These organizations displayed a clear willingness to integrate several disciplines into their Nipah research portfolio, but still represented a relatively small number of organizations.

Similar changes occurred in the type of organizations involved in the network.[20] Over the 13-year period, universities and government agencies were the dominant type of organizations publishing research on Nipah and the connections between the two got stronger over time. Government agencies were the most numerous organizations involved in collaborative research for the first publication period (1999–2003). However, university departments took over by 2003 as the dominant type of organization in the network, but with government departments and the private sector (mainly pharmaceutical laboratories) also acting as important players. By contrast, the number of hospitals, NGOs and international organizations remained comparatively small during all three publication periods. This could be explained by the fact that these organizations are typically involved during, or just after, disease outbreaks, where they tend to conduct rather isolated research. Universities are involved in more long-term research initiatives, and governments certainly play a role of coordinator between different organizations. This may suggest that in the current One Health movement, international organizations might have an overestimated role while the significance of government agencies may be substantially under-appreciated.

Another important network characteristic involved the geographical location of research organizations. As with knowledge brokers, the proportion of LICs and MICs decreased from 1999 to 2011 (from 36 per cent to 24 per cent) and became progressively more marginal, situated at the edge of the main network in the last period. Organizations from LICs did not publish in collaboration with organizations from MICs during the first period of analysis, only partnering with organizations from HICs. Then, a few links appeared in 2003–2007 but diminished in 2008–2011. In contrast, HICs became more important in the network, with greater numbers of collaborations with LICs and MICs. This also reveals the dominant knowledge broker role of HICs in terms of linking organizations from countries with different economic backgrounds. A clear linguistic, historical and cultural divide was also observed in publishing trends. Organizations from Cameroon, Madagascar and Cambodia were connected with each other and with actors in France during the period 2003–2007. All three are former French colonies. By contrast, Ghana (when entering the network in 2008–2011) was collaborating solely with English-speaking countries, such as the USA, UK and Australia.

Conclusions

This chapter raises some important questions about how central tenets of the One Health movement, namely collaboration and interdisciplinarity, have become institutionalized in scientific research networks. The first SNA presented in this chapter looked at the global scientific research network associated with One Health. This allowed us to ask: who are the research advocates? Where do they come from? And what disciplinary focus do they have? This analysis exposed some of the limits to current notions of collaboration and cross-disciplinarity, revealing that One Health is dominated by veterinarians and animal health scientists and is predominantly driven by actors situated in the Global North. Relatively few institutions and individuals act as leads, and brokers, between otherwise disconnected clusters of researchers. This is, of course, not universally the case, but it is a striking pattern that merits reflection.

In the second part of the chapter, we looked at trends in Nipah virus research over time – a virus that has been at the forefront of much current One Health thinking and advocacy. This revealed some interesting features that allowed us to explore what favours and impedes One Health principles in zoonoses research networks. We found the co-authorship network growing over time, which is in line with another recently published bibliometric and social network analysis on zoonoses research worldwide (Hossain *et al.*, 2015). The network evolution showed greater internationalization of COPs, an increase in cooperation between fields, types of organizations and between MICs and HICs. Researchers first became integrated into small networks involving a few organizations, which allowed them to create communities of practice. These small networks progressively joined together with others to form bigger networks. As the number of knowledge brokers grew and new organizations joined, national clusters became internationalized. This might have contributed to a better circulation of knowledge among scientists from different regions and a more diverse, potentially more innovative network. This growth paralleled greater One Health advocacy more generally, such as international conferences, funding initiatives and more attention to emerging infectious diseases.

In contrast, we also found a number of shortcomings in the evolution of Nipah research networks inconsistent with the One Health concept. We found that there was no increase in the rate of interdisciplinary publications, a weak involvement of the environmental field and a marginalization of developing countries in the network. Interdisciplinary research clearly requires time to understand different professional languages, framings and, perhaps more difficult, the socio-political context that different researchers operate in and have to respond to. Fostering relationships between experts from different fields, and between scientists and practitioners from different cultures, tend to have hidden transaction costs. Everyone cannot form partnerships with everyone else, especially when trust is needed to maintain these relationships. Some connections might be easier to sustain than others. Institutions need to think about how to enable collaboration, which requires very deliberate changes in leadership, reward systems, funding streams and even physical workspaces (Buntain *et al.*, 2015).

A more concerted effort needs to be made to understand the process of exclusion of developing country researchers acting as knowledge brokers in the One

Health research network. The fact that Nipah emerged in Malaysia supported the growth of Malaysian research nodes in the network, who originally acted as knowledge brokers. The University of Malaya (together with the ICDDR, B) was one of the last organizations from LICs or MICs that remained an important knowledge broker as other LICs and MICs were progressively displaced from the centre of the network. LICs and MICs always appeared very dependent on HICs to publish, which is something that is noted in wider scientific publishing trends and not unique to the One Health field (Safahieh *et al.*, 2012). The ability of closed communities to circulate information rapidly and efficiently is indubitably an asset for interdisciplinary cooperation and swift dialogue with policy-makers during an emergency, but also represents a potential barrier for international cooperation. These observations raise concerns about the exclusion of LIC and MIC research organizations, running counter to longer-term capacity-building efforts needed in these regions to help institutionalize the One Health concept.

Knowledge broker positions confer significant power to control knowledge distribution (Burt, 2001). If LICs and MICs find themselves excluded from these key positions, it can distort research agendas and reduce their ability to be heard in policy circles (Ollila, 2005). International collaboration can also be compromised by the sheer workload of the key knowledge brokers, who balance various research grants across the globe as well as having teaching, administrative and other commitments at their home institutions. Global public health risks, like emerging and endemic zoonoses, are unevenly distributed and typically located in poorer regions of the world. Socio-economic and institutional realities, such as the huge gap in available resources and lack of established national research funding bodies, are certainly a major reason for low research productivity (e.g. publications) in developing nations. But scientists in HICs, from different linguistic and cultural backgrounds, can also find collaborating with organizations with limited scientific capacity, expertise and foreign language skills cumbersome and difficult, especially on short-term research projects.

Barriers to international collaboration are not only associated with physical, linguistic and socio-cultural boundaries, but also importantly with economic and professional disincentives. Perception of the much higher salaries of HIC researchers compared to their LIC and MIC counterparts can generate latent conflict, as can issues surrounding authorship and knowledge attribution. Different institutions also have different reward systems. HIC academic institutions, especially in medical and veterinary sciences, are often grant- and research-based, whereas many LIC and MIC institutions emphasize teaching and clinical work. Hierarchical bureaucracies are also damaging. Government employees tend to focus on their own ministries in order to get rewarded and promoted. Where competent southern researchers are few, they can quickly become over-burdened while juggling too many responsibilities. Past experiences of HIC researchers 'flying in' to collect, or take, blood samples to bring back to their own labs or even large government data sets can lead to a sense of post-colonial scientific dominance, or even abuse and deception (see Tilley, 2011). These can all contribute to closed knowledge systems, which push networks toward disciplinary and geographic isolation (Reagans and Zuckerman, 2008), which have damaging long-term effects on the interconnectivity and strength of global preparedness and response systems for emerging diseases.

With this in mind, what type of 'network(s)' does One Health need? Should the focus be on establishing a 'global network' or a more decentralized approach? Who should push the agenda? How should the relationships between networks be fostered and cultivated? There are trade-offs to consider, albeit establishing networks at global, regional and national levels are not necessarily mutually exclusive. International networks that bring together a diversity of actors and interests tend to be more demanding and have higher transaction costs compared to national-level or even regional networks (Schmoch and Schubert, 2008). Supporting the development of localized communities of practice, which differ according to their cultural and historical background and politico-economic contexts, could promote unique and diverse perspectives on what One Health means, how it should be conceptualized, institutionalized, utilized and transformed, especially in developing country contexts.

Notes

1 Knowledge flows involve much more than co-publication. They involve physical meetings and conferences and a large number of informal discussions in person or by virtual exchange. In recent decades, international organizations have established panels of official cooperation networks involving close interactions. With the information and communication technology revolution, researchers have been increasingly connected with each other in virtual networks and there has been a proliferation of web-based platforms (for example, the World Animal Health Information Database (WAHID) and the Global Early Warning System (GLEWS) developed by UN agencies).

2 Research networks are typically represented as structures consisting of actors (e.g. individuals or organizations) and the relationships between these actors (e.g. co-authorship or citations).

3 Despite its usefulness to analyse and visualize network structures and quantify the level of cooperation among scientists, SNA does not provide information on the nature of the relationships depicted, nor show the extent to which norms and values are shared. That is why more qualitative methods are needed to complement such studies. Although this was done for the Nipah virus network, the results were excluded from this chapter and will be published elsewhere.

4 The information related to the articles was accessed and retrieved from the Thomson Reuter Web of Science website (www.isiknowledge.com) on 25 March 2014. For additional methodological details see: http://steps-centre.org/publication/one-health-2.

5 This has had an impact on the scientific literature, with a rise of mentions of One Health in titles and abstracts of published articles over time, and a particular increase in 2009 when articles on swine flu, as well as broader reflections post-avian influenza, were being published. This table is based on a literature search of the Web of Science for the years 2007–2013.

6 The titles, abstracts and keywords for all 737 articles were checked manually to verify that the reference to One Health was relevant for the study. Only publications relating to the One Health concept and/or containing the keyword One Health were kept.

7 To assess which regions mainly contributed to the scientific discourse on One Health, all the countries linked to a publication via the author's institutional address have been aggregated. If a publication had multiple institutions and hence countries associated with

it all countries were included. Likewise, if an author had multiple institutional affiliations, the countries associated with the author's institutional addresses were all included in the analysis.

8 Note that while the network maps are based on co-authorship patterns between institutions, the links may very well be the result of the publications of very active individuals rather than institutions *per se*.

9 A publication's disciplinary affiliation was determined by the journal in which it was published, using Web of Science's categories as a proxy for scientific disciplines. If all Web of Science categories related to the same discipline, the publication was assigned to that discipline. If a publication was associated with different disciplines, no discipline was assigned and the publication was coded as 'ambiguous'. It is important to note that while Web of Science categories and journals can be used as proxies for disciplines, they are not disciplines *per se*.

10 A notable limitation of the data set is that it only contained peer-reviewed journal articles from the Web of Science database. Including other document types and/or non-English publications would have provided a more comprehensive data set and hence understanding of the scientific discourse around One Health. When interpreting the co-authorship patterns, the time period from 2007 to 2014 and the small sample size of 157 publications must be kept in mind. Relatively small changes in the data (e.g. new publications) could significantly alter the structure of the co-authorship networks. Therefore, collaboration patterns are likely to change and the network should be revised as new publications on One Health become available.

11 Ribonucleic acid qualifies the virus' genetic material.

12 Nipah and Hendra viruses constitute the *Henipavirus* genus.

13 Publicly available bibliometric information from articles published in peer-reviewed journals was extracted from Scopus online database. Articles and reviews containing the words 'Nipah virus' in their titles, abstracts or key words were selected. In total, 160 organizations participated in the publication of 514 papers from 1999 to 2011 – 1 to 15 papers each. For the purpose of a time-based analysis, the initial 13 years have been separated into three periods of four or five years: 1999–2002; 2003–2007; and 2008–2011. Each period represents a 'publication wave' in which the number of works (and following publications) rose substantially, and then stabilized or decreased. It is unclear why this happened. For additional methodological details, see: http://steps-centre.org/publication/networks-2.

14 As well as one organization from Papua New Guinea.

15 The density corresponds to the actual number of connections in a network divided by the potential number of connections (if all the nodes were connected). The measure of density for the three periods is 0.09 for 1999–2002, 0.05 for 2003–2007 and 0.03 for 2008–2011.

16 Equal to the average number of links per organization (sum of the number of links for each organization divided by the number of organizations). The average degree centrality was 6.1 for the period of 1999–2002, 4.4 for the period 2003–2007 and 7.0 for the period 2008–2011.

17 Equal to the number of brokers divided by the total number of organizations (nodes).

18 We followed the 2013 World Bank classification.

19 The term 'interdisciplinary' was used to qualify organizations that were carrying out research that directly contributed to knowledge in at least two different field categories (e.g. among veterinary medicine, human medicine and environment/ecosystem health). This was done by looking at the research interests of each research organization, which included visiting official websites.

20 Five categories were defined: universities (universities, schools and colleges); government agencies (national and sub-national public institutes); hospitals (government-funded hospitals and other medical treatment facilities); private sector (commercial firms, private laboratories and private clinics); and others (non-governmental organizations (NGOs), foundations and intergovernmental institutions, such as the OIE).

4

CONTESTED HISTORIES

Power and politics in trypanosomiasis control

Ian Scoones

Introduction

Current One Health rhetoric focuses heavily on the need for 'integrated' control approaches that bring together diverse stakeholders and expertise. The assumed narrative is that an inclusive politics of collaboration is desirable and possible. While intuitively appealing, and perhaps economically sensible, often hidden from view is how scientific networks are formed and sustained by power and politics, and so prevent integration from happening. Most diseases have multiple control modalities, and divergent communities of research and practice compete for funding and influence. These science-policy controversies make collaboration inherently challenging.

This chapter explores these issues in relation to African trypanosomiasis, a complex disease with an equally complex history.[1] Trypanosomiasis is a devastating vector-borne disease of both humans and animals. It is, in fact, multiple diseases, involving various trypanosomes, protozoan parasites carried by different variants of the tsetse fly.[2] It appears in different forms, affected by different epidemiological and ecological processes. Over the last 100 years, a massive effort to fight the fly and control the disease has been undertaken using a wide array of techniques, from draconian colonial policies, aerial spraying, baits and traps, drugs and vaccines, and the breeding of resistant cows and sterile flies (Maudlin, 2006). But these technologies and approaches have sometimes been accompanied by conflicting aims, and tensions between them are apparent.

Colonial authorities were horrified by the consequences of human trypanosomiasis or sleeping sickness, investing huge effort and resources in trying to tackle it. Around a quarter of the colonial research budget was focused on sleeping sickness control, either major treatment campaigns for people, or wider efforts to push back the fly belts (Rogers and Randolph, 2002). Today, some 50 million cattle are potentially at risk from animal trypanosomiasis, and the economic losses of the disease amount to an estimated US$4.75 billion per year, suggesting massive gains to be made for development from control operations.[3]

However, since the peak of colonial efforts, human African trypanosomiasis has slipped down the list of priorities. Today it is classified as a 'neglected disease', one that is underreported, poorly understood and not allocated significant global resources, and so of lower prestige than other current priorities in global health (Maudlin *et al.*, 2009). That said, there is still plenty of action around trypanosomiasis control – global coordination groups, pan-African initiatives, national programmes and dedicated branches, commercial public–private partnerships (PPPs) for drug and vaccine development and research projects galore on facets of vector and parasite biology.[4]

In many ways, trypanosomiasis is an ideal candidate for a 'One Health' approach. The different fly vectors are highly dependent on particular habitats for their survival, and so ecological and land use change has a major impact on fly populations, and the associated disease risks. Equally, the probabilities of infection by people and livestock are influenced by the presence and distribution of hosts, including wildlife, and so disease dynamics are equally affected by ecology, but also the social, economic, cultural habits of people and their livestock. This makes designing interventions very difficult, and open to controversy about what is the best approach.

This control quandary was posed by John Ford in his 1971 book, *The Role of the Trypanosomiases in African Ecology* (Ford, 1971). Ford was a brilliant, lateral-thinking, big-picture ecologist who argued that wider development was the answer to the tsetse problem, and that pre-colonial, indigenous systems were highly effective. He strongly objected to *Pax Britannica*, that peace brought by colonialism had improved development; indeed he argued that the early colonial epidemics of trypanosomiasis were a direct result of changing ecological dynamics influenced by colonial conquest. He argued instead that colonial science 'almost entirely overlooked the way considerable achievements [had been made by] the indigenous peoples in overcoming the obstacle of trypanosomiasis [through] tam[ing] and exploit[ing] the natural ecosystem of tropical Africa by cultural and physiological adjustment both in themselves and their domestic animals' (p9). He argued that, 'a policy based on elimination is not a practical one' (p10).

In his advocacy of a 'systematic' integrated approach based on 'joint investigation', he was in many ways an inspired forerunner of the One Health argument of today. But for a number of reasons this more holistic perspective on trypanosomiasis has been a footnote in a larger saga dominated by often narrow 'techno-fix' narratives, and policy drives centred on tsetse eradication and area-wide control. While these have, in many quarters, brought considerable benefits, they have also been accompanied by trade-offs and many failures.

This chapter examines several ongoing, and long-running, debates about vector and parasite, focused on zoonotic and animal trypanosomiasis in eastern and southern Africa. By tracing the histories behind particular technologies, it reveals the ways in which control methods are embedded within contests of power, prestige, funding and institutional politics. Engendering collaboration and integrated approaches, forming the basis of a One Health approach, seem an unlikely proposition unless these contested histories are made explicit and concerted efforts are made to address them.

Colonial 'scorched-earth' policies

Following the devastating rinderpest epidemic of the 1890s, trypanosomiasis became a major concern for colonial authorities. The East Africa Commission (1925) claimed that, 'the ravages of the tsetse fly are the greatest menace to the development of tropical Africa' (Ford, 1971, p1). In southern Africa, tsetse infestations were hampering colonization, especially the expansion of settler ranching. Colonial authorities ordered large-scale bush clearance and wildlife extermination programmes. These involved armies of people, clearing bush with machetes and trapping and shooting wildlife. The scale was phenomenal; around 750,000 animals were shot in Zimbabwe between 1932 and 1961 (Ford, 1971, p322). A close alliance between veterinary departments and hunters was struck. Presented as a project of taming, conquering and transforming wilderness into a productive alternative, efforts very much coincided with the colonial vision, and substantial resources were allocated.

They met some success. For example, in Zimbabwe the fly belts were pushed back significantly (Lovemore, 1994).[5] The settler population backed these efforts, as land became available and was cleared. Yet local people were not part of this picture, except as enlisted workers for the huge operations. The memories of these campaigns are often evoked, with strong nostalgia by some: 'It was a really massive effort. There were thousands of people, tens of trucks, dozers. If you lead the department you imagine that you can revive the department to that level of capacity. But it won't happen' (interview).

These approaches were not without their critics. While an environmentalist lobby did not exist as it does today, many white settlers and colonial officers had a romantic attachment to wildlife in Africa, and so the clearance policies were seen as unreasonably destructive. Even within the ranks of colonial veterinarians there were debates. For example, John Ford argued that regular, but low, levels of challenge fostered trypanosomiasis resistance among both cattle and people and when combined with vegetation management, settlement site choice and herding behaviours, this offered a better route to a longer-term solution.[6] This did not go down well with the more macho, scorched-earth advocates in the colonial tsetse and veterinary service.

The scale, depth and organization of colonial policies were witness to the disciplining power and control of the colonial state, and the institutionalization of tsetse control branches, often the most prestigious section of the agricultural ministry, with the most resources and personnel, reflective of the ambition. This created in turn professional cadres, and associated career trajectories, committed to such a control response. The funding and operation of tsetse control branches was thus dependent on justifying a particular style of response. While control measures have changed, and with them styles of intervention, the importance of tsetse and trypano-somiasis, especially for veterinary departments, is still significant. The justificatory narratives that attempt to mobilize resources – if not to return to the glory days of the colonial era, at least to sustain a commitment to control – are important.

The chemical revolution

Overlapping with this period was the promotion of insecticide applications, both from the air and through ground spraying operations. The chemical revolution accel-erated following the Second World War, when new chemicals, notably the organo-chlorines, DDT and dieldrin, became available thanks to the war effort. This was a period when land allocation to white settlement began in earnest, especially in British colonies like Zimbabwe. War veterans from the UK and elsewhere were offered land, often in the more marginal areas, and colonial authorities needed to expand 'African' land to accommodate them. Tsetse clearance became a greater imperative:

> In the 50s and 60s tryps was a serious veterinary problem. In Zimbabwe they were looking to open up new places for communal areas. When the flies came back after rinderpest, it was a problem. The white farmers of Matabe-leland North put serious pressure on the government.
>
> *(Interview)*

The ground spraying operations followed a similar pattern to the earlier bush clear-ance and wildlife extermination campaigns, and were often combined. Vast numbers of people were mobilized, often in very unsafe working conditions, to spray huge areas: 'The amount of dieldrin they put on was extraordinary. It was mixed with fuel and came out of the exhaust of the planes. It was in quantities that were unim-aginable. They were so enthusiastic' (interview).

Again this was presented as human mastery over nature, the deployment of tech-nology to conquer a scourge that lay in the way of a colonial vision of moderniza-tion. The military scale of the operations, and the involvement of former armed forces personnel as pilots, logistics operators and so on, gave a particular image and flavour to these efforts, reflected in turn in the language used – campaign, front, operation and so on. The full force of colonial power was being exerted, confront-ing and taming a dangerous and threatening Africa.

Both the intensity and scale of these efforts did again have results, boosting the argument for a top-down, hierarchically organized, military-style operation. But these efforts came at a cost: in terms of human health and wellbeing (for ground spraying operators with backpacks of chemicals), the risk of death (for pilots flying in low in difficult country) and for the environment (in terms of the impact of residual chemicals).

Rachel Carson's book, *Silent Spring*, published in 1962, raised the consciousness of a nascent environmental movement (Carson, 1962). DDT in particular became a watchword for environmental destruction: extensive studies, particularly in Zimbabwe, have shown the negative impacts of the use of residual chemicals as part of spraying campaigns (Douthwaite and Tingle, 1994; SEMG, 1997). Even though with time air spraying switched to endosulfans and other less toxic chemicals, such as synthetic pyrethroids with lower residual effects, the image of aircraft releasing gallons of chemicals on the African bush was not good PR. Ground spraying, too, was seen as expensive, dangerous and environmentally damaging, even if again the approach to chemical application had become more and more selective and targeted.

In Zimbabwe ground spraying with DDT continued until 1991, and in the Okavango delta of Botswana a major air spraying operation continued through the 1980s and 1990s using endosulfans: 'There were 17 successive years of spraying. It did not work. They couldn't get enough of it. It went on and on. It was just madness. They could have done it for centuries', commented one observer. But eventually the Botswana efforts had success thanks in particular to another technological development – the emergence of GPS systems for highly site-specific spraying (Kgori et al., 2006). It has since become the poster-child for pro-aerial spraying advocates.

Spraying efforts today are limited, and subject to many more controls than in the past. Environmental impact assessments (EIAs), toxicity appraisals and health and safety procedures are all part of the new requirements (Grant, 2001). Today, spraying operations are not part of large government-led, military-style campaigns, but are still being done, and planned, in some locations. The veterinary departments simply do not have the resources or expertise, and instead private contractors have taken on the role.

An alternative use of chemicals has evolved in parallel, however, particularly following the development of low-toxicity pyrethroid compounds, and this involves application on animals. Insecticide-treated cattle approaches can be highly effective against tsetse, particularly as the knowledge about fly behaviour has evolved (Vale, 1974; Vale et al., 1988; Hargrove et al., 2003, 2012; Hargrove, 2004; Torr et al., 2007, 2011). This means that pour-on application techniques can be highly targeted, and managed by herders (Swallow et al., 1995).[7] With the flies having such low reproductive rates, the kill rate needs to be relatively low in order to have a major control effect. 'Actually it's quite simple. Look after your cattle, spray the front legs, perhaps once a month, even every three months. It might cost two cents to spray', explained one researcher. The approach can also be combined with tick control, thus making any investment much more cost-effective for livestock-keepers to implement (Bardosh et al., 2013). Concerns have been raised, though, about resistance, and ongoing research on this continues.

Baits and traps

As a response to the destructive land clearance, wildlife extermination and chemical spraying alternatives, trap technologies were developed. The earliest 'Harris traps' were used in South Africa (Swynnerton, 1933), although they did not use odour baits, and simply used visual stimuli. It was only through the work on fly behaviour and how they are attracted to odours in particular that new, more effective technologies were developed. This particularly took place in Zimbabwe from the mid-1960s through the persistent and innovative scientific efforts of Glyn Vale and colleagues.[8]

The Rukomichi research station in the Zambezi valley became a hub of activity. An incredible body of research was developed, based on detailed studies of fly movement, population ecology and disease epidemiology:

> They had some very clever people who worked there – Vale, Hargrove, and so on. They could do experiments on a gargantuan scale. They had money to support them. Vale had hundreds of people working for him, collecting flies and so on

explained one informant. 'Zimbabwe was the epicentre of the tsetse world'. Vale explained:

> We wanted something that was non-polluting. We didn't want to use DDT or dieldrin, to plaster tonnes and tonnes across the bush. The environmental people didn't like it, nor indeed the tsetse people. Shooting all the game animals was another option. Some of the wildlife people liked this. They were keen on hunting. Bush clearing was highly destructive. We wanted something else.
>
> *(Interview)*

When Zimbabwe became independent in 1980, the basic infrastructure, and many of the former staff, including Vale, remained. Recalling this period in southern Africa, someone joked:

> It was white guys in baggy shorts and knee length socks. A particular type of science. A great gig. You could be in the bush, drive around in Landrovers. . . . They don't even touch the socio-political aspects. It was a very British, ex-colonial scene.

Another informant observed: 'It was all very top down. And it was dominated by whites. For a long time it was always whites at the top in Zimbabwe, even after Independence.' Another commented on the social dimension: 'The white males stuck together. They were a tribe.' The gendered nature of expertise was also commented on: 'It was white males, mad on flies.' Yet despite the racialized and gendered context for science and policy in the transition to independence in southern Africa at least, there was also continuity in the science, and the unquestionably high-quality work on fly behaviour and traps continued.

This was given a massive boost with the inception of the Regional Tsetse and Trypanosomiasis Control Programme (RTTCP) operating in southern Africa

(Malawi, Mozambique, Zambia and Zimbabwe) from 1986 to 1998. The RTTCP was seen by the European Union (EU) as part of the support to the front-line states during the apartheid era in South Africa, but suitably 'apolitical', focused as it was on flies, cattle disease and development. Significantly, the RTTCP also supported the bureaucratic and professional interests of veterinarians (and, to a lesser extent, entomologists):

> It was led by vets. This was a time when veterinary services were being privatised, and they were fighting for funds. They needed the funds to continue to justify their own existence. They wanted funds for vaccination, for mass prophylaxis. They didn't always see the broader goal.
>
> *(Interview)*

The RTTCP fitted a number of political objectives. First, it was an opportunity to support the newly independent Zimbabwe, and to capitalize on the very considerable research and operational expertise developed there. The end of the Zimbabwean liberation war meant that there was an opportunity to invest in control measures linked to a process of re-establishing national control and the demining of borders. Second, a grand mission to push the fly belt back over an area of over 300,000 km² was a sellable proposition. The RTTCP became a platform for the rolling out at large scale of the odour bait trap technology developed in pre-Independence Zimbabwe, presented as an alternative to aerial spraying. It thus was presented as a pro-development operation, with technologies that were environmentally sound, cheap and efficient.

It was a large aid commitment, and with hindsight some have questioned its focus: 'That many euros! What were they thinking? They were just chasing the fly.' The whole operation was highly dependent on external funds, and longer-term sustainability became an issue:

> After 1980 Zimbabwe was swimming in funds. Once something is moving you don't stop it. So all these people were hired after 1980s to do tsetse control.... But when the cash started to dry up ... you now have a huge tsetse department, but no operating costs.

RTTCP was a major test of the bait technology approach. Thousands of traps were distributed across vast areas. Because of the reproductive biology of the tsetse fly, killing very few flies could result in a diminution of populations in a relatively short period. When well organized, again with a top-down, hierarchical approach, the trapping worked reasonably well. As Vale explained: 'It has to be organised and planned properly. When it first started in the 1980s it worked magnificently.'

Elsewhere, however, things did not always go so well. This was particularly the case where the capacity of government services to implement and sustain such a large-scale programme was weaker, even with the considerable resources available from the RTTCP. Local people often did not understand what the traps were for, and did not in any case rate trypanosomiasis as a major problem. One observer commented: 'Trapping – it's more trouble than it's worth. It's a logistical night-mare. There are all sorts of other uses for blue or black cloth.' Another recalled that villagers found better uses for the traps: 'The netting used on some designs was perfect for fishing nets. The blue cloths were good curtains. And the aluminium frames were perfect for door posts and window frames.'

Community compliance and sustainability became a big issue. In the Lambwe valley of Kenya, a site of extensive and long-term research on tsetse and tryps, community programmes facilitated by the International Centre on Insect Physiol-ogy and Ecology, based in Nairobi (ICIPE) took off (Ssenyonga et al., 1996; Barrett and Okali, 1998). These involved community participation from the start – from trap construction to placement to management. This had a great effect, but required local-level community organization and buy in. Participatory development was, however, not a strong point of the average veterinary department. The institutional culture and the professional training ran against interacting with people.

With the trap technologies, there were always challenges of reinvasion. Trap-ping was a long-term solution that had to be sustained, particularly in border areas, for years. Some suggested that this was a 30–40-year challenge. As African govern-ments became more and more reliant on donor support, projects would last a few years at best. Even a massive prestige project such as the RTTCP had only one renewal, and was wound down in 1998–1999. As one informant explained: 'In retrospect, the targets didn't produce the results that they hoped for. In the end, RTTCP was a lot of money down the drain.' Perhaps this assessment is too pess-imistic. Vale counters: 'If we didn't have the bait system, the whole of Zimbabwe would have gone down. All gone down.'

Enter the nuclear solution

In the tsetse control field there seems to always be some group somewhere who has managed to convince someone that 'their' solution is going to work, and should be the next big thing. The Sterile Insect Technique (SIT) promoted by the Inter-national Atomic Energy Authority (IAEA) – based in Vienna with a UN mandate – gained prominence through the 2000s (Feldmann and Parker, 2010), just as other options and their funding were faltering.[9] This came from an unusual source, and was presented as part of the IAEA's advocacy of 'peaceful uses' of nuclear technology.

Based on successes in the Americas with screwworm, SIT is based on irradiating male insects and releasing them in very large numbers; it is an 'area-wide' eradica-tion approach. This was presented as part of a strong narrative of eradication by the African Union (AU), specifically the Pan African Tsetse and Trypanosomiasis Erad-ication Campaign (PATTEC). John Kabayo, then PATTEC coordinator, argued: 'the application of the area-wide principle that is planned [has a] goal to continue the interventions in each identified area until confirmation of local elimination of the tsetse populations' (Kabayo, 2002, p474). As one commentator recalled:

'PATTEC provided a renewed spurt of interest. It was like Godzilla rising out of the ashes.'

The idea of eradication goes down well with veterinarians and policy-makers. Getting rid of the vector of a major infectious disease is a great achievement; everyone wants to replicate the iconic eradication campaigns for smallpox and rinderpest. Selling this potential is very much part of the rhetoric, even if the likelihood of this ever happening is exceedingly slim: 'SIT needs to be seen as part of a success story. This is what attracts people', explained Feldman of the IAEA during an interview. He went on, acknowledging the limitations, 'Of course it depends on the situation.... SIT is not applicable everywhere.... It is always part of an integrated approach.'

The IAEA had tested their approach on the island of Zanzibar – in fact in a fairly isolated patch of forest – and through prior suppression of the population by 95 per cent using traps. The elimination of tsetse from the island required the repeated release of sterile males over several years, and with the expenditure of perhaps millions of dollars – but they eventually managed to eliminate the tsetse fly from the area (Vreysen *et al.*, 2000; Vreysen, 2001). This was glorified as 'winning the battle' and 'waging a war'– the final solution to the scourge of the tsetse fly across Africa.[10]

But as someone commented: 'SIT in Zanzibar worked. It was one species, on an island, with 1000 km sq of infestation. But on the mainland it's a different story.' Everyone, of course, likes a success story, no matter how peculiar, context specific and expensive. The details can be brushed under the carpet for the purpose of the big sell, and then the subsequent details worked out. The IAEA are not the only organization, and SIT not the only technology that has used such a tactic in the harsh world of competitive funding. As one informant mentioned: 'The key is generating success stories. Everyone wants to be part of a success. Then donors will want to be involved. And governments. Research is needed to demonstrate tangible successes.' Gaining a strong political ally in the AU, deploying an articulate African advocate in John Kabayo and inveigling your way into the international bodies was also part of the strategy.

The SIT approach, and the role of the IAEA and PATTEC's advocacy of SIT, provoked massive controversy, outrage and anger among the small tsetse and tryps community. According to some: 'The SIT approach has been massively oversold.' Some of this was of course jealousy: how dare they capture the increasingly scarce funds when we have worked so long and hard working out solutions? But part of it was legitimate scientific concern. One scientist reflected: 'SIT is only applicable if eradication is the objective.' A vicious war of words ensued, with a variety of papers, vitriolic responses and harsh critiques offered. David Rogers and Sarah Randolph from Oxford University responded in scathing terms: 'PATTEC's proposals ignore the lessons of history, deny certain undeniable ecological facts, require a degree of coordination that seems unlikely, and will surely lead to increasing foreign exchange debt with very little to show for it' (Rogers and Randolph, 2002, p534). The controversy sparked big debates in the scientific literature. In particular there was a to-and-fro of different models, each arguing for and against the efficacy and efficiency of the SIT approach, especially in comparison to others (Vale and Torr, 2005; Barclay and Vreysen, 2011; Hargrove et al., 2011; Bouyer et al., 2013; Shaw et al., 2013).

My interviews almost inevitably turned to this subject. Views were heart-felt and strong: 'Now it's a big political thing. This is my view. It's a sexy way of giving nuclear power a jolly green ecological face. Nuclear power, as a green, alternative, clean solution', argued one informant. Another commented: 'IAEA is distorting what is happening. SIT is hugely expensive. It requires massive suppression to work at all. And why would you do SIT when you have other perfectly good and cheaper alternatives?' Another observed: 'It's all ridiculously complicated and expensive', while another commented: 'Anyone who believes this can work is crazy.' Accusations of skulduggery were often not far below the surface:

> It's a political game. It is the basis for an awful lot of corruption. SIT involves a lot of funds. The fly factory that comes to your area brings benefits, they say. But the Ethiopian one has not released a single fly.

Others were more compromising: 'I have nothing against SIT. A tool, we have it. Under certain conditions it can work. If the tsetse population is isolated, and the chance of reinvasion is zero, and suppression can be implemented, then, yes, SIT can work.' Indeed, the overall evolution of the debate was acknowledged by some, and heavily emphasized by IAEA. An outsider commented: 'PATTEC has evolved.... A shift from eradication to sustained control ... it's more sensible now.'

Drugs and vaccines

Another suite of alternatives has focused not on the vector but on the parasite itself through the development of prophylactic and therapeutic drugs for animals, as well as that ultimate Holy Grail, a vaccine. A range of drugs were developed from the 1950s, and later came off-patent, and have been produced as generics for very low cost since the 1990s. Also, over the last 40 years there have been attempts to produce an animal vaccine.

The drugs (notably diminazene aceturate (mostly for chemotherapy), isometamidium chloride (for chemoprophylaxis) and homidium salts (for chemotherapy)) are reasonably effective and relatively easy to administer, and especially as generics very cheap.[11] This can be, advocates argue, a livestock owner-led solution, delivered through agro-vets and the private sector drug companies, and so not reliant on large-scale government-led control campaigns, at least for animal trypanosomiasis. A unique mass treatment campaign for cattle has also been used to control the zoonotic parasite in Uganda.[12]

A private sector solution, especially developed through PPPs, is very much in vogue. GALVmed, for example, is modelled after approaches that have been successful in the human health domain.[13] GALVmed articulated an argument for a medical solution, using the latest recombinant genetics technologies, cutting-edge drug development platforms and novel approaches to private sector development and delivery. As a technology development broker and market initiator, they have argued that they could be the missing piece of the puzzle in the task to deliver new technologies to tackle neglected livestock diseases in poor areas of the world.[14]

The new class of drugs will, they argue, meet the increasingly stringent regulatory requirements that national governments and international protocols require. Such regulations, they claim, will make their new products competitive. While the market is relatively small, it is not insignificant, and as producers have higher-value animals to protect the incentives to protect them will increase, they contend.

There are quite a few uncertainties in this argument. Much relies on the control of the cheaper, lower-quality generics (and counterfeit) market, and the convincing of producers that a higher-quality product is worth paying for (Bardosh *et al.*, 2013). Others question the push for greater regulation, arguing that the informal markets are actually providing reasonably good-quality products:

> There is a real push back from vets and companies. The market is so small. There is just enough cash in trypanocides to attract the private sector, but only just. They want quality control. More vets, more cars. Our work showed in West African markets in the mid-2000s, formal and informal, we didn't find anything bad. Counterfeits are rare. Generics are low price, so there's a low incentive. They have been off-patent for 10–15 years, so there is a mature market now.
>
> *(Interview)*

Clearly much hangs on the extent of low-quality and counterfeit products in the market, and the implications this has for longer-term problems of resistance, that is in turn compounded by widespread underdosing.[15] Disputes remain over the extent of the market for new products, given the mature generics market, the level of local demand and ability to pay and the scale and impact of under-dosing, sub-standard products and drug counterfeiting.

As with many technology-driven efforts, the investment in drug development has gone into the upstream science, and not into the downstream market testing and delivery. As one informant noted:

> There is a gap. Ideas are developed in isolation of thinking about the delivery systems. Unless you develop the technology with a delivery system in mind, it will end up too expensive, and sit on the shelf. Tryps falls into this problem.

This would not be the first time a new technological solution, even if it worked well, met an early fate, as the assumed mass of consumers refused to buy it. The real challenge, often poorly recognized and understood, is the social and political context of such markets (Kingsley, 2015). There are plenty of vested interests in not regulating drugs, and keeping poorly performing generics and counterfeits. Even if these were overcome, the ability to regulate drug markets in remote rural settings is very limited. And in any case the costs of off-patent drugs are so low that competitors would have to offer very substantial added value. While some claim that low-quality drugs, counterfeits and under-dosing is a real problem, others argue that it is not such a problem, and that livestock keepers have developed capacities to discriminate between drug types, and have good knowledge of application processes.

Most commentators regard the pursuit of new drug discovery channels as a useful thing to do, although questions are raised about how much de-risking support should be offered to large private pharmaceutical companies from public aid or philanthropic money. However, the same view is not shared when the technology development is focused on a vaccine, which has recently regained some traction.

Vaccine development for trypanosomiasis has a chequered history. Part of the Consultative Group on International Agricultural Research (CGIAR) system, the International Laboratory for Research on Animal Diseases (ILRAD) spent the best part of 30 years from the early 1970s in pursuit of a trypanosomiasis vaccine (ILRAD, 1991). The effort failed completely, and the work was finally shutdown in the early 2000s after a thorough-going review (e.g. Budd, 1999). An International Livestock Research Institute (ILRI) insider commented: 'There was good science, but it was a random walk. There is no point in fiddling around with more and more responses. There was not a rational basis for continuing.' In a similar vein: 'We spent the whole of the twentieth century learning that [tryps] vaccines don't work ... donors don't have technical advisors who can say "hang on a minute". It's a tragedy of Shakespearean proportions. So much money wasted!'

There are good reasons why vaccine development is difficult, if not impossible. This has to do with the way trypanosomes change their antigenic covering, making it virtually impossible to generate a vaccine response:

> Now we have the Gates programme, and silver bullets and grand challenges. Everyone wants a new vaccine or drug ... ridiculous.... There have been some very clever people over 20 years doing research on tryps showing that they change their coat – not even in response to antibodies. There are thousands of genes controlling the coat, and it changes all the time.... It will be a total waste of money.
>
> *(Interview)*

Certainly the allure of the technological silver bullet is strong. However, unregulated drug markets are difficult ones to compete in. Beyond the technical difficulties of achieving a vaccine solution, there are other delivery questions that have yet to be addressed. The prospects of a commercial vaccine emerging look slight and vaccine development is a way off. That the well-funded institute ILRAD failed over 40 years is witness to the steepness of the challenge. Sceptics argue that there are cheaper solutions that are possible, and the funds could be better invested elsewhere, while others counter that pursuing all options is essential.

Breeding resistance

Another long-running story in tackling animal trypanosomiasis has been focused on breeding. There are a number of indigenous cattle breeds, most notably the N'dama and West African Shorthorn breeds, that show characteristics of trypanotolerance (Roberts and Gray, 1973).[16] The International Trypanotolerance Centre was established in The Gambia in 1982 to build on this.[17] Making use of this genetic material in cross-breeding efforts was, it was hoped, a route to producing better-quality (larger, with greater meat and milk production potential) breeds that were also trypanotolerant. The International Livestock Centre for Africa (ILCA), and then ILRI, were engaged in this research in The Gambia and Senegal and had a number of core breeding herds across West and Central Africa that were integrated into the cattle breeding programmes over a number of years (Murray *et al.*, 1984). The results were mixed. As many have argued, small, indigenous, low-productivity animals that have repeated tsetse challenge are often resistant to trypanosomiasis.

This is why trypanosomiasis is not regarded as a major animal health priority by people in tsetse areas, especially if the challenge is slight, occasional or can be avoided (Torr *et al.*, 2011). It is only when people and animals move in from outside, or when susceptible breeds are used as in large-scale ranching operations, that it becomes a big problem, it is argued. It is a question less of disease challenge than of type of production system. Indigenous systems for a range of reasons were always quite resilient, and with a judicious combination of approaches, including the use of local breeds, this could be the same again.

This approach of course does not chime well with the objectives of technology centres who seek a technical solution, and see their role primarily as focused on milk and meat production. As someone put it: 'These resistant breeds are too small and unproductive for the breeders.' Trypanotolerance evolves through co-existence with the disease, and so is not easily transferrable: 'Over time, trypanosomes become tamed, domesticated. They become used to domestic livestock. Where you give it time, where tryps and livestock live together in a farming landscape there is less of a problem; it goes away.'

The search for a generic technical solution, however, continues. Breeding in particular has been given a new lease of life by a new generation of biotechnology solutions, allowing genetic screening and the ability to insert transgenes and so speed up the process of selection dramatically. From Dolly the sheep to Tumaini the cloned calf, some important scientific developments have occurred. A collaboration between ILRI, the Roslin Institute in Scotland and Michigan State University resulted in a transgene from the trypanosomiasis-resistant baboon being inserted into a cow.[18]

Is this the genetic silver bullet everyone has been waiting for, or yet another interesting scientific diversion, involving lots of funds, plenty of scholarly papers but no useful product? Only time will tell. Certainly the motivation and incentives towards a technical solution remain strong, and the biotechnology advocates will not shy away from making massive claims about the potentials.

Conclusions

In a global policy debate centred on an inclusive politics of collaboration and integration, the history of trypanosomiasis and tsetse research and control reminds us of how prevailing institutional politics and entrenched interests remain very much embedded within narrow scientific and practitioner networks. A parasite and vector very much amenable to a One Health approach, trypanosomiasis reveals the entrenched world of tropical disease research, and its contested social arenas. This story is often told in terms of scientific 'facts' or economic 'models', but it is one where science is deeply conflated with competing power, prestige, control and authority. Disease and vector control options support careers, professional interests and institutional positions. All research and intervention efforts are thus deeply political, and socially embedded in long personal and institutional histories. Scientific practices are often co-constructed with political and institutional power; scientists assert control over the problem, and so the solution. While there is much rhetoric about integrated solutions, holistic approaches, and 'One Health' policies, the practice, as this chapter has shown, seems to be very much about a narrow control framing, a technological focus, the defining of territory and so the capturing of resources – so essential for African veterinary departments whose budgets have been squeezed.

Despite the nods towards broader systems understanding, integrating veterinary, medical and environmental disciplines and holistic solutions, the tsetse and trypansomiasis community remains narrow and compartmentalized. The earlier calls for integration, and listening to local livestock keepers, of John Ford and others have not been widely heeded. Claims of 'One Health' and 'integrated pest management' are ever present, but most activities are fragmented, unconnected, poorly integrated, and too often based on limited data, evaluation and review. Attempts at integration and coordination either get captured or become talking shops of limited value. One of the major problems is that the politics at play prevent the more long-term approaches often needed to successfully control the disease and build capacity at the local level with district teams, livestock-keepers and communities. Funding is tied to a particular narrative and project: of a problem, a solution, a technology, an approach and a scientific network; and competition among the epistemic community enacts turf wars, feuds and animosities.

This tells us something relatively straightforward about the rhetoric of 'collaboration' and 'integration' dominating the One Health agenda. First, navigating political and institutional barriers is key to getting over the unhelpful competition between control approaches. Funding and governance pathways, if re-directed and re-envisioned in ways that account for contested histories and the ultimately political processes at play, may co-construct the scientific network in ways that incentivize new forms of collaboration and integration. Second, realizing the rhetoric of a more integrated One Health approach in practice would require moving beyond the science, towards a better linkage between the disease and those affected by it. What do livestock keepers think? What constraints do they face? What control modalities would work best, in what combinations, where and for whom?

Building a One Health approach would require investing in more capacity building and institutional strengthening at the local and national levels (Smith *et al.*, 2015). In this way, the problem is not so much centred on the fly and the disease, but on the lack of infrastructure, governance, markets and wider development activity. Debates and agendas currently dominated by global donor and research institutions need to be re-directed towards more locally grounded perspectives that emphasize the need for collaboration and integration in practice. Realizing this demands diverse views to be incorporated into the scientific and social networks of disease control – beyond the narrow cliques focused on control methods and associated technologies. Understanding the limitations of past technologically centred approaches, and the way science and policy have been co-constructed, as has been attempted in this chapter, can help us open up approaches to alternative pathways that are more integrative and sustainable, and more genuinely embracing a One Health perspective.

Notes

1 This chapter is based on a close reading of a range of material, including archival documents, classic papers and books, and is complemented by a set of 20 interviews with key actors in research and policy. Interviews were carried out largely via Skype during June and July 2013, with a review process during October 2013. Informants were predominantly based in Europe, the USA and international organizations, and thus represent those with power and influence over research agendas, policy and funding in global arenas. The chapter draws from an earlier Working Paper (http://steps-centre.org/wp-content/uploads/Trypanosomiasis.pdf, accessed 10 July 2015) where anonymized details of all interviews quoted here are given, including location and date of the interview.

2 Trypanosomes are unicellular protozoa parasites. Human African trypanosomiasis (or sleeping sickness) refers to two subspecies: *Trypanosoma brucei gambiense* (occurring in West and Central Africa, mainly through human–tsetse contact) and *Trypanosoma brucei rhodesiense* (confined to East and Southern Africa, where wildlife and livestock act as zoonotic reservoirs). Between 2000 to 2009, more than 170,000 cases of sleeping sickness were reported from 21 African countries, with only 5086 cases caused by the zoonotic parasite (Simarro *et al.*, 2010). In contrast, animal African trypanosomiasis (AAT) is caused by a group of other trypanosome species that do not affect people: mainly *Trypanosoma brucei*, *Trypanosoma congolense* and *Trypanosoma vivax*. Estimates are that the disease kills some three million cattle across the continent every year, although other livestock and wildlife are also affected. Trypanosomes are spread by 23 different species of tsetse fly, divided between savannah, forest and riverine habitats.

3 www.fao.org/ag/againfo/programmes/en/paat/disease.html, accessed 10 July 2015.

4 The University of Edinburgh also has a major social science research project (2012–2017) to investigate the history and politics of trypanosomiasis research and control from the Second World War to today: Investigating Networks of Zoonosis Innovation.

5 www.sacema.com/uploads/tsetse/tsetse-project/tsetse-project-reprint-1387.pdf, accessed 10 July 2015.

6 The idea that 'healthy carriers' of human trypanosomiasis explained the relatively low incidence among the local population in the Zambezi Valley, for example, had been a subject of discussion over many years (see Ford, 1971, pp358–366).

7 A rather lower-profile effort led by ICIPE involved the development of repellent collars. Rather than killing the flies, the idea was to repel them, and this involved fitting collars to animals. This has involved research over a number of years, although the efficacy of the technology is disputed.

8 There were parallel efforts in the Francophone parts of Africa, with the Laveissiere trap being a prime output (Laveissiere and Couret, 1981).

9 SIT had of course been tested on tsetse populations before, both in Nigeria and in Burkina Faso from the 1980s.

10 www.iaea.org/newscenter/multimedia/podcasts/tsetse-flies-and-sterile-insect-technique, accessed 10 July 2015.

11 www.fao.org/docrep/006/x0413e/x0413e05.htm, accessed 10 July 2015.

12 www.stampoutsleepingsickness.com, accessed May 2015.

13 www.GALVmed.org; www.gavialliance.org, accessed 10 July 2015.

14 This was part of a wider package of support involving the Bill and Melinda Gates Foundation, as well as DFID: www.GALVmed.org/2012/03/gates-foundation-dfid-award-GALVmed-51-million-to-combat-livestock-disease-2, accessed 10 July 2015.

15 See van Gool and Mattioli (2010) for a discussion of sub-standard and falsified trypanocide drugs.

16 Of course the challenges of bovine trypanosomiasis can be traced much further back to the pre-colonial era and the introduction of *Bos indica* and its crossing with the much more tolerant indigenous *B. taurus*.

17 www.itc.gm, accessed 10 July 2015.

18 www.ilri.org/ilrinews/index.php/archives/10937; see also: www.ilri.org/breadtrypanosome, accessed 10 July 2015.

5

THE LIMITS OF RAPID RESPONSE

Ebola and structural violence in West Africa

Kevin Bardosh, Melissa Leach and Annie Wilkinson

> [Ebola is] the most severe acute public health emergency seen in modern times.... I have never seen an infectious disease contribute so strongly to potential state failure ... [the outbreak represents] the dangers of the world's growing social and economic inequalities ... [where] the rich get the best care [and] the poor are left to die.
>
> *(WHO director general, Margaret Chan, during an Ebola conference in late 2014)*[1]

Introduction

Begun in December 2013 in the Republic of Guinea, the West African Ebola epidemic has attracted unprecedented global attention. As it devastated families throughout the Mano River Region, the disease dominated media headlines around the world and, albeit belatedly, international debate at the highest levels of economic and political power (seen in the opening quote by the WHO's director general). By far the deadliest and most protracted Ebola outbreak in history, by May 2015 the virus had infected some 27,085 people and killed 11,157 – more than all previous outbreaks combined.[2] Ebola crippled the economies of Sierra Leone, Guinea and Liberia – the hardest-hit states – in ways that were far from linear. With initial estimates of over one million future cases and potential spread to other African countries and regions, mass hysteria culminated in economic breakdown in mid-2014 (Meltzer *et al.*, 2014). In a region still recovering from decades of civil war, this severely compromised already vulnerable populations and livelihoods.

Less than a month after the World Health Organization (WHO) became aware of the epidemic in March 2014, a group of scientists – including veterinarians and one anthropologist – investigated the outbreak's origin in the small town of Meliandou, located in the Forest Region of Guinea, not far from the border with Liberia and Sierra Leone (Saéz *et al.*, 2015). Unlike in Central Africa, where Ebola outbreaks are typically preceded by deaths in chimpanzee and gorilla populations, they found no concurrent epidemic in other wildlife.[3] The team concluded that the outbreak was likely caused by a 'single zoonotic transmission event' between a two-year-old boy, the 'index case' named as Emile Ouamouno, and a colony of insectivorous free-tailed bats who inhabited a large hollow tree some 50 metres from his house.[4] Although many hunted these bats, Emile was too young to do so, and his father was not a known hunter. He did, however, play regularly in the tree. With this in mind, the researchers concluded that Emile caught the virus through contact with the body fluids or excretions from these bats – although the exact transmission mechanism from bats to humans remains ambiguous. While they did sample bats in the area, the scientists were not able to isolate any Ebola virus, either in the village or its surroundings, suggesting that the biological origins of the epidemic may never be known for sure.[5]

But as efforts continue to untangle the biological and social origins of the epidemic, such research does little to tell us why the crisis unfolded the way that it did. Since its discovery in the forests of Central Africa in 1976, a mythology of gory clinical symptoms and heart-pumping thriller movies have surrounded this single-stranded RNA virus, making it a major zoonotic disease of global concern and a candidate for a future pandemic (Leach and Hewlett, 2010). Fear of Ebola spreading throughout the world has helped drive major global surveillance and outbreak response systems, such as the WHO's Global Outbreak and Response Network (GOARN) that was used during the West African crisis.[6] Previous Ebola outbreaks have been contained through rapid, often military-like, containment strategies, although predictions that a major crisis would occur if the virus were to enter African cities have often been emphasized. In parallel, communities in areas of repeated outbreaks in East and Central Africa have learned how to cope, with local social protocols and cultural logics helping to limit spread to, in most instances, tens of cases or fewer (Hewlett and Hewlett, 2008).

Despite the global media and policy imagination surrounding Ebola, it took over eight months for a coordinated global response to the West African outbreak to fall into place. Clear warning signs were present early on that the epidemic was soon to turn from bad to worse, but were masked by complacency, confusion and politics (MSF, 2015). As the virus spread to Texas and infected two nurses, this belated response relied more on hype and fear-mongering among citizens of richer, more privileged countries than a concern for social justice or local impact. As such it followed the well-trodden path of the 'outbreak narrative' where the dominant concern is of 'exotic' diseases exploding onto the global stage (Wald, 2008; Dry and Leach, 2010). But beneath the hype, was this a natural course of events for a newly emergent pathogen in a region that had yet to experience it, or could things have gone very differently? What does the Ebola crisis tell us about the ways in which zoonotic epidemics unfold in contexts of poverty and inequality, and in turn, how we should understand the relationship between those 'pockets' and the 'global stage'? What does this reveal about the aspirations of 'virus hunters' to prevent the next global pandemic before it emerges? And what can we learn from this dramatic set of events about the political economy of zoonotic disease containment, and 'One Health'?

The scale of the outbreak has been variously described, like the biological origins in Meliandou village, to a number of social and political factors: weak health systems, a lack of resources, the element of surprise, cultural traditions and the high-level of regional population mobility. Again, while these causative descriptions are not inaccurate, conceptualizing the crisis from these normative standpoints is woefully decontextualized, and possibly even dangerous.[7] Building on other recent commentaries (Wilkinson and Leach, 2015; Leach, 2015), this chapter locates the source of the epidemic in a different set of explanations structured around the concept of structural violence: the interlocking of socio-political, economic and historical processes that have effectively perpetuated deep-seated inequalities in income, health and political inclusion in West Africa. The chapter explores a longstanding crisis of development and political economy that underpins different legacies of mistrust and dysfunction that interacted in multifaceted, yet often predictable, ways during the Ebola crisis. This allows for reflection on what the epidemic tells us about the types of systems and approaches needed to prevent and respond to zoonotic 'spillover' events more effectively in the future.

A slow response to an unprecedented outbreak

Once Emile Ouamouno became sick in Meliandou, Ebola quickly infected his unsuspecting family members and staff at the local under-equipped rural clinic. For three months a mysterious disease spread around the Eastern Guinea Forest Region, until health workers in Guéckédou and Macenta, in the south-east of Guinea, alerted public health officials and NGOs to a deadly disease that killed 'like lightning'. The Zaire Ebola strain was finally identified on 22 March 2014, nearly three months after its first appearance. The virus then crossed into new territory, using the 'porous borders and dense transnational trade networks' of the region (Moran and Hoffman, 2014): the Guinean capital, Conakry, as well as neighbouring Liberia (also in March) and Sierra Leone (in May).

According to the International Health Regulations (IHR), the only legally binding set of international 'rules' for infectious disease control, a single case of Ebola counts as an outbreak, which should precipitate a rapid response from national and international agencies to contain it (WHO, 2005b). Learning from past outbreaks, the WHO, the Centers for Disease Control and Prevention (CDC) and Medecins Sans Frontieres (MSF) had developed standardized medical and public health response strategies to contain the virus. Past Ebola outbreaks typically involved highly trained teams parachuting from outside to establish isolation units, contact tracing and health education to address unsafe burials and homecare of the sick. In the early 2000s, anthropological expertise and community engagement strategies had been added to increase local acceptability (Hewlett and Hewlett, 2008). But national governments need to first sound the alarm.

The actual implementation of rapid response is, however, a different matter. As in many situations, it is beset with personal, organizational and national politics that make collaboration elusive when it is most needed. Fearful of economic uncertainty, the government in Guinea dismissed MSF's warnings and played down the outbreak (Nossiter, 2014). The slowness of the WHO to relay the urgency between their country, regional and Geneva headquarters has been widely critiqued (WHO, 2015a).[8] Institutional resistance to admitting things were out of control, and organizational hierarchies that prevented fieldworkers and officials from reporting to their seniors how badly things were actually going, acted as perverse incentives. On top of the three-month lag in identifying Ebola, early coordination struggles and delays were amplified as there were soon three governments, three WHO country offices, multiple ministries, NGOs, and disease specialists shipped in by different agencies, all of whom had different interests and approaches to managing the epidemic. Operating on a shoestring until at least September, the 'response' was 'running behind' the epidemic from the beginning.[9]

As the crisis unfolded (Table 5.1), several patterns emerged. First, it appeared that health messages about the new virus were fragmented, confusing and largely 'top-down'. The original emphasis disproportionately focused on telling people to avoid bushmeat, but this generated significant suspicion as local people had long consumed forest animals as an important protein source without human disease. Second, the health system quickly became overloaded. Patients overwhelmed local clinics that lacked supplies, training and support systems, and fearful health workers who had heard, or witnessed, the high death rates among their colleagues abandoned their posts, often in haste. This included deaths at the region's only Lassa fever isolation ward: experienced laboratory technicians and most of the ward's nursing staff died, as well as Doctor Khan – Sierra Leone's only hemorrhagic fever expert. As the virus reached burgeoning cities and case rates ballooned to a few hundred each week in September and October, the modellers' graphs went

TABLE 5.1 Total cases of Ebola during the West African epidemic to end of May 2015

Country	Total cases (suspect, probable and confirmed)	Laboratory confirmed cases	Total deaths
Sierra Leone	12,745	8614	3911
Liberia	10,666	3151	4806
Guinea	3644	3216	2425
Nigeria	20	19	8
Mali	8	7	6
USA	4	4	1
Other (UK, Spain, Senegal, Italy)	4	4	0
Total	27,085	15,015	11,157

Source: CDC Data from 29 May 2015, www.cdc.gov/vhf/ebola/outbreaks/2014-west-africa/case-counts.html.

exponential, predicting epidemic doubling times of 28–30 days. The sense was of a crisis soon to reach apocalyptic proportions. A WHO-affiliated arbovirus expert was at the centre of a media storm in Europe when he predicted an inevitable five million deaths in Guinea, Liberia and Sierra Leone – the time had passed for effective containment and the virus now needed to 'burn itself out'.[10] The disease crossed into Nigeria, Senegal and Mali and foreign medical volunteers, who had to be transported back to America and Europe for treatment, became infected.

Once the WHO declared the outbreak to be a Public Health Emergency of International Concern (PHEIC) in August 2014, a concerted global response finally gathered momentum. International agencies, NGOs and foreign governments set up a series of emergency response activities. A mounting discourse of global health security followed in the establishment of airport checkpoints and the deployment of the US and UK militaries to Sierra Leone and Liberia to establish Ebola Treatment Centres (ETUs). This followed historic-colonial trends with the USA in Liberia, UK in Sierra Leone and France in Guinea. With fears that the number of beds in ETUs would not be sufficient, and amidst evidence that people found these alien and inaccessible, local Community Care Centres (CCCs) were also set up to triage and isolate suspect patients. Accompanying these care facilities were information campaigns, new laboratories to process the vast numbers of samples and fast-tracked ethical clearances to test experimental vaccines.

But many of these outreach efforts and medical infrastructures only came online well into November. While teams were being deployed and supplies sent, woeful inadequacies remained on the ground during the peak of the epidemic: a lack of healthcare workers, treatment beds, functioning triage and test facilities, burial teams, ambulances, laboratory staff, contact tracers and infection and prevention control (IPC) supplies. As the number of ETUs and CCCs finally blossomed, by December 2015 the epidemic curve had largely passed, first in Liberia and then in Sierra Leone – although ongoing cases and small outbreaks went on occurring in Sierra Leone and Guinea at least until the summer of 2015.

The epidemic ruptured the social and economic fabric of the region. As with the wars that preceded it, Ebola created a suspicion of strangers and physical distance – things like handshaking, hugging, burying the dead, caring for the sick and making love were seemingly outlawed (Richards *et al.*, 2015). The virus also represented a series of personal tragedies for the women, men and children who lost loved ones and now had to endure the consequences as survivors and their communities were stigmatized. The total economic consequences of the outbreak were dramatic; a World Bank study estimated that economic impacts for 2015 alone were at more than 12 per cent of the combined GDP for Liberia, Guinea and Sierra Leone (Thomas *et al.*, 2015). Airlines stopped flying, mines and schools closed, fields went fallow and village markets and clinics shutdown; in Sierra Leone the government enacted a range of measures which interrupted routine social and economic life: restrictions on trading hours, parties, sports and public gatherings. At the same time laws against hiding the sick, road checkpoints, curfews and massive quarantines became the norm, sometimes forcefully implemented by the military.

A legacy of exclusion and inequality

The Ebola epidemic provides a unique vantage point to inspect the processes that transform a 'single zoonotic' spillover event into a transnational medical humanitarian disaster in some localities but not others. The concept of structural violence, first proposed by Galtung (1969) and refined by Farmer (2005) in relation to global health, refers to the ways in which institutions inflict avoidable harm to people by barring access to basic human needs, often in ways that normalize these practices to those most affected. Structural violence is manifest and maintained by a set of interlocking institutions that, across different spatial and temporal planes, act as vectors for interrelated patterns of economic, political, judicial and social exclusions and injustices. Locating these interlaced domains helps contextualize the extreme vulnerability to epidemic disease of the Mano river region, and how these compromised the resilience of peoples, places and systems during the Ebola outbreak. Viewed through a lens of extremes and inequality, disease does know borders.

It is no secret that Guinea, Sierra Leone and Liberia are among the poorest nations on the planet; they consistently rank at the very bottom of development indexes, such as low per capita income, life expectancy, literacy rates and infant mortality (Table 5.2). This level of dispossession has been fuelled by a long history of conflict, instability and political repression that stretches back to the slave trade and colonial era, when the region supplied labour and commodities like timber, rubber and cocoa to the British and French colonial powers (Fyfe, 1962; McGovern, 2012; Fairhead and Leach, 1996). Decades of authoritarian rule and military coups in Guinea followed independence from France in 1958. Brutal civil wars took hold in Liberia (1989–1996 and 1999–2003) and Sierra Leone (1991–2002), known for their use of child soldiers and 'blood diamonds'.[11] War metaphors were ubiquitous across the region to describe the spread of Ebola just as political commentaries began to fear that the virus itself could precipitate state failure and further regional conflict.

But not everyone is poor in West Africa. Inequalities are situated across a spectrum of socio-demographic profiles that shape advantages and disadvantages in nuanced, place-specific ways. Large income gaps are maintained between the elite and poor. Securing enough rice to eat, either through subsistence farming or raising

TABLE 5.2 Key development indicators for the Mano River region

Country	Population (millions)	Per capita GDP income	Life expectancy (years)	Literacy (%)	Population below the poverty line (%)	Infant mortality rate (per 1000 live births)
Liberia	4.1	$900	58	48	64	69
Guinea	11.5	$1300	60	30	47	55
Sierra Leone	5.7	$2100	57	48	70	73

Source: CIA's World Factbook.

'small money', is a daily struggle for most. In contrast, others maintain conspicuous signs of accumulated wealth in the form of new iPhones, $4 \times 4s$, and gated compounds with security guards. Precarious rural and urban livelihoods are maintained by longstanding neglect of the agricultural, education and health sectors, while urban and rural elites disproportionately monopolize state resources and economic wealth. Major social barriers exist for young people and women in land and labour rights, perpetuated both by state hierarchies and customary institutions. It was disenfranchised youths, after all, who revolted in the face of urban elites amassing mineral wealth, and land and labour barriers instituted by ex-colonial chiefs, that precipitated civil war in Sierra Leone in the 1990s (Richards, 1996).

People's disenfranchisement is both material and political. Nationalism, sectarianism and tribalism have often been used to rally mass political support in West Africa. This 'politics of the belly' involves politicians distributing goods in exchange for loyalty, which obviates moral and institutional forms of accountability (Bayart, 1993). Governments may follow donor-directed policies to enact decentralized governance in an attempt to widen inclusive political processes, but 'shadow state' systems still link these efforts to existing patronage networks (Reno, 1995, 1998; Højbjerg *et al.*, 2013). Such non-inclusive politics have major repercussions during times of crisis. The fact that the Ebola outbreak in Sierra Leone originated in the east of the country, an opposition stronghold, led to popular fears that the virus was part of a politically motivated genocide campaign and contributed to the government's tardy response. While mass shortages of protective gear were being reported in Freetown in October 2014, a massive shipping container with supplies sat unopened at the docks for two months, reportedly due to its being organized by an opposition politician.[12] The legacy of Guinea's Marxist state apparatus contributed to fears that outbreak control teams were pumping viruses, and not chlorine, into crowded market places (Fairhead, 2015).

Inequalities become institutionalized in bodies and societies. Severe inequalities produce social and psychological stresses which impact on health outcomes and on social capital and cohesion, especially on levels of trust (Wilkinson and Pickett, 2009). Similar interactions between corruption, inequality and trust have been described as a 'vicious cycle' (Rothstein and Uslaner, 2005). At its height, Ebola exemplified this vicious cycle, only at high speed. The ethnographic literature on West Africa has documented how lack of inclusion drives fears, suspicions, anxieties, and even rebellion, and how it has shaped logics and institutions based on ambiguity and secrecy to protect from extraction and violence, and to explain unequal (or ill-gotten) gain (Fairhead and Leach, 1996; Richards, 1996; Ferme, 2001; Shaw, 2014). Numerous recent corruption scandals in all three countries reinforce these logics. It was on these foundations that people viewed government motivations as self-serving, coercive or dangerous. As one ex-civil servant commented during the Ebola crisis: 'The Liberian government [is] like a buffet service, in which those who control the government and their relations eat all they can eat for free while the majority of Liberians look through the windows with empty stomachs.'[13]

Moneymaking – by governments, ghost workers and NGOs – was a recurring theme of local perceptions about the virus and it influenced every level of the response.[14] In Sierra Leone, social mobilizers complained that one of their biggest challenges in Ebola sensitization was the communities' belief that they were just trying to make money. Also in Sierra Leone, the allocation of jobs and 'fabulous' salaries at the CCCs was felt to be unfair (Oosterhoff *et al.*, 2015). Liberian nurses protesting that they were not being paid pointed to the higher wages of expatriate staff and noted that school closures did not affect government employees because they sent their children to private schools abroad.[15] Such reflections complicate the idea that 'we are all in this together'. In the forest region of Guinea (a heartland of political opposition), a message was sent around to local phones to warn people that doctors were being paid to infect people with Ebola (see Figure 5.1). Much Ebola

FIGURE 5.1 Picture of an Ebola message in Sierra Leone. The message read: 'A vaccination will soon be used against Ebola but this product contains Ebola virus to contaminate the Forest peoples. There are doctors paid to pass from house to house to give this vaccination. We must categorically refuse to be vaccinated so that all of the Forest peoples are not eliminated' (credit: James Zingeser)

commentary has focused on the militarization of the response, seen in roadblocks, quarantine, curfews and roadblocks. However, while heavy-handed tactics did little to build trust, and may have fostered memories of war, the experience of inequality and the related concern with moneymaking, coupled with the politicization of the response in some parts of the region (Fairhead, 2015), was arguably more corrosive.

Inequalities in West Africa are maintained by resource scarcity and socio-political exclusion, which is explicitly and implicitly manufactured by the elites that will benefit from them (Leach, 2015; see also Mehta, 2011). In this way, the aid industry and foreign direct investment are implicated in these local worlds, creating surplus for some and want for many. This sense of disenfranchisement has not been well navigated by the post-conflict period, where the UN, humanitarian and donor agencies have often driven partial, fragmented and inadequate state re-building policies and practices, often driven by geopolitical agendas (Fanthorpe, 2006). In fact, in some quarters, Ebola fears drew directly upon a history of popular suspicion about the motivations of foreign organizations, rooted in the region's past and current relationship with resource extraction and local elite capture (Fairhead, 2015).

The mass deployment of foreigners during the epidemic carried with it a sense of overt sorcery – those arriving dressed in masks, sprinkled water ceremoniously and concealed material in ways that mimicked the activity of local secret societies (Fairhead, 2015). People variously ascribed the virus to a man-made scheme to profit the pharmaceutical industry in the West and/or reduce the African population. The Lassa fever lab in Kenema was widely implicated in these rumours (see Wilkinson, this book). These fears extended to outbreak response teams who, dressed in spacesuits, were seen as extractors of body parts, blood and lives to sell on the global market. These suspicions, located in political and economic exclusion and a history of local and international extraction, gave logic to the early avoidance of ETUs and the dramatic stoning of humanitarian response vehicles and other acts of resistance and violence.

Accompanying the startling interactions between inequality and mistrust being played out during the epidemic was an equally startling lack of acknowledgement of those dynamics. So in the face of initial doubts that the virus was real, people were repeatedly told that 'Ebola is real', which did little to allay their fears that the outbreak was, in some way, a political or financial ploy by their government or foreigners with hidden motives. Meanwhile a sub-current of local commentary continues to further such connections and question Western intentions. As one stated in a Liberian newspaper the day before the country was declared Ebola-free by the WHO:

> The deadly Ebola virus is a myth created by the US and Canadian dark secret services to instigate an atmosphere of fear mongering ... there is no deadly Ebola ... [just] a cocktail of pathogenic viruses genetically modified and/or created by contract laboratories in [the West to make money] ... [but] what most westerners do not realize is that neoliberalism is infinitely deadlier than these man-made viruses.[16]

The article's reference to the 'dangers of neoliberalism' went on to implicate free-market capitalism as the driver of a 'genocide against Africa'. Although using different language, many scholars equally locate the roots of an array of current social problems in the often criticized post-cold war structural adjustment policies implemented by the global financial institutions as part of the Washington consensus. These emphasized the need to retract education, health and agricultural services in order to balance budgets, which created 'blindspots' in governance and equity for the poor (Keshavjee, 2014).

Economic recovery in the region has improved lately through large-scale mining operations, but again the benefits are skewed and unequal. World Bank and International Monetary Fund (IMF) supported policies have fuelled huge economic growth rates of upwards of 21 per cent in Sierra Leone in 2013. Schemes to annex huge tracts of land for biofuels, palm oil, agriculture and mining have become major drivers of economic growth in the region, including iron ore supported by major multinational mining companies like Rio Tinto, Arcelor Mittal and London Mining. But several projects have been beset with corruption scandals, and even when mines have opened local employment and infrastructure benefits have been limited, tempered by adverse effects on artisanal producers and land displacement (Maconachie, 2014). Furthermore, they have not proved to be stable: a global crash in iron ore price has deepened economic woes which, combined with Ebola, has caused London Mining to file for bankruptcy.[17] In some parts of Guinea, people believed that Ebola was introduced by foreigners complicit with the government to destroy local communities in order to better extract mineral wealth.

As rural livelihoods and institutions are unsettled, urban areas expand to present new challenges. Unplanned urbanization, entailing both increased population density and urban sprawl, can increase inequality (McGranahan and Satterthwaite, 2014). Those escaping rural poverty can encounter new economic and livelihood opportunities, but also new forms of exclusion in cities and towns. Blind-spots in state administration, and government policies which simplistically attempt to discourage urbanization, can push people into precarious living conditions and a reliance on informal economies and services (McGranahan and Satterthwaite, 2014). Indeed, rather than consolidating geographical divides, urban expansion sees urban–rural relationships becoming increasingly complex, and livelihoods increasingly transect them. Once in cities, Ebola highlighted how poor housing, inadequate water supplies, hazardous conditions and dense concentrations of people in slums and peri-urban settlements – partially the remnants of dislocation cause by instability – exacerbate the potential for disease spread (Hoffmann, 2011). It made clear how the expansion of urban populations in this region has occurred under the nose of the state – and indeed in full view of urban-based politicians – but without its engagement. The failure to manage this process has led to interlinked rural and urban exclusions, which meant Ebola was especially difficult to control as it travelled in 'pendulum' patterns between towns and villages (Richards et al., 2015).

Whose health governance?

The Ebola outbreak revealed the systemic inadequacies of West Africa's healthcare system and the shortcomings of global pandemic response capabilities. Beyond the community level, the culture of the response itself severely limited effective control. By June 2014 there were 60 separate locations across these three West African nations with Ebola cases, prompting MSF (who was leading the response on the ground) that a massive infusion of resources was desperately needed to address a situation that had become 'out of control'.[18] But a 'global coalition of inaction' followed, as the international response was still sluggish, under-resourced and lacking in leadership and vision (MSF, 2015). High-pledged donations took time to translate into effective field activities; desperately needed 'stuff, staff and systems' were slow to follow (Farmer, 2014).

Much of the blame has been directed at the architecture of global health governance, specifically the WHO. Despite the fact that the organization should have been, given its mandate, leading the response (especially through GOARN), the agency originally downplayed the scale of the crisis and then dropped the ball (MSF, 2015; WHO, 2015a). This had devastating consequences. Poor communication, delayed logistics, bureaucracy and difficulties negotiating with partner countries and organizations, especially by the Africa WHO office, meant it took eight months after the first confirmed case and five months after MSF publicly expressed concern at the slow response to draw a comprehensive roadmap for control. Peter Piot, who helped discover the Ebola virus in 1976, stated, 'What should be [the] WHO's strongest regional office because of the enormity of the health challenges, is actually the weakest technically, and full of political appointees.'[19] The issue of disjointed regional and country WHO offices with a lack of emergency funds required that fear and panic was needed in Europe and America to spur action from above.

This situation has historic-political roots. The politicization of WHO appointments, especially in the Africa office, contributed to a decline in the organization's legitimacy. Relatedly at the global policy level, the WHO has seen its authority and capacity to address global public goods further eroded over time by funding cuts, bilateral donations that come with strings attached and the proliferation of other global health actors who sometimes operate at odds with its broader mandate and goals (Farmer, 2005; Keshavjee, 2014). This includes the World Bank's focus on 'selective primary healthcare' in the 1980s as well as hugely bloated vertical programmes like the Global Fund to Fight AIDS, Tuberculosis and Malaria (GFATM). Due to the financial crisis, in 2011 the WHO saw massive restructuring and funding cuts that included dropping nearly two-thirds of its emergency response unit staff, including nine of the 12 emergency specialists based at the Africa office (Gostin and Friedman, 2014). Concurrent epidemic emergencies (Middle East respiratory syndrome coronavirus (MERS-CoV), polio and avian influenza) together with humanitarian emergencies in the Central African Republic, Iraq, South Sudan and Syria, also stretched the agency thin as it struggled to respond to multiple threats and disasters (WHO, 2015a).

Perhaps more acutely, the Ebola crisis also exposed the health system in West Africa. Existing policies on surveillance and outbreak response may exist on paper but are rarely known outside a small cadre of technocrats in the capitals of Monrovia, Conakry and Free Town, and haphazardly implemented during times of crisis (Petit *et al.*, 2013). Even before the virus hit, there was a tenuous shortage of health staff; Liberia, Sierra Leone and Guinea ranked at the bottom of statistics in terms of doctors per population. A 2011 assessment in Liberia found that for a country of over four million, there were only 5346 front-line health workers, including 90 physicians, 1393 nurses and 412 midwives (Downie, 2012). These were unevenly distributed in urban areas, with very little specialist training – the country had one psychiatrist, two paediatricians and three obstetricians. Hence medical services rely on the aid industry, which funds and manages major hospitals and other facilities. In 2009, government expenditure in Liberia made up only US$19 million of the US$179 million spent on health, with the majority supplied by donors and charities (Downie, 2012). But international funding has tended to prioritize particular diseases and health issues rather than address the systemic dysfunction of the systems that drive them. Unfortunately, the sustainable restructuring of salary structures, education and training, management and a focus on quality tend to be overlooked. These conditions underlay the reason why healthcare workers at the few ETUs functioning at the beginning of the international response threatened to strike in Sierra Leone and Liberia at the peak of the epidemic. But this gap also persists at more localized levels, with their lack of accessible networks of rural health outreach workers and paramedics that might have served as key nodes in the Ebola response, linking rural and peri-urban communities to response partners.

For villagers, seeking care in rural areas often involves distant travel, sometimes on foot and hammock through bush tracks, to under-equipped facilities where small 'fees' are needed for donor-provided 'free' drugs (Petit *et al.*, 2013). A lacklustre leadership and staff, and a harrowing lack of basic supplies and drugs, from gloves to functioning latrines, portray the gravity of the situation at many of these facilities. Even before Ebola, many people avoided formal clinics in the region, given the lack of drugs, nurses and quality care. In the region's pluralistic therapeutic landscape, traditional doctors, healers and informal drug vendors have significant community trust and legitimacy, partially due to their availability, bedside manner and socio-religious symbolism; these actors also combine herbs, pharmaceuticals and incantations in ways that speak to logical aetiological understandings (Jambai and MacCormack, 1996; Leach *et al.*, 2008). Plural understandings of health, wellbeing and disease predominate, and are linked to socio-ecological orders that shape production, reproduction and the afterlife (Fairhead and Leach, 1996). But socio-economic and ideological tensions between traditional practices and biomedicine ensured that the Ebola response made little use of these alternative structures, despite their significance for local people.

Chronic underfunding and neglect contributed to the health systems of Guinea, Sierra Leone and Liberia effectively being 'vectors for Ebola' (Abramowitz, 2014). The lack of basic infection prevention and control material and training created dangerous circumstances where health workers had to triage and isolate suspected patients with substandard resources, and under duress. This contributed to further spread at clinics. Clinics were then shut down and healthcare workers fled. Without ambulances, calls to the Ebola hotlines went unanswered for days. Nearly 900 healthcare workers were infected with Ebola during the crisis, and 500 died (MSF, 2015). This further compromised already fragile health systems. Without access to basic medical care of any sort during the peak of the crisis, more people likely died from other preventable conditions than from the Ebola virus itself. The region, after all, is endemic for other infectious diseases that occur in seasonal outbreak cycles. Reports on the region's common disease killers like malaria, respiratory infections and diarrheal diseases ceased for months during the crisis (Table 5.3). A study in Liberia found that antenatal visits and deliveries in clinics came to a near standstill (Iyengar *et al.*, 2014). Measles and other preventable childhood diseases have surged (Takahashi *et al.*, 2015). The undocumented personal tragedies of people suffering from these illnesses, many of which mimic certain Ebola-like symptoms, reveal the unexpected consequences of the epidemic.

Sub-standard care, like socio-political trends, has provided little ground for trust between clinics, public health authorities and communities. Communities are often seen as passive recipients of biomedical knowledge, an idiom that perverts local understandings and obstructs ways to involve local people in meaningful ways. There were good reasons for people avoiding ETUs during the crisis – there was a lack of transport, unsafe triage, lack of food, a lack of effective therapy and fear of undignified – but more importantly socially damaging – burials (Abramowitz *et al.*,

TABLE 5.3 Top ten causes of death across the Mano River region

Ranking	Sierra Leone	Liberia	Guinea
1	Malaria	Malaria	Malaria
2	Lower respiratory infections	Lower respiratory infections	Lower respiratory infections
3	Protein-energy malnutrition	Diarrheal diseases	Diarrheal diseases
4	Diarrheal diseases	Protein-energy malnutrition	Protein-energy malnutrition
5	Pre-term birth complications	HIV	Pre-term birth complications
6	HIV	TB	Diarrheal diseases
7	Cancer	Sepsis	Neonatal encephalopathy
8	Stroke	Pre-term birth complications	Meningitis
9	TB	Stroke	Sepsis
10	Ischemic heart disease	Meningitis	TB

Source: Global Burden of Diseases, Injuries and Risk Factors Study (2010), www.thelancet.com/global-burden-of-disease.

2015). This goes some way to explaining why villagers obstructed control teams, removed patients from health clinics and hid sick relatives at home. These suspicions continue into the latter stages of the epidemic, with resistance continuing in Guinea, and rumours that a mass vaccination for a resurgent measles outbreak is a ploy by opposition parties and foreign elites to spark a return of the epidemic.

Community-based responses

Community engagement in West Africa suffered from a lack of dialogue and multiple layers of mistrust between governments, response agencies and citizens. From the beginning, state communication was largely a one-way street and messages were confusing and inadequate. This was shown in the prevailing emphasis on not eating bushmeat (despite the human-to-human spread) in comparison to other hygiene measures, for example (Figure 5.2). Blaming the same rural communities that suffered from infection for deforestation and bushmeat hunting provided an inaccurate depiction of environmental change processes in the region, as well of the drivers of the outbreak (Fairhead and Leach, 1996). People and bats have long cohabited in a region that has historically been a mosaic of forest, savannah and farmland (Fairhead and Leach, 1998), and not recently deforested as so many Ebola commentators have assumed (Bausch and Schwartz, 2014). Increased viral spillover

FIGURE 5.2 Ebola messaging poster, Liberia. Note the emphasis on bushmeat in two of the five pictures (credit: Kevin Bardosh)

between bats and people cannot be attributed solely, or for that matter largely, to subsistence farmers; studies have shown that large agricultural schemes and mining operations have a more pronounced effect on ecological disruptions, and likely also on viral transfers (Wolfe, 2005).[20]

A geography of blame ensued (Briggs and Mantini-Briggs, 2003), accusing 'backward' cultural traditions and 'ignorant' populations of being primary drivers of the epidemic – much was said of hugging and kissing bodies infected with Ebola, rituals and medicine men, fanciful rumours and the pilfering of clinics with Ebola patients, for example in West Point slum, Monrovia, as if these were bizarre exotic behaviours and not typical human responses to social experience and context. Efforts by Sierra Leone's president, Ernest Bai Koroma, to 'cancel Christmas' and spread blame-based messages was premised on the notion that unruly populations, steeped in superstition, were the major problem. An unpopular policy of mass cremation of Ebola-dead bodies in Liberia, to deal with an ineffective response system, likely drove many infections underground and certainly spawned a trade in fake death certificates, ascribing death to other causes. International media tended to obscure the region as disconnected and backwards, despite a long history of regional and global connectedness (McGovern, 2012). But the involvement of local communities and even existing networks of volunteer health workers (who typically deliver donor-funded public health campaigns, like dewormers and childhood vaccinations), were not well involved until late in the outbreak.

In mid-September, Sierra Leone instituted a massive three-day nation-wide lockdown that involved training thousands of community volunteers who went door-to-door spreading information, although concerns were voiced that the strategy could backfire because of its coercive implementation. With current data, it is impossible to know whether authoritarian policies such as this lock-down or externally imposed quarantines helped or hindered. What they certainly showed, however, was a lack of trust on the part of the government as to the capacity of local populations to understand and act appropriately. It seemed the dominant belief was that Ebola control was only possible by force. Huge amounts of resources were needed to make quarantines liveable, to provide adequate food supply, to monitor contacts[21] and ensure sanitation was adequate.[22] Meanwhile the fear of quarantine, which meant jobs, livelihoods and farms were at risk, may have stopped people reporting cases (ACAPS, 2015) and quarantine 'escapees' have been associated with Ebola spikes.[23] A different approach would have been to spend the same resources on engaging with communities and building a trust-based response which did not rely on the use of force. As the WHO's own external review of the Ebola response commented:

> Bleak public messaging emphasized that no treatment was available and reduced communities' willingness to engage; medical anthropologists should have been better utilized to develop this messaging. It must also be realized that the fact that communities were already in a post-conflict situation manifested itself in high levels of distrust in authority. Owing to an extent to a lack

of involvement on the part of the broader humanitarian systems, the non governmental organization resources, such as community development workers and volunteers, many from the countries and communities themselves, were not mobilized in the early stages. Given WHO's extensive experience with outbreaks, health promotion and social mobilization, it is surprising that it took until August or September 2014 to recognize that Ebola transmission would be brought under control only when surveillance, community mobilization and the delivery of appropriate health care to affected communities were all put in place simultaneously.

(WHO, 2015a)

The epidemic's spread, and ultimately its containment, occurred for the most part before the belated aid machinery hit the ground. In retrospect, most models that predicted massive influxes of case rates into the hundreds of thousands did not account for the ways in which communities themselves adopted innovative and life-saving strategies to deal with infection risk under compromised circumstances (Abramowitz *et al.*, 2015). People have knowledge, expertise and practical experience to bear on epidemic response, to deal with life, death and health through individual and collective efforts, such as community-level institutions. This has been well documented during Ebola outbreaks in Central and East Africa by Hewlett and Hewlett (2008). Just as Ebola spreads through social acts, like caring for the sick, physical contact, following social networks across borders and burials (Richards *et al.*, 2015), so too is its control a social act. Local people supported caring, burial, isolation and mobility restrictions, where culture was made flexible despite deep social logics (Abramowitz *et al.*, 2015). This included the institution of local organization structures, like local Ebola task forces, to carry out neighbourhood surveillance and quarantines implemented by traditional leaders and concerted efforts by local health workers who facilitated social learning (Richards *et al.*, 2015). Word of mouth spread messages about 'makeshift PPE' (personal protective equipment): the importance of plastic bags and long clothes as local 'chlorine economies' sprang-up. People kept their distances in public and avoided strangers. Furthermore, once communities became familiar with Ebola transmission pathways and trusted the messengers who brought them, they often complied readily with exceptional quarantines and medical burial teams. Over time, the relationships between national authorities, such as Sierra Leone's District Ebola Response Commands (DERCs), and local communities improved to the degree that, on the whole, new cases were quickly isolated and cared for, and food and non-food provisions given by NGOs for any quarantined houses.

This is not to say that resistance and evasion to these measures were not practised; a small number of reports persisted of households hiding the sick, turning to traditional medicines and ceremonially burying bodies well after the response was coordinated and adequately funded, and resistance driven by political-economic fear has also persisted in some parts of the region. But the eventual focus on taking adequate time to engage communities, through involving multiple sources of local leaders and experts, had a profound result. CCCs were eventually built as facilities close to the community, where triage and testing would be done and where patients were cared for close to their families (Kucharski *et al.*, 2015). But these were constructed late in the game, and often in ways that were never truly 'community-led' but maintained social distance between staff and communities. In practice, the model showed that implementing agencies were sceptical of having trained lay people care for the sick.

Response activities frequently fell foul of local politics and power dynamics, sometimes in subtle ways but sometimes dramatically. For example, the notorious murder of eight outreach workers in Womey, Guinea, should be seen as a result of socio-political tensions and ineffective community involvement (Fairhead, 2015). In this case, 'big men' politicians joined a sensitization visit, but were attacked after telling people to not be afraid of Ebola and to cooperate with the authorities. No attempt was made to listen to their concerns and perspectives. Tragically, armed youths then attacked the delegation, and eight bodies were later found in a latrine. This experience contrasts with other equally 'resistant' communities who had similar concerns but where things turned out differently. In mid-2014, 26 Kissi-speaking villages in an area of Guinea effectively cut themselves off from the Ebola response by stoning vehicles and barricading bridges (Anoko, 2014). The area had historical tensions between the ruling Muslim Fulani and Malinke elites and local ethnic groups in the Forest region, which could have easily precipitated a violent outcome. But efforts were made to identify, understand and involve a wide range of locally influential actors, including secret society members, hunters, elders, healers, street vendors and others, which shifted the tensions and then generated successful Ebola response activities (Anoko, 2014).

Another case involved a pregnant Kissi woman who died of Ebola in Guéckédou Hospital in Guinea (Faye, 2014). The family and village elders demanded the body before complying with necessary contact-tracing activities. To avoid socio-spiritual consequences for other pregnant mothers in the village, who had already fled in fear, mother and baby needed to be buried separately by sterile or menopausal women, according to Kissi tradition (Fairhead, 2015). But response teams considered the infection risks much too high, and refused. Things were at a standstill, until another anthropologist brokered a solution with initiation societies to address the needs of the ancestors and dead through a reparation ritual. This was financially supported by the WHO to allow for the procedure, and maintained local socio-religious norms.

Conclusions

Ebola provides a mosaic of domains, from the economic, social, cultural, political, biological and ecological, to reflect on how notions of collaboration, cooperation and interdisciplinarity can better be operationalized in global health and development. At its core, the crisis reveals a simple and intuitive axiom: the spread of epidemics is caused by unequal social and political-economic conditions (Farmer, 2005). Structural violence, as a set of overlapping institutions and practices, provides a conceptual lens by which these inequalities, across multiple scales, can be exposed, and their repercussions during a crisis understood. These are not 'natural' conditions, but are repercussions of a set of actors and actions that have co-created deeply unequal health, state, business and international systems over time and space. When epidemic-prone viruses emerge, these conditions then act as the primary vectors for further spread.

Ebola challenges some of the recurrent priorities sketched out in the One Health literature on how effective disease control activities should be conceptualized and implemented. In his book, *The Viral Storm: The Dawn of a New Pandemic Age*, Wolfe (2011) calls for the prioritization of a new 'holy grail' for modern public health: pandemic prediction. Coupled with this new scientific aspiration – to predict epidemics 'just as meteorologists predict the course of hurricanes' – is an often vague and yet repeated claim that scientific knowledge will enable public health officials, sometime in the future, to actually prevent pandemics from occurring in the first place. This is the ultimate philosopher's stone of much current One Health research and policy. The assumption is that through cross-disciplinary scientific research and new wildlife-based surveillance systems, forecasted knowledge about disease ecologies and trends will enable targeted prevention of potential spillover events. While the science may improve, it is likely that uncertainties will remain in complex human–animal–social–ecological landscapes, confounding the best-laid prediction models. Precautionary and adaptive approaches that relate local knowledge and wider-scale scenarios may be more appropriate to realities 'on the edge' (cf. Roe and Schulmann, 2008) in zoonosis – vulnerable places like West Africa.

More significantly, though, the Ebola crisis shows that the rhetoric of pandemic prevention must engage more readily with unequal political economies that are at the roots of societal distrust, neglect and imbalances. These are the conditions which make it harder to spot disease spillovers and which exacerbate the scale of resulting epidemics. The danger here is that One Health proposes a new set of expert-driven solutions that appear to be all-encompassing in terms of interdisciplinary science, but become compartmentalized from wider and more complex systems of health, poverty and politics.

As One Health scholars and practitioners grapple with what pandemic prediction and prevention mean in the real world, there is a need to involve more plural forms of expertise in disease systems that stretch across multiple scales. In this way, the foundational notions of interdisciplinarity, collaboration and complexity that underpin the One Health movement have much to offer. Epidemics like Ebola are effectively 'mirrors held up to society' that showcase fundamental differences in ideology and power between different social groups (Briggs and Mantini-Briggs, 2003). Inequalities, systemic dysfunction and top-down approaches not only inhibit the controllability of epidemic diseases but they help to exacerbate them. They reveal a failure of development to support effective and inclusive health, governance and livelihood systems. While the WHO argues that Ebola reveals that 'business as usual' and 'more of the same' is a perilous path for future global health security (WHO, 2015a), more attention to the nexus of health, humanitarian, security and development crises which goes well beyond institutional and ideological silos is needed. Greater action to promote the global public good aspects of international governance systems is key, but it must have an engagement with power and politics at its heart.

The foundation for epidemic control should be located in inclusive institutions and economies that generate trust, justice, equality and security in social milieus. Building inclusive institutions demands 'people-led' politics: taking seriously the challenges and claims of communities, activism and grassroots ingenuity to dominant modes of power. The lack of transformational politics is a glaring shortcoming to current aid modalities, and Ebola highlights how these glaring shortcomings perpetuate epidemic disease. This is not to propagate some romantic view from below, but merely to suggest the need for alliances that re-configure power and expertise in ways that address inequalities and their corollaries.

As organizations like the WHO assess their response to Ebola and look for reform, the conversation should therefore not just be about improved coordination or budgets for emergency response, but about how they can institutionalize plural forms of knowledge and involve local communities meaningfully from the start. Accepting the counter-intuitive notion that effective epidemic response might not rely on everyone accepting the same worldview is a prerequisite.

There are signs that this is happening. A network of anthropologists, some directly involved in 'outbreak ethnography' in West Africa, others bringing long-term regional and local contextual knowledge, formed in response to the Ebola epidemic. They crowd-sourced knowledge and provided expert advice, briefs and input on a wide range of issues: guidelines for safe and dignified burials, support for community-led action, caring for the sick, addressing stigma and the design of clinical trials (www.ebola-anthropology.net). They interpreted and showed the logic in social and cultural practices, anxieties and rumours. They were able to feed this knowledge into high-level government strategies (Whitty *et al.*, 2014) and to international scientific committees, including at the WHO, and were listened to and heeded.

When Margaret Chan gave her statement on the WHO's learning from the Ebola crisis, she strikingly said:

> We have learned lessons of community and culture.... This is not simply about getting the right messages across; we must learn to listen if we want to be heard. We have learned the importance of respect for culture in promoting safe and respectful funeral and burial practices. Empowering communities must be an action, not a cliché.

And that:

> We will create a Global Health Emergency Workforce – combining the expertise of public health scientists, the clinical skills of doctors, nurses and other health workers, the management skills of logisticians and project managers, and the skills of social scientists, communication experts and community workers.

Has the Ebola crisis marked a turning point, then, in appreciation of the value of social science in epidemic response – and perhaps more broadly One Health policy – as part of collaborative multidisciplinary approaches? One would like to think so. Yet it is salutary to recall that global institutions like the WHO and CDC have long had social scientists in their midst, yet have remained dominated by biomedical expertise. Government agencies tend to prioritize quantifiable indicators like the number of beds over the quality of community engagement and participation. Institutional pathways to bring social science intelligence into an unfolding medical humanitarian emergency remain nascent, and not always easily accepted, while One Health policy aimed at preventing zoonotic outbreaks remains dominated by the voices and perspectives of medics and vets. So although the Ebola crisis may have been a wake-up call, sustaining the momentum of social science engagement will require better understanding of its role, and its embedding in institutional routines and resourcing. In this sense, the Ebola crisis reveals the need to move beyond principles to focus on processes – to how collaborative disease control actually happens, and to the political economy of science, social science and local knowledge within this.

Finally, though, the crisis reveals that the knowledge required to inform immediate epidemic responses is only one piece of a much larger puzzle. More efforts are also needed to build plural forms of knowledge to address deeply laced structural violence in areas where epidemic diseases, and potential future pandemics, are most likely to emerge. It is here that the political economy of knowledge within epidemic responses must engage with the political economies and histories of localities, countries and regions, and knowledge of these, in order to contribute to a more sustainable future.

Notes

1 WHO's director general, Margaret Chan, during an Ebola conference in late 2014, http://who.int/dg/speeches/2014/regional-committee-western-pacific/en, accessed 18 July 2015.

2 Ebola is often considered one of the most 'deadly diseases' on earth, and was first discovered in 1976. It has been responsible for various outbreaks in Central and East Africa, in Gabon, Congo, DR Congo, Angola, Uganda and Sudan. Prior to 2014, Uganda had reported the largest outbreak in 2000, with 425 cases. Fatality rates have ranged from 50 per cent to 90 per cent, depending on which of the five different Ebola virus species are present and the availability of supportive clinical care. The viral incubation period is 21 days.

3 Ebola is a major threat to the conservation of great apes. Before the outbreak in West Africa, more great apes had died from Ebola than people.

4 The causal association of bats with Ebola rests on sporadic Ebola RNA and antibody detection in fruit bat species, the high-levels of viral abundance and diversity in bat populations more generally and the high frequency of human–bat contact in Ebola epidemic zones, for example hunting bushmeat (Wood et al., 2012). But large gaps still remain in understanding of the specific disease and host ecologies of the virus.

5 Curiously, the hollow tree had unfortunately been burned a few days before they arrived in the village for unknown reasons, preventing any sampling of that particular bat colony.

6 Established in 2000, GOARN provides a set of formalized technical and operational procedures to assist with the detection, verification, alert and response to disease outbreaks. This includes a wide range of partners: scientific institutions, surveillance initiatives, regional technical networks, laboratories, UN organizations like UNICEF and UNHCR), the Red Cross and humanitarian NGOs like MSF.

7 The assertion that the outbreak was so severe because it had never been in the region before overlooks a few facts. First, the region is known to be 'endemic for epidemic diseases'. Despite Ebola never having been detected, Lassa fever, a related haemorrhagic fever, and other major epidemic diseases like cholera and typhoid, are widely endemic (see Wilkinson, this book). Efforts to control these endemic diseases could easily have transferred to Ebola, if they were adequate, which they clearly were not. Second, a recent study of blood samples taken in the mid-2000 from the Lassa laboratory in Kenema, Sierra Leone, showed that Ebola and Marburg antibodies were present, implying that Ebola could have been circulating for some time in the region (Schoepp *et al.*, 2014).

8 See:www.bloomberg.com/news/2014-10-16/who-response-to-ebola-outbreak-foundered-on-bureaucracy.html, accessed 18 July 2015.

9 See: www.theguardian.com/world/2014/oct/09/ebola-who-government-cuts-delays-in-dealing-with-outbreak; http://uk.reuters.com/article/2014/10/16/ukhealth-ebola-un-idUKKCN0I51XO20141016, accessed 18 July 2015.

10 These comments were made by the German scientist, Jonas Schmidt-Chanasit.

11 A poignant example of this political repression is the case of Liberia's Charles Taylor, perhaps the most successful and ruthless African warlord-politician. During the inter-war period in Liberia, he successfully campaigned on the slogan: 'He killed my ma, he killed my pa, but I will vote for him.' With bribes and intimidation, a fearful population, thinking that he would resume the war if not elected, voted for him en-masse (Gberie, 2005).

12 See:www.nytimes.com/2014/10/06/world/africa/sierra-leone-ebola-medical-supplies-delayed-docks.html, accessed 18 July 2015.

13 See: www.huffingtonpost.com/2014/07/31/ebola-outbreak-causes_n_5638503.html, accessed 18 July 2015.

14 See: www.theguardian.com/world/2015/feb/16/ebola-sierra-leone-budget-report, accessed 18 July 2015.

15 See film by Sorius Samura and Clive Patterson for Africa Investigates: http://africainvestigates.insighttwi.com/episode-one-liberia.html, accessed 18 July 2015.

16 'Ebola is a Big Lie', *Independent*: Monrovia, 8 May 2015.

17 See www.bbc.co.uk/news/business-29650186, accessed 18 July 2015.

18 MSF deployed 1300 MSF international staff and 4000 local staff during the crisis, caring for nearly 5000 confirmed Ebola patients.

19 See: www.theguardian.com/world/2014/oct/17/world-health-organisation-botched-ebola-outbreak, accessed 18 July 2015.

20 Most Ebola outbreaks have occurred in places with high forest cover: Democratic Republic of Congo, Republic of Congo and Gabon. These were contained because of their low human population and remote location.

21 In some quarantined households in Sierra Leone multiple people fell sick but their condition was not reported to the visiting surveillance officers, illustrating the extent to which relationships between response actors and the public continued to be deeply problematic. See ACAPS (2015) for more details.

22 Quarantines could mean that households of 20 or more were kept in close confines, with poor sanitation and often sharing latrines. Keeping people in such conditions, some of whom had high exposure risks while others did not, arguably increased the chance of transmission. See ACAPS (2015) for more details.

23 www.nytimes.com/2015/03/01/world/africa/nearly-beaten-in-sierra-leone-ebola-makes-a-comeback-by-sea.html?_r=1, accessed 18 July 2015.

6

STEPPING TOWARDS A POLICY RESPONSE TO RIFT VALLEY FEVER

Pastoralists and epidemic preparedness in Kenya

Erik Millstone, Hannington Odame, Oscar Okumu and Kevin Bardosh

Introduction

Rift Valley fever (RVF) is a viral haemorrhagic fever affecting domestic livestock, wildlife and humans. Transmitted by mosquitoes, RVF is characterized by sporadic but significant epidemics that are associated with changes in land use and climate, specifically extensive flooding that precipitate pathogen and vector spread. Though intermittent, RVF has generated much scientific and policy interest. Outbreaks have had severe social and economic consequences, enhancing the vulnerability of marginalized pastoralists in East Africa (Rich and Wanyoike, 2010). The economic costs of the most recent epidemic in 2006/2007 were estimated at some US$60 million for the East African economy (Anyamba *et al.*, 2010). The disease has become endemic in several sub-Saharan African countries, and has been the subject of livestock movement bans given its potential to spread to other countries and regions, such as the Arabian Peninsula.

RVF is interesting, in part, because it is a relatively novel disease characterized by long and irregular periods between outbreaks (Britch *et al.*, 2013). Before 1977, RVF was primarily considered an animal disease causing abortions in sheep but, for unclear reasons, it has increasingly affected people and spread to new regions. RVF spread has tended to be in places where climate changes are already having significant adverse effects on local livelihoods, and where land use changes, such as the expansion of irrigated farming and the introduction of more susceptible livestock breeds, are taking hold (Grace and Bett, 2014). Climatic fluctuations and cycles play an important role, and efforts have been made to model and predict these bioclimatic relationships and delineate their influence on RVF epidemiology.

RVF illustrates some of the challenges of disease prediction, forecasting and the operationalization of early warning systems in contexts of poverty, vulnerability and uncertainty. The disease ecology of the virus contributes to a certain type of knowledge fragmentation – it is incompletely understood not only by pastoralists, but also by scientists and policy-makers. Prediction of RVF outbreaks is currently very imperfect; major disease ecology questions also remain unanswered. Furthermore, the disconnect between predictive models and pastoralist livelihoods, the veterinary and public health sectors and policy-making in East Africa complicate RVF epidemic preparedness. RVF typically occurs in very remote and poor regions where veterinary and public health capacity, as well as local governance structures, are particularly weak. In this context, the uneven intervals between outbreaks leads to losses of institutional and community memories concerning responses to, and consequences of, RVF outbreaks. Consequently, governments need to develop and implement clear intervention strategies during non-epidemic periods and to set aside resources for building resilience in the outbreak response system and the livelihoods of pastoralists. But these goals remain somewhat elusive for a variety of reasons. Long inter-outbreak periods ensure that resources are re-allocated to other diseases or more pressing problems.

This chapter focuses on the evolution and characteristics of RVF policy-making in Kenya.[1] Kenya has been the epicentre of several RVF outbreaks and has put into place specific policies to prepare for and address future outbreaks. The chapter pays particular attention to the ways in which knowledge claims in Kenya have become articulated and defended by different actors, including pastoralists, veterinarians, public health officials and senior policy-makers.[2] Identifying the congruencies and incompatibilities between these diverse perspectives, we argue for the need of more inclusive policy-making processes to address the social, as well as the microbial, aspects of RVF vulnerability. Understanding the limitations of scientific authority, and their practical manifestations in political processes surrounding RVF in Kenya, is important when exploring future avenues for more effective policy development.

Disease dynamics: climate, trade and livestock in Kenya

A viral zoonosis, RVF is poorly understood, and unfamiliar to many, even in Kenya. Following drought and flood cycles, outbreaks are intermittent and not accurately predictable. During periods of drought the infectious phlebovirus resides in the eggs of flood-water *Aedes* mosquitoes. In Kenya, the major vector is *Aedes mcintoshi*. These eggs, which effectively act as reservoirs, can survive for several years in dry conditions, but when heavy rainfall occurs the eggs hatch, vector populations increase and the virus spreads rapidly to animals. Other species of mosquitoes and biting insects can then also play a role in transmission (MLD, 2010). The amount of rainfall and local soil types are both important. Outbreaks are often triggered simultaneously in adjacent countries because of climatic fluctuations, and livestock movements are known to spread the virus to new areas.

RVF affects many different species of animals, including sheep, goats, camels, buffaloes, cattle and others. Outbreaks cause severe disease, including high abortion and mortality rates in livestock. Sheep appear to be most affected, with a 90 per cent mortality rate among lambs and nearly 100 per cent abortion rate with ewes.[3] RVF can also be transmitted to people, which normally causes mild influenza-like symptoms but can develop into meningoencephalitis and haemorrhagic forms in a small percentage of patients (roughly 1 per cent).[4] Transmission is mainly through direct contact with the bodily fluids of infected livestock: blood, meat, viscera, faeces and raw milk. Those engaged in slaughter, butchery and veterinary occupations are especially vulnerable (see Figure 6.1).

Though its emergence is intermittent, RVF has become endemic in several African countries. The first outbreak was reported in 1915 in Kenya, although it

FIGURE 6.1 A woman slaughtering and skinning a goat, Kenya (credit: Oscar Okumu)

was not until 1931 that the virus was identified and isolated. Outbreaks have now been reported in six of eight Kenyan provinces. The most recent epidemics occurred in 1997/1998 and 2006/2007, with the epicentre in Northeast Kenya and South-west Somalia (Figure 6.2). During the 1997/1998 outbreak, over 400 human deaths were attributed to RVF in Kenya alone. Underreporting of RVF remains a big challenge for both animal and human infection. Although RVF is seen as having killed 'millions of animals and thousands of people' (Grace and Bett, 2014), there is currently no reliable and comprehensive estimate of RVF burden worldwide.

The impact of RVF on Kenya's pastoralist community is multifaceted; livestock in Kenya provide nomadic pastoralists, who largely inhabit the arid north of the country, with income, social standing and nourishment.[5] These communities are often remote, lack basic veterinary and social services and are far removed from official Kenyan policy-making processes. With few veterinary services, pastoralists have been severely affected by RVF not only due to animal deaths and production losses (abortions, reduced milk production and emaciation), but also by reduced demand for meat as well as market and livestock movement bans. In the event of an RVF outbreak, severe movement restrictions are imposed by the government and veterinary authorities that inhibit access to local and cross-border markets. Income declines are abruptly and severe.

But RVF is a 'trans-boundary' disease, having found its way into Southern Africa and the Arabian Peninsula. In September 2000, an outbreak was confirmed in Saudi Arabia and Yemen. The assumption was that RVF had been imported from East African livestock. Animals, such as cattle, camels, sheep and goats, are often sold by East African pastoralists, and increasingly by powerful individuals and companies, into the export trade which passes through Djibouti, Ethiopia and Somalia into the Middle East. This trade, estimated at some US$1 billion annually, has significant impacts on the livelihood and the food security of pastoralists and the burgeoning livestock and dairy industry in Kenya (OIE, 2007). Furthermore, Arabian countries are also almost entirely dependent on imported livestock, and meat prices can be notoriously volatile when supplies fail to meet demand.[6] Out-break reports of trade-sensitive diseases, like RVF, have considerable adverse impacts on this export market through movement bans and quarantines, which have wider geopolitical implications.

Framing a policy response

For many years, RVF was not a high priority for policy-makers in East Africa; it occurred sporadically and mainly affected pastoralists in remote rural areas. Official responses were characterized by considerable delay in investigating, acknowledging and responding to these epidemics. In practice, RVF has only come to the notice of senior Kenyan government officials when human deaths have risen conspicuously, which is typically several weeks after viral emergence in livestock. Despite the emphasis on bioclimatic forecasting systems, during the 2006–2007 outbreak human cases were in effect 'sentinels', which brought the outbreak to official attention (MLD, 2010).

Rift Valley Fever in Kenya, Somalia and the United Republic of
Tanzania, as of 9 May 2007

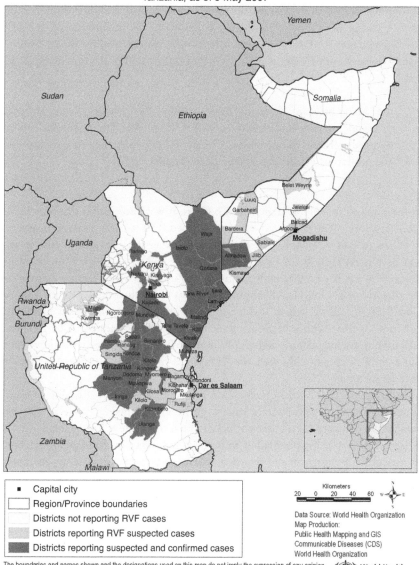

- ■ Capital city
- ☐ Region/Province boundaries
- ☐ Districts not reporting RVF cases
- ☐ Districts reporting RVF suspected cases
- ■ Districts reporting suspected and confirmed cases

Kilometers
20   0   20   40   60

Data Source: World Health Organization
Map Production:
Public Health Mapping and GIS
Communicable Diseases (CDS)
World Health Organization

World Health
Organization

FIGURE 6.2 RVF outbreak map, 2007 (source: WHO)

With restrictions on the livestock trade with the Middle East, RVF has risen up the policy agenda. Economically influential elites, increasingly involved in the Kenyan livestock export business, are clearly interesting in avoiding future export bans. A conspicuous sign of this higher salience was the publication of the *RVF Contingency Plan* (RVF CP) in April 2010 by the Ministry of Livestock Development's Department of Veterinary Services (MLD, 2010). The document explained that,

> the last outbreak in Kenya occurred in 2006/2007 and was associated with severe socio-economic consequences that went beyond the immediate effects on producers and public health. A total of 158 people died in the outbreak, and numerous market actors were severely affected.
>
> *(MLD, 2010, p4)*

Threatening to spill across regions and borders, it was also around this time that a growing chorus of scientific experts characterized RVF as an important disease for an enhanced policy response, one that joined together public health and the veterinary sectors (WHO, 2010; Dijkman *et al.*, 2010; Jost *et al.*, 2010; Munyua *et al.*, 2010). This has been followed by an increasing use by the Kenyan government of the rhetoric of a 'One Health' approach. Kenya established the Zoonotic Disease Unit (ZDU) in 2011, which involves the Ministry of Agriculture, Livestock and Fisheries together with staff from the Ministry of Public Health.[7] Charged with establishing and maintaining active collaboration between sectors in the prevention and control of zoonotic diseases, the ZDU has a mandate that covers 17 different diseases, including RVF.

Included on the World Organisation for Animal Health (OIE) list of transboundary diseases, RVF policies have been heavily framed by trade and export standards in comparison to other priorities (Aklilu and Catley, 2009; Dijkman *et al.*, 2010; FAO, 2011). To pastoralists, there remains a sense of marginalization, both to current RVF detection and response policies, and to the wider socio-economic contexts that shape their implementation and outcome. Official preparedness and responses to RVF outbreaks are situated within the contested policy landscapes of the livestock sector in Kenya. This has broadly been dichotomized between the interests of poor livestock keepers and cross-border trade markets and phytosanitary regulations, which are supported by urban elites and wealthier countries (Scoones and Wolmer, 2006). As we will see, RVF policy and practice in Kenya tends to predominately focus on the latter.

Prevailing discussions about the characteristics of a national RVF emergency fund focus largely on the ability of key government sectors to make funds available rapidly in response to early warning systems detecting specific outbreak indicators (ILRI and FAO, 2014). The range of potential interventions include: enhanced outbreak forecasting, surveillance and diagnostic activities; mosquito control programmes including distribution of mosquito nets and use of insecticides sprayed onto water bodies; risk communication and awareness creation; and rapid livestock vaccination (Amwanyi *et al.*, 2010; Jost *et al.*, 2010). But there remains considerable uncertainty about the effectiveness of these measures in remote pastoralist communities, due to various scientific, technical, policy and social factors. Furthermore, a focus on controlling 'outbreaks' tends to overlook and under-prioritize the broader systemic conditions that influence RVF risks in Kenya.

Forecasting outbreaks

Early warning systems have been enthusiastically promoted for zoonotic disease preparedness. The World Health Organization (WHO) considers them vital to guide RVF surveillance in livestock and wildlife, and to enable authorities to rapidly implement suitable measures to avert impending epidemics (WHO, 2007). To be effective, local climate monitoring and 'hotspot' disease surveillance need to be linked with a national and regional response system that can mobilize adequate resources and responses (Clements *et al.*, 2007; ILRI and FAO, 2009). However, global meteorologists as well as members of local communities who have access, in very different ways, to some relevant information and understandings cannot predict when and where RVF outbreaks will emerge with sufficient accuracy and precision. Eruptions of RVF infectivity are influenced by abrupt changes in the weather and by land-use changes that, for example, introduce cattle in areas not previously used for livestock farming and that change the distribution of ground and surface water (Bett *et al.*, 2014). Early warning systems that monitor climatic and meteorological indicators have been developed, but changes in weather from drought to flood cannot yet be forecast with sufficient precision or reliability.

Some progress has certainly been made. Outbreaks of RVF in East Africa have been linked to the heavy rainfall that occurs following the appearance of warm ocean currents off the South American coast, known as the El Niño phenomenon (Britch *et al.*, 2013). That insight has underpinned the development of several forecasting models using satellite images and weather and climate data. This includes a joint initiative of the NASA Goddard Space Flight Centre and the US Department of Defense's Global Emerging Infections Surveillance and Response System (DoD GEIS), which utilizes various remotely sensed data from global databases. Other attempts to establish early warning systems have relied more on climate-based disease prediction models, relating changes in variables like water and vegetation to vector population increases; for example, the Normalized Difference Vegetation Index (NDVI).[8] However, incomplete knowledge of the interactions between what Fastring and Griffith (2009) have called the 'epidemiological triangle', namely the agent, host and environment, have hampered the applicability of remote sensing and epidemiological models for predictive purposes. It has not yet been possible to estimate the predictive reliability or precision of the forecasting models, or the rates at which they generate false negatives or false positives (WHO, 2009).

Critics of the adequacy, reliability and utility of RVF early warning models have argued that, being developed mainly by international organizations, they are based on fragmented and de-contextualized knowledge that has little applicability at a local East African scale. Furthermore, there are gaps between models and available national and local response and preparedness capacity. Dijkman *et al.* have argued that:

> the US team behind the RVF early warning system are both physically and culturally distant from the actual situation on the ground ... the scientists clearly inhabit a very different world to that of the pastoralists of the Horn. The RVF early warning mechanisms are not embedded in local, national or regional knowledge networks, nor are they provided directly to the pastoralists. Rather, the RVF risk assessments are simply generated on a monthly basis and posted on the DoD GEIS website for anyone to use as they wish.
>
> *(Dijkman et al., 2010, p24)*

A 2009 report of a joint FAO–WHO expert consultation acknowledged that 'RVF warnings are given two months in advance, but six months are needed between the forecasting alert and outbreak onset in order to implement preventive measures, including social awareness and mass animal vaccination' (FAO and WHO, 2009, p5). Novel models used in 2006/2007 did provide some increased accuracy, but still delayed the warning until after the apparent onset of the outbreak (ILRI and FAO, 2014). By the time these warnings were generated and distributed, more than a month had passed since pastoralists had reported the first suspected cases in their livestock. Dijkman *et al.* (2010, p24) have argued that the funding currently being directed into RVF models, instead of helping to develop appropriate tools to inform public policy and outbreak responses, is rather a case of 'a technology seeking an application'. This has led some to question the focus on satellite image-based technologies and climate modelling in favour of a more locally grounded system. As Jost *et al.* have pointed out

> the observation by local communities of climatic, entomologic, and clinical events consistent with RVF within the known risk-prone areas were more timely and definitive risk indicators than the global early warning system in place at the time of the 2006–07 outbreak.
>
> *(Jost et al., 2010)*

Constructing RVF preparedness in Kenya?

Programmes of scientific work on RVF, funded by major donors, have made advances in virology, vaccines, epidemiology, socio-economic assessments and the designing of surveillance systems. But the ecology of the RVF virus and the most appropriate tools and strategies to control it remain uncertain. Breiman *et al.* (2010) outlined a few important scientific questions that remain unanswered; for example, the role of animals in the maintenance of the virus during non-epidemic periods, the significance of natural immunity in livestock populations and the role of mosquitoes in transmitting symptomatic and asymptomatic infections. There are also important social and technical dimensions at play that influence the operational effectiveness of existing diagnostics, vaccines and other strategies, which are dependent on different types of knowledge, interests and priorities.

While pioneering virologists have identified and isolated RVF pathogen(s), there is debate about whether RVF is one, or several, varieties of virus. This has left unresolved the question of whether RVF is caused by a single serotype of a virus, or whether the pathogen has differentiated. As the district veterinary officer (DVO) in Ijara District, Kenya, discussed:

> There is need to carry out more research on the possibility of RVF being caused by different strains of viruses, or the possibility of the virus mutating in other forms ... there is a lot we don't know.... This disease is a minefield of research waiting to be mined. Who knows the full extent of the reservoir of this disease and who knows why the disease survives in eggs or mosquito larvae for many years?
>
> *(Interview, Ijara District)*

There are gaps in testing, which is required to confirm or refute provisional diagnoses of RVF. The OIE *Manual of Diagnostic Tests and Vaccines for Terrestrial Animals*, as of April 2014, referred to seven distinct methods to test for RVF (OIE, 2013). Several have been developed into portable rapid diagnostic kits which, while reliable (with rates of false positives and false negatives estimated to be below 5 per cent) are not yet cheap (LaBeaud *et al.*, 2007). Field veterinarians are able to recognize the clinical signs of RVF, which they treat as suspect cases, but it is difficult to differentiate RVF from other viral fevers without laboratory testing and confirmation. The official declaration of an RVF outbreak in Kenya is made only after confirmation by the Central Veterinary Laboratory, the Kenya Medical Research Institute (KEMRI) or the Centers for Disease Control and Prevention (CDC). Laboratories in rural areas have limited capacities or equipment to test specimens and samples for RVF.

Vaccination is perhaps the most challenging issue for RVF control. To be effective, RVF animal vaccines need to be administered rapidly before outbreaks.[9] Once an outbreak has started, animal vaccination becomes increasingly problematic, and most campaigns have actually had very limited impact (Breiman *et al.*, 2010). Two main types of RVF vaccines have been developed, both intended for veterinary use, but come with different caveats. For the live attenuated vaccine, only one dose is required for immunity of up to a year, but the vaccine is known to have significantly increased spontaneous abortion rates in pregnant animals (Munyua *et al.*, 2010; Jost *et al.*, 2010). This has tended to increase the suspicion and distrust between veterinary authorities and pastoralists during mass RVF vaccination campaigns, and fostered avoidance and conflict. The inactivated viral vaccine does not have those adverse consequences, but multiple doses are required to provide sustained protection, which is difficult to achieve with nomadic herds in remote areas.

Perspectives on vaccination vary among Nairobi-based policy-makers, international agencies, district veterinary authorities and pastoralist communities. The

WHO explicitly recommends that, 'once an outbreak has occurred animal vaccination should NOT be implemented' (WHO 2010; emphasis in the original). This highlights the importance of early warning systems; for example, in the 2006/2007 outbreak in Kenya an FAO-EMPRES (Food and Agriculture Organization's Emergency Prevention System for Animal Health) early warning system issued an RVF alert in November.[10] But the earliest RVF livestock cases had occurred in mid-October, implying that vaccination campaigns should have been in place by the end of September (ILRI and FAO, 2014). A recent document prepared by the International Livestock Research Institute (ILRI) and FAO indicated that the multiple challenges involved in implementing such a campaign may be 'so great that they effectively preclude the use of vaccines to prevent/control RVF outbreaks in this region' (ILRI and FAO, 2014). There is also a fear of amplification. Animal health workers may inadvertently transmit the virus between animals through the use of multi-dose vials and the re-use of needles and syringes (WHO, 2007). Another problematic feature of the available vaccines are their shelf lives. The fact that RVF epidemics occur unpredictably in intervals of 10–20 years generates problems in maintaining sufficient up-to-date stocks, when and where they would be needed. The ILRI and FAO (2014) report recommended that a large regional organization should fund a strategic regional vaccine stock to address this problem. However, even if stored in stable refrigerated conditions, these vaccines have shelf lives of six months to four years. There are also very few refrigerators in the most vulnerable districts. RVF typically erupts at times of flooding precisely when road transport becomes exceptionally challenging, creating severe logistical challenges for rapid transport and distribution.

According to Ogodo (2007), there was a significant shortfall in funding for a programme of vaccinating livestock in vulnerable districts during the 2006/2007 epidemic. In 2007, Kenya had some 1.5 million doses of vaccine, but three million doses were required to cover all vulnerable livestock. The government's response was admittedly slow, in part because funds designated for use during emergencies had already been exhausted dealing with the preceding drought that killed huge numbers of livestock in pastoralist regions (Ogodo, 2007). However, policy documents emphasize that RVF vaccination should be a routine activity, conducted annually in high-risk areas and ahead of predicted outbreaks in medium-risk areas (DVS, 2014). But a shortage of vaccines result in hard decisions about which species of animals to target (either small or large ruminants) and in which region(s). The Department of Veterinary Services (DVS) is responsible for buying and distributing vaccines to DVOs. During vaccination drives, the resources available have never been adequate:

> When we suspect that there will be heavy rains and floods, we would vaccinate in the risky areas. We have 25,000 doses of RVF vaccine in store. These doses are not enough when we need to vaccinate all animals. In case of any signs of RVF risk factors, we only vaccinate sheep and goats.
>
> *(Interview, Ijara District)*

Many local veterinary officers also have difficulty identifying both the exact number of livestock in their area and local patterns of livestock movements; they have neither the staff nor the mobility that would be required. So they are unable to be sure which areas and animals to emphasize or avoid. Since the 2006/2007 outbreak, risk maps have been developed indicating high-risk RVF areas to prioritize during potential outbreaks, but it is unclear how reliable and useful these maps will be.

Vector control strategies face similar problems. Towards the end of the 2006/2007 outbreak, Kenyan government officials were spraying bodies of water suspected of harbouring infected insects with oil-based synthetic pyrethroids, to diminish RVF spread (Ogodo, 2007). Although such larvicides are thought by some entomologists to be an effective form of vector control, the tactic could only be applied once specific breeding sites had been identified and if the sites were limited in size and location. The relevance of larvicidal sprays to the lifestyle of nomadic pastoralists, however, is clearly problematic. They are often dispersed, remote and mobile. In the long run, insecticide spray programmes would also need to take into account the possibility of vector populations becoming resistant, if used over long periods of time.

The examples of vaccination and vector control show that effective RVF control requires raising awareness among livestock owners, especially in high-risk areas. Before the 2006/2007 RVF outbreak, there were low levels of awareness about the importance of vaccination among pastoralists. During a focus group discussion in Ijara District, we learned that pastoralists held diverse views about RVF vaccines. One farmer explained that he had assumed that vaccinating all his animals would result in the death of some of them. Consequently, he separated his healthier animals and drove them into the bush, but left those that appeared weak or sick to be vaccinated. Unfortunately, many of those that were not vaccinated, and were taken to the bush, died of RVF while most of his vaccinated animals survived, despite their prior weakness. Such experiences have challenged pastoralists' perceptions and some are consequently more receptive to vaccination in the event of an RVF alert than they were previously. Nonetheless, some remain resistant, especially during the dry season, because their livestock are then weak and so might be less able to withstand the effects of the vaccine. Resistance is also influenced by low levels of trust in formal professional veterinary services and by several socio-economic disincentives involved in reporting and seeking vaccines, such as strict RVF quarantine measures.

RVF vaccination campaigns have run into serious institutional, infrastructural and logistical problems because of the limited veterinary and medical capacities of remote districts in Kenya. Very few veterinarians are in established government posts and there are major capacity gaps at district hospitals. For example, during the 2006/2007 outbreak in Ijara District, nurses had to be brought in from outside the district to reinforce staffing at the district hospital. The Ijara DVO also reported that his office had just one vehicle, which was not road-worthy because of a lack of maintenance and spare parts. He explained that they sometimes had to use donkey carts to transport equipment to suspected areas to contain the RVF outbreak. To address this, community animal health workers (or CAHWs) were recruited to assist with the vaccination programme, but once the outbreak subsided they were increasingly marginalized and ignored. With an ambiguous legal status, prevailing tensions between CAHWs and professional vets (who are seen as scarce and prohibitively expensive by pastoralists) reduce opportunities to strengthen service delivery in RVF-endemic regions, where untrained or nominally trained CAHWs are nonetheless the main animal health providers (K'Oloo *et al.*, 2015).

Policy from above: the Kenyan *Contingency Plan*

To understand RVF policy-making in Kenya, it is imperative to explore the most comprehensive statement of the Kenyan government's RVF policy. The RVF CP emerged in April 2010 from the DVS, located in the Ministry of Livestock Development (MLD) (MLD, 2010). Shortly after publication, it was officially adopted by the government, and its creation can be understood in large part as a reaction to the 2006/2007 outbreak.

The RVF CP's characteristics drew on the 2002 FAO document *Preparation of Rift Valley Fever Contingency Plans* (FAO, 2002). In March 2008, another influential contribution emerged jointly from the DVS and ILRI, reporting the findings of a study funded by the US Agency for International Development (USAID) that sought to identify lessons from the 2006/2007 outbreak (ILRI and DVS, 2008). One month after ILRI's *Learning the Lessons of Rift Valley Fever*, the RVF CP was published. The RVF CP was prepared by the DVS, but with support from the FAO and USAID and by specialists working at the Nairobi-based offices of the ILRI (MLD, 2010). The RVF CP envisaged a sequence of four decision points or stages for action, mainly – but not entirely – by central government organizations:

> In this contingency plan key decision points have been identified, subdivided into *normal, prediction* (investigation and alert), *outbreak* (operational) and *step-down* phases. Key activities during the normal phase include capacity building, disease surveillance, developing early warning systems (sentinel herds and climatic monitoring) and building livestock immunity through mass annual vaccinations in high risk areas. Early warning systems that will be set in the normal phase will enable accurate prediction of a potential disease outbreak at which point implementation measures will be taken. In addition, mosquito surveillance and control will be critical, especially when heavy and prolonged rains result in flooding. Once the outbreak occurs in animals, measures will be geared towards preventing human infections through animal movement restrictions, closure of livestock markets and slaughter bans.
>
> *(MLD, 2010, Executive Summary, p4 (emphases added))*

While the RVF CP offered a roadmap to an effective RVF response, it is framed from a conspicuously technocratic perspective, which was understandable given that it had been based on an FAO template. The perspectives of pastoralists themselves and public health authorities were largely marginal, making it premature to suggest that RVF policy-making in Kenya has become sufficiently integrated that it should be labelled as exemplifying a 'One Health' approach. The RVF CP was prepared by the DVS, with puzzlingly little contribution from the Ministry of Health (although since the writing of the RVF CP, the ZDU has been established and the Ministry of Health has prepared a document entitled *Guidelines for Rift Valley Fever Preparedness and Response*). The RVF CP did, towards the end, refer to 'rural communities' but only in terms of 'Community based animal disease surveillance and response groups', which were to operate under the leadership of 'Chiefs and their assistants, Community leaders and departmental animal health staff' (MLD, 2010, p40). Pastoralists were largely cast in the passive role of information providers, able to identify clinical signs and inform early warning systems. The document continued:

> To mitigate potential socio-economic impacts of a future outbreak, it is important that measures for preparedness during the normal phase are taken seriously, as little can be done once an outbreak occurs. Enhancing the response capacity of veterinary services as spelt out in the resource plans in this contingency plan will be critical. Financing of RVF prevention and control requires an increased budgetary allocation during normal times while some emergency funds will be set aside through the Veterinary Services Development Fund. This will assist implementation of heightened measures at prediction phase while awaiting access for contingency funds from treasury once the chance of an outbreak is very likely. In addition to finances this contingency plan highlights the gaps in technical personnel capacity which will be addressed during the normal phase.
>
> *(MLD, 2010, p4)*

As the policy makes clear, significant financial and human resource investments are needed over the long term if these rapid response activities are to occur (MLD, 2010). But resources have yet to be allocated, let alone invested, in the types of systems described and advocated for. A large disparity in human and financial resources are at the core of RVF preparedness and response. The veterinary sector, for example, remains significantly understaffed in comparison to the public health sector in Kenya (ILRI and DVS, 2008, p5). There is also scant evidence of improved communication between professional groups with distinct types of expertise, or between the central government, local officials and representatives of pastoralist communities. During the 2006/2007 RVF outbreak, contingency teams were formed, called 'Disaster Rapid Response Teams', that drew on local representatives from the Ministry of Health, the Ministry of Public Health (MoPH), the District Veterinary Office and a representative of the district commissioner. Some resources were mobilized and the teams trained. But in the absence of a serious and widespread outbreak of RVF, few preparations take place, and these emergency groups dissolve. While the Ministry of Livestock has established a new Veterinary Services Development Fund (VSDF), which obtains some of its revenue from meat inspection services, the size of that fund is dwarfed by the magnitude of the task of preparing for RVF and other threatening zoonoses.

Despite the technical detail of the RVF CP, RVF uneasily occupies a policy space characterized by nominal attention from some but a low priority for many. Its long periods of inactivity place it 'off the radar' for many years, and even in the context of an outbreak it can be difficult to mobilize the required resources. This lack of investment is likely caused by competing demands on limited resources and the anticipated up-front costs of addressing systemic institutional shortcomings in the veterinary sector in Kenya (McSherry *et al.*, 2007). Moreover, given that significant resources were eventually provided by international donors during the 2006/2007 outbreak, some interview informants wondered whether government neglect was effectively related to aid-dependency, and a perception that investments could diminish the impact of subsequent requests for urgent aid during a future outbreak. Ministers need to adjudicate between many competing claims on public resources. They not only have to, in effect, rank RVF in relation to other zoonotic infections, but also to rank zoonotic infections against other challenges faced by pastoralists, such as food insecurity, drought and conflicts, and the needs of pastoralists in relation to other groups and stakeholders who stake claims to official policy support and resource allocations.

But a prevailing tendency for top-down knowledge processes is also responsible for perpetuating large disparities between policy ideals and conditions on the ground. For example, we found huge gaps in knowledge about the RVF CP during our research. Veterinary staff in Ijara and Tana River Districts had little, or no, familiarity with the policy, suggesting that it has not been widely disseminated beyond Nairobi-based experts, national policy-makers and international agencies. The lack of an inclusive policy process will surely create major challenges during future outbreaks. Implementing the RVF CP, which is a complex and multidimensional policy plan operating on different scales, surely needs a huge amount of support from local technical and political authorities, both to implement it and to advocate for resources and investments over the long-term. But without knowledge of the plan, these activities will not take place.

Interestingly, the new 2010 Constitution may have an influence on future RVF resource allocation, since it promotes greater devolution of power from central government to the newly established counties (although this is officially expected to take until 2017 to be fully implemented).[11] In 2008, ILRI argued that devolving powers to deal with RVF to local communities would be beneficial. They stated that:

> Decision making power should be entrusted at the appropriate level so that early prevention and control actions are possible. In the case of RVF in Kenya, the authority of local level decision makers in the districts to declare and take actions to control a potential RVF outbreak based on local early warning indicators ... needs to be recognized.
>
> *(ILRI and DVS, 2008, pp6–7)*

Under the new dispensation, 47 newly designated counties will replace the provinces (which are being abolished) and the districts. But these new geo-political divisions, while helping to decentralize government resources, may also create a new set of challenges for RVF preparedness and response. The new location and control of borders between local jurisdictions will be important, since they are fundamental to implementing livestock movement restrictions. With the counties in place, it is not yet clear how authority and responsibility will be divided between the county government and local veterinary departments during an epizootic event. Different interests and norms are at play in the control of trade-sensitive transboundary diseases like RVF (Scoones and Wolmer, 2006). This could generate significant divergences of opinion, and conflict, between local vets, national technical staff and political authorities on 'correct' control measures during an outbreak. In 2014, the Directorate of Veterinary Services of the Ministry of Agriculture, Livestock and Fisheries prepared a set of *Standard Operating Procedures*, which included guidelines for livestock vaccination, quarantine and surveillance for RVF. A conspicuous feature of those documents is that they attribute numerous responsibilities for setting and enforcing control measures to county-level authorities, but without any indication that resources would be made available to meet these responsibilities. As discussed above with the RVF CP, it is highly unlikely that these directives, created in Nairobi, will be adequately and rapidly funded and implemented by local-level government during an unfolding RVF epidemic.

The view from below: pastoralist perspectives

A number of authors have commented on the importance of 'empowering livestock owners' in RVF surveillance and control (Butcher *et al.*, 2012). While there is no evidence that pastoralists have any awareness of the RVF CP, the policy contains a number of provisions on capacity-building and resource provision that would be very much welcomed by pastoralists. On the other hand, even if the policy were adequately resourced and put into practice, there are important alternative pathways to address RVF risk that need to be acknowledged. These have, for the most part, been relatively marginal in the policy debate.

During and after the 2006/2007 outbreak, many local NGOs, government bodies and international organizations invested in providing RVF training and awareness raising to veterinary and public health staff and to pastoralists in some of the worst affected areas. It is difficult to estimate the impact of those efforts, but our research in 2013 in Ijara and Tana River Districts in north-eastern and coastal regions of Kenya showed that many pastoralists were relatively well-informed about RVF. Most considered diseases of livestock, and the consequent risks to health and livelihoods, to be major obstacles to sustainable livelihoods, but ranked brucellosis and foot-and-mouth disease as a more significant zoonotic infection than RVF. Although there are a number of diseases that may be clinically confused with RVF, pastoralists knew that the most distinctive symptoms of RVF in livestock is nose bleeding and abortions in pregnant females, while other symptoms are characteristic

FIGURE 6.3 A young pastoralist in Ijara district herding RVF susceptible shoats (credit: Oscar Okumu).

of many different fevers. This fits with other studies on pastoralist perceptions of RVF (ILRI and DVS, 2008; Jost *et al.*, 2010). In particular, we found that cattle keepers knew enough about RVF and animal health in general to contribute effectively, and possibly improve upon, disease surveillance. In 2008, ILRI reported that: 'Herders recognise that outbreaks [of RVF] are associated with large black and white mosquitoes … as opposed to, for example, the smaller mosquitoes associated with malaria' (ILRI and DVS, 2008). In our study, pastoralists explained that they recognized that 'dotted' mosquitoes are most likely to carry RVF. They were also aware that moving animals could spread the infection.

Through local-level research, we identified a number of mitigation strategies and 'grassroots innovations' that local populations used that could reduce exposure to, and spread of, RVF during an outbreak. Cultural and religious taboos against eating meat from sick animals, to which Muslims subscribe, are perceived as a measure that can protect against zoonotic diseases such as RVF. A pastoralist in Ijara District explained: 'We Muslims don't butcher dead animals. When we feel like eating an animal, we slaughter and butcher a healthy one at home.' While poverty often drives pastoralists to consume sick animals before they die, during outbreaks these norms change, and many bury animals suspected of having RVF in a safe location away from water sources in order to contain the disease. Pastoralists also have traditional methods for reducing exposure to biting insects, such as enclosing livestock overnight (if only with rudimentary barriers) and setting fires downwind to use the smoke, especially with material from acacia trees, to repel insects. When RVF erupted, they tried using traditional herbal ointments on fevered animals, but subsequently reported that they found those remedies to be ineffective. But not all livestock keepers have the same type of local knowledge. For example, we found that recently settled communities of sedentary agro-pastoralists located in the Tana River District, coming from arable farming communities, have less experience of livestock and knowledge of animal health than traditional mobile pastoralists in Ijara District.

Innovations were also developed in collaboration between pastoralists and local veterinarians to diminish RVF risk. We found that in several small settlements, where pastoralists bring their livestock for sale and slaughter, changes had been introduced in the design, layout and practices of slaughter facilities. Traditionally in Ijara District, individual pastoralist households would slaughter and butcher their own animals. During the most recent outbreak of RVF, pastoralists realized that if they relocated their slaughtering to shared facilities that were better designed and equipped, it would reduce exposure risks. Several such facilities were built after the 2007 outbreak in Ijara District in collaboration with local authorities; protective gloves and new staff trainings were then provided. This changed the ways in which pastoralists handled their animals before slaughter, as well as ways of handling carcasses, meat and waste, thus avoiding potential high-risk exposures. While several individuals took initiatives to invest in those new facilities, they did so on concessionary terms. In some localities, the communities refunded the butchers' investments and adopted forms of collective ownership of the facility, where the butchers remained as custodians and service providers. In others, they paid for the service at, for example, a rate of 20 KSh per shoat, and 100 KSh for cattle and camels. More recently, however, the use of protective gloves has apparently diminished, and it is unclear exactly how often infection prevention and control procedures are followed.

Other avenues for RVF transmission, however, have been harder for pastoralists and local authorities to address. Our research revealed a number of major systemic livelihood vulnerabilities related to climate change that would likely compound efforts to control an RVF outbreak: water and grassing land shortages as well as physical insecurity from aggressive and heavily armed groups, including Al Shabab. There are also major challenges in managing water sources around human–livestock–wildlife interfaces. In areas with sufficient pasture and water, such as Boni Forest close to the border with Somalia, there are frequent interactions between people, livestock and wildlife. This is problematic once an RVF outbreak begins. As a National Park warden explained: 'fewer water pans lead to congregation of livestock, wildlife and humans at water points. As a result of this interaction, it was possible for RVF to spread with ease.' To address this, donor and aid organizations, such as World Vision, have constructed separate water pans and boreholes for humans and livestock to diminish the risks of cross-infection. But these have not addressed the significant declining number of water sources and water availability in these remote areas. Environmental change and increased numbers of livestock are having significant adverse effects on pastoralist groups in Kenya, driving more frequent and closer interactions between wildlife and livestock during dry periods, especially in fall-back grazing areas.

The lack of government services in these areas is similarly a major challenge, and fosters a certain degree of distrust between pastoralists and the central government (Waller and Homewood, 1997). Professional veterinarians in Kenya often maintain that farmers should benefit from the services of trained professionals rather than poorly trained or equipped CAHWs (K'Oloo *et al.*, 2015). Some veterinarians consider CAHWs as competitors who undercut their prices while providing inferior services. On the other hand, pastoralists, especially nomadic ones, see vets as scarce and prohibitively expensive and tend to prefer CAHWs. ILRI's 2008 report acknowledged that livestock owners would only participate in RVF surveillance if they could benefit directly from it, and that this could only be achieved through improved delivery of veterinary services, including the strengthening of CAHWs in rural areas (ILRI and DVS, 2008, p29). But the RVF CP fails to refer to CAHWs. From the pastoralists' perspective, that would be a puzzling omission. Building CAHWs capacity would be an important pathway to generating trust and involvement of local communities, and could promote increased information dissemination to livestock keepers and generate more reliable surveillance data, among other things.

The RVF CP overlooks the major issue of community distrust of policy-makers and government officials. But pastoralists have incentives to delay (or even refuse) RVF control measures and to ignore or discount some of the official advice and instructions. Historically, pastoralists in many parts of Africa have been less than trusting of government officials due to cultural stigma, tax and forced relocation and destocking (Waller and Homewood, 1997). If reporting suspected cases of RVF entails the imposition of local movement controls, compulsory vaccinations and bans on the export of livestock from East Africa to lucrative markets in the Middle East, it is understandable that pastoralists might hesitate before reporting their earliest suspicions, and why they might be reluctant to comply fully with subsequent movement restrictions. The prevailing incentive for pastoralists, according to some, is to evade detection and rapidly sell livestock before an outbreak is officially declared, when prices collapse and markets close. If pastoralists were provided with some form of government-supported livestock insurance scheme or compensation for loss of diseased livestock and/or livelihoods (including assistance with re-stocking) then higher levels of cooperation would be more likely. Implicit in the RVF CP is that there is little prospect of pastoralists being provided with much in exchange for the valuable surveillance data they are supposed to deliver. Even when samples have been taken from fallen stock, surviving herds or human tissue, the results obtained in laboratory tests are never reported back to communities. This is a common problem with much scientific research in rural Africa, and perpetuates a sense of exploitation and mistrust. If the results of RVF tests are shared with local communities, it would likely enhance their ability to distinguish cases of

RVF from other viral fevers, and consequently improve surveillance and diagnoses. It would also help to generate stronger social bonds between the authorities and pastoralists that could form the basis of a more effective RVF epidemic response in the future.

Conclusions

Making appropriate and effective preparations for epidemics of zoonotic disease, such as RVF, is challenging, in part because of uncertainties of when and how the disease is going to emerge, but also because of ecological and socio-economic complexities and resource constraints. Developing a plan for effectively responding to RVF requires understanding more than virology, epidemiology and immunology; it also requires an appreciation of the socio-political challenges, incentives and opportunities with which pastoralists, as well as veterinary and public health staff, are confronted as they attempt to design effective systems of response and enrol the support of politicians and funders to support them.

The Kenyan government's 2010 *Contingency Plan for RVF* contained many promising provisions, but in several important respects it remains incomplete.[12] Much of that incompleteness arose as a consequence of failing to adequately engage with the perspectives of pastoralists and district officials, as well as the broader institutional and resource constraints of the veterinary and public health sectors. Policy development has largely been a top-down process. This has generated a significant gap between policy rhetoric, what is plausible on the ground and marginalized pathways of response, such as the incorporation of pastoralist and district-level knowledge, needs, and innovation.

A recurrent theme has been the difficulty of enrolling support from the government of Kenya to allocate the necessary resources for RVF preparedness. In this context, it is clear that RVF prevention and control measures will be selected and implemented in a context of resource constraints and competing demands. Persuasive arguments about the cost-effectiveness of investing in systemically strengthening disease surveillance, enhanced diagnostic capabilities and outbreak controls formed the backbone of the 2010 RVF CP, but so far they have had limited effect. Low levels of investment impose restrictions on the extent and viability of vaccination initiatives, not only due to the technical characteristics and costs of vaccines, but also because the logistical and infrastructural requirements needed to deliver them are simply not in place.

Building an adequate and sustainable human and animal health infrastructure in Kenya that could effectively reduce the risk, exposure and spread of RVF will not be a simple task. This would need to include vital components such as more effective management as well as risk analysis, disease surveillance and enhanced diagnostic capacities, as well as a set of appropriate and acceptable measures that could be implemented and enforced to control outbreaks. Such a system would benefit from research and development, all of which requires investing financial resources to enhance levels of human capital in scientific, technical, local government and pastoralist communities. In a context of resource constraints, building capacity for RVF preparedness would also benefit from considering how to integrate key aspects of the plan with other animal, human and ecological health initiatives and systems, instead of only focusing on one virus. In this sense, there is a need to consider how to build more inclusive and resilient institutional networks for RVF disease preparedness in Kenya that stretches across different scales.

As this chapter has shown, there also remain several uncertainties and gaps in knowledge about RVF outbreaks and their persistence that need to be addressed. Control tools are also inadequate, and could certainly be improved. Given the unpredictability of virus dispersion and uncertainties about RVF epidemiology, there is a need to fill these scientific gaps by developing targeted agendas for RVF research. Aid agencies and donors have a role to play in supporting these efforts. One key area is in vaccine development. Thermo-stable vaccines that could be stored, transported and administered at ambient temperatures would be remarkably helpful. If vaccines could be developed that provided sustained protection, without regular re-inoculation, and which did not threaten adverse reactions such as spontaneous miscarriages, they would be enthusiastically welcomed by pastoralists and settled livestock farmers alike. But these improvements might not be possible, or easily forthcoming.

There is a need to consider the trade-offs involved in an over-emphasis on vaccine development with other forms of technological, research and institutional capacity investments. For example, much current RVF risk could be diminished if a better supply of current vaccines were available in key locations to respond to early surveillance outbreak indicators. Targeted vaccination of the most vulnerable livestock in high-risk areas is currently recommended but rarely implemented on a consistent basis. One potential funding innovation would be to involve the more affluent countries in the Arabian Peninsula, which normally rely on importing livestock from East Africa, in supporting a sustained programme of preventative vaccination in the Horn of Africa. This could help Arab countries secure a more stable meat supply, enhancing domestic price stability.

But while national, regional and local capacities need to be enhanced and coordinated, the costs of doing so remain difficult to estimate, as do the potential costs of failing to implement an effective plan. A resilient preparedness plan, first and foremost, requires enhancing information flows between national and local officials, in both veterinary and public health areas, and between officials and local communities. Roles and responsibilities need to be defined. To maximize the likely success of RVF control, effective coordination will be critical, alongside adequate infrastructures, trained local personnel, effective regulatory enforcement and community involvement. As this chapter has argued, the incentives for pastoralists to report an RVF outbreak, whether economic, cultural or political, affect whether and when an outbreak is officially recognized and addressed.

If policy-makers and public officials were to engage more effectively with the perspectives of pastoralists, they would recognize that pastoralists have incentives and some means to innovate. Providing them with resources and incentives to do so, and showing willingness to adapt plans to take account of such innovations, would be beneficial to all groups. Establishing and supporting community-based early warning systems, and providing official support to CAHWs and other local stakeholders, would be an important step forward. Such changes could enable DVOs to capture and share larger and more reliable sets of data, and improve RVF surveillance. In this regard, it would seem that RVF preparedness cannot be separated from the need to strengthen veterinary service provision in rural Kenya. Enhancing the resources for, and responsibilities of, CAHWs, perhaps under the supervision of professional veterinarians, would enable Kenyans to improve their ability to withstand multiple challenges posed by zoonotic and animal infections alike. CAHWs might themselves also contribute by facilitating learning and innovation on the part of their pastoralist communities. As scientists and public officials continue to anticipate the next RVF epidemic, enabling such institutional changes is clearly needed to move the One Health concept forward in Kenya.

Notes

1 This chapter is based on data collected in 2012–2013. A comprehensive analysis of key policy documents and the scholarly literature was done first. Subsequently, we conducted 21 key informant interviews with key Nairobi-based veterinary, public health, research and policy actors. Interview and focus group data with pastoralists and district officials were then collected in 2013 – some five years after the last officially reported outbreak of RVF in Kenya. These focused on outbreak response, the capacity of the veterinary sector and key aspects of the livestock system. This included exploring how differences among pastoralists may influence RVF spread and response, for example issues of gender, socio-economic status, herd or flock size, and nomadic and sedentary livelihoods. This research was done in Ijara and Tana River Districts in the north-eastern and coastal regions of Kenya, respectively. We first conducted a scoping study in Ijara, where we mapped key policy actors and conducted 16 key informant interviews and four FGDs with pastoralists. After this initial period, we conducted a further 20 key informant interviews, five FGDs and a survey with 102 households in Ijara District. We also conducted ten key informant interviews, three FGDs and 100 surveys with households in Tana River. For the key informant interviews, we targeted a range of informants: officials from the Ministry of Livestock, Ministry of Agriculture, Ministry of Health, Hospitals, NGOs, public administration, livestock traders and butchers, local health facilities, pastoralists and farmers. For the household survey and FGDs, we mainly targeted pastoralists and farmers, including herd owners, herders and livestock product traders.
2 To enhance our understanding of different local perspectives, we purposively selected two districts with contracting characteristics. Ijara was chosen for a number of reasons: history of RVF, large livestock population, domestic animal–wildlife and human interaction, proximity to Boni forest, high-levels of insect vectors, presence of drought-prone hotspots, numerous natural water bodies and constructed water pans and the presence of Somali pastoralists and Pokomo farmers. Tana River District was selected because of: the presence of numerous water bodies (such as irrigation schemes and water pans), animal grazing routes that enable animal from different areas to interact, increasing population of livestock and livestock markets in the area and the presence of Pokomo, Orma and Wardey agropastoralists.
3 www.who.int/mediacentre/factsheets/fs207/en, accessed 11 July 2015.
4 www.who.int/mediacentre/factsheets/fs207/en, accessed 11 July 2015.
5 Pastoralism in Kenya is a major economic production system that contributes about 12 per cent of GDP (GoK, 2010). It is oriented around the arid and semi-arid lands that

make up 80 per cent of the country's landmass. These support roughly one-third of the human population, and 70 per cent of the nation's livestock. Major pastoralist groups include the Pokot and Turkana.

6 See: http://halalfocus.net/uae-over-dependence-on-imported-food-is-dangerous, accessed 11 July 2015.

7 See http://zdukenya.org/about-zdu, accessed 11 July 2015.

8 See: http://earthobservatory.nasa.gov/Features/MeasuringVegetation/measuring_vegetation_2.php, accessed 11 July 2015.

9 To date, there are no licensed commercially available vaccines to protect people against RVF.

10 FAO EMPRES stands for 'Emergency Prevention System for Animal Health', and is a flagship global surveillance network for transboundary animal diseases coordinated by the FAO: www.fao.org/ag/againfo/programmes/en/empres/home.asp, accessed 11 July 2015.

11 www.kenyaembassy.com/pdfs/The%20Constitution%20of%20Kenya.pdf, accessed 11 July 2015.

12 There is also insufficient clarity as to the precise conditions under which the Kenyan government would declare an official outbreak of RVF. How many cases of RVF, judged by reference to which kinds of epidemiological and microbiological data, would be deemed necessary and/or sufficient for an outbreak to be declared have yet to be officially specified in published documents.

7

BEYOND BIOSECURITY

The politics of Lassa fever in Sierra Leone

Annie Wilkinson

Introduction

In 2014, the Ebola outbreak in West Africa once again brought zoonotic diseases to the forefront of the international community's attention. The surprise and horror that the Ebola epidemic provoked, including in Sierra Leone, was a reminder of the value of One Health, but also of considerable unmet challenges in realizing it. This chapter examines science-policy processes for Lassa fever, a rodent-borne viral haemorrhagic fever (VHF) in West Africa, and explores some unique practicalities and politics of zoonotic disease control. In certain zones of Sierra Leone, a country that has consistently reported some of the highest incidence rates in the region, Lassa fever was considered one of the country's most feared infections: it had, as one survivor put it a 'big name'.[1] Now described by local outreach workers as Ebola's 'little brother',[2] it holds clues to the way events unfolded in 2014; more than that, though, the story of Lassa presents both questions and opportunities for applying One Health in extremely low-resource contexts.

Since the discovery of Lassa fever in 1969, only Sierra Leone, Liberia, Guinea and Nigeria have recorded regular cases.[3] Lassa was long thought to be confined, mysteriously, to these few hotspots in West Africa and consequently it was not high on international policy agendas. Post 9/11, and the US anthrax attacks, however, Lassa virus was assessed for its use as a bioterrorist agent (Borio *et al.*, 2002) and is now categorized as a 'Category A' agent by the US Centers for Disease Control and Prevention (CDC).[4] Category A is the highest risk level of 'select agents' with potential bioterrorism use on account of their ability to spread easily and cause major public health impacts. Lassa is considered a threat as fatality rates in symptomatic cases are high, diagnosis is difficult, treatments are not widely available and vaccines do not exist. Most of all, although airborne transmission is not considered to be a routine mode of transmission, it could not be ruled out (Borio *et al.*, 2002).

Unusual among the list of today's bioweapons, Lassa also causes considerable endemic human disease in West Africa.[5] Recently, Lassa fever's home territory appears to be growing, with cases identified in Ghana, Benin and previously non-endemic areas of Sierra Leone and Nigeria, revealing new dimensions to the region's viral make-up (Gire *et al.*, 2012; Sogoba *et al.*, 2012; WHO, 2015b). As a rodent-borne virus, whose host is the *Mastomys natalensis*, Lassa fever is of particular interest from a One Health perspective since it displays complex, and yet still unknown, social and ecological dynamics that drive periodic epidemics and maintain steady states of endemicity.

The heightened concern around Lassa is an illustration of how the biosecurity agenda reframes – 'securitizes' – health problems as existential threats (Elbe, 2010b). In securitization debates, biosecurity priorities are often portrayed as being in opposition to those of public health (Elbe, 2010b; Lakoff and Collier, 2008). Two basic points are made about framing health problems as security issues: on one hand, it successfully raises awareness and mobilizes resources, but on the other these resources can be limited, privileging defence priorities instead of civilian ones. The case of Lassa fever provides an opportunity to broaden these debates, as the disease occupies a space at the intersection between biosecurity agendas, neglected diseases, standard public health and emerging One Health perspectives. In light of commentary on the failure of preparedness and global health governance to prevent the Ebola crisis, this is timely.

Public health efforts and investments in biosecurity have improved the management of Lassa fever but not in ways that have translated into sustained and wide-ranging health systems strengthening, or in improved understandings of the interactions between human and animal health needed for effective disease management. Indeed, we see how the uncertainty of emerging diseases makes policy action difficult and, in this case, appears to have led to a 'retreat into the laboratory', with basic-science research the only interest able to raise substantial investment. Prevention, based on understandings of environment–human–rodent interactions has been relatively neglected and is actually very poorly understood. One Health can provide a more holistic approach but its effectiveness, for Lassa at least, will depend on finding ways to address the politics that accompany the ambiguity and complexity of the disease.

Central to this analysis is the sense that diseases are complex systems, involving interlocking social, technical, cultural, political, economic, ecological and biological dynamics, which are often not easily discernible (Leach *et al.*, 2010a). Different values, assumptions and knowledge-making processes cause problems to be framed in distinct ways (Jasanoff, 2005). Policy narratives, which combine different framings, are mobilized by actor networks to promote specific courses of action (Roe, 1994; Keeley and Scoones, 2003). As displayed in the populist discourse on emerging diseases (Wald, 2008), the preponderant concerns of biosecurity hinge on an 'outbreak narrative', where the sudden emergence of a new disease (often in remote African landscapes) triggers a global pandemic, seeping across international borders and causing mass panic and economic disintegration. Underpinning this narrative is the critical role of epidemiological science and military-style responses in tracking and containing the disease. The dominance (and shortcomings) of this discourse in policy approaches devised by international agencies and Northern governments for epidemic disease has been pointed out elsewhere (Leach *et al.*, 2010b). This critique has highlighted the need to contrast the 'view from above' with alternative, local-level perspectives. Collier and Ong's (2005) concept of 'global assemblages' is relevant here. 'Global assemblages' describe the configurations of people, artefacts, brokers, economies, normative frameworks, styles of reasoning and more, through which global forms (such as biosecurity, see also Lakoff and Collier, 2008) are brought to life in particular settings. In this way, the concept emphasizes how distant policy priorities and frameworks are manipulated and (re)constructed in line with local contexts.

To understand how local and global concerns interact, this chapter not only looks at the role of different narratives in defining the research and control landscape for Lassa fever, but also at the socio-technical processes and contexts through which they emerge. Drawing on ethnographic research in Kenema, Sierra Leone, it explores these critical but poorly understood dimensions of science-policy processes.[6] The 'Lassa ward' at Kenema Government Hospital (KGH) is the world's longest-running dedicated Lassa isolation facility; in 2005 work began to supplement the dilapidated 'Lassa ward' at KGH with the 'Lassa lab' (Khan *et al.*, 2008). The combined facilities serve as a field site for international research collaborations on Lassa and other viral haemorrhagic fevers, and so offer a unique window to contribute to the debates.

From neglected disease to priority pathogen

Lassa fever was first identified in the town of Lassa, Nigeria, in 1969 after missionary nurses fell sick from a mysterious new illness. As scientists began to investigate, there were two laboratory-based infections in the USA: a laboratory technician at the Yale Arbovirus Research Unit died and a senior researcher contracted Lassa fever but survived. In light of these events, ad hoc protective procedures were applied (Fuller, 1974).[7] Informal biosafety arrangements have since matured into formal standards with pathogens classified according to their perceived risk. Lassa virus has been classified as a biosafety level 4 (BSL-4) pathogen, and requires the highest possible containment facilities. In 2007, there were only 20 BSL-4 laboratories in the world and when research on Lassa began there were even fewer (Gronvall *et al.*, 2007). None of these were in West Africa.

From these early discovery days, two worlds of Lassa fever research begin to take shape. In Europe and the USA, biosecurity norms and practices predominate as stable electricity supplies made establishing highly controlled environments feasible and the necessary resources – expertise and finance – were easier to come by. In the Mano River, these standards were not achievable. Even when investments (including solar power) were made to build the 'Lassa lab' in Kenema, it only reached BSL-3 standards at best (Khan *et al.*, 2008). Meanwhile, education in laboratory sciences in Sierra Leone remains constrained so the production of scientific know-ledge for Lassa fever is geographically anchored in the Global North, to where samples need to be shipped from 'field stations' like the Lassa lab. This has implica-tions for science-policy processes as field contexts, and the complexities of the disease–environment interactions, fade from view.

Central to this disease–environment nexus is the reservoir of the virus: the rodent host, *Mastomys natalensis* (Figure 7.1), which was identified in 1972 after outbreaks in the towns of Tongo and Panguma in Eastern Sierra Leone (Monath *et al.*, 1974). These settlements and the area surrounding them have been known as the 'Lassa belt' ever since, with some of the highest incidence rates in West Africa. After the 1972 outbreaks in Sierra Leone, the CDC set up field research stations in Segbwema, Kenema and Panguma. The main treatment programme was based in Segbwema at the Nixon Memorial Mission Hospital, and run by Dr Aniru Conteh. But as civil war erupted in 1991, spilling over from the Liberian border not far from Segbwema, Lassa activities moved to KGH, where they remain despite KGH being outside of the hyper-endemic Lassa belt.[8] Civil instability, which would continue for over a decade, caused the CDC to close their programmes and pull out of Sierra Leone entirely in 1993. They moved some of their work to Guinea but the inci-dence of Lassa was lower there and the organization's interests were soon diverted. By 2003 the Guinea programme was also closed. After the departure of the CDC

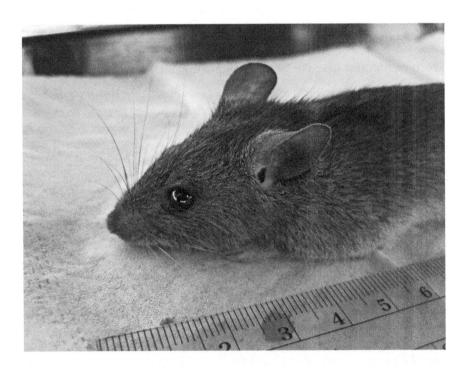

FIGURE 7.1 *Mastomys natalensis*, the reservoir of Lassa virus (credit: Lina Moses)

from Sierra Leone, the Lassa ward was left largely without support. It was kept going on a shoestring by Dr Conteh. In 1996, in the wake of a steep rise in cases, and with the country still blighted by war, the British medical relief organization, Merlin, took the reins in Kenema by providing health promotion and treatment activities, but not laboratory support (Khan *et al.*, 2008).

On one level, the trajectory of Lassa fever's emergence – the first cases in Nigeria, the US infections and subsequent outbreaks in the Mano River region – provided the key events for a typical 'outbreak narrative' (Wald, 2008). On the international stage, Lassa was considered an emerging infection that followed this logic of outbreak and containment, with CDC field stations doing pivotal work to understand and control the disease. Books such as *Fever! The Hunt for a New Killer Virus* (Fuller, 1974) and *Level 4: Virus Hunters of the CDC* (McCormick *et al.*, 1999) reflect such storylines. The ongoing problem of Lassa fever in Sierra Leone proved trickier to narrate and manage. Lassa fever disease control was dependent on international whims and humanitarian assistance, made worse by the regional conflict. By the end of the war, Lassa was proving itself to be an 'unheralded problem' (Birmingham and Kenyon, 2001) and the 'poster child of neglected diseases' (Donaldson, 2009). Yet the steady stream of cases was not matched by resources.

The confluence of the outbreak narrative with a range of security concerns, at local and international levels, meant that Lassa was not destined to remain a typical neglected disease. The year 2004 was a devastating one for Kenema, but one which marked the beginning of a new phase. With stability returned to Sierra Leone, Merlin, primarily an emergency relief organization with no mandate to provide long-term support, was looking to leave. The virus, however, was wreaking havoc with renewed vigour. A nosocomial outbreak linked to KGH's paediatric ward saw 95 paediatric cases admitted to the Lassa ward between 1 January and 24 April 2004 (WHO, 2005a). There were also cases among expatriates and peacekeepers. With the ward overflowing, a further blow was the death of Dr Conteh after he contracted Lassa fever through a needle stick injury.

The Office of United States Foreign Disaster Assistance (OFDA), part of USAID, then set up a task force to deal with Lassa fever. They brought stakeholders from Sierra Leone, Guinea, Liberia, the World Health Organization (WHO), the European Union (EU), and INGOs together to develop a regional strategy. In 2004, the Mano River Union Lassa Fever Network (MRU-LFN) was formed to strengthen scientific cooperation, patient management, surveillance, laboratory capacity and information communication and education. OFDA gave a small amount of funding to the WHO to coordinate this and to set up a laboratory in Kenema. A member of the WHO team recalled that the death of Dr Conteh was a 'tipping point' in setting up the MRU-LFN – previous WHO missions to Sierra Leone had come to little and there was a sense that Dr Conteh had been 'left in the lurch, without any help' and they wanted to 'put this right' to ensure that it would not happen again. Central to the WHO/OFDA plan was the idea of building a laboratory in Kenema that could be a research campus where international researchers would pay to use the facilities. The Kenema laboratory was to be connected to laboratories in Guinea and Liberia through the MRU-LFN, with governments cooperating on surveillance. There were also plans for a new isolation ward at KGH for which the EU had committed funds (WHO, 2005a).

The MRU-LFN was part of wider efforts to strengthen surveillance for global health security post-SARS (severe acute respiratory system), and in the wake of outbreaks of avian flu in the early 2000s. WHO revised the International Health Regulations (IHRs) – to control diseases *and* avoid interference with international traffic and trade – and established structures like the Global Outbreak Alert and Response Network (GOARN) to ensure global public health security (Dry, 2010) through surveillance and early warning systems. Lassa fever was included as a notifiable disease under the revised IHRs due to its potential to 'cause serious public health impact and to spread rapidly internationally' (WHO, 2005b). The Ministry of Health and Sanitation (MOHS) also adopted the WHO's Integrated Disease Surveillance and Response[9] (IDSR) in order to implement the IHRs, under which Lassa fever was included as a 'priority' 'epidemic-prone' disease. But is Lassa really a threat to global health security? And can Sierra Leone really abide by the standards of the IHR? These governance tools worked on the principles of detection and containment at source, but they have been criticized for prioritizing the safety and interests of Northern populations (Calain, 2007b; Dry, 2010; Elbe, 2010b) while overlooking the social and material circumstances which produce disease in specific contexts (Hinchliffe, 2014). In the case of Lassa, most agree that the virus is much less infectious than Ebola and secondary infections in imported cases are rare. Many scientists, therefore, do not even believe the natural risks of international spread are high. Potential use of the virus as a bioweapon, discussed below, is considered by many to be sensationalism and 'paranoia' which is useful to raise grant funds – although this is not an uncontested view and some scientists do maintain that it is a threat which should not be dismissed.[10]

Hence the events of 2004 were, from the start, entwined with a collection of biosecurity concerns that took place in a global health landscape that was increasingly security conscious. As one long-term researcher recalled:

> In 2004 a lot of things were happening simultaneously. There was epidemic spread in the Sierra Leonean population. There were cases in UN peacekeepers. There were cases in relief workers. There was a Red Cross surgeon who got Lassa and died. In the United States side of things people were of course worried about Lassa as a Bioterrorist agent … [then] culminating with Aniru Conteh, who ran the Lassa ward, getting Lassa and dying.

During the MRU-LFN inception phase further security anxieties emerged. After the war, with the influx of aid workers and peacekeepers, Lassa was painted as a threat to post-conflict redevelopment. A Weekly Epidemiological Record from the WHO, which played a key role in setting up the MRU-LFN, spelled this out:

Civil unrest in the Mano River Union region created newly vulnerable populations, including refugees and humanitarian relief workers. There have
been several recent fatal cases of Lassa fever among United Nations peace-
keeping forces. The return of areas to government control and the rebuilding
of civil society in Liberia and Sierra Leone puts aid workers at risk of contracting Lassa fever.

(WHO, 2005a)

By the risks it posed to the humanitarian relief and reconstruction efforts, Lassa was
framed as a threat to a fragile new peace. Indeed, the doctor employed to replace
Dr Conteh in running the Lassa ward recalled senior staff in the MOHS persuading
him to take up the post by warning him that 'the peacekeepers will leave if they
don't have a [Lassa] doctor'.

The creation of the MRU-LFN also saw Lassa fever control dovetail with
regional post-conflict diplomacy. As countries where Lassa fever was endemic,
Sierra Leone, Liberia and Guinea also made up the Mano River Union economic
sub-region.[11] Staff from WHO saw an opportunity to use that entity to get leverage
for Lassa fever work. High-level ministry staff from each Mano River government
were invited to participate in developing the five year MRU-LFN strategy. The
hope was that tackling the mutual problem of Lassa would foster and capitalize on
inter-country cooperation in a historically volatile region. However, as the WHO
staff coordinating this reflected, there was relatively little input and engagement
from the three governments themselves, which in hindsight was not enough to
realize the network's broader aims.

The establishment of the MRU-LFN did a great deal to improve the situation
in Sierra Leone. Diagnostics have been available routinely to suspected Lassa cases
in Kenema since 2007. Yet, outside of laboratory diagnostics, progress on the
MRU-LFN's objectives of surveillance, case management and education have been
much more limited. The laboratory established in Kenema continues to run, but
programmes in Liberia and Guinea either never materialized or could not be maintained. The fact that the laboratory was even built was down to the 'sheer will of a
few' rather than effective stakeholder cooperation. Many of the original commitments made by the MOHS and NGOs were not fulfilled. The laboratory was finished in the end with the help of Pakistani peacekeepers who were stationed near
Kenema and who offered their help after some of their troops contracted Lassa
fever. They donated supplies and arranged for the biosafety cabinets, which could
not be taken over the dirt roads from Freetown, to be airlifted in the UN helicopter
to Kenema.

Both past and present WHO staff describe difficulties in getting original stakeholders, including the MOHS, to stick to their commitments. The foundations of
the new EU-funded ward were laid but never completed as match funding from
the government did not materialize. Eventually the WHO, both Country Office
and Geneva staff, pulled back. The WHO country representative was moved to
another position, the Geneva-based staff were sent back from time to time but, as

a former staff member recalled, 'somewhere down the line when the glow of the outbreak was done', attention was turned away from Lassa (see also Khan *et al.*, 2008).

Biodefence dollars: technology deficits and counter threats

Of the various security 'problems' attached to Lassa the one which has raised the most resources, and eyebrows, is US biodefence interests: the laboratory in Kenema has been called a 'US anti-terror outpost'.[12] However, while the headlines may refer to bioterrorism, on closer inspection the biodefence assemblage reflects a more complex set of interests and politics surrounding knowledge and technology.[13]

When the MRU-LFN was set up, diagnostics were identified as a priority. Cumbersome and expensive to produce, routine serological tests were unavailable in West Africa. Classification of the Lassa virus as a Category A pathogen created funding incentives and possibilities for researchers and biotech companies to work on an otherwise neglected disease, marking a gear change from the activities carried out by humanitarian and international agencies up to that point. However unrealistic the widespread transmission of Lassa fever may appear, that classification frames Lassa fever as a threat to US national security due to its potential to spread and cause panic, therefore necessitating 'special action for public health preparedness'.[14]

The greater part of the billions of dollars which have been raised and spent on biodefence by the US government since 2001 have both biodefence applications and non-biodefence applications – for instance in health care, public health or other security applications (Franco, 2009). The Tulane University-led research proposal to the United States' National Institute of Health (NIH) to develop Lassa 'Diagnostics for Biodefense' exemplifies this 'dual-use' purpose:

> The potential use of LASV as a biological weapon directed against civilian or military targets necessitates development of, *'effective, rapid, highly sensitive, specific, easy to use, adaptable, and cost-effective medical diagnostics for public health laboratories, hospital-based clinical laboratories, and point-of-care use (RFA-AI-08-001)'* to diagnose individuals exposed to and/or infected with LASV. The impact of Lassa fever in endemic areas of West Africa is immense, and a safe and effective diagnostic can also provide a very significant public health benefit.
>
> *(Garry, 2004, p64, emphasis in original)*

With a budget of approximately US$9–10 million, this was one of the first grants using the new Lassa lab in Kenema for field research. Another five-year grant, focusing on the role of humoral immunity in the protection or pathogenesis of Lassa fever (which has implications for developing effective treatment), was awarded from NIH's biodefence allocations in 2009/2010 for US$15 million.[15] The portfolio of biodefence-related projects in Kenema also includes those of Metabiota, a private for-profit company run by 'virus hunter' Nathan Wolfe. Metabiota focuses on monitoring 'viral chatter' in emerging disease hotspot, where intensive

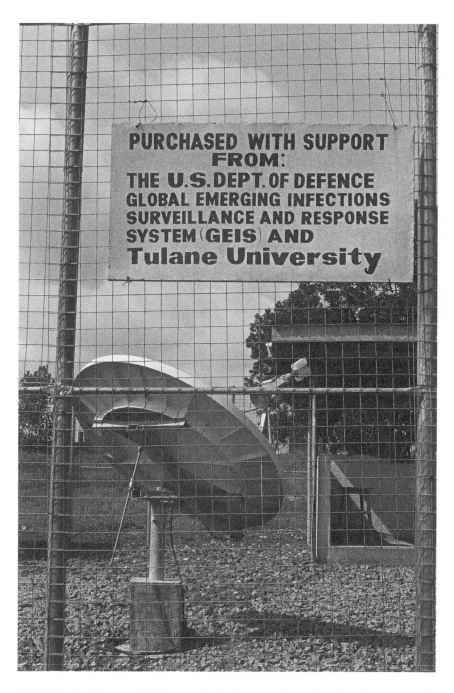

FIGURE 7.2 Satellite on KGH grounds funded by biosecurity-related grants (credit: Annie Wilkinson)

contact between humans and wildlife, for example through bushmeat hunting and trade, take place. The hope is that by being able to identify and mitigate viral spill-over events before they take place, the 'next HIV' can be stopped in its tracks.[16] Metabiota had at least three grants from the Defense Threat Reduction Agency (DTRA) and Cooperative Biological Engagement Program (CBEP), both of which are US Department of Defense (DOD) agencies. Work in Sierra Leone initially concentrated primarily on the pathogenesis of Lassa fever, with applications for treatments and vaccines. More recently, Metabiota has carried out modelling research to understand the cycle of transmission in relation to climate. To put all of these Lassa grants into perspective, the Sierra Leonean MOHS was allocated approximately US$19,562,598 in 2009 to run the national health system for a country of 5.6 million people.[17] The significance of these well-funded research projects to a small site in Eastern Sierra Leone is considerable.

In 2010, the Viral Haemorrhagic Fever Consortium (VHFC) was established, bringing together US universities and research institutes, biotech companies, KGH and Irrua Specialist Teaching Hospital in Nigeria. The driving force behind this consortium was to understand mechanisms related to the human immune response to Lassa virus infection.[18] Collectively, the general approach has been to do research oriented towards the development of products, such as diagnostics, drugs or vaccines. A senior scientist at one of the Consortium's biotech firms summarized this in an interview: 'You're never going to eradicate the virus', he said, 'what we want to do for the next ten years is just get into a system where we can diagnose them quickly, treat them quickly and reduce the mortality rate'.[19] Consortium partners at Harvard University are also carrying out genomic studies of the virus and exposed humans as improved understanding of genetic factors may help in the development of effective treatments and interventions.

Vogel (2008) argues that, post 9/11, the US approach to biodefence has been captured by a 'science-based approach' that emphasizes the development of bio-technology as the most effective way to deal with uncertain threats stemming from complex socio-political factors. Preparedness is conceived of in terms of scientific capabilities. The 'tech fixes' hoped to arise from investments in research are thought to be the most rapid and robust way of overcoming threats. Understanding the social and political drivers of such threats is not a significant part of the agenda. In Sierra Leone, research trends reflect this. With the CDC's pre-9/11, pre-Sierra Leonean civil-war field investigations halted, the focus of recent work has been on the development of medical countermeasures as funding flowed for research on pathogenesis and genomics for diagnostics and treatment. On the ground in Sierra Leone, biodefence concerns are largely alien but they provide an injection of otherwise scarce resources. A MOHS doctor explained:

> The average Sierra Leonean won't see LF as a bioterror threat. Only in the Western world do they see it like that. They see it coming from here as a weapon.... All the knowledge produced here could be used to help counter bioterror. But we do not see it like that.

For KGH, the research funds flowing into the Lassa laboratory provide opportunities to improve clinical practice. During development, using samples from Sierra Leonean populations, the prototype diagnostics are provided to KGH for free. The research projects have created work and skill development opportunities for Sierra Leonean staff employed at KGH. Research funds have also supported the outreach and surveillance team to do critical but often overlooked community sensitization on Lassa. This reflects a broader trend whereby the traditional roles of defence and health agencies are blurred as defence actors become involved in humanitarian and development work. In this case, research, defence and health system strengthening are brought together in an uneasy blend under the auspices of 'white coat diplomacy'. Yet when grants are primarily for research, the diplomatic spillovers are not always clear-cut. In particular, the provisions within research projects for longer-term capacity development and training of national staff have jarred with local expectations, especially over training and educational opportunities. Diplomacy is also undermined by inter-organizational disputes with national staff having to mediate between, for example, Metabiota and Tulane conflicts. One clinician commented, 'Now we have the troubles of one organisation to another, it is giving me a headache.'

Further complicating the research–defence–health system strengthening nexus are the uncertain financial incentives driving innovation, which for tropical diseases in poor countries have traditionally been minimal. While biodefence can provide a cash injection for developing drugs, vaccines and treatments for otherwise neglected disease, bringing products to the market has proved tricky. Members of the VHFC have made considerable progress in developing laboratory-based and rapid diagnostic kits. The innovation process has been driven by expectations of a market for these products in wealthier Nigeria as well as with US troops in Africa. However, in Sierra Leone there are questions about the sustainable supply of these kits. The provision of diagnostics is currently tied to the availability of research programmes but there is no formal agreement between the MOHS and Tulane and their partners about how the diagnostics will be supplied once research and development is completed. This ambiguity about ownership brings to mind another infamous example. In 2007, the Indonesian government famously refused to share their H5N1 samples in a protest about the inequity of international virus-sharing agreements. They argued that poorer countries supply the raw materials – i.e. samples – which are then used by Northern pharmaceutical companies to develop and sell drugs, vaccines and diagnostics at a profit, often at prices too high for those same poor countries (Elbe, 2010b). It is hard not to see the rumours about a US-created Lassa–Ebola hybrid virus (as circulated during the Ebola outbreak) as a reflection of the ambiguous interests and outcomes of international viral research and the unequal power relationships it transects.

Becoming a national public health problem: from unknown to known

While on the international stage Lassa fever is an emerging disease and potential bioweapon, in Sierra Leone it is an endemic disease largely associated with the east of the country. There is a local version of the disease's exceptional status; it has, as one survivor put it, a 'big name'; however, compared to malaria or typhoid, which are common throughout the country, Lassa fever is not a 'national disease'. Professionals residing in Freetown spoke of Lassa fever as located in 'that little corner of Sierra Leone' and 'so far off'. Parts of the country are designated as being the 'Lassa belt', understood to run across the 'Kenema–Kailahun axis' or the 'axis of Kenema and Segbwema'.

Although money has gone into laboratory research, it has been shadowed by chronic underfunding in the wider health system. For significant periods of field-work in Sierra Leone there was no thermometer on the Lassa ward in Kenema, despite the fact that temperature readings are a key part of the case identification protocol. Nurses had to reuse needles on patients over the course of their treatment (although not between), which puts nurses at increased risk of infection as they 'recap' the needles. In health clinics elsewhere across the country neither gloves nor clean water are routinely available, let alone electricity. This is shocking but not surprising in a country that has faced ten years of civil war in recent memory, and is consistently ranked near the bottom of the Human Development Index.[20] Sierra Leone has some of the highest rates of maternal and child mortality in the world. In this context, Lassa fever is simply one problem on a long list of pressing concerns. Understandably, priorities are constructed in terms of geographic distribution and prevalence. A senior MOHS official emphasized that as long as the virus was considered to be geographically limited, resources would be limited: 'I'll be very frank with you, [resources are] not forthcoming because [Lassa] is not being perceived by all as a nationwide threat, yet.'

Scientists emphasized the patchy evidence base: the lack of good-quality diagnostics and the absence of extensive prevalence studies contributed to a knowledge vacuum. Many of the established facts are dismissed as 'dogma' by some research groups. One US researcher summarized the situation like this, 'Seriously, everything about Lassa, I think, needs to be re-examined. Everything published before 2000.... There is a big gap, at least in field research on Lassa.' The patchy evidence base was not sufficient to translate into sustained policy support. There are moments, such as the death of Dr Conteh, when attention is drawn to the plight of Lassa in Sierra Leone but these focusing events tend not to last long.

In a country with multiple health and development problems, high-level policy interest has been episodic. After 2004, the MRU-LFN was formed and there was supposed to be regular regional meetings. But seven years lapsed before the next regional meeting, held in 2011. This meeting came about largely because of a spate of infections in the north of Sierra Leone, including the death of a South African engineer working for a biofuels company, which provoked concern about the disease's appearance outside of the traditional eastern zone and with negative consequences for the country's investment prospects. By 2012, however, a nationwide cholera outbreak had become the pressing concern. WHO country office staff reported that little had been done since the second regional meeting and that people and funds had once again moved on. Likewise, Ebola replaced cholera.

Within the usual policy ebbs and flows, the events of 2011 created a new discourse about Lassa fever. Conventional wisdom had located Lassa only in the east of the country, but it was now 'everywhere but Freetown'. As such the disease was now a nationwide problem that needed nationwide resources and attention. A senior MOHS official described what this would look like:

> A new approach would be for us to just take the country as it being endemic. Not only do you have the hyper-endemic areas but you really have it all over the country. And as such each and every health worker should be trained to look out and diagnose and pick out cases of it. Now more than ever the nursing barriers should be in place at all times. It also calls on all health institutions to provide the personal protection equipment for nurses, for health workers. It goes a long way in terms of the entire system … it means community sensitisation in previously non-endemic areas should be on-going and not a one-off issue. It is a disease that does not forgive you if you make mistakes.

This was a new conceptualization of the disease prior to which the Sierra Leonean government's approach to Lassa could be described as 'policy-less'. The new narrative, that Lassa was a national disease making inroads to Freetown, challenged the implicit politics of the status quo which was that Lassa was a disease of the rural East and thus of little concern to Freetown policy-makers and donors. Technological change played a pivotal role in creating the conditions needed to shift the politics of this emerging disease. Before the Lassa lab was set up there were no routine diagnostics available for Lassa in Sierra Leone, or indeed the Mano River. Samples could be tested for research, mainly in laboratories abroad, to provide a retrospective diagnosis at best (Khan *et al.*, 2008). The first routine laboratory-based tests – enzyme linked immunosorbent assays (ELISAs) – were introduced in KGH in 2007 but they still took the best part of two days to process the results, making them of limited clinical use. The Tulane-led 'Diagnostics for Biodefense' grant to develop ELISA kits saw the two-day wait reduced to a few hours.[21] The new ELISAs were not only quicker but more specific and therefore reliable (Branco *et al.*, 2011). The speed and availability of new diagnostics improved clinical care and surveillance, which in turn provided the evidence needed to make new policy claims. The lack of diagnostic know-how and associated knowledge deficit was one of the reasons that researchers had focused so heavily on diagnostics. As one international researcher commented in 2010:

> I was really impressed that the only way we were going to be able to get any sort of handle on things was to not jump right into community education or

prevention measures because all those things require you to have some base line data, you know, what are you preventing, are you using your resources wisely; if you say we're going to go out and do community education or prevention, where are you going to do it? How much Lassa is there really in one particular region, or one village? The only way you could know, answer any of those questions was to have reliable diagnostics. And then start to collect information that was objective and could be verified and say here is where our Lassa cases come from, here is what is real and here is what is not real.

Public health prevention and disease control relies on statistics to improve epidemiological understandings but also to raise funds, secure policy attention and to make investments accountable through monitoring. These concerns were also emphasized by a senior MOHS official:

So resources for Lassa sensitisation, Lassa training, are not forthcoming. Last year we approached WHO and we have thrown this to some NGOs working in some of these districts to pick up this as an issue. But you know before even things become a priority you need to see data, case notes, and its coming and by all means the focus on Lassa will soon take place but it won't take place immediately because there are other priority diseases which have [more] attention.

He added later that '[Lassa] is an unknown.' Hard data is required before, and in order for, Lassa to compete with other diseases for attention and resources. There were disagreements about the direction of the LFN-MRU at its outset and some stakeholders wanted to focus on community-based prevention or improving the ward. However, the focus on diagnostics and surveillance won (Khan *et al.*, 2008). Lassa needed to make the transition from an *unknown* to a *known* disease, and diagnostics were the building blocks to enable improved understandings of the disease profile, incidence and prevalence.

The differing attitudes towards uncertainty between biodefence and public health helps to explain the dominance of biodefence-funded projects for Lassa fever up until now. The public health resistance to act in contexts of uncertainty contrasts with the knowledge processes propelling biodefence interventions. Biodefence is, as argued by Vogel (2008), built on preparing in the face of ambiguous, potential threats – as a policy framework, it deals in the unknown and thrives on uncertainty.

Beyond containment: the scope for One Health

As the knowledge base for Lassa matures, the disease is increasingly caught between different problem framings and on the boundaries of policy assemblages in global health. Much of the research up to now has been based on a premise that Lassa is a rare and deadly disease which needs to be contained. It is this view which has enrolled biodefence interest. However, both the virus' geographic spread and its clinical presentation look to be wider than once thought. Improved diagnostics are finding evidence of milder infections, reshaping the diagnostic profile of the disease (Branco *et al.*, 2011). Integrating a more nuanced understanding of what the disease looks like in a patient is a complex task and it has implications for the health system as a whole. The scary 'bleeding disease' image so useful for attracting resources may be less helpful in meeting this objective. Sensationalized accounts about Lassa, and indeed Ebola, can prevent them being dealt with in a calm and measured way. It was common to hear nurses talk about how they feared, and tried to avoid, nursing jobs in the Lassa belt. Doctors at KGH described cases being declined admission to other hospitals if there was the slightest suspicion that they may have Lassa. Inaccurate images of bleeding orifices and rapid death run counter to helping the public and healthcare workers understand the varied way the disease actually presents, and the need to extend treatment, infection control and suspicion beyond Kenema and the East.

Aside from the clinical and diagnostic work going on in Kenema, there was also a core group of staff carrying out (passive) surveillance, community outreach and rodent-trapping, supported by US research funds. Some of these frontline workers have worked on Lassa for decades. They embody the deep history of Lassa fever research in Sierra Leone and have unmatched expertise of the disease in local context. Working in close contact with the laboratory and ward at KGH, and with visiting scientists, they provide a bridge between the community and hospital settings and are the backbone of clinical, prevention and research activities. When a positive case is confirmed it triggers both human contact tracing and, if possible, rodent trapping. Community outreach is done by members of this team, and so benefits from their extensive knowledge of the local terrain. In many ways the integration of spatial (villages, bush, hospitals, labs) and knowledge domains (bioscience, human health, rodent ecology) achieved at KGH, in 'that little corner of Sierra Leone', is what One Health aspires to. Yet this team are based in Kenema and though they have kept admirably on top of case-loads, the geographical expansion of Lassa fever means such a set-up is unlikely to be feasible for much longer. They are also constrained by out-of-date and unsophisticated field research on Lassa.

Even before Ebola hit, the limitations of the joined-up but small-scale and vertical operations in KGH were increasingly clear. After the flurry of early CDC research when the virus was first discovered, field studies on Lassa have since been scarce. By 2010, some researchers were beginning to question the diversity of research in Sierra Leone:

> The problem is a lot of money is being devoted to Lassa in terms of therapeutics, vaccines, diagnostics. But there is no money whatsoever for prevention, education, for health promotion. For understanding the epidemiology and transmission dynamics of Lassa, nothing.

As a result, little is known about patterns of exposure and disease vulnerability. The lack of clarity about the drivers and consequences of expanded disease territory (Gire *et al.*, 2012) highlights this. Significant questions remain concerning the apparent disparity between the distribution of *Mastomys* habitat and recorded incidence of disease and whether this is due to occurrence of vertical or horizontal transmission within *Mastomys* populations (Moses *et al.*, 2012). Fichet-Calvet and Rogers (2009) investigated climatological influence on the distribution of Lassa by compiling data on human infections from 1952 to 2007 and using it to draw predictive maps. Their results suggest that heavy rainfall and temperature impacted on Lassa fever distribution, with rainfall exerting the most influence. However, their models did not include rodent data, and it has been suggested by Moses *et al.* (2012) that these maps may be biased towards where humans get diagnosed rather than the actual ecological niches of the virus.

Understandings of social, economic, technical and environmental drivers of Lassa prevalence in human or rodent populations are further constrained. The impact of the civil war and development trends towards large-scale agriculture or mining activity are unknown. However, in Sierra Leone, well-known hotspots for Lassa overlap with long time mining areas, such as Tongo Fields, and new cases in the north were detected in areas undergoing transitions to large-scale farming. Research looking at macro socio-economic or ecological trends that may drive exposure, either due to major changes in land-use or seasonal agricultural practices, would be valuable. Patterns of transmission linked to farming practices and livelihood strategies, old and new, and across gender roles are not known.

The result is that plausible disease control and prevention strategies based on an understanding of everyday practice and differential vulnerability, as documented in recent modelling work (Iacono *et al.*, 2015), are not possible. Instead, the prevention work carried out by the outreach team is based on CDC work from before the war, mostly from the late 1980s. It can be summarized as: don't eat rats, keep your environment clean and go to the doctor if you have a fever. Of potentially greater significance is the fact that *Mastomys* are burrowing animals. Dirt floors are common where cement cannot be afforded, making poverty itself a potential indicator of risk. Moses *et al.* (manuscript in preparation) found that houses with mud walls were nine times more likely to have rodent infestation than houses with concrete walls. Existing prevention messages advocating hygiene amount to little in the face of these socio-economic conditions.

Medical historian Charles Rosenberg distinguishes between 'contamination' and 'configuration' models of disease (Rosenberg, 1992). Configuration is concerned with the interacting social, medical and economic factors in particular contexts. Contamination models tend to put more emphasis on tracking and treating pathogens – through surveillance and counter threats – rather than understanding the conditions in which they thrive, and where changes could produce or reduce vulnerability. While much of the work done under the umbrella of the VHFC and the MRU-LFN has been in contamination mode, the research portfolio at KGH has begun to diversify and include more field studies to complement the counter threat work and to inform prevention. Metabiota is modelling the influence of climate on disease incidence using rodent and human data. The genetic work done by Harvard University and their collaborators is bringing a long-term perspective to Lassa fever. In 2011, the Dynamic Drivers of Disease Consortium, which this case study is a part of, began multi-method and participatory research into the ecological, epidemiological and environmental drivers of Lassa virus transmission, focusing especially on local livelihood and ecosystem service processes, including land-use patterns, climate, biodiversity, geography and lifestyle patterns.[22] In 2012, a Tulane researcher obtained UK Department for International Development (DFID) funding to work with GOAL, an Irish NGO, to test rodent control methods in an effort to update disease prevention messages and techniques. Collectively, these efforts are broadening the research base, providing an enriched understanding of the disease in its social and ecological context which One Health requires. Unfortunately, many were disrupted by the Ebola outbreak, so progress may be set back.

Promising research on the configuration of the disease should be matched with efforts to understand and influence the configuration of the policy environment. Dominant narratives about Lassa fever in Sierra Leone contain some troubling patterns. The persistence of the idea that Lassa fever is located only in that 'little corner of Sierra Leone' sees Lassa fever located in rural backwaters of little concern to urbanized areas such as Freetown, where most business, government and NGOs are based. This also relegates Lassa fever to an area associated with the civil war which began in the east.[23] Furthermore, Lassa fever's infection route is easily stigmatized and it converges with the perception that rural people living 'up country' are less civilized. The reason Lassa fever is only in the east, it is said, because that is where people are driven by ignorance, a lack of education and tradition making them behave in risky ways: eating rats and practising poor hygiene. Although common across rural Sierra Leone, the consumption of rodents as a source of protein receives considerable scorn; as one Freetown professional said, 'there is no better way of getting the disease than by eating its carrier' (see Figure 7.3).

These perspectives on Lassa, which attribute responsibility to individual behaviour as opposed to socio-economic conditions or long-term socio-ecological change, are troubling in a context where ideas of disease and development can so easily become entwined. Post-war Sierra Leone has sought to move up from the bottom of the human development index and discard its 'blood diamond' label by achieving growth. The Sierra Leone Investment and Export Promotion Agency (SLIEPA) was formed in 2007 and seeks to promote investment opportunities in the country, particularly from foreign investors. It has focused on agriculture, identifying sugar cane and oil palm as priority investment areas. Commercialization and diversification of agriculture by the private sector is proposed as a key means of achieving change (GOSL, 2005). Large-scale land deals, farming and mining are the order of the day.

Changes to the landscape may well influence rodent populations and disease ecology, but debate about the implications of these environmental and economic

FIGURE 7.3 Local rodent trap, in Mende, with mock rodent (credit: Annie Wilkinson)

changes is absent, discouraged even. Institutional reluctance to consider different possibilities was evident from key stakeholders. During interviews, farming and mining industry actors did not see connections between their work and zoonotic diseases such as Lassa fever. Both London Mining[24] and Octea Mining[25] staff interpreted questions about the potential health implications of their operations as concerning staff getting sick. Otherwise, they saw their activities as unrelated and argued, for example, that Lassa fever was simply about people's culture and behaviour. As one stated: 'It is society generic not mining operation specific.' The mining companies, and the EPA who oversee their licences, view the impact of mining activities through the limited lens of the environmental, social and health impact assessments (ESHIA). This covered only those issues which were described as 'mining related health issues', like noise, dust and human resettlement. Health outcomes are framed as immediately observable with direct causal links. Messier, longer term and indirect outcomes are not contemplated and are not included in impact assessments. The direct links between Lassa fever, rodent consumption and poor hygiene are preserved as the primary drivers of infection and consideration of long-term and non-linear impacts of changing land use are avoided.

Advocating for a broader, deeper conceptualization of One Health, Hinchliffe (2014) emphasizes that there is not one world, but many different worlds full of different perspectives. Putting this into practice means integrating plural forms of knowledge, especially bringing the views and experiences of local people into research and disease control. If outbreak narratives dominate on the global stage, and episodic, and at times stigmatizing views of Lassa fever are held in Freetown, very little attention has been paid to the perspectives of those who are most affected by the disease, making health messaging very unidirectional. Ethnographic research in eastern Sierra Leone uncovered some rather different understandings and reasons for susceptibility (Wilkinson, 2013; also DDDAC, unpublished). Although the message that Lassa is caused by rodents has diffused relatively well, there is a common misconception about which rodent carries Lassa. *Tuile* is the local name for an unpleasant smelling common pest, known to eat rice, on which Lassa is blamed. *Tuile* is more likely to be a shrew and the *Mastomys natalensis* is most likely known as *fogbetei*, although identification of rodent species is challenging, especially distinguishing *Mastomys* from other similar rodents. For example, DDDAC research has determined that *fogbetei* is not associated with homes and is considered to reside mostly in fields, swamp or the bush (unpublished). However, *M. natalensis* has routinely been trapped in homes in high numbers in Sierra Leone: in a study by Moses *et al.* (forthcoming) rodents were captured in 63 per cent of houses sampled, of which 47 per cent were *M. natalensis*. Rodents are eaten but people avoid *tuile* due to its unappealing smell and assumed Lassa connection. No such restrictions apply to *fogbetei*, and in general people report a preference for eating rodents found in the field or swamp instead of those around houses. This has implications for prevention messages, especially making information about rodent exposure more relevant to local categories of food and hygiene.

In village settings, Lassa fever was explained within existing disease landscapes where categorizations of sicknesses correspond, less to causative agents, and more to the available treatment options and social relations of sickness. In Mende areas, Lassa fever is known, along with other similar fever-producing illnesses, as a 'big fever', as opposed to a 'small fever'. A key distinction is that a 'big fever' is considered to be a 'hospital sick' which requires expert, most likely biomedical, attention, as opposed to an 'ordinary sick' which can be managed at home. There are some practical issues relating to if, and how, these categories can be realized. Whether someone has sufficient funds to travel and pay for treatment is a critical factor in determining whether a 'hospital sick' can actually be dealt with at a hospital. However, the circumstances surrounding sickness or death are also important. As is characteristic of Mende social life (Ferme, 2001), much about disease causation is ambiguous and biomedical information, even a positive diagnostic result, is not considered to be the end of the story in many cases. Fitting into existing ideas about misfortune and witchcraft, the deaths of pregnant women from Lassa (a group who are particularly vulnerable to the disease) are often said to have broken important social, ecological or ritual rules. In other cases, the questions hint at ideas about unknown environmental exposures. The role of rodent consumption, the discouragement of which is a key part of Lassa fever health prevention messages, is often disputed. Questions about the surrounding environment, for example the quality of water sources, are common. As such, the experiences of local people mean explanations for vulnerability to Lassa are grounded as much in social, economic and ecological dynamics as they are in biomedical mechanisms. This suggests that prevention methods and communication relying solely on giving biomedical information overlooks the realities and perspectives of people at risk of the disease, and will have limited effect.

Conclusions

The question of whether Lassa's expanded territory is truly 'emerging' or caused by improved diagnostics hints at the socio-technical processes underpinning Lassa fever's discovery and recognition. It is not simply a new virus disease of man coming out of Africa. The co-evolution of science, technology and policy has constructed different versions of Lassa fever over time. This chapter has identified policy and knowledge processes that have underpinned the transition from a neglected disease to an exceptional high-priority pathogen, through to a national public health threat. This progression has been shaped by shifting assemblages of people, tools, economies, framings, styles of reasoning, interests and values (Collier and Ong, 2005). While Lassa can no longer truly be called a 'neglected disease', scrutiny of the distribution and direction of disease control efforts in the Sierra Leonean context is needed.

The scale of the Ebola crisis necessitates reflection on preparedness and bio-security. Strong critiques have been made of how the tropes of pandemic preparedness, bioterrorism and emerging diseases have dealt in imaginary threats (Vogel, 2008) and produced imaginary interventions (Lachenal, 2014). In Sierra Leone, the threat of bioweapons may have been largely imaginary, but the problem of Lassa was real and tangible, and biodefence agendas have contributed to significant developments in diagnostics. The nascent articulation of Lassa fever as a national public health problem establishes a version of preparedness based on health systems, which is broader in scope than that of biodefence, but it is still lacking depth. So far, this national public health framing has involved talk of surveillance, training and a consistent flow of protective equipment for health workers. Missing from the discussion has been the vector itself, *Mastomys natalensis*, and its relationship with social, economic and environmental processes at community, regional and national levels. This may be due to *Mastomys natalensis* being considered a pest instead of livestock, removing it from linear discussions about 'economic value' that tend to define the priorities of the veterinary, public health and livestock sectors.

Lassa also highlights the need for One Health proponents to engage with uncertainty – an area where the paradigms of biodefence and public health, as applied in development contexts, means that influential disease dynamics are overlooked. Biodefence funding and science has been pivotal in establishing a valid evidence-base for Lassa fever. However, the uncertainty narratives that have been told about Lassa fever, which emphasize a knowledge and technology deficit, overlook important alternative sources of knowledge which should now be integrated. Both biosecurity and standard public health approaches prioritize laboratory knowledge and have come to focus on reducing contagion; but they do so on the basis of impoverished understandings of human to animal transmission that pay little heed to configuration in the 'real-world'. Unpicking the configuration of the disease in field contexts, in particular the interaction with gender, socio-economic status and forms of 'development' has been marginal at best. As Lassa proves itself to be a more common and complex disease than first assumed, plural forms of evidence can contribute to contextually appropriate, diverse and more resilient response pathways.

Recognizing and integrating the knowledge of a broad range of actors, especially frontline workers, field staff, social and political scientists, and urban and rural populations is essential. The Lassa ward suffered appalling losses in the Ebola epidemic, as did the general health sector in Sierra Leone, but those remaining have gone on to play pivotal roles in turning Kenema's fate around and now have a deepened knowledge of viral haemorrhagic fevers in the local context. Local communities have also learned rapidly and developed effective protective community-based responses (Abramowitz *et al.*, 2015). Ebola has demonstrated how fragile local expertise is if not nurtured and supported, while also revealing the problems caused by weak health systems which local populations do not trust or feel connected to (Wilkinson and Leach, 2015). Applying such a lens is urgent as Lassa emerges as a national disease, as the MRU-LFN ends its first decade, and as the Mano River region recovers from Ebola. It should address not only the socio-economic conditions that drive disease, but also the ways in which these conditions can be systematically overlooked by dominant policy perspectives.

Notes

1 This chapter draws from an earlier Working Paper (http://steps-centre.org/publication/lassa-fever-the-politics-of-an-emerging-disease-and-the-scope-for-one-health-2) where anonymized details of all interviews quoted here are given, including location and date of the interview.

2 A phrase coined by members of the Lassa fever outreach team in Kenema, Sierra Leone.

3 Lassa infection appears to be mild in approximately 80 per cent of cases and severe in 20 per cent, with an overall fatality rate of 1 per cent, but these are crude estimates; see: www.cdc.gov/ncidod/dvrd/spb/mnpages/dispages/fact_sheets/lassa_fever_fact_sheet.pdf, accessed 10 July 2015. Symptoms for severe cases include high fever, sore throat, red eyes and, in some circumstances, haemorrhaging, with death occurring within 10–20 days from the onset of symptoms. In hospitalized cases, the fatality rate has been recorded to be as high as 69 per cent.

4 Other Category A agents are: anthrax, botulism, dengue, plague, smallpox, tularemia, and viral haemorrhagic fevers, which includes Lassa fever, along with others like Ebola, Marburg and Machupo. See: www.bt.cdc.gov/agent/agentlist-category.asp, accessed 10 July 2015.

5 Estimates of disease burden are unsatisfactory and out of date. Variation in estimated annual infections is huge, ranging from 100,000–300,000 cases each year with as many as 5000 deaths, to up to three million new infections each year with 67,000 deaths (Richmond and Baglole, 2003).

6 Details about the fieldwork and research methodology that informed this chapter are discussed at length by Wilkinson (2013).

7 For example, staff with young children were not allowed to work on the investigations (see also Fuller, 1974, p142).

8 The Sierra Leonean civil war lasted between 1991 and 2002, and involved a series of coups, continued rebel insurgency, new governments and broken peace.

9 IDSR was developed by WHO African Region as a way of integrating health system strengthening and global surveillance.

10 That Lassa fever could cause a serious international epidemic is generally considered unlikely, especially as the virus is not associated with routine (or indeed any conclusive evidence of) airborne transmission. Small outbreaks, like that in Benin (WHO, 2015b), and imported cases, such as from Liberia to New Jersey, USA, in 2015 do raise concern and are not uncommon (Sogoba *et al.*, 2012).

11 Ivory Coast joined in 2008.

12 See: http://reut.rs/1GCh96Q, accessed 10 July 2015.

13 Indeed, this association contributed to the rumours circulating in Sierra Leone during the Ebola epidemic that Ebola, or some mutant Lassa–Ebola hybrid, had been created and released from the Kenema laboratory itself, either deliberately or as biowarfare gone wrong (see Bardosh, Leach and Wilkinson, this book).

14 See: www.bt.cdc.gov/agent/agentlist-category.asp, accessed July 2015.

15 See: http://bit.ly/1A7TllW, accessed July 2015.

16 See Wolfe's TED talk: www.ted.com/talks/nathan_wolfe_hunts_for_the_next_aids?language=en, accessed July 2015.

17 Figures taken from Save the Children UK and the Budget Advocacy Network's budget tracker (2012): www.savethechildren.org.uk/sites/default/files/docs/Sierra_Leone_Health_and_Sanitation_Budget_Tracking_2012.pdf, accessed July 2015.

18 See http://vhfc.org/home, accessed July 2015.

19 See www.dailycamera.com/business/ci_17601956, accessed July 2015.

20 In 2009, at the start of this research, Sierra Leone was ranked 180 out of 182 in the Human Development Index, having moved from the bottom in 2007.

21 Rapid diagnostic tests have been developed since fieldwork was carried out, which has speed the process up even further and allows for decentralized diagnosis away from KGH.

22 www.espa.ac.uk/files/espa/ESPA-Evidence-Note-DDDAC-ESPA-2011.pdf, accessed July 2015.

23 The border with Liberia and eastern Sierra Leone saw the brunt of the fighting in the ten-year civil war.

24 London Mining mined and exported iron ore from Tonkolili district. It went bankrupt in 2014.

25 Octea Mining mine diamonds in Kono district.

8

RESPONDING TO UNCERTAINTY

Bats and the construction of disease risk in Ghana

Linda Waldman, Audrey Gadzekpo and Hayley MacGregor

> Bats were the forgotten species. No-one thinks of them as posing a threat to human life.
>
> *(Ghana Wildlife Veterinary Specialist, 2012)*

Introduction

Significant international attention on emerging zoonotic diseases has, since the late 1990s, been complemented by the modelling of disease emergence and policy interest in a standardized approach to disease mapping, risk assessment, surveillance systems and regulation. Identifying the causal links between human health, wildlife and livestock diseases, environmental change and ecosystem dynamics remains challenging, as causality is deeply complex and uncertainties high. For instance, in examining animal migration and zoonotic disease risk for humans, Altizer *et al.* (2011) demonstrate numerous unanswered questions relating to pathogen emergence, resistance, and pathogen shedding. Dudley (2008), too, identifies many uncertainties relating to avian influenza, including questions about the ecology and epidemiology of the viruses, the dynamics and mechanisms of transmission, vagueness around 'spillover' and 'spill-back', vaccine effectiveness, and risk factors associated with human involvement. Such uncertainties have led to a focus on 'science-based' risk assessment methods that measure and define disease risk based on 'outcomes' and 'probabilities' (Stirling and Scoones, 2009).

International organizations, such as the World Health Organization (WHO) and the United States Centers for Disease Control and Prevention (CDC), have sought to improve formal surveillance systems, by revising the International Health Regulations (IHRs) in 2005, targeting initiatives for global, regional or cross-border surveillance and expanding reporting of informal, rumour and syndromic (or symptom-based) events (Calain, 2007a). Although a One Health approach seeks to 'integrate human and animal data in one surveillance initiative', wildlife disease emergence is often not prioritized to the same extent as human health (Vrbova *et al.*, 2010). Surveillance of emerging zoonotic disease remains challenging as it requires the 'effective integration of surveillance [in] both human and animal populations' (Halliday *et al.*, 2012, p2872). But a plethora of barriers, some more challenging than others, persist: weak detection and reporting capacities; limited opportunities for participation; poor communication between stakeholders; sectoral boundaries; weak incentives; limited funding; an emphasis on treatment rather than diagnosis; and international regulatory bureaucracies (Calain, 2007a; Sawford *et al.*, 2012; Halliday *et al.*, 2012). Surveillance of emerging infectious disease is thus frequently based on a lack of knowledge, and hence underreported (Halliday *et al.*, 2012). In this regard, different actors have different perspectives on uncertainty and opinions as to the degree of risk and best avenues for surveillance efforts, which shape the ways in which policy-makers, scientists and others respond.

This chapter examines uncertainty, the assessment of the risk of zoonotic disease emergence and associated policy responses, through the example of fruit bats and *Henipavirus* (Nipah and Hendra)[1] in Ghana.[2] It argues that a 'politics of precaution' has operated around this uncertainty in which the control of knowledge has became a sensitive issue. As discussed below, the discovery that Ghana's bats hosted zoonotic pathogens revealed the many latent tensions between the preservation of human health and of wildlife, and militated against immediate public disclosure. Furthermore, uncertainty around the emergence of bat-associated zoonoses facilitates a lack of clarity over which government sector should take responsibility and which type(s) of surveillance activities should be prioritized. Broad plans for 'big system' surveillance, currently proposed by the WHO and other international players, pose additional challenges surrounding detection and public health system constraints.

Fruit bats have become iconic species in the unfolding drama of emerging zoonotic disease. Bats are sentinel creatures in the search for new viruses because they demonstrate extreme potential for zoonotic disease emergence, and are known reservoirs of multiple existing viruses (Leroy *et al.*, 2005; Jones *et al.*, 2011). High-profile spillover events in Bangladesh, Malaysia, Singapore, India, Cambodia and Australia have been traced to fruit bats (Gurley *et al.*, 2007b; Montgomery *et al.*, 2008; Luby *et al.*, 2009). Links have also been established between bats and the spread of coronavirus responsible for Middle East Respiratory Syndrome (Doucleff, 2013), and a bat reservoir has been associated with the 2014 Ebola outbreak in West Africa.[3] For these reasons, bats connect a variety of actors with different interests and perspectives. Global organizations are interested in bats because of their potential to help scientists manage zoonotic disease spillover. Local and national actors, such as in wildlife, veterinary and human health sectors, are concerned about bats for career-oriented, personal and conservation reasons. The international media, too, has made much of bats and virus hunting in remote, exotic 'hotspot' locations (Gale, 2009; Cruzan Morton, 2013).

Galaz argues that the interplay between environmental change, ecosystem dynamics and human behaviour and health are particularly difficult to unravel as, 'uncertainties are high and causalities complex' (Galaz, 2010, p2). In Ghana, this is further complicated by the fact that, while pathogens with zoonotic potential have been identified in bats, spillover of disease from bats to humans has been suspected but not confirmed. Bats sampled in Ghana are reservoirs of Henipa (Hendra and Nipah) viruses, but spillover to humans has not been confirmed (Hayman *et al.*, 2008a). This national context is not unique. Nipah virus, for example, has been found in many Asian and African countries since its emergence in 1998 in Malaysia, but significant chains of human-to-human transmission have not been widely established (Luby *et al.*, 2009). At the time of research in 2012 – that is, before the West African Ebola outbreak – the risk of spillover and the identification of viruses in bats as a source of new emerging infectious disease was not known beyond specialist research circles in Ghana.

Research into how Ghana's fruit bats, and their associated viruses, are connected to health and policy concerns offers an opportunity to consider how socio-ecological issues get framed in a context where generalized disease risk from emerging infections is not strongly established, resources and capacities to detect new pathogens are limited and where, despite potential for infection, no large-scale definitive outbreaks have occurred in humans (cf. Halliday *et al.*, 2012). These uncertainties result in risk being assessed differently by different policy actors, which has implications for resources, the degree of planning for, and the extent of, zoonotic disease surveillance.

This chapter explores these issues, focusing on the difficulties and anxieties policy-makers face around communicating bat-associated zoonoses risk to the public in Ghana, and the media's role in relation to this. It interrogates the diverse kinds of evidence required by policy-makers in different sectors, and how the focus on evidence leads them to frame zoonotic disease differently. The emphasis on evidence leads, in turn, to processes which favour endemic diseases over emerging ones; in which zoonotic disease transfer from livestock is prioritized over that of wildlife; and in which other forms of wildlife (birds, for example) received attention while bats – despite their international attraction as viral hosts – remained neglected. In these ways, the chapter demonstrates how different appreciations of risk filter through to different policy landscapes, and how unknowns and uncertainties create a disjuncture between the interests of scientists and policy-makers' knowledge, awareness and prioritization of emerging microbial threats.

Context: bats and Ghana

Ghana is populated by several bat species. The migratory straw-coloured fruit bat (*Eidolon helvum*) roosts in extremely large colonies comprising several million inhabitants, in both urban and rural areas (Hayman *et al.*, 2010). There are several Eidolon colonies in Ghana which are also eco-tourist sites. These include roosts at Buoyem, BrongAhafo Region, Shai Hills in the Greater Accra Region, Wli Falls in the Volta Region and 37 Military Hospital in the capital, Accra. Although large bat populations exist throughout Ghana, little is known about most of the roosts. In terms of conservation status, the International Union for Conservation of Nature (IUCN) identifies the fruit bat as 'near-threatened'. This is primarily due to over-hunting and bushmeat trading, with an estimated 128,000 bats consumed annually in Ghana, in conjunction with habitat loss, climate change, deforestation, roost destruction, and increased pesticide use (Kamins *et al.*, 2011; Kunz *et al.*, 2011). The roost at 37 Military Hospital, in Accra's city centre, has between 250,000 and one million bats (varying seasonally). This roost is situated in trees surrounding one of Ghana's most important hospitals. There is a well-known explanation for the bats' presence in this urban environment: they accompanied their chief who sought treatment at the hospital. The chief died, but the bats still wait for their chief. In some versions, the bats had lived in trees surrounding the chief's palace and these trees have subsequently died.

There are many other Ghanaian beliefs about bats (Ishmael, 2005). Some people associate bats with sacredness, burial and chiefly authority. In this conceptualiza-tion, bats reside in sacred groves, chiefs' palaces and royal burial sites, have super-natural powers and have forewarned ancestral persons of danger. Others link bats with evil and witchcraft. Beliefs include: if a bat brushes against you, it might be taking away your soul; that unnatural deaths are forecast by the presence of bats; and that killing bats in sacred groves can result in sickness. Bats are also considered to be a nuisance, noisy, polluting and smelly. Yet they are also a source of food and a delicacy. Similarly, bats are linked to health and illness in different ways. For example, there is a belief that eating them can bolster a person's immunity, but they are also known to spread rabies and, according to some, ringworm.

Since 2000, scientific research on Ghana's bats has increased, focusing specifi-cally on bat virology and ecology. Several collaborative research teams, involving British, German and Ghanaian partnerships, have produced academic publications linking bats to disease (for example, Epstein *et al.*, 2008; Hayman *et al.*, 2008a, 2008b, 2010, 2012). These studies have associated bats in Ghana with the Lagos Bat Virus, Hendra, Nipah and Ebola. As one Ghanaian official commented:

> Increasingly everyone is a little worried because of interacting with us.... They ask more and more if these bats don't pose a health risk. As we begin to dig deeper people ask, why are you looking, why are you taking blood?

In Ghana, as shown above, there is widespread knowledge of bats accompanied by diverse beliefs about their potential to prevent or initiate misfortune. Far less is known about bat-related scientific research and the potential for bats to cause zoonotic disease spillover; this information is more restricted, privy to specialist research and policy circles who also have, as the following section demonstrates, distinct perceptions of bats and disease.

Framings of zoonotic disease risk

Zoonotic diseases from wildlife pose particular challenges when examining the relationship between emerging disease, risk and policy. Conservation, veterinary services and public health, each of which has sectoral and disciplinary boundaries, responsibilities and priorities, are involved. Sectoral approaches are thus of limited value when·dealing with an emerging zoonotic disease as the situation is highly complicated, involving social, ecological and technological systems as well as 'the messy political complexities of disease-risk governance' (Stirling and Scoones, 2009).

Indeed, this research occurred in the midst of a muddled, contingent process of natural science research, knowledge generation and policy response in Ghana. As scientists searched for new viruses in bats, seeking permission from, and feeding back information to, influential officials in government ministries, new knowledge was acquired by a select circle of scientists and government officials.

For the most part, public officials regarded scientific knowledge about the risk of potential spillover of Henipa as relatively benign, partly because of the lack of evidence of human suffering. In early 2010, it became evident that Ghana's bats can harbour the Ebola virus (Hayman *et al.*, 2010). Ebola was familiar to Ghana's public officials and this knowledge was seen by them as potentially explosive. It was therefore disseminated only to relevant public officials and was not widely known at the time of our interviews. We were cautious not to reveal this information to informants while seeking to understand their knowledge of bats, potential spillover and how this related to veterinary, wildlife and health sectoral responsibilities.

The scene for examining Ghana's policy responses to emerging zoonotic disease, and the scope for a One Health approach, was set in the late 1980s and early 1990s in Accra, a time when the bats around 37 Military Hospital attracted great policy and media attention. The military, concerned about their polluting, noisy and smelly presence, decided to remove the bats. But their attempts to shoot the bats failed dismally. The government departments of Wildlife Services and Veterinary Services were not initially involved, and neither were conservation NGOs such as the Wildlife Society. After considerable upheaval and serious discussion, collaboration between the Ghana Armed Forces and Veterinary and Wildlife services was established, and continues to this day. Bats still roost at 37 Military Hospital, where the military now acts as their guardian, using tree coppicing to limit the size of the colony (Figure 8.1). Despite initially wanting to remove the bats, the military did not consider bats a source of risk for zoonotic disease. This assumption, that bats pose a negligible risk, was still prominent in 2012 among most policy-makers and scientific actors – at least those outside a small, inner circle of actors closely connected with researchers investigating bats and disease spillover.

Biologists from the University of Ghana were not involved in bat research and therefore did not associate bats with serious disease threats. During interviews, they pointed to the government's tendency to prioritize human needs over conservation, to the lack of enforcement of environmental protection rules and regulations

FIGURE 8.1 The bat colony at 37 Military Hospital in Accra, Ghana (credit: James Wood)

and to forests being preserved in name only. As people hunt in protected forests, an 'empty forest syndrome' is created in which there is forest canopy but no animals. As one biologist stated, 'people are protecting a forest which is not there'. In particular, they identified poverty as a major cause of ecosystem decline. Poverty-induced migration meant that people lived in areas where they had no obligations to respect traditional laws on land and hunting, and hence no long-term commitment to the land or natural resources. These biologists reported that communities react negatively to wildlife officials and to conservation in general, perceiving conservation activities as a direct threat to their ability to exploit land and resources. This framing of conservation and the 'downward spiral' view put forward by biologists in Ghana prioritizes wildlife and ecology, with little appreciation of the complex dynamics between poverty, conservation and political representation (Scherr, 2000).

Ghana Wildlife Services are also concerned with conservation and it sees the bats as a species requiring protection. For Wildlife Services, bats are framed as providing critical ecosystem services. Their vital role in seed dispersal (bats were described as having planted neem trees throughout Accra), the usefulness of these trees as firewood and the ecological importance of bats was pointed out. As one official mentioned, 'every creature [has] positives and negatives, we need to balance these. [There is] no perfect creature. We would not have fruit without bats.' Additional ecological contributions of bats, widely documented in the scholarly literature,

include forest regeneration, pollination, suppression of insect and arthropod popu-
lations, provision of fertilization through guano mining, and eco-tourism (Kunz *et
al.*, 2011). As biologists, Wildlife Services did not support the eradication of bats
and, as suggested in the above quotation, emphasized the need to 'live with' bats.
They were highly concerned with the reduction in bat numbers caused by hunting.
Their protective stance towards bats is widely known. As one informant from 37
Military Hospital commented, 'wildlife [authorities] are preventing the shooting.
They say we are infringing the bats' rights. We are destroying the ecosystem.' The
news that bats harboured Ebola viruses renewed Wildlife officials' need to manage
the interface between wildlife and humans; they began to think about how to communicate risk to tourist sites close to bat roosts in order to inform, but not frighten,
the people most at risk of exposure.

Ghanaian conservation NGOs were also interested in bats, not least because the
United Nations had launched the 'International Year of the Bat' in September
2011. Bat Conservation International, a US-based NGO, promoted bat conservation both internationally and in Ghana.[4] These conservationists' framings echoed
those of Wildlife Services, emphasizing bats' role in ecosystem services, their seed
dispersal and pollination roles (see Duncan and Chapman, 1991) and the ways in
which community livelihoods relied on bats. The Conservation Alliance in Ghana
similarly emphasized bats as an endangered species frequently hunted for bushmeat.
These conservationists knew of scientific literature documenting bats as a source of
Henipa spillover and of bats' harbouring Ebola. In contrast to Wildlife Services,
they saw bats as a 'big threat to public health in Ghana', in which potential spillover
was shaped not only by the lack of medical evidence of disease contagion, but also
by the continued destruction of bat habitats and their growing presence in urban
areas. Thus bats were framed as endangered species requiring urgent conservation
action. From their perspective, the Ghanaian government paid insufficient attention to bats and their spillover potential. As one commented: 'The time has come
for the government to take serious steps to bat conservation which should be on the
agenda.'

In Ghana, the Government's Veterinary Services and Wildlife Services are closely
aligned, with shared responsibilities around Accra Zoo and staff seconded from Veterinary to Wildlife Services. The framings of these two government departments are
also closely aligned, with vets stressing that all wild animals have the potential to serve
as a reservoir of viruses, but that a stable relationship exists between host and virus
unless disturbed by environmental stress. Veterinary Services is primarily interested in
zoonotic disease from livestock and domestic dogs. Officials argued that Ghana's
biggest zoonotic disease threats are rabies, trypanosomiasis,[5] rinderpest[6] and avian flu.
Zoonoses affecting cattle and horses are of strategic importance because of their economic impacts. Senior Veterinary Services personnel were very aware of the possibility of zoonotic disease spillover from wildlife. For instance, Dr Akunzule, the
principal veterinary officer of the Ministry of Food and Agriculture, was quoted in
the media as pointing to an 'unprecedented worldwide impact of emerging and
re-emerging zoonotic and other Trans-boundary Animal Diseases'.[7] In interviews,

veterinary scientists posited that humans had to live in harmony with animals and that bats did not pose a special threat. This resonated with Wildlife officials who framed the issue in terms of a balance between humans and animals. Veterinary framings acknowledged the importance of bats' ecological role, but prioritized human health: 'My concern is health protection first ... veterinary medicine is preventative human medicine.' Nonetheless, most veterinarians interviewed, in both the military and Veterinary Services were unconcerned about spillover from bats to humans despite awareness of the recent research on Henipa. As one government vet commented:

> These endemic diseases ... are very serious animal diseases that attract their [vets'] attention. So before [vets] can appreciate [the importance of spillover from bats], you really have to have evidence that the disease is killing either animals or humans. It is difficult to direct attention away from what they know is a threat.

This lack of concern is replicated in the routine surveillance of animal diseases provided by the Ministry of Agriculture. As one animal husbandry specialist explained, diseases from wildlife are not a significant concern to the Ministry and bats are considered only a very minor rabies risk.

Ghana's public health priorities are oriented around known threats, like cholera, HIV/AIDS, meningitis, hepatitis, TB and malaria. The focus on these priorities crowds out an interdisciplinary approach to zoonoses. As stated by one medic, 'zoonotic infections, we leave that to veterinarians'. Nonetheless, officials at 37 Military Hospital and Ghana Public Health Services recognized zoonotic disease as a potential area of concern: 'Zoonosis is becoming increasingly more important in the world, you always wonder what the next infection will be, where the next outbreak will come from.' Their framing focuses on human health as the most important variable, as articulated by one very senior military official: 'Human heath should triumph in the preservation of bats versus humans.' The primary public health zoonotic concerns reported in 2012 concerned influenzas, rabies, yellow fever and Lassa fever.

The knowledge, among those closely connected to the bat research teams, that bats carry the Ebola virus, brought renewed public health attention to the risk of emerging zoonotic diseases in Ghana. Unlike Henipa, Ebola raises considerable concern. 'We are', stated one medical official (in hindsight, prophetically), 'sitting on a time bomb.' Nonetheless, as public health officials relayed in interviews in 2012, the lack of evidence that bats transmit Ebola to humans (together with the absence of Ebola outbreaks in West Africa), made it difficult to take action. The lack of certainty as they saw it – about which diseases were involved, the potential for spillover of new infections and the scope for ongoing human-to-human disease transfer – made this a nebulous area for any precautionary public health responses.

But the recent research into bats and spillover has led to increased collaboration between Public Health officials, Wildlife Services and the Noguchi Institute for Medical Research (a semi-autonomous institute of the University of Ghana).

Although respondents from Ghana Public Health reported that they wished to undertake human studies to ascertain if bat-borne diseases have infected humans, Ghana Health Services has very little capacity in the required microbiology expertise and necessary equipment for such studies. The Ghana Ministry of Health could turn to the CDC, which operates a small office within Ghana, for additional support, but it has not done so.[8] The CDC was thus providing only 'small and fragmented' support to Ghana's national health management information system, mainly related to HIV/AIDS, and was not undertaking active surveillance for emerging infectious diseases (CDC, 2011b, p3). Nonetheless, research collaboration between the Noguchi Institute, the CDC and the United States Naval Medical Research Unit (NAMRU) does exist. Although not focused on bats, NAMRU and the CDC have helped Noguchi set up a sentinel system for avian influenza, actively monitoring poultry farms and migratory wild birds and provided funding for establishing laboratory capacity for testing influenza in humans and animals.

As the following quote by a member of the Ghana Health Service indicates, the onus has been on Wildlife and Veterinary Services to undertake surveillance and to track the levels of disease within bats:

> Now we take zoonotic disease more onboard.... We have not seen the Ebola virus and we are hoping that it's not there. If we do find it, we will try to find the source. Our veterinarians follow the virus reservoirs in animals, monitoring rabies and anthrax. We are however on our toes now for the Ebola virus – the study has put us on our toes and since every animal is a carrier of disease we are watchful. We are watching cows and dogs, although the animal side belongs to the vets, cows and dogs are on our radar, we are now aware.

As is evident, growing awareness of bats' potential for zoonotic disease transmission has been accompanied by disagreement on the seriousness of the threat, on whether surveillance is needed, and on the nature of evidence required prior to effecting policy. Select scientists and government actors within Ghana debated these issues at length. Yet media dissemination and public knowledge was more constrained.

Public awareness of risk

Policy actors in Ghana view the media as an important source of public information and awareness on zoonotic disease, and some have appeared in media reports as expert sources on rabies, avian flu and swine flu. But they adopted a more cautionary approach in providing the media with information on bats and disease, primarily because they lacked confidence in the media's ability to treat the subject competently. Interviews with most policy actors betrayed a fear that moral panics would result if media coverage on bats and disease risk was 'mishandled'. Some recalled dissatisfaction with media reportage on avian influenza: 'People got into a panic, there were exaggerations about side effects; the media went on overdrive', said one health official. Another health official, who acted as an expert source for the media, complained that some reports on avian flu were inaccurate, for example one article advised against eating eggs because of avian flu, and thus provided the public with incorrect information. Such experiences have influenced the kind of information public officials provide on bats. As a consequence, media reports have focused on bat conservation and on recognizing that bats have ecological value.

On the few occasions when public health officials have tried to engage the media on the risk of disease posed by bats to humans, the media have failed to pick up on the information. One official who mentioned to journalists that bats are carriers of rabies, Nipah and Hendra said that they did not put this information into the public domain. Another official explained that when, in 2008, journalists came to a national stakeholders' workshop where links between bats and Henipa were discussed, there were no published reports because journalists 'did not consider it big news'. In July 2012, no journalists were invited to the workshop at which research findings on Ebola in Ghana's bats were shared.

Content analyses of the Ghanaian media confirm the dearth of information on bats and zoonotic diseases. A scan of key news sources[9] indicates that stories published on bats rarely make reference to the threat of zoonotic diseases, while stories on zoonoses refer to rabies and avian flu, but not to threats from bats. Media stories were generated mostly from press releases or local and international meetings, at which the threat of emerging zoonotic diseases (avian flu, swine fever, etc.) were mentioned.

Wildlife officials, veterinarians, public health officials and scientists engaged in zoonotic or conservation research have been the primary sources of zoonotic disease information. Still, few media articles quote these sources as associating bats with zoonoses. The exceptions were an online radio article which quoted a researcher working on a collaborative project between the Kumasi Centre for Collaborative Research in Tropical Research (KCCR) at Kwame Nkrumah University of Science and Technology and Ulm University, Germany[10] and an April 2013 article, in which Richard Suu-Ire, a veterinarian with the Wildlife Life Division of the Ghana Forestry Commission revealed that antibodies to the Ebola virus had been detected in Ghana's bats (based on research by Hayman *et al.*, 2010, 2012).

Typically, media reports on bats are framed within narratives of conservation. These perceived bats as being threatened by human activities and as important species for ecological balance and eco-tourism. For example, one article, entitled 'Bats: Ghana's best-kept wildlife secret' noted that bats were 'one of the most important players in regenerating Ghana's degraded forests' and were 'facing a major threat through hunting'.[11] Several such stories cover the standoff between bats, the military, conservationists and veterinarians in the late 1980s/1990s at 37 Military Hospital. This coverage acknowledged bats as a public nuisance ('activities of the bats and their droppings were causing a lot of anxiety and environmental concern, as they continued to defoliate the trees in the area and made a lot of noise that disturbed patients'); conservationists' opposition to the military's attempts to shoot the bats ('bats by themselves do not cause nuisance except they are disturbed'); and hinted at the ineffectiveness of the military ('therefore it does no good to frighten them').[12]

Stories on zoonoses, in contrast, contain narratives on human public health and veterinary concerns, with some citing officials warning of the threat of zoonoses from domestic animals (chickens, dogs, cattle) and increasingly from wildlife. One article reports a Ghana veterinary expert identifying the wildlife sector as a 'major factor in the outbreak of emerging zoonoses', and stating that '71 per cent of zoonotic diseases were of wildlife origin'.[13] Another, by the president of the Ghana Veterinary Medical Association, noted there were 'over 134 zoonotic diseases of viral, bacterial, fungal, parasitic or rickettsial origin which can be transmitted from animals to man'.[14] Many well-known and less well-known diseases were included in the list, but not Henipa or Ebola.

An online radio article reporting the views of a local researcher on the collaborative KCCR and Ulm University project was one of few media reports on the risk of animal–human spillover from bats.[15] The researcher was quoted as stating:

> It has become important for us to study the bat because if these bats are known to harbour these viruses and human beings interact with these bats, definitely there might be some transmission from these organisms to the humans and therefore there is the need to look at the extent of this inter-action, the levels of occurrence of these viruses in the animals, so as to determine whether transmission do actually occur and whether some of the diseases that are found in humans, being caused by viruses, are actually coming from transmissions that are coming between bats and humans.[16]

Passing reference to disease-carrying bats was made in another report sourced from the KCCR, although the dominant media frame was conservationist. A third story linking bats with disease emerged from 'Ecotourism Week' celebrations, where bats were identified as carriers of Ebola virus antibodies. Like the Farm Radio story, the framing was conservationist and reported Suu-lre from Wildlife Services down-playing the risk; arguing that though bats had antibodies to Ebola virus, their presence in the environment was not a risk to human health.[17]

Clearly, the evidence from local media and official sources of information (health and wildlife officials) suggests little interest in creating public awareness on emerging threats of diseases from bats. The only meaningful media analysis on the subject of bats and zoonotic disease risk was found on the Ghanaian online site Ghanaweb, which occasionally aggregates news on research findings from international scientific journals, such as *Nature*.[18]

With the media focused on bats and conservation, these articles downplay the role of bats in potential spillover events. This is unsurprising, given public officials' lack of confidence in media reporting on outbreaks (cf. Briggs, 2003) and their determination to keep the link between bats and Ebola contained. As a consequence, only isolated articles provide framings of risk and uncertainty relating to bat-zoonoses, and the public remain largely unaware of these links. As such, the media failed to influence how people think about bat viruses and their threat to human health, and did not question 'who or what is to blame ... who is at risk and ... what can be done' (Degeling and Kerridge, 2013).

Policy responses associated with bats and zoonotic disease emergence

The scientific attention on bats and zoonoses, and the sharing of this information with key actors, led to some proactive policy development in Ghana. The Wildlife Regulation Act of 1963 was revised, to list bats as a 'scheduled species', enabling Wildlife Services to prosecute illegal hunting and ensuring that protected area managers pay attention to bats. Wildlife Services has also facilitated community responsibility towards bats and natural resources through the passing of a new bill that provides a legal framework for Community Resource Management Areas (Agidee, 2011).

The presence of avian flu in Ghana's wild birds and poultry led to the establishment of a National Task Force for Avian Influenza in 2006 (GNA, 2006). Funded by donors, this was the first multi-stakeholder ministerial group for zoonotic disease and human health. Using a One Health approach, it created a framework for increased collaboration between the military, Wildlife Services, Veterinary Services and Public Health. Collectively these departments and ministries undertook exercises in pandemic disaster training. In addition, a government agency, the National Disaster Management Organisation (NADMO), was created as a coordinating body for national disasters, and zoonotic outbreaks were placed within its remit. This has created greater alliances between Ghana's government departments, and greater knowledge of different roles and responsibilities. It has also reduced government agencies' competition for funding. According to interviewees, participating in NADMO gave public health officials greater appreciation that rabies management cannot be limited to human exposure and treatment. They therefore advocated for greater resource allocations to Veterinary Services to ensure a multidisciplinary approach to rabies prevention.[19] Participants also valued the new cross-sectoral relationships: 'We are changing our perception of disease control, not only solving issues at a departmental level but ... bringing in other partners.'

With the legal mandate to deal with disasters, NADMO provides the muscle to mobilize for education, financial support and material supplies that cuts across government departments and sectors in Ghana. But NADMO staff were unaware of bats as a potential source of zoonoses. According to one member, bats are a threat to public health only because they are clustered around a hospital. In 2012, NADMO was not connected to any researchers working on bats. However, from a NADMO perspective, it was not the bats *per se* which mattered in terms of a risk profile. Their concern focused on the proximity of bats to medical experts and equipment at 37 Military Hospital. Because of its strategic importance, if the area were the epicentre of an epidemic and cordoned off, Ghana's ability to contain the outbreak would be significantly compromised.

This emphasis on outbreaks was echoed by academics at the Ghana University School of Public Health. They were highly aware of zoonoses and the potential for a mass outbreak. As one senior staff member explained: 'The problem is that we are susceptible, there are huge peri-urban groups, one drop of infection and there will be disease.' These academics knew that wildlife acted as a disease reservoir and that there may be spillover from bats, yet felt that this was not a priority. Indeed, it was unlikely to be a priority unless or until 'it explodes' and receives emergency international support. Nonetheless, the School of Public Health has created a one-year course in field epidemiology, bringing together medical doctors, veterinarians and lab scientists. This course trains field epidemiologists in different disciplines, to conceptualize disease problems from a One Health perspective. Students undertake field studies, engage in public health practice and are linked into national policy. They are also expected to participate in any outbreak that occurs in the course of their studies, working under the coordination of NADMO and with classes suspended to facilitate any fieldwork.

Finally, research collaboration between the CDC, NAMRU and the Noguchi Institute, which focuses on disease surveillance and laboratory capacity for parasitology, bacteriology and virology coupled with epidemiology expertise, has helped Noguchi set up a sentinel system for avian influenza. While funding has been provided for laboratory capacity to test influenza and identify unusual cases in human health, there is no focus on Henipa or Ebola.

Intersectoral challenges and uncertainty

We found that many of Ghana's public officials were aware of the need to develop an interdisciplinary and collaborative approach for emerging zoonotic diseases, as well as established priorities such as TB. In relation to bats and emerging diseases, meetings had been held with key actors as scientific findings emerged and information was disseminated. Yet, different interpretations of the data were shaped by how different actors framed the problem, and this created bottlenecks that limited a One Health approach.

Wildlife Society officials stressed that more research was necessary to investigate the possible links between bats and disease, to establish the level of risk and to understand why bats harbour viral diseases, but do not die from them. As trained biologists, they questioned whether better understandings of bat immunity might offer solutions for human exposure. They cautioned: 'it has not yet been established that [bats] can transmit [Henipa]. It is possible to harbour the disease, which is species specific, so there is no risk to humans.' The wildlife sector was concerned about how it would handle a situation in which bats were strongly associated with human disease. It feared that scientific research on emerging zoonoses could create a backlash and result in people shooting animals and negatively affecting the ecosystem. Their solution is to encourage communities and bats to live together, through greater community responsibility of natural resources.

In contrast to the Wildlife Services' views, which emphasized the unknowns associated with bats as a viral host, human public health perspectives emphasized the need for more evidence and scientific proof of the risk to humans, such as sero-logical evidence of infection:

> I don't know that bats can transfer airborne disease. We don't have signs and haven't done any research to prove [risk]. . . . It is good to leave the bats, there is no harm, apart from their droppings because as I'm talking now, there's no scientific proof. If there is a disease they can transmit, in an air-borne way, we don't know unless we do some research.

Because of the lack of evidence of human infection from bats, in 2012 public health officials emphasized that Veterinary and Wildlife Services should monitor the prevalence of anti-bodies in the bat population to achieve a detailed picture of the infection dynamics. One senior health representative was reported to have said, 'this is your problem, you handle it'. The Department of Public Health was, as one informant described it, 'very neutral' and 'not keen to take it on'. The public health framing, which emphasized that there was as yet no firm scientific evidence of spill-over, or substantial risk, was echoed in veterinary specialists' framings:

> Most reports from the researchers are just precautionary, they haven't put their hands on anything firm. We don't have to cause panic and can just say that bats, like any other animal, could be dangerous. Until we get evidence.

Veterinarians recognized the need for conclusive evidence before convincing public health officials of any urgency or generating policy change. As one stated, 'for us to receive attention, we really have to prove that Ebola is killing people. Politicians will only release funds when humans die.'

Thus, while researchers identified bats as a reservoir for zoonoses and the poten-tial for spillover, these messages were refracted through different sectoral and sci-entific framings in the policy world: wildlife officials were worried about stigmatizing bat populations; health officials stressed that it was a wildlife and veterinary problem; and veterinary officials were frustrated by the need for evidence of human disease in order to attract political attention and resources. An impasse existed between veterinarian concern and medical evidence. In addition, known existing zoonotic diseases such as Ebola generated more interest than the risk of diseases hitherto unknown in Ghana, such as Henipa. One expert summed up the problem as follows.

> The Government is paying attention to zoonotic diseases. They do because that's one of our main concerns. CDC asked if they need assistance and the vets said no. They said they know what they need to do, what they need is resources. The agencies mandated to deal with zoonotic infections know what they are doing. . . . Veterinarians and doctors all work together, at the national level, all sit on the same committee, do research to find out what's happening and it works. It is not about vets establishing a threat level in

animals, rather any unusual cases of disease in humans are supposed to be investigated. The catch is we do not have specific systems in place [to diagnose particular zoonotic infections] like Lassa, Ebola, etc.

This summary points to a high level of uncertainty regarding the ability of the existing public health system to detect and diagnose cases of known, endemic zoonoses as well as suspicious infectious symptoms that might herald an outbreak of a new condition. In rural Ghana, where people's livelihoods involve close proximity to bats and other wildlife, the public sector health system is under considerable strain. Infrastructural, human resource and other material constraints, such as shortages of diagnostic test kits and reagents, mean that many illnesses are likely to be treated based upon a clinical assessment of the syndrome (Jephcott, 2013). Febrile illnesses are typically treated as malaria, even in the absence of laboratory confirmation, so that it is hard to assess the extent of misdiagnosis. A prominent public health academic interviewed spoke of diseases being labelled as 'Not Yet Diagnosed'. This NYD acronym sometimes remains on the death of a patient in the absence of resources to pursue a more definitive investigation. Diagnostic practices and constraints make it unlikely that fevers of unknown origin would be thought of as potentially indicative of a new emerging disease, and people do not always seek diagnosis or care at public sector biomedical facilities (Jephcott, 2013). While the use of the NYD category acknowledges the constraints to achieving certainty, discussions with public health academics suggested that the existing surveillance system is unlikely to identify potentially unknown diseases (cf. Calain, 2007a; Halliday et al., 2012).

Local surveillance capacity in Ghana also involves a network of community-based surveillance (CBS) volunteers who watch for HIV, cerebrospinal meningitis, hepatitis, TB and malaria.[20] There are incidences of CBS volunteers identifying and reporting well-known disease outbreaks, such as meningitis in 2008 and addressing rabies surveillance (CDC, 2003). However, such an extension of reach is unlikely to be effective in relation to new or emerging diseases until much closer attention is paid to improving the system of health care and incentives for reporting in rural areas. The weaknesses of surveillance, and the lack of attention to emerging zoonoses (Halliday et al., 2012; Sawford et al., 2012) is significant given that regional initiatives such as the Integrated Disease Surveillance and Response Strategy (designed by the WHO and CDC) relies on early detection of disease at facility level. As Calain (2007a, p9) argues: science can only help define and limit the complexity of zoonotic disease spillover 'and feed decision-makers with facts and pondered uncertainties. Prioritization of health programmes is thus ultimately a matter of judgement, considering … the balance between known scourges and elusive disasters.'

Conclusions

As scientists search for new viruses that could cause the next pandemic, bats are important sentinels for zoonotic disease spillover (Leroy et al., 2005; Jones et al.,

2011). In 2012, prior to the Ebola outbreak in West Africa, the international media used headlines such as 'The Virus Hunter', 'Virus Hunters Find Ebola', and 'Marburg Source in Fruit Bat' (Gale, 2009; Cruzan Morton, 2013), while Ghana's media remained ill-informed and silent on the disease significance of bats. This was a reflection of the sectoral divisions within government and of the different framings these actors have of wildlife disease and risk to humans. It was also a reflection of the considerable uncertainties that Ghana's policy actors were grappling with and of the difficulties of making key decisions in such a context.

As this chapter has shown, in 2012 an appreciation of the risk of endemic or emerging zoonoses from bats in Ghana was confined to a core group of academics and policy-makers linked into a bat research network. Other actors, in wildlife, veterinary and public health services, perceived bats very differently, particularly with respect to the level of disease risk. Across institutional and disciplinary affiliations, concerns foreground human health, livestock health, or wildlife preservation, respectively. Bat-related research had catalysed some awareness of the complex dimensions to the assessment of disease risk from bats, but policy-makers spoke of requiring more certain evidence before they would be willing, or able, to take action. A politics of precaution thus operated around this uncertainty regarding the extent of risk.

In a context of uncertainty, certain trade-offs are evident that make the control of knowledge a sensitive issue. For example, the discovery of antibodies to Ebola virus in bats in Ghana generated tensions between the preservation of human health and wildlife, which militated against full public transparency. The degree of uncertainty regarding the extent of the implications of these research findings makes the politics of knowledge and response even more complex to navigate.

The case of bats in Ghana thus raises important questions about how policy is made around disease threats when the extent of the risk is not yet known. However, at the same time, the different sectoral gazes and framings create impasses that make it hard to link and assess evidence across the disciplinary divides. This reality facilitates a situation in which no one sector takes full responsibility so that unknowns hover uneasily in the space of current policy. Furthermore, the existing regional surveillance systems suggested by the WHO and other international players presuppose a particular set of conditions on the ground that rarely exist in a stretched public health system, where resource constraints of various kinds make facility-based detection of new infectious diseases unlikely.

Our research suggests that intersectoral collaboration on policy and the strengthening of surveillance systems for emerging zoonoses is still limited. The devastating Ebola outbreak in West Africa has affected zoonotic disease policy in Ghana, public and media perceptions of bats and disease and informed the mechanism for coordinated international response to confirmed outbreaks with epidemic human-to-human spread. Whether a politics of precaution will continue to operate for unconfirmed emergent zoonotic disease, and whether surveillance for such occurrences will receive greater attention and what forms they take, remains to be seen.

Notes

1 Hendra and Nipah cause severe encephalitis in humans, beginning as a mild fever, headaches and muscular pain before progressing to coma and death over a period of ten days. The ratio of cases to fatality is 40–76 per cent (Montgomery *et al.*, 2008). The viruses are transmitted directly to humans through contact with bat urine, saliva and guano.

2 Qualitative research was undertaken in Accra between May and October 2012, when there was no definitive evidence of disease spillover from bats to humans, although international researchers had alerted Ghanaian government officials to this possibility. Twenty-six open-ended interviews were conducted with policy-makers (veterinary and human public health officials and a NADMO representative); academics undertaking bat research, public health and disease surveillance; doctors and a veterinarian employed by the Ghana military; and state wildlife officials and conservationists in the state and NGO sectors. Ethical approval was received from the Noguchi Memorial Institute of Public Health, stipulating that informants be kept anonymous. When Ghanaian officials' statements about zoonotic disease are disseminated by media, they have been named. A media search, undertaken in 2012, identified the sources of information on bats and zoonotic disease.

3 The Ebola outbreak occurred after the research reported in this chapter. While it has shifted policy norms and the framing of bat-related zoonotic disease, no Ebola cases have been reported in Ghana.

4 See: www.batcon.org, accessed 10 July 2015.

5 Although Ghanaian officials identified trypanosomiasis as zoonotic, the occurrence of zoonotic trypanosomiasis in West Africa is widely debated in the scientific literature.

6 Rinderpest was declared the second eradicated disease on earth in 2011; however, in 2012 Ghana examined whether animals still acted as hosts.

7 www.ghanaweb.com/GhanaHomePage/health/artikel.php?ID=162784, accessed 10 July 2015.

8 The CDC's collaboration with the Ministry of Health is HIV-related, building capacity and strengthening laboratory systems (CDC, 2011b); developing HIV/AIDS-related surveillance systems and improving HIV-related services.

9 An initial Google search, using 'bats' and 'Ghana' as key terms selected only media articles. The term 'bats' was also matched with Ghana's main news sources – *The Daily Graphic*, Ghana News Agency (GNA) and Ghanaweb. This covered Ghana's most widely circulated newspapers, the foremost aggregated news site and its most influential media sites. After eliminating non-Ghanaian articles and articles which contained a spurious mention of bats, there were 12 articles dating from 2002 to April 2013.

10 myjoyonline, 20 August 2010 (Ghanaian internet news media outlet).

11 *Daily Graphic*, 11 April 2013.

12 *Daily Graphic*, 25 May 2004.

13 GNA, 25 April 2008.

14 *Daily Graphic*, 8 May 2009.

15 myjoyonline, 20 August 2010.

16 Ibid.

17 GNA, 19 April 2013.

18 Ghanaweb, General News of Monday, 3 October 2011.

19 Although Ghana Veterinary Services used to coordinate free annual rabies vaccinations for dogs, this policy was amended in the early 1990s. Current policy efforts are attempting to address the low dog vaccination rate by reinstating these campaigns.

20 In interviews, representatives of the Ghana Health Service claimed that 27,000 CBS volunteers had been trained and that every community had a CBS volunteer.

9

WHOSE KNOWLEDGE MATTERS?

Trypanosomiasis policy-making in Zambia

Catherine Grant, Neil Anderson and Noreen Machila

Introduction

This chapter explores the political economy of African trypanosomiasis knowledge and policy in Zambia. Using key informant interviews with a wide range of stakeholders, it focuses on multiple framings of the disease, and the historical and contemporary consequences of these different narratives.[1] Trypanosomiasis is transmitted by tsetse flies of the genus *Glossina* and its distribution consequently reflects that of its vector. Human African trypanosomiasis (HAT) can be a fatal disease and African animal trypanosomiasis (AAT) can also be fatal in all livestock species, but commonly causes chronic debilitating disease and loss of production. It is a pertinent time to examine this disease in Zambia as growing land pressure, human population growth and other factors have led to migration into tsetse-inhabited areas with little historical influence from livestock. This is bringing people, their domestic animals and wildlife into greater contact, and reducing biodiversity. These anthropogenic changes could potentially destabilize transmission cycles, resulting in as yet unknown disease changes and spread into previously unaffected areas.

This chapter largely focuses on two dominant narratives that frame the trypanosomiasis policy debate in Zambia. First, the 'protection narrative' maintains that trypanosomiasis is protecting the national parks surrounding game management areas (GMAs) and gazetted forest reserves from being invaded by people and livestock. According to this viewpoint, policy decisions that prioritize the environment, but support inaction in relation to eradicating the disease, are important and preserve the 'African wilderness'. Second, the 'poverty narrative' maintains that trypanosomiasis is causing poverty in potentially productive agricultural areas and that the parks, GMAs and forests must be cleared of trypanosomiasis to protect livelihoods and help with poverty alleviation. According to this perspective, trypanosomiasis in wildlife is a continuous 'spillover' threat to the rural economy that must be addressed, and the resulting policy aim is for disease eradication over control. Two alternative narratives are also discussed. The 'Zambian narrative' maintains that the international community has historically put a lot of emphasis and effort into eradicating trypanosomiasis, but now responsibility for this has passed to the Zambian state. Problems remain with this shift, as governance and funding shortfalls persist, leading to fragmented control activities and a lack of capacity. Efforts to address this gap, however, run up against policy debates about funding prioritization in Zambia. Lastly, the 'wider health narrative' maintains that Zambia has multiple health and environmental issues and that limited funding means that trypanosomiasis is not a priority area of concern.

These four narratives propose conflicting views on the best control methods and different reasoning behind the pathways of response. They are based on apparently incompatible priorities of people, land, animals, the economy and the environment in a complex and shifting landscape. Trypanosomiasis interventions are difficult to design and, as the different narratives show, are open to controversy about which offer the best solution. Although evidence should be the basis for policy-making, the dominance of different viewpoints driven by competing power plays overshadows the possibility of truly balanced 'evidence-based' policy. Understanding the ways in which these narratives have shaped policy decisions and funding are key, as the focus, support and funding for trypanosomiasis has changed over the years, not necessarily for scientific reasons.

Within this polarized policy landscape, a lack of focus and funding for trypanosomiasis is a major barrier to progress. There is a key tension between the two dominant narratives because an ecosystem of human settlement, cultivation and livestock keeping opposes the wildlife, woodland savannah and tsetse ecosystem that naturally sustain the persistence of trypanosomiasis. Competing ideologies will push for differing policies, which will have a vastly different impact on tsetse, human and livestock populations, thereby affecting disease levels.

Control efforts have ranged across killing wildlife, setting up game fences to control wildlife movements, aerial spraying with insecticides, deploying trap technology and drug treatments targeting animals. This chapter reveals how these control efforts have been, and continue to be, influenced by diverse framings of tsetse and trypanosomiasis. These span very different perspectives: from wildlife and environmental protection, agricultural development, poverty alleviation and veterinary and public health. This chapter unpacks why specific narratives have become dominant in Zambia, the power relations involved between stakeholders and how the past continues to influence the present.

The chapter goes on to argue that while tsetse and trypanosomiasis control would benefit from interdisciplinary and collaborative efforts characterized by a One Health approach, institutional structures and capacity are not set up to work accordingly. Outside a specific, noteworthy disease threat, challenges persist in mobilizing cross-sectoral momentum for endemic diseases; this is especially pronounced when shifting disease dynamics are inherently uncertain and blur the consequences of future scenarios and hence the actions that are needed to address them.

While One Health highlights the need for interdisciplinary thinking about zoonotic disease problems like trypanosomiasis in Zambia, present incarnations of the paradigm appear to offer only scant advice on how to actually address these complex systems, especially when shifting disease ecologies are being primarily driven by larger social, political and economic changes. Without addressing the fundamental structural causes of 'collapsing health ecologies' – which are historically and culturally embedded, and also involve circuits of capital and their influences on environmental change – there are big limitations on how far the rhetoric can go (Wallace et al., 2015). In this sense, the chapter reflects on the challenges involved in a more expansive 'structural One Health' agenda, and its relevance to shifting epidemiological patterns at new human–wildlife interfaces.

The Zambian context: trypanosomiasis as a complex problem

HAT is almost always fatal if untreated, and involves a prolonged recovery if successfully treated. It mainly affects rural communities with poor health infrastructure and can be easily confused with other diseases like malaria and HIV/AIDS. Many cases remain undiagnosed or under-reported and the true disease burden remains unknown (Welburn and Maudlin, 2012). Approximately 400,000 people in Zambia are at moderate risk of infection (Simarro et al., 2012). Risk areas are distributed, but commonly located near national parks or GMAs, notably the Luangwa Valley. The disease is endemic at a low level in north-eastern Zambia, punctuated by occasional epidemics (Anderson et al., 2015). Districts that have reported HAT cases recently are Mpika, Chama, Nyimba and Rufunsa (Mwanakasale and Songolo, 2011).

The focal distribution of trypanosomiasis can have great socio-economic effects. A significant proportion of HAT patients are active adults, often because their work brings them into contact with tsetse. Their illness, need for care and possible death affect their families and livelihoods. AAT causes severe production losses and sometimes death in livestock. The costs of living with trypanosomiasis among pastoralists or small-scale farmers are diverse because of livestock's multiple functions in these livelihood systems. They include milk and meat for household consumption; cash from livestock sales or livestock products; manure; draught power; social values; and trypanocide treatment costs. This affects poverty levels; with livestock production worth over US$1.5 billion in Zambia, approximately 50 per cent of the rural population depend on livestock (Government of Zambia, 2013). This sector has experienced steady growth recently, with beef and dairy products growing 5–7 and 10 per cent per annum, respectively (Government of Zambia, 2013). Significant economic and health gains could be realized through control of production-limiting animal diseases and zoonoses, including trypanosomiasis. A major focus of trypanosomiasis is in Eastern Province, where cattle are the primary food source for tsetse on the plateau, given the low wildlife densities (van den Bossche, 2001).

Wildlife constitute an important trypanosomiasis reservoir in Zambia, with most host species capable of supporting asymptomatic infections due to co-evolution over many centuries (Anderson et al., 2011). Zambia has a vast wildlife estate covering 29.2

per cent of land, comprising 6.4 per cent national parks, 15.6 per cent GMAs and 7.2 per cent forest reserves (Chileshe, 2001). GMAs differ from national parks in that they are zoned for wildlife utilization, mainly commercial safari hunting, and allow human residency. Some have large and expanding populations, accompanied by widespread habitat loss (Lindsey *et al.*, 2014). However, in both zones wildlife is state property, and hunting in GMAs requires expensive licences. The 1998 Wildlife Act fails to recognize communities as the owners of land or wildlife in GMAs, despite some laws in the 1980s introduced to partially decentralize authority to communities (Fernandez *et al.*, 2010). This denial of access to animals used for protein causes negative feelings towards government wildlife policies among residents (Lewis *et al.*, 1990).

There are differing views on how conservation policies have influenced trypanosomiasis risk. Some claim that the creation of national parks led to an increase in wildlife and, consequently, expanded tsetse distribution (Munang'andu *et al.*, 2012). However, as monitoring has been limited there is insufficient evidence. The Luangwa Valley has long had trypanosomiasis and had one of the highest tsetse densities in southern Africa before the creation of game reserves (Kinghorn *et al.*, 1913). Others claim that habitat destruction is exacerbated by shifting agriculture, charcoal production and mining. Wildlife is under immense pressure from poaching and data from aerial censuses indicate that wildlife populations in protected areas are relatively low (Lindsey *et al.*, 2014).

Trypanosomiasis risks are influenced by human settlement patterns and herding practices in relation to this complex wildlife–tsetse relationship. This includes an increasing trend of human migration and resettlement into relatively 'untouched' tsetse-infested lands. Migrations into GMAs, generally with low human population densities and where livelihood strategies have typically not involved cattle-keeping, are considered a concern. Alternatives to livestock-keeping, used successfully in the Luangwa Valley by inhabitants like the Bisa, are now being threatened by 'outsiders' who are introducing cattle. However, some anthropogenic activities could reduce tsetse habitat; when woodland savannah is cleared and land is burned for livelihood activities, habitat loss makes tsetse and wildlife retreat. This transition period, when migration is occurring and land is slowly being cleared, is considered 'risky' as the flies are still prevalent, and opinions on the best course of action are extremely divided. Given the wide host range of species, the Luangwa and Zambezi valley ecosystems are likely to sustain trypanosomiasis for the foreseeable future.

Different narratives, different interests

Stakeholders held very different views on trypanosomiasis, which was found to be at the heart of the different disease narratives circulating in Zambia. The prevailing emphasis of international organizations, the cotton sector, researchers and others focused on animal trypanosomiasis, and so the focus of this chapter, is often on AAT rather than HAT.

The tsetse control and ecology sections of the government, and the cotton industry, in particular focused on the 'poverty narrative', stressing the disease's economic impact. For example, a tsetse control official emphasized that the big focus is that 'areas stay tsetse free'. They believe it is in the economic interests of rural populations to expand areas that can be used for animal rearing. Livestock are critical for their livelihoods; acting as buffers (i.e. cash income) in times of need, ploughs, transportation, manure producers and protein sources. Historically, colonial powers saw tsetse as the bane of development, and policy aimed for eradication (Rogers and Randolph, 1988). The poverty narrative still frames tsetse as a threat to rural livelihoods. As the Tsetse Section, part of the government's Veterinary Department, explained:

> When the fly spreads to these areas, people and their livestock are forced to move out to relatively tsetse-free areas, thereby rendering such areas unproductive. People have to move into marginal, unproductive areas. This means that poverty increases and livestock numbers reduce. This is a vicious circle and poverty will go up if people cannot own livestock ... without them farmers will be poverty-stricken and dependent on the government. They need help and are dependent on food relief. Fertile areas become no-go areas because of trypanosomiasis. If we don't deal with this problem we will depend on donors to feed our citizens.

Sceptics of this approach believe that many tsetse-inhabited areas are unsuitable for productive farming and that immigration, in the end, is a grave threat to the environment. For example, when we interviewed hunters, those from the hunting industry, environmentalists and environmental activists, they maintained a 'protection narrative'. This perspective, also documented in the wider literature (e.g. Rogers and Randolph, 1988), saw tsetse as preserving the natural environment from human intervention: 'Tsetse are keeping the area natural and wild' (interviewee). Trypanosomiasis has prevented arable and livestock farming from being established which, according to this view, has avoided the grave consequences of over-stocking that has been observed in fly-free areas: 'The presence of tsetse ... prevented these mistakes from being more widespread and now provides a window of opportunity for sensible development that acknowledges the uniqueness of African soils and ecosystems' (Rogers and Randolph, 1988). An interviewee stated:

> Tsetse are still the biggest obstacle to wild areas being taken over by farmers and cattle. Tsetse protect the environment and stop farmers encroaching on land so I don't want tsetse control. Farmers move into areas and then hit the tsetse zone and cattle die. This protects the land.

Although contrasting perspectives about tsetse, the environment and economy were dominant themes, there were also two other narratives that emerged from the interviews. In contrast to the poverty narrative, most medical and public health actors were dismissive about HAT. It was seen as a low priority, confined to specific locations, only sporadically occurring in high-risk groups at the fringes of wildlife areas. This represented a 'wider health narrative' that viewed trypano-somiasis within a broader health system landscape with limited resources and other priorities. According to this view, resources should be directed to more prevalent diseases – however, under-reporting may also be influencing this perspective. One interviewee stated: 'The main health problems are HIV and malaria. Trypano-somiasis isn't on the radar. The government do not have the resources to keep areas tsetse-free and we should focus on more prevalent diseases.'

The final identified narrative contrasted with this, stressing the need for 'owner-ship' of tsetse and trypanosomiasis control by the state. Although this perspective shares a similar critique that historically the government was unable to maintain 'tsetse free zones', this was viewed within a broader context of the international aid system. According to this view, control was previously dominated by donors and international agencies fixated on eradication. Due to shifting global priorities, donors largely pulled out in the 1990s, and the government needed to conduct control measures. This represented a 'Zambian narrative', focused on the need for ownership, sustainability and improvements in governance.

In sum, we identified four narratives about tsetse and trypanosomiasis in Zambia, centred on poverty, health, governance and environment (see Figure 9.1

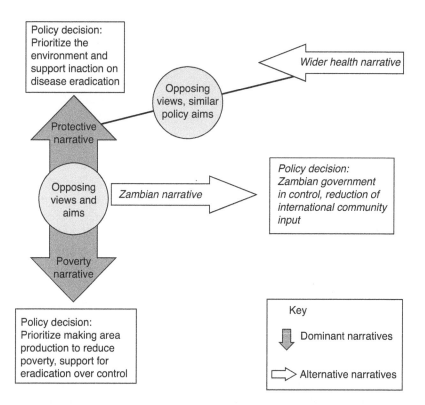

FIGURE 9.1 Schematic diagram of the four identified policy narratives

TABLE 9.1 Summary of the four policy narratives

Narrative	Actors who support this	Summary	Policy they support
Protection	Professional hunting industry, environmentalists and environmental activists	Tsetse protect the environment from anthropogenic change	Prioritize the environment; inaction over disease control
Poverty	Tsetse control and ecology section, livestock sector, NGOs and the cotton industry	Tsetse is a threat to rural livelihoods	Prioritize making areas productive to reduce poverty
Wider health	Medical and public health actors	More prevalent diseases are a priority	Inaction over disease control
Zambian	International community, Zambian activists	Zambian government 'ownership' of policy	Zambian government in control, reduction of international input

and Table 9.1). These differing views on the importance of trypanosomiasis mean there has been, and remains, great controversy about how to control the disease. The next few sections focus on how control techniques are prioritized, funded and deployed and how these are shaped by competing, and often incompatible, views on people, environment, politics and poverty. These depend greatly on stakeholder narratives, especially those in positions of power with influence to direct the agenda, such as decision-makers, lobbyists and industry.

Scourge or saviour? Competing views on controlling tsetse

The history of trypanosomiasis in Zambia, and specific tensions between environmental conservation and tsetse control, goes some way to explaining current divergences in policy and decision-making, as well as showing the grave effects that these decisions can have on people and the environment. Ford (1971) argued that wider development was the answer to the tsetse problem and pre-colonial indigenous systems were effective. He believed colonial authorities overlooked the 'considerable achievements of . . . indigenous peoples in overcoming the obstacle of trypanosomiasis' by adjusting themselves and their domestic animals to enable them to utilize the ecosystem (Ford, 1971, p9). He believed tsetse was not an insurmountable problem, and challenged the assumption that tsetse deprived people of a huge proportion of inhabitable land in Africa.

Control became institutionalized during colonial times, when elimination of wildlife was seen as a favourable policy due to the 'Great Rinderpest Epizootic'. This devastating outbreak reached Zambia in 1892 and contributed to the decline of wildlife and livestock, which drove tsetse down to near-eradication levels in many areas (van den Bossche *et al.*, 2010). Most of eastern Zambia was then made tsetse-free, and cattle-rearing then became viable in the Luangwa Valley towards the end of the nineteenth century (Hall, 1910). From 1897, the first game reserves were introduced by the British to, 'save Africa's game' (Vail, 1977). The first set of regulations were adopted in 1900 and the first game reserve was created in the Luangwa Valley in 1904. However, no development took place and it reverted back to its unprotected state in 1913 (Anderson *et al.*, 2015). This greatly affected poverty levels, as laws preventing hunting and trapping of animals and forbidding the sale of gunpowder to Africans were made at the same time as their cattle had been killed by disease or seized, cutting off livelihood options and causing extreme poverty (Vail, 1977). It was not until 1942, when control of the wildlife estate was passed over to the Department of Game and Tsetse Control, that game reserves were once again created in the valley (Anderson *et al.*, 2015).

However, small tsetse populations survived and spread. Wildlife re-population was quick, resulting in increased tsetse. Higher tsetse density in the Luangwa Valley then drove expansion southward and eastward onto the plateau areas, and resulted in outbreaks (Munang'andu *et al.*, 2012). This historically embedded experience, of complex social and ecological factors, was not considered in official explanations of the time (Vail, 1977). Rather, the government blamed wildlife movements, a policy emphasis that drove the creation of the Department of Game and Tsetse Control in 1942. Their main aim was the elimination of wildlife hosts; public opposition led to its abolition in 1960.

Wildlife groups criticize past control efforts. A major policy of contention has been game fences introduced in the 1950s to limit wildlife movements following the recovery of game and tsetse. One interviewee stated that there were, 'game and cattle fences where ... a hunter [was] stationed every mile to unnecessarily shoot everything that came over the line'. This was counter to emerging scientific knowledge, showing host preferences for tsetse. Some informants expressed anger at 'a failure to use available evidence'. As one stated: 'Shooting all these animals was irrelevant as the tsetse didn't feed on them.' Experiments showed that selective culling failed to control tsetse as the fly changed host. In other words, host preferences are not as strong as early authorities believed (Hargrove, 2003).

To further restrict and regulate interactions between man, animals and fly, colonial authorities implemented a number of other physical barriers, such as fly gates. However, these tended to act more as symbolic representations of authorities' attempts to regulate nature and social order than effective tsetse control methods. As one informant put it: 'Tsetse barriers only have a social function ... but there is no use or point of them for tsetse.... [They] are only there so people can show that they are doing something.' Despite this, fly gates still nominally exist, with one interviewee stating that a guard at a gate said they had only found one tsetse fly this year. Research has shown that technical difficulties, high construction and maintenance expense and the challenges of tsetse reinvasion make it ineffective. This reveals that antecedent approaches die hard in tsetse control.

The advent of new control technologies led to a reappraisal of tactics. By 1968, endosulfan spraying began, followed, in 1970, by odour-baited targets. Together, game fences, aerial spraying, bush burning and use of odour-baited targets aimed to reduce the expansion of tsetse from the Luangwa and Zambezi Valley. These control strategies were confined to communal areas, while in the national parks wildlife and tsetse were left to interact (Munang'andu *et al.*, 2012).

This expanding control toolbox has generated controversies and challenges, as policy actors and practitioners hold different views on their relative effectiveness. The Tsetse Section, coming from a 'poverty narrative', stressed the importance of aerial spraying. As one official stated:

> The best method is aerial spraying – this is very expensive but very effective. Targets work … but they only suppress the fly. When you go for control you go back to where you started from. We need to eradicate the fly.… We really want to start aerial spraying.… We want to do 5000 to 10,000 sq km annually. We just need to get the funding to do this.

Preference for aerial spraying was rationalized through an emphasis on eradication and creating 'tsetse-free zones'. These zones are envisioned as sustainable trypanosomiasis-free areas, where freedom from tsetse will lead to improvements in livestock rearing and farming. These areas require agricultural activities to proceed quickly, preventing reinvasion; as one official stated: 'if an area is eradicated from flies, we must use it to ensure it stays tsetse free'; however, this requires huge financial investments and coordinated technical expertise. The Tsetse Section, for example, has a three-year strategic plan but lacks funding to implement it. Sustainability is a huge issue and one informant warned that 'if you leave any pockets of tsetse, you would experience re-infestation'.

Dealing with tsetse re-invasion was believed to require the continuous, strategic use of insecticide-treated targets. Others emphasized that targets need to be used in conjunction with veterinary drugs, the main rural control method, to have lasting impact. Drugs are highly used and easily accessed, which has contributed to misuse, under-dosage and drug resistance (Chitanga *et al.*, 2011). It is estimated that some 35 million trypanocide doses are administered every year in sub-Saharan Africa (Geerts and Holmes, 1998). Eighteen countries have reported drug resistance and there has been a five-fold increase in resistance over seven years in Eastern Province, but mostly confined to endemic areas (Delespaux *et al.*, 2008). Others emphasized that infected livestock are not well regulated and can bring trypanosomiasis into new areas. In Uganda, uncontrolled cattle movements precipitated a large epidemic in the 1990s (Selby *et al.*, 2013).

However, the overarching preoccupation of current government policy seems to be most concerned with clearing land for settlement coming from the 'poverty narrative'. Government motivation for clearing tsetse is affected by population growth and the need for more areas for settlement, crops and cattle. In terms of the focus of those in power, some interviewees mentioned that the government tends to override environmental policies in favour of promoting economic growth, including large-scale disease control efforts like tsetse control. Examples abound of how disease and poverty are intricately connected with environmental issues and ecosystem services. For example, growing land pressure and human activities in Eastern Province are bringing people, their domestic animals and wildlife into contact. Changes in land use, wildlife abundance and livestock numbers, as well as the use of insecticides, are impacting on tsetse populations. The anthropogenic changes have potential to destabilize trypanosomiasis transmission cycles, resulting in an increase in prevalence and spread to previously unaffected areas.

Environmentalists emphasized the need to preserve local ecosystems. This 'protection narrative' focused on different funding and control options compared to those concerned with eradicating tsetse to bolster economic growth and livelihoods. This highlighted the intrinsic value of preserving biodiversity, including tsetse. People and livestock should be kept away from uninhabited land, which should be protected and left to wildlife. This perspective emphasized that the disease helps to maintain natural vegetation from migration, and that tsetse eradication schemes could have devastating effects on biodiversity and tourism. In fact, viewing tsetse as 'saviours of the African wilderness', these actors stressed that tsetse prevented the effects of deforestation from charcoal burning, poaching, killing of wildlife and other environmentally destructive practices. Some informants clearly had their own financial interests in mind – for example, from hunting and tourism – but this was also the major perspective of environmentalists. In reality, the link between humans, animals and the environment is key, as their welfare is interrelated.

However, there tends to be very little direct management of conservation areas in Zambia, and many commented on the destructive and unsustainable use of natural resources. Commenting on potential efforts to manage land use as a control method, one interviewee commented:

> From the 1970s until now there have been no rules about what people can do in rural areas. People do whatever they like and take land, shoot animals, burn trees and there's no effective system to manage them. This is having grave ecological effects.

In the 1940s, wildlife ownership changed from traditional to state control. Now, in GMAs and national parks wildlife are constitutionally state property, and hunting in GMAs requires expensive licences, restricting traditional hunting. However, legal denial of access to protein resources causes negative sentiments among residents towards government wildlife policies and has not helped poverty (Lewis *et al.*, 1990). Related to this is, as a result of hunting, much wildlife retreat to national parks, contributing to their high tsetse density; low altitude and lots of vegetation cover also contribute to habitat suitability. However, low human population density in the valleys means there are not high levels of competition for natural resources between humans and wildlife, and GMAs can also support high tsetse densities (Munang'andu *et al.*, 2012).

Hence tsetse control officials emphasized that efforts aimed at preserving natural resources through wildlife conservation and biodiversity could serve as a long-term trypansomiasis reservoir. The principal factors that influence tsetse populations are host availability, climate and vegetation (Robinson et al., 2002). Current conservation strategies, such as those aimed at reducing poaching to increase the wildlife population, favour enrichment of the wildlife/woodland savannah/tsetse ecosystems that sustain the persistence of the disease reservoir. This ensures that trypanosomiasis will remain a threat in boundary areas and has been described as one of the three main reasons for endemic sleeping sickness in the Luangwa Valley (Buyst, 1977). Other reasons are a lack of game animals in the northern edge, forcing tsetse to feed on humans, and game movement patterns. Tsetse thrive and increase in the rainy season but starve in the dry season, leading them to accumulate in villages where they depend heavily on livestock, and people, for their blood-meals (Buyst, 1977). This change is important as cattle potentially have a role in maintaining tsetse. They will feed readily from cattle and if cattle densities become high enough there will be no need for wildlife to maintain fly populations.

With complex relationships between humans, animals, ecosystems and vectors, there were clear trade-offs, tensions and ambiguities involved between eradicating tsetse, preserving the natural environment and providing livelihood activities to local people. These different narratives articulate divergent policy pathways, framing the nature of the problem and possible solutions.

Prioritization, funding flows and ownership

Funding issues are viewed differently by the different narratives, which have a major impact on possible interventions. Issues of prioritization, funding and ownership are key. Following current development trends that focus on 'country-ownership' and disease control capacity, international organizations have moved away from funding and coordinating large-scale tsetse eradication to emphasize that the government should have power and responsibility, with nominal international support. All informants stated that currently only the government is trying to clear tsetse.

Interviewees gave varying critiques about the 'transfer' from donor-led to national ownership. Many informants were critical of current activities, revealing that control efforts had largely been 'forgotten' during this transition. As one informant mentioned: 'retired professionals have not been replaced. There is a big human-resource issue [since the donors left]'. In the absence of policy development and the allocation of sufficient resources, this transfer of responsibility was believed to be more a discursive technique aimed at justifying donor-funding withdrawal. As one official stated: 'Projects can keep systems going but when they leave everything stops working. When donor funding runs out and everything is handed to the government it stops functioning.'

Another criticism of government management was that 'they do big schemes ... if they don't work, they just carry on. There is no evaluation' (interviewee).

However, not everyone had such dismissive perspectives about the state. Those who advocated for the importance of moving from a donor-led agenda emphasized the need to look at how donor-led development itself operates according to its own interests. Policies conceived abroad, whether for environmental conservation or tsetse control, were believed to not consider community priorities. For example, one informant mentioned:

> They used the national parks legislation which came at the same time as tsetse control. Both came from outsiders and had colonial influence. Neither is Zambian. Hunters wanted to protect the land and their businesses and this is why the national parks were made. It is useless for outsiders to come in and say, 'Don't use the trees'. Local people know the importance of not depleting their resources and they have the knowledge to protect them and not overuse. Outsiders do not have this knowledge. Zambians need to develop policies and know what is best.

From 1986, donor assistance was directed through the Regional Tsetse and Trypanosomiasis Control Programme (RTTCP). The original objective was to eradicate tsetse from the common fly belt, initially using aerial spraying, and later odour-baited and insecticide-impregnated target technology. Targets were progressively deployed to 'roll back' tsetse. However, economic instability and donor fatigue led to funding shortages. This, combined with a relative lack of success in 'area-wide' control, resulted in a change from widespread eradication towards community-based interventions requiring disease management, including a focus on animal drug treatments, rather than purely on vector control (Robinson *et al.*, 2002). As the project continued, RTTCP adopted a more participatory approach, which had gained currency in tsetse control in the 1990s. However, soon after this was implemented, community activities declined and eventually stopped. Interviewees stressed that finances and interest dried up as donor projects shifted and the state focused on what were perceived to be more pressing health issues. Passing responsibility to the state led to fragmentation and discontinuities, threatening the sustainability of past efforts. As one Tsetse Section officer reflected:

> By 1992 a lot had been achieved [by the RTTCP] but funding ran out and the project was handed over to the government ... which shows the dwindling interest and funding.... The EU pulled out.... We [only] had [government] funding until 2006.... Now we can only do surveillance. We try to target the vector with very little funding, but it's hard ... to undertake sustainable tsetse control under these conditions.... This means that areas where the fly was eradicated have become populated again. We know of better control methods but we can't afford to use them.

This lack of government funding causes frustration, as underdogs in a policy landscape with multiple priorities, vets and tsetse control officials stressed this was a major problem. For example, one official claimed that only 30 per cent of the trypanosomiasis budget was approved in the last financial year, then reduced to only 10 per cent. Contrary to health officials and others who considered trypanosomiasis a low priority, these actors stressed its far-reaching influence on livelihoods and rural economies. It is estimated that many livestock have trypanosomiasis in Zambia. A study conducted in Eastern Province showed that prevalence differed substantially between livestock species. A polymerase chain reaction (PCR) analysis revealed trypanosomiasis prevalence of 33.5 per cent, 6.5 per cent and 3.3 per cent in cattle, pigs and goats, respectively (Simukoko *et al.*, 2007). As human encroachment into high tsetse density areas continues, the importance of livestock, especially cattle, as tsetse hosts will increase.

Despite the donors pulling out, there have been a few other funding options that have emerged recently, such as the Pan African Tsetse and Trypanosomiasis Eradication Campaign (PATTEC) established in 2000. African heads of state agreed to a continent-wide campaign coordinated by the African Union, funded within Africa, and mobilized with local resources. This follows the 'Zambian narrative' as the plan was renegotiated with regional governments to eliminate the vector from the southern tsetse belt: 'Botswana has provided staff, expertise ... Namibia has used [a] specialist airfield for aerial spraying, Zambia and Angola have [given] ... US$8.5 million of funding' (Senior, 2009). Aerial spraying and localized use of insecticides has eradicated the tsetse fly that carries *Trypanosoma brucei gambiense* and *Trypanosoma brucei rhodesiense* from 36,000 km^2 across Botswana, Namibia, Angola and Zambia. However, there seems to be latent politics at play within PATTEC itself. One interviewee attended a PATTEC meeting, which he described as being 'all over the place' regarding control measures. In Zambia and Zimbabwe, PATTEC seems to be concentrating on the use of what is often considered a controversial control modality: the Sterile Insect Technique (SIT) (see Scoones, this book). But Zambia is struggling to fund this – several interviewees commented that there are lots of ideas without any funds attached.

Challenging the perspective that more trypanosomiasis funding is needed were those who prescribed to the 'wider health narrative'. They stated that Zambia has multiple health issues, and that limited government funding should not be focused on a marginally important parasite – although under-reporting of trypanosomiasis makes it difficult to gauge the extent of the burden of human trypanosomiasis (Odiit *et al.*, 2005). Government priorities, they say, should be on prevalent diseases, such as HIV/AIDS and malaria, and increasingly focused on cancer and lifestyle diseases such as diabetes and high blood pressure. Interestingly, these actors also highlighted a donor-driven funding landscape swayed by political trends. It was mentioned that focus

> is not based on research but on the issues important to those in power. For example, when the president's son died of AIDS, it was talked about more and there was lots of donor funding. People are interested in whatever issue donors want to give money for. The donors control what issues are seen as important.

It was also mentioned that if people have a fever they automatically say it is malaria, which is what HAT resembles in its early stages; later the symptoms are similar to AIDS (Odiit *et al.*, 2005). Trypanosomiasis is not publicized or talked about. Some even questioned its existence in humans: 'If you asked urban people they would not know about it.' This may be affecting the belief that trypanosomiasis is unimportant, something of the past, and relegated to colonial times when people were 'backwards'. The disease is neglected because people are ignorant about its effects, and because it hides among the rural population residing 'out in the bush'.

These debates highlight important relationships between government decentralization, funding flows and control activities. Driven by wider trends in governance and development, state funding is now regional and funding decisions decentralized down to the district level. Contrary to a situation where local government can provide support for local disease problems, meagre financial resources are spread too thinly with little impact. As stated by an interviewee of the tsetse control section: 'This makes implementing control programmes difficult as you are at the mercy of regional decision making; it makes it very difficult to make an impact.' A lack of health system capacity means that basic drug kits are absent, even in highly prone areas. Rural clinic staff regularly report shortages of equipment, facilities, training and a poor work culture, while veterinary staff comment on the lack of funds for fuel and transport inhibiting community outreach.

A dominant theme here was a failure of government management within a wider, shifting political landscape that was predominately urban focused. Gould (2010, p137) has argued that state concerns are dominated by urban elite where 'persistent agrarian stagnation might be better understood as an unintended consequence of a structural logic of social exclusion that divides Zambian society with ruthless consistency'. For example, gains from active participation in natural resource management are large but unevenly distributed. Often, the poor do not seem to gain even when they participate actively. More even distribution of gains from GMAs across households near different park systems should be a continuing goal of national policy-makers (Bandyopadhyay and Tembo, 2009).

Various efforts dating back to the end of colonialism have attempted to strengthen local governance, but many have been thin on the ground. For example, from the 1960s, tensions emerged between chiefs and state-supported leaders:

> There was a native autonomy system based on local chiefs, and then when Kaunda came into power he wanted to … replace this with village development committees affiliated to the party. This replaced traditional power structures with political ones but this did not work well.

Kaunda led the fight for independence and was Zambia's major political figure from 1964 to 1991. In 1972, Zambia became a one-party state and Kaunda, the only candidate, became president. Increasing opposition led to the rise of the Movement for Multiparty Democracy (MMD). Kaunda signed a constitutional amendment for a multi-party state and elections were held in 1991. MMD candidate Chiluba won the presidential election. As one interviewee recalled:

> This new multi-party state led to another change in the political structure and there was a proliferation of committees.... However it is always the same people on each committee, and they need to harmonise them in order to make them effective.

In 2001, MMD presidential candidate Mwanawasa won the elections and remained president until his death in 2008. Interviewees described this time as a period of mismanagement:

> In the mid-2000s it was really wild. The Chinese came ... and went everywhere ... exploited the system, lack of controls and oversight. It is really bad. They use chainsaws to mow down entire forests in a week. They get licences ... which are corrupt and no one can stop them.... The forestry department is corrupt.

After Mwanawasa's death, Banda succeeded him. Recently, Sata of the Patriotic Front was elected in 2011, ending 20 years of MMD rule. During this time, many interviewees stressed the lack of adequate local governance of natural resources and disease control more generally as major barriers to effective trypanosomiasis and tsetse control.

These examples, from different points in history, show the ways in which trypanosomiasis control in Zambia links up with both local and global political economy issues. Despite different interests, all groups agreed that control used to be higher on the agenda, better funded and the subject of more programmes. Most felt other countries, especially Zimbabwe, had a better model. Those in international organizations emphasized that should there be a disease outbreak, extra funding is always available. But as each new disease threat emerges, prior threats are forgotten and endemic scenarios are allowed to fester without much attention.

These wider political and governance challenges are important. They reveal a mixed context where management and coordination of rural concerns, of which trypanosomiasis is one, are effectively marginalized due to a wider political economy. Without local political structures to manage programmes and enforce regulations concerning relationships between land, animals and people, there can be little hope of a more long-term and integrated One Health approach.

Structural change: tsetse, poverty and environment

One Health perspectives that transcend vertical disease control programmes advocate for holistic engagement with the complex drivers of disease dynamics, as situated within ecosystem and socio-economic systems. Zoonotic HAT in eastern Zambia is considered by some to have potential to become an 'emerging zoonosis' due to shifting land-use patterns in the Luangwa Valley. Human and livestock migration, according to this view, may drive increased transmission. Alternatively, others propose that increased land use, especially when involving cotton growing, will drive significant tsetse reductions over time that will likely eliminate, or at least control, it. However, the transition period is risky. Uncertainties are maintained, as multiple factors and their interactions are complex or unknown. Resources, planning and long-term strategies are considered key to management, even when the threat is not directly visible. However, due to weak governance and lack of forward thinking, this may prove to be easier said than done.

Informants provided important reflections on future processes, and their interrelated challenges. These come from a wider consideration of the ways in which environment, economy, livelihoods and pathogens are connected, much in the same way as One Health proposes a need for interdisciplinarity and sectors working together. They also stressed the embedded challenges of addressing wider structural changes, many of which had indirect or hidden effects on trypanosomiasis and tsetse.

Central to this were discussions about the influence and effect of changing land-use patterns. For example, clearing forested areas to provide land for cotton growing, sanctioned by the government, can be a control measure in itself as it disrupts the ecosystem needed to provide tsetse habitat. The cotton sector emphasized this:

> There have been changes to the environment. Cotton growing has increased. This means that vegetation that supports the fly ... goes away and is replaced by farmland, this pushes the fly away. There is a link between an increase in farming and fly reduction ... there is less trypanosomiasis now because the flies have gone.

Cotton production is tied to larger socio-economic trends, and is an unstable commodity (Figure 9.2). One informant stated: 'multinational [cotton] companies are powerful.... Farmers are not happy with the prices and their volatility.' Links between land productivity, livelihood and tsetse were also related to an absence of an enabling economic platform for farmer-based innovation to grow and transform the rural economy. The Cotton Association pointed to services that the land could provide to help poverty levels, but blamed industry and the international system for the lack of economic development in the region. These structural processes of exclusion coalesced with placing the blame for a stagnant rural economy on farmers, who were accused of practising 'traditional farming'. This perspective under-appreciates the ways in which power and politics disable agricultural change in rural Zambia (Gould, 2010).

Examples were also given of how disease affects cotton farming, and of the interconnectivity between livestock, farming, health and poverty. As one informant discussed:

> When livestock disease strikes, a lot of farmers lose out and hectares of cotton grown is reduced because farmers do not have cattle to till the land.... If you don't have them then you have to rely on tractors which are expensive and difficult to maintain. If an animal falls sick ... then you get a lower cotton yield and are forced to reduce the hectares you can grow on.

FIGURE 9.2 Cotton harvest in Mambwe district, bordering South Luangwa National
Park (credit: Catherine Grant)

The link with human diseases was also made: 'If the husband is sick then the
woman can't work … as she has to look after him. If the woman gets sick and dies
then you lose the cotton producer' (interviewee). Livelihoods, land, disease and
poverty levels are intimately related, not only for disease but also for efforts to
bolster productivity. A major discussion related to the effect of large-scale cotton
production on tsetse populations, given heavy reliance on insecticides. Like spraying cattle with insecticides, cotton chemicals may be a cause for disease reduction.
Opening up new land and providing a steady cotton-production base could have
long-term effects on maintaining a buffer zone between wildlife and migrant
populations.

The potential role of cotton farming on tsetse highlighted how local practices,
albeit in this instance precariously integrated into the global economy, have differential effects on tsetse. But there are other ways in which people's activities can reduce
tsetse – although some can have hidden consequences. Human encroachment of protected areas in Zambia is worse than in most other African countries: 2500–3000 km^2
of land are deforested annually (Lindsey *et al.*, 2014). Deforestation due to charcoal
extraction, clearing of land for cultivation and livestock, burning for wild honey collection and hunting are contributing to loss of wildlife and tsetse habitat. When trees
are cut down, people plant crops and conduct other livelihood activities, which have
an impact on tsetse, human and livestock populations, affecting disease levels. Every

interviewee stated that the biggest ecosystem issue is deforestation in Zambia, and that there is an increasing need for 'socially sustainable charcoal … and reforestation'. As one official stated, it is a major societal and environmental issue: 'Zambia has one of the highest deforestation rates in the world, driven by charcoal.' As another informant discussed: 'Urban dwellers are driving deforestation, they use charcoal. The end users … benefit but producers make very little profit.' Studies highlight dramatic consequences, including Zambia's 0.3 per cent per annum forest loss. The largely undocumented charcoal and timber trade nevertheless contribute to rural livelihoods and income, providing important sources of income for the rural poor (Gumbo *et al.*, 2013). Furthermore, land-use changes have an impact, including the consequences of new roads and settlements brought about through mining. This shifts landscape dynamics, with long-term consequences.

Bringing people into new areas affects trypanosomiasis incidence. Land encroachment leads to new forms of human–animal–tsetse contact. Wildlife is an ecosystem service, but can also be a disservice. Hunters and those in the wildlife industry pointed out the benefits of wildlife for hunting. However, having shifted in the 1940s from traditional to state control, local people resent their exclusion from official oversight and use. Some tourist industry representatives stated that 'local people believe … they can use them. They believe that no one can own the animals.' These actors, typically maintaining a positive role of tsetse as wildlife regulators in an unregulated policy landscape, advocated for stronger wildlife protection to maintain a competitive image as a wildlife viewing and hunting destination for tourists. As one stated: 'Police often benefit from poaching so they don't prosecute. There's corruption … even though the law provides good punishment it is very seldom applied … there's still lots of poaching and … problems.' However, this criticism of local people as environmental degraders and illicit poachers contrasts with some local knowledge about community environmental practices, as well as negative consequences of wildlife on livelihoods. For example, our participatory research in Mambwe district, bordering South Luangwa National Park, showed that most communities do not actively hunt in the GMAs. Rather, due to competition for space and resources, increasing interactions between people and wildlife have led to greater human–wildlife conflicts, promoting opportunistic hunting. Wildlife crop damage has a negative effect on food and livelihood security due to nutritional supplement shortages and inadequate food reserves. This is exacerbated by ineffective and corrupt agricultural extension services, especially those associated with hybrid maize seed and fertilizer subsidies (Jayne *et al.*, 2002). In a context of limited state services and market access, crop losses from wildlife often lead to negative perceptions, potentially leading to retaliatory killings. Farmers' perceptions are, therefore, a critical socio-dimensional component of human–wildlife conflicts (Nyirenda *et al.*, 2013).

This local-level analysis reveals a different picture of the social and environmental relationships that determine future scenarios for trypanosomiasis. Considering the multitudes of local risk factors, involving local people in disease control was a largely neglected aspect of informants' emphasis, which tended to abstract control away from communities. The complex interplay between policies protecting wild-life and the environment, providing land to secure livelihoods and controlling disease, has led to close contact between wildlife, tsetse and people as part of many socio-economic activities for local people in tsetse-infested areas. These activities predispose individuals to infection. This is an issue not just for hunting and wildlife conservation activities, but also for other activities such as herding, fishing, fire-wood collection, producing charcoal and crop farming (Rutto et al., 2013). These have clear gendered and socio-cultural dimensions that have not been readily acknowledged, or addressed, in much of the policy and expert-driven debates thus far.

Conclusions

Each of the narratives described in this chapter have different perspectives on how environmental, health, poverty and economic issues influence and affect trypano-somiasis incidence and control. These compete in a context where data on inci-dence and impact are uncertain, funding is limited and scientific controversies about the best course of action continue to unfold (see Scoones, this book). Into this 'neglected' field of trypanosomiasis and tsetse, decision-makers are influenced by the fashions of donors, scientific debates and the 'push-and-shove' of different stakeholders, all of which operate within wider political processes. This makes understanding the different perspectives on control decisions and their multiple impacts on disease, poverty and the environment an important step in beginning to think clearly about the relevance, and practicalities, of a more 'joined-up' One Health approach to emerging zoonotic diseases.

Looking at the perspectives of these four narratives, it is clear that increased disease surveillance and burden assessments that account for both animal and human trypanosomiasis together are essential to opening up the debate. There is still under-reporting of trypanosomiasis, and without accurate information on disease burden and impact it is difficult for decision-makers to plan and manage disease control, identify hotspots and drive the prioritization process forward. But the monitoring also needs to shift from a focus on the *disease* to the wider *social-ecological interactions* that surround it. This requires rethinking the foundations of disease surveillance – what are we, in fact, monitoring?

Disease dynamics for animal and human trypanosomiasis in Zambia, and the fragmented policy and control landscape that surrounds it, challenge linear notions of disease causation – trypanosomiasis is historically embedded, shaped by multiple ecological and livelihood contexts and influenced by different interests, values and priorities. While 'bringing together' different stakeholders is certainly important and necessary to acknowledge the ways in which biological transmission is medi-ated by complex human–animal–ecosystem interfaces, normative One Health per-spectives largely overlook the complex structural unsustainabilities and imbalances at play. The socio-ecology of trypanosomiasis, and its control, is influenced, to a considerable degree, by the wider context of interlaced local and global political economies – from cotton growing and urban charcoal markets, to tourism and game hunting, human and animal migratory patterns, local livelihood practices, governance challenges and disciplinary priorities. Left off the radar in current policy debates, and hence much field control effort, have been the very people, in villages, forests and towns, who are most likely to suffer from the disease. So far, local involvement in tsetse and trypanosomiasis has often stopped short of including communities' knowledge in understanding disease dynamics or involving them in policy decisions. This can lead to reductionist understandings of the factors that are actually driving emergent disease dynamics, of the different future possibilities and of the trade-offs between policy decisions (Mwacalimba, 2012).

Hence, to understand the divergent factors that compose trypanosomiasis as a potentially re-emerging 'disease system' in Zambia, there is an important role for understanding, and incorporating, the connections and disconnections between many different biosocial scales. Wallace *et al.* (2015) have challenged us to trace the 'proximate mechanisms of emergence' that drive 'collapsing health ecologies' in places like eastern Zambia, locating the 'deep-time histories', 'cultural infrastructures' and 'circuits of capital' involved, so as to challenge mainstream policy framings about causation. But aside from an interesting research agenda, how can such an approach translate into more effective modalities on the ground for those who are most at risk from both the human and animal disease? This is a difficult question to answer, but seems to hinge on the need for new organizational forms that prioritize diverse expertise and a more holistic understanding of the trypanosomiasis puzzle in local contexts. Hence tracing the proximate 'structural' causes behind trypanosomiasis, as this chapter has done, is certainly the first step. The next, then, is to complement this understanding with a more ethnographic perspective of how global, regional and national political economies intersect in 'bushy places' where the disease is actually circulating.

Note

1 A qualitative case study methodology was used to examine the narratives on trypanosomiasis in the Zambian policy context. A series of 20 key informant interviews were completed in 2013 with officials from international organizations, different government sectors, agrobusinesses, academic researchers and local activists from a variety of perspectives. The chapter was also informed by parallel epidemiological and social research on trypanosomiasis being conducted in and around South Luangwa National Park in Eastern Zambia, see: http://steps-centre.org/wp-content/uploads/Zambia_RU_230913_WEB.pdf, accessed 22 July 2015.

10

LIVING LABORATORIES

The politics of 'doing' brucellosis research in Northern Nigeria

Marie Ducrotoy, Anna Okello, Susan Welburn and Kevin Bardosh

Introduction

> The future for nomadic pastoralism is bleak. If we do not learn how to change, only the big farmers will remain and nomads will be boxed out of their livelihoods and forgotten.
>
> *(Elderly chief, Kachia Grazing Reserve, Nigeria)*

This quote was uttered by a local Fulani chief in 2011 as he described the cycle of political marginalization, ethno-religious crises, climate change and land-use conflict that have come to increasingly threaten pastoralist livelihoods in Northern Nigeria, and indeed across the Sahel.[1] The chief lived on the Kachia Grazing Reserve (KGR) in Kaduna state; the product of concerted state policies aimed at sedentarizing the nomadic Fulani, begun in the 1960s. Fondly referred to as *Ladduga* in Fulfulde, or 'wilderness' in English, the chief's concerns about the KGR community, and of the Fulani in general, were made near the end of a high-profile European–African One Health initiative focused on the neglected zoonotic diseases (NZDs). ICONZ operated in the KGR, as well as six other African country sites, between 2009 and 2014 with the goal of building evidence and fostering policy momentum for the NZDs (Okello *et al.*, 2015).[2] But while the chief concisely summarized many of the challenges faced by the Fulani, his comments also reflected a growing awareness among a group of Nigerian and UK-based researchers (including the authors of this chapter) about the many difficulties of 'doing' One Health research in a remote corner of Northern Nigeria.[3]

A major critique about global health is that so much research is being funded and generated by actors in the Global North about the Global South (Crane, 2013; Geissler, 2013). Like the colonial era, developing countries are, so the accusation runs, becoming mere objects of research, or 'living laboratories' (Tilley, 2011). As

Geissler (2005, p178) noted, the very act of global health research itself reveals a 'hierarchy of power, wealth, education and mobility' that spans from rural villages to the universities and international agencies that increasingly act as knowledge brokers in the global health and development apparatus. Social distance and competing priorities between different actors can generate tensions in these research agendas, the process of data collection itself and the ways in which knowledge is legitimized and used; hence, there is an important politics at play within notions of collaboration and partnership.

As a set of global research projects aimed at understanding health and wellbeing in the context of interrelationships between humans, animals and ecosystems, One Health requires new types of research methodologies (Schelling and Hattendorf, 2015). The issue is not only with generating innovative knowledge tools and techniques to push the boundaries of science, but also with greater reflexivity in how these research approaches intersect with local worlds. The ambitions of One Health as *research* are often difficult to separate from the needs of intervention, and so many projects aim to bridge the knowledge–action–policy divide (Mazet *et al.*, 2009; Goldberg *et al.*, 2012). In this sense, the push for 'holistic health projects' (Mazet *et al.*, 2009) will generate new forms of research ontologies that impact how researchers design their research, engage study sites and communicate with different stakeholders (Dakubo, 2010). Understanding these projects will require moving beyond the normative, to consider issues of researcher positionality, power, histories, community dynamics and locally relevant priorities (Wendland, 2012; Geissler, 2013).

This chapter attempts to do just that. Our research in the KGR centred on brucellosis – a quintessential neglected and endemic zoonotic disease. A bacterial infection caused by several species of the genus *Brucella*, brucellosis causes chronic human morbidity and significant reductions in livestock productivity.[4] Although brucellosis is considered one of the most widespread zoonoses in the world, with an estimated 500,000 cases annually (Pappas *et al.*, 2006), its epidemiology and burden in Africa is poorly documented and likely grossly under-reported in both humans (Dean *et al.*, 2012) and animals (McDermott and Arimi, 2002). Brucellosis is transmitted to humans through the consumption of raw dairy products and contact with bodily fluids (especially aborted material) from infected animals. While the disease has been largely controlled or eradicated in developed countries through concerted veterinary public health campaigns, disease control remains very challenging in the African context (Marcotty *et al.*, 2009). A number of factors are involved, including the nature of husbandry systems, keeping of mixed species, close contact with humans, poor veterinary inputs, limited movement controls and lack of pasteurization.

In this chapter, we reflect on the process of 'doing' a One Health approach to brucellosis in the KGR – a context of resource-limitations, uncertain epidemiology and vulnerable livelihoods. We describe what can be called an 'insider account' of how the policy rhetoric of One Health – of integrating animal and human health research and designing and implementing locally appropriate interventions – becomes increasingly difficult and muddled in socio-economically marginalized contexts. This allows us to explore a number of interrelated themes in how researcher–community relationships, interests and expectations are steeped in power dynamics, cultural perspectives and politics, and how these influence the One Health research process. We argue that greater attention to the social context of knowledge production is an essential path forward in better linking One Health research to scientific rigor, community concerns and policy relevance.

ICONZ: a big project with big goals

ICONZ was a five-year collaborative research project funded by the European Union's FP7.[5] This ambitious project was the long-awaited fruit of lobbying by a group of scientists, seen in a series of international meetings, to raise the profile of endemic zoonotic diseases within the global health agenda, which involved the European Union (EU) Parliament, international agencies (World Health Organization (WHO), World Animal Health Organisation (OIE), Food and Agriculture Organization (FAO) and others. As with policy rhetoric for the neglected tropical diseases (NTDs), attention and funding for the NZDs were considered to be 'overshadowed' by the 'Big Three' (namely HIV/AIDS, TB and malaria) and emerging zoonoses such as highly pathogenic avian influenza (Maudlin *et al.*, 2009). While several scientific groups were celebrating the improved political attention and funding towards the NTDs, the NZDs remained the 'poorer cousins' of the neglected diseases. There were multiple reasons for this, but they were largely considered in researchers circles to be the result of patchy evidence regarding their true societal burden, as well as an under-appreciation of the feasibility of control, both of which resulted in cycles of underfunding and neglect.

ICONZ stepped into this political landscape, and attracted significant attention. The project aimed to improve both human health and animal production in seven case-study sites across Africa: in Morocco, Mali, Mozambique, Uganda, Tanzania, Zambia and Nigeria. This was to be done through a series of 'integrated' interventions in animals against a suite of NZDs. Marketing itself as a protagonist of One Health, the project soon gained wide recognition in international One Health and zoonoses circles via its unique 'selling points' around interdisciplinarity and integrated approaches, undertaken by an impressive consortium of 21 European and African partner organizations and leading scientific experts (see Okello *et al.*, 2015). A major focus was on offering a holistic analysis of the societal costs of zoonotic disease and the cost-effectiveness of animal-based interventions – partners developed various methodologically rigorous frameworks to help individual field researchers, who tended to be PhD students interested in One Health, to do this (see Figure 10.1). Aside from capacity building, the focus was on generating a cohort of evidence, across countries and diseases, that would convince donors and policy-makers that NZDs should be prioritized – there was, so to speak, a need to 'remove the N from the NZDs'.[6]

ICONZ was big in vision, big in ambition and big in size. Despite the philosophy being very clear and appealing, the reality of implementing the approach was

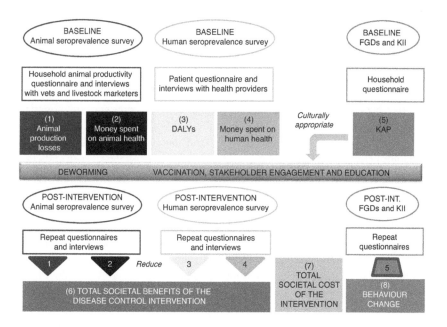

FIGURE 10.1 The conceptual framework for the Nigerian case study (adapted from original figure by Alexandra Shaw)

far less straightforward. Indeed, it was never exactly clear how the various interacting domains and tasks were to be integrated. This included 12 different 'work packages' on areas such as policy, culture, economics, diagnostics, epidemiology and communication that were to be managed, albeit somewhat ambiguously, across the seven different case-study countries. There were different 'leaders' – leaders of the project coordinating team, leaders of the case studies, leaders of each of the four disease clusters and leaders of a number of 'cross-cutting' work packages. The management challenges of such a large project are certainly not unique to ICONZ. One Health projects – by their very definition – will all face rather unique organizational challenges due to their broad objectives and the often differing priorities and mandates of different disciplines and partners (see Cummings and Kiesler, 2005). Managing these differences across spatial and cultural spaces – between Europe and Africa – also presents unique challenges that need to be negotiated. The remainder of this chapter highlights some of these broader issues by reflecting on the activities of the Nigerian ICONZ case study.

Diagnostic dilemmas: untangling brucellosis in Nigeria

The original ICONZ vision encouraged case studies to embrace the disease 'cluster' approach.[7] This emphasized the added value of integrating research and control activities for multiple diseases in a single study site. The Nigerian case study, as with others in Morocco, Mali and Mozambique, was to focus on three major bacterial zoonoses: anthrax, bovine tuberculosis (BTB) and brucellosis. The integration mantra has become fairly common rhetoric in the One Health movement, one that has been especially promoted for the control of BTB and brucellosis due to their fairly similar risk factors and the potential to integrate brucellosis vaccination with test and slaughter strategies for BTB (Maudlin *et al.*, 2009). The effort to integrate these three NZDs, however, was largely abandoned in the context of the Nigerian case study, where activities overwhelmingly focused only on brucellosis.[8]

The reasons for this were three-pronged, and involved a significant degree of negotiation between different research partners in the UK, Nigeria, Spain and elsewhere. First, although anthrax is endemic to Nigeria, it only occurs in isolated outbreaks, which does not lend itself easily to the type of survey design needed to investigate either BTB or brucellosis. The second reason involved the challenges of BTB control – a disease that has been largely eliminated from developed countries, although wildlife reservoirs, like badgers in the UK, have proved rather difficult and controversial to control (Cassidy, 2012). In the African context, the test-and-slaughter regiments that have become the mainstay of traditional BTB efforts have been deemed unacceptable – there is a lack of resources for farmer compensation and a history of state suspicion around culling livestock, especially with pastoralist communities. This was deemed too challenging to implement in the KGR. The third reason had more to do with the group of researchers involved. The Nigerian case-study team, including Nigerian and European partners, had a specific and long-standing expertise and confidence in brucellosis that did not readily extend to either BTB or anthrax.[9]

Whether brucellosis was, or was not, a high-priority disease in the pastoralist system of Northern Nigeria was something that was not widely debated at the time when ICONZ was selecting an appropriate study location, despite a lack of appropriate data in the wider region. The Nigerian partners, with a sound publication record on brucellosis in Nigeria, took the lead in defining appropriate study sites.[10] The decision to select the KGR[11] (Figure 10.2) was supported by a prior pilot serological study done by the Nigerian team, which demonstrated a high individual brucellosis prevalence of 8 per cent in cattle owned by 'settled agro-pastoralist'.[12]

Despite selecting the study site, it took a further two years before field teams were mobilized to undertake the baseline seroprevalence and socio-economic surveys. These were, according to the ICONZ vision, fundamental to the design, piloting and evaluation of the disease control intervention that would fulfil the bulk of the required project deliverables. Such delays in case study activities were a common theme in ICONZ, and one of the major perceived challenges to achieving its broad and ambitious goals. Many of the partners, including the Europeans and Nigerians involved in the KGR research, had not previously worked together, and it took time for personal relationships to develop. The management structure also required that research protocols had to be assessed and agreed by a panel of experts from a range of disciplines. The work was largely to be carried out by PhD students, and training issues arose. This all led to lengthy delays that were nevertheless considered a 'necessary evil' in

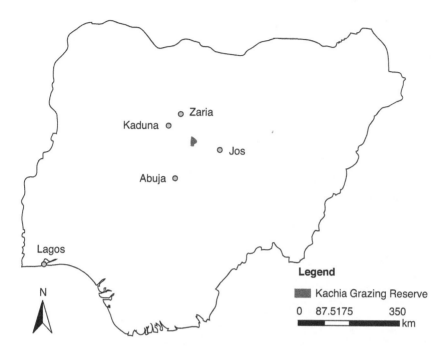

FIGURE 10.2 Location of the Kachia Grazing Reserve, Nigeria (credit: Ward Bryssinckx)

the quest to achieve interdisciplinarity and build research capacity. In short, the complex organization of ICONZ meant that it took time for the project to 'get off the ground'.

After deliberation, fieldwork commenced in March 2011 (Figure 10.3), and all baseline blood and questionnaire surveys, covering cattle, sheep, goats and humans, were completed by October 2011.[13] Of the range of brucellosis diagnostic tests available, the Rose Bengal Test (RBT), a serological test detecting antibodies to *Brucella*, was chosen, given its simplicity and alleged familiarity by the field team.[14] However, instead of providing a clear epidemiological picture from which to build an intervention and to propel brucellosis into the policy limelight, the outcomes of field screening were perplexing and unexpected; brucellosis individual prevalence in cattle was found to be low and negligible in small ruminants.[15] Even more surprising, despite our survey data showing that the Fulani engaged in widespread 'risky behaviour' such as preparing and consuming raw dairy products, assisting in animal births and slaughtering animals at home, there were no confirmed cases of human brucellosis. Running parallel to ICONZ, the Nigerian Health System (government) organized screening of over 1000 people – approximately 20 per cent of the resident KGR population and a statistically significant proportion – and did not find a single case. These results were in direct contradiction with the previous pilot survey that served as the justification for selecting the KGR as a high-priority brucellosis area. But more importantly, they were also in direct disagreement with a

FIGURE 10.3 Team members taking part in the first blood sampling survey in the KGR, 2011 (credit: Marie Ducrotoy)

widely held scientific discourse that motivated the Nigerian and European partners: that poor pastoralists bear a high burden of brucellosis because of their herding practices and socio-cultural traditions.

A number of steps had to be taken to verify these unexpected findings. Questions were raised about the possibility of having missed positive cases due to the sub-optimal field conditions.[16] The first step was to rescreen all blood sera, stored at the Nigerian research station, under laboratory conditions. This was no small task given the approximate 10,000 samples collected from humans, cattle, goats and sheep. Government strikes, in the volatile Nigerian public sector, meant that it took longer than expected for the research lab to re-run these tests. But once the results of a subset were analysed, researchers were no closer to solving the 'brucellosis puzzle' – the cattle herd prevalence had jumped to almost 100 per cent, and the individual human prevalence was also high at 7 per cent. To the Nigerian institute, this sudden prevalence increase was due to the large number of false negatives obtained during the sub-optimal field conditions that produced the initial low figures. From the perspective of the research–policy nexus, this high prevalence maintained an overarching narrative about the heavy burden of brucellosis in Fulani populations; ICONZ partners were primed and ready to commence a brucellosis vaccination intervention.

But the disparity between the two sets of results rang alarm bells with the ICONZ brucellosis diagnostics experts, and a blind serological experiment was done to clarify the confusion; the Nigerians would rescreen the sera with RBT and send all positive samples – plus a random selection of negatives – to a Spanish brucellosis laboratory for parallel testing (a costly exercise given import permits and cold-chain requirements for travel). In the end, the samples sent to Spain were in line, for the most part, with those obtained during the 2011 fieldwork. Researchers considered different options for this. One likely reason involved the out-of-date RBT antigen used at the Nigerian institute and a 3:1 serum to antigen protocol (which has never been validated for use in cattle or humans, only small ruminants) used for the in-country laboratory processing.[17] There may have also been an overconfident assumption that the Nigerian *Brucella* team was familiar with RBT protocols, highlighting the importance of training lab staff more carefully.[18]

The bottom line for the ICONZ Nigeria case study was that vaccination could not go ahead, given the low prevalence of animal brucellosis – and more importantly – almost no human cases that would benefit from an animal-based intervention. Moreover, in the absence of human disease and the lack of statistically significant differences in productivity between infected and non-infected herds, it was not possible to calculate the societal burden of brucellosis, nor demonstrate the cost-effectiveness of an intervention. In the absence of a sound economic argument, the Nigeria case study could not provide policy advocacy for bacterial zoonoses, as originally intended by ICONZ.

But this muddled epidemiological experience – mediated by the available diagnostic tests and training of the Nigerian partners – nonetheless questioned some important aspects of the received wisdom on brucellosis in Nigeria. This drove new lines of inquiry, as the ICONZ partners began to wonder about the broader evidence-base on brucellosis in Nigeria and where future researchers should prioritize their quest for *Brucella*. An analysis of the available literature was undertaken in an attempt to contextualize the KGR findings (see Ducrotoy *et al.*, 2014). Despite a relatively large body of published literature on the subject in Nigeria (127 papers were reviewed), only one study (looking at seroprevalence in cattle) was based on probability sampling methods and would have passed stringent scientific criteria for inclusion. In this sense, untangling the evidence available on brucellosis, a lot of which was contradictory and outdated, was almost as difficult a task as understanding the diagnostic issues in the KGR. An interesting political dimension regarding the interpretation of brucellosis knowledge and evidence quickly began to unfold.

Stigmatizing nomads: the Fulani and the Nigerian state

It became apparent that scientific reasoning about brucellosis in the KGR, and in Nigeria more generally, was being clouded by political bias about the 'backwards' Fulani. In this sense, prevailing scientific discourses were embroiled in a 'geography of blame' (Briggs and Mantini-Briggs, 2003) that implicated pastoralism and Fulani culture as a main 'reservoir' for *Brucella* infection and a 'driver' to settled farmers and commercial farms. Mobility, cultural norms and poverty were implicated as vectors for spread. However, the evidence from the KGR appeared to suggest the opposite: that the pastoralist system had little brucellosis. Understanding the discourse requires appreciating this complex political history.

The pre-colonial era in Northern Nigeria was dominated by an extensive and nomadic pastoral system, where livestock production was central to the regional economy. With the coming of the Islamic Sokoto Caliphate in the 1800s, the Fulani ruled the largest state south of the Sahara until the arrival of the British in the early 1900s (Falola and Heaton, 2008). Land was then nationalized, rather than awarded under prevailing Islamic inheritance laws. These new land laws clearly favoured farmer rights in the sub-humid zone; having not been well integrated into the burgeoning colonial education and civil service system, the illiterate Fulani were mostly left out of the new state-building project. This was a major blow, as Fulani lost their land rights and political prestige, which continues to be at the centre of current inter-ethnic conflicts that plague Northern Nigeria today.

Despite a lack of confirmation, the circulation of *Brucella* among Fulani herds was alluded to by early British colonial researchers (Banerjee and Bhatty, 1970). British rule saw the establishment of government livestock improvement centres and ranches, which continued into independence. These policies were implemented to support colonial commercial dairy and beef herds and were matched by an investment in veterinary field and research centres, where crossbreeding with exotic bulls and artificial insemination was carried out (David-West, 1978). It is, therefore, not surprising that a peak of brucellosis research and scholarly publications (almost exclusively conducted in government-owned herds) was from this time. Brucellosis outbreaks were reported regularly from government livestock farms, where disease was reported 'to have become hyperendemic on account of close domestication and overcrowding' brought about by new 'scientific' and 'modern farming', especially revealed in the devastating occurrence of brucellosis 'abortion storms' (Banerjee and Bhatty, 1970, Esuruoso, 1974).

However, the spread of brucellosis at the time was not linked to intensification, but rather blamed on the unruly nomadic Fulani, whose herding of animals was described as being 'largely traditional and unscientific' (Alausa, 1980). The Fulani have long been known as the major cattle-keepers of West Africa – the common estimate is that 90 per cent of all cattle in Nigeria are from Fulani herds. Despite limited evidence, researchers maintained that Fulani migratory habits were the root cause of the brucellosis problem in Nigeria, resulting in disease control narratives heavily focused around restricting pastoralist migration (Rikin, 1988).[19] Increasingly, a number of contemporary studies continue to support the notion that Fulani suffer from a high burden of brucellosis compared to the intensive farm system, although issues in study design, location and the degree of nomadism of these study groups are the most likely explanation for this disparity (e.g. Mai *et al.*, 2012; Maurice *et al.*, 2013).[20]

During our time on the KGR and in interviews with policy-makers and others in Nigeria, we found that narratives about brucellosis and Fulani migrations were hard to separate from wider cultural perceptions and political conflicts around land (Okello *et al.*, 2015). Unlike farmers, the Fulani still have little or no formal land rights, or rights of inheritance, to pasture, water or cattle tracks in the country, where access depends on their relationship with the local *indigene* community (Stenning, 1957). In the middle-belt region of the north, populations from minority Christian tribes – the '*indigene*' – have claimed supremacy over land rights since independence in 1960, and in many cases prevent Hausa and Fulani from owning land or businesses (IDMC, 2009). Discrimination runs deep; land rights of settled Fulani (not to mention the many who maintain year-round or semi-nomadic livelihoods) are not considered to be as legitimate, so Fulani are forced to move out if land becomes scarce (Oxby, 1984). It is no secret that the indigenes are politically backed by the predominantly Christian 'power-house' of Southern Nigeria, further frustrating Fulani and Hausa.

At the same time, grazing zones and transhumance routes have become increasingly encroached by farmland, leading to conflict, especially when migrating herds destroy crops. Fulani communities have to contend with shifting climatic conditions that are driving desertification, decreasing access to water and pasture and food insecurity in the Sahel region (Blench, 1996). Previous interdependences that facilitated more symbiotic farmer–pastoralist relationships have been eroded. Artificial fertilizers and new livestock markets have marked the end of an era when a farmer wanted Fulani cattle on his land. Religious and political leaders have exploited these pressures to their advantage by driving people to vent their frustrations through acts of violence, religious extremism and increasing terrorism (IRIN, 2009a).

One solution promoted by policy-makers has been grazing reserves, like the KGR. Following the British, successive Nigerian governments have made minimal attempts to preserve transhumance corridors (known as the *burtali* system). Rather, the focus has been on getting the Fulani to stop moving around, through promoting a series of sedentarization policies during the 1960s and 1970s. In total, 415 grazing reserves have officially been established throughout Nigeria, although only one-third of these are currently in use (IRIN, 2009b). A number of policy justifications support this, including that reserves prevent farmer–pastoralist conflict, increase access to social services and help control livestock diseases (Oxby, 1984). The success of the reserves, however, has been poor at best, achieving little to resolve farmer–Fulani conflict (Oxby, 1984; Blench, 1996). Social services, so important to incentivize the Fulani to take-up residence, have been erratic and inadequate. The number of grazing reserves is also vastly insufficient to meet the needs of the 15 million or so pastoralists in Northern Nigeria (IRIN, 2010).

In this sense, it became all too apparent that the prevailing scientific discourse about the Fulani being 'vectors' for brucellosis was driven more by politics and history than epidemiological fact. Our research on the KGR suggested the opposite: that the government's drive to stop the Fulani from migrating might paradoxically be facilitating brucellosis transmission on grazing reserves and in the intensive and agro-pastoralist systems. This raised important and complex questions about the trade-offs in pushing sedentarization policies, not only in relation to zoonotic disease, but also on the wider context of Fulani livelihoods and wellbeing.

Why the KGR? Choosing a study location

In as much as brucellosis being selected as a 'priority disease' was dependent on prevailing researcher and state perceptions and interests, so too was the selection of the KGR as a study site. The KGR was chosen by our Nigerian partners, in part at least, because it was 'where you go' in Northern Nigeria to study the Fulani. Since opening in 1967, the KGR has attracted significant political attention and development funds, including a series of World Bank-funded livestock, crop and infrastructure projects implemented by the International Livestock Centre for Africa (ILCA) (von Kaufmann, 1986). This was presented as immensely positive by our Nigerian collaborators: the KGR was 'sensitized' to being on the receiving end of global research and development. A common phrase from our partners was that: 'they are used to seeing Westerners, so they will not be suspicious. They will certainly cooperate with us.'

The KGR was also a 'known place' to Nigerian policy-makers, having been one of the first gazetted grazing reserves in Nigeria. This gave it significance to our research partners, who were affiliated to one of the leading government-funded research institutes in Nigeria, focused on producing livestock vaccines and controlling economically important animal diseases. The only prior interactions between this institute and the KGR had been in the sporadic delivery of vaccines. Their prior brucellosis research had been done in the intensive commercial sector, as is the accepted norm. The mandate of ICONZ, however, was to improve the livelihoods of poor livestock-keepers.

In our early meetings, it was emphasized that the KGR community were 'sedentary agro-pastoralists' who had long abandoned their nomadic habits – the KGR was described as a 'closed system'. This made them amenable to a vaccination intervention, which would have been much more difficult in truly nomadic or transhumant populations. As we later found out, however, the social and livelihood system on the KGR was far more complex (Majekodunmi *et al.*, 2014; Okello *et al.*, 2014b). The Nigerian researchers were very much motivated by the desire to pilot a vaccination campaign using the S19 brucellosis vaccine administered via the conjunctival route (as opposed to the licensed subcutaneous route), which had never been trialled before in Nigeria and was a potential avenue for policy development.[21] The KGR was also deemed a 'safe place' to work, given that the KGR does not suffer cyclical bouts of Fulani–*indigene* conflict. Despite our field research team having two Fulani Muslim members, it was almost entirely composed of Christians from other southern ethnic groups. There were clear concerns about safety for both the European and Nigerian team members. For these reasons, the Nigerian partners 'sold' KGR as a site suited to the ICONZ vision of rolling out a vaccination intervention.

From suspicion, to trust, to disappointment

The socio-political context of the Fulani also shaped our own research in a number of complex ways, especially in terms of our relationships with the KGR community.

As with other biomedical research projects in Africa, issues of community access, compliance and engagement quickly become politicized (Geissler, 2005; Fairhead *et al.*, 2006). Attempts to impose standardized sampling protocols on pastoralists, collect blood, map out risk factors and understand the hierarchical social system of the KGR were fraught with power and politics. This required adapting to local forms of gate-keeping, and learning how to mediate between the worlds of science and development.

The Nigerian partners first visited the KGR in 2009 and held meetings with the District Head and *Ardo'en* (village leaders) outlining the project and our plans. Three of the European researchers, including a brucellosis expert, also visited the KGR in December 2010, informing community leaders of the purpose and design of the research and seeking their consent. Things went smoothly, and the expectation was that a livestock *Brucella* cross-sectional prevalence survey ($n = 88$ households) could be quickly organized and completed in four weeks in March 2011. But a number of issues prevented adherence to the original cluster sampling protocol.

The overarching problem was an intense level of community suspicion and poor cooperation of the KGR community with our work, at least during the initial stages. It became quickly apparent that the prior community 'sensitization' had had little impact. For example, contrary to original claims, the KGR was not a 'closed system' at all – as we began the survey in March 2011, we slowly realized that approximately 50 per cent of the resident cattle population was on dry-season trans-humance, leaving a biased sub-sample of females, calves and the herds of 'elite' KGR leaders with priority over dry grazing lands. As we attempted to follow our sampling protocol, other issues emerged. There was an inability to match household head names listed on a 'comprehensive' (so we were told) census done in 2010 by the KGR project office, staffed by one member of the State Ministry of Agriculture without a work vehicle. We had aimed to randomly select households from this census with the aim of achieving probability sampling. But the lack of financial and human resources together with the perpetually strained state–pastoralist relationship (not helped by unkept promises around water, roads and schools from the state) called into question the accuracy of the census.

Three other issues emerged with our sampling strategy. The first had to do with our original aim to geo-reference households to identify spatial patterns of brucellosis and human demographics. The KGR community was familiar with GPS through previous use by the state KGR office, and was concerned that the research team was posing as spies, tracking livestock migration routes. This was especially inflamed by fluctuating population dynamics and land ownership patterns inside the KGR itself, which we observed during our fieldwork. The population of the KGR, for example, increased by over 30 per cent during our research in 2011, as it became a safe haven to some 3000 Fulani pastoralists fleeing post-election violence in the north – at least 800 people were killed and 65,000 displaced in the region.[22] The Nigerian Red Cross had to set up temporary classrooms, and distributed food, blankets and other supplies (Figure 10.4). But this was not the first time conflict had

FIGURE 10.4 Temporary housing erected by refugees during the mass KGR influx of May–June 2011 as a result of post-election violence (credit: Marie Ducrotoy)

increased the population of the KGR. Each cycle of conflict and migration into the KGR, however, had generated tensions within the local political hierarchy. Although the KGR project office was technically responsible, existing village leaders, influenced by clan affiliations, negotiated new land arrangements with the migrants. In such a context, geo-referencing was a difficult proposition, and had to be quickly abandoned.

Overall, there was an extreme reluctance from community leaders to mobilize the wider KGR community for our research.[23] Two issues, also related to our study design, were especially inflammatory, the first of which culminated to crisis point whereby the field team was asked to leave the KGR by the District Head. This was the undertaking, not long after our attempt to use geo-referencing, of focus group discussions with women groups, which challenged the patriarchal order (Okello *et al.*, 2014c). KGR leaders could not understand why the views of the women were required to discuss livestock issues, given this was clearly a male domain. The role of women in transferring knowledge to communities and in preventing zoonotic diseases – particularly food-borne infections like brucellosis and BTB – is, of course, fundamental.

Working through the ten village heads on the KGR, we also met stiff resistance in our attempt to follow random sampling; the district head insisted on preferential sampling herds only from elites. This was likely due to a misconception of what blood sampling would involve, and the assumption that money and free drugs would be given. A culture of 'incentivized participation' had clearly been encouraged in previous NGO projects; leaders had gained other benefits such as boreholes and preferential access to inputs. This was not helped by the promises, relayed by our Nigerian partners, of an impending but 'small-scale' vaccination intervention.

The lack of community sensitization, coupled with the early failure to employ social science research, resulted in the loss of valuable time and funds, and damaging first impressions. This is not to say that the whole experience was not valuable. In fact, it proved to be an important turning point in the ICONZ project, moving past a rhetorical acceptance of social science research. Part of the problem was that social research was planned in parallel to the epidemiological surveys, which were pre-designed. If time had been taken to better understand the 'living laboratory' of the KGR beforehand through a more participatory approach (see Catley *et al.*, 2012), we would have discovered not only that the Fulani of the KGR are not as 'sedentary' as the Nigerian government would have us believe, but also that they were in fact well aware of key aspects of brucellosis (known as *Bakale* in Fulfulde), and considered it to be a low-priority disease.[24]

In the end, the need to maintain probability sampling and to account for livestock away on transhumance required that ICONZ repeat the baseline study in June 2011. This allowed researchers to learn from their mistakes, build relationships and address community suspicions. A number of specific events and people helped. The first was a series of formal and informal meetings with the *Ardo'en* and other leaders. For example, we spent considerable time trying to explain the importance of 'random sampling'. Conceptually, this involved using a bag of stones of different sizes to illustrate the point.[25] However, we also had the issue of 'incentives' to address. During our original March survey, many Fulani did not allow all their livestock to be sampled – due to the length of time it took and concerns about the health of their animals after taking blood. In order to increase compliance to allow for all livestock in a herd to be sampled, we decided to provide cattle anthelmintics.

In order to make sure that this sampling would be random and not only involve the family and friends of the *Ardo'en*, we organized a large community workshop for over 200 people. We provided a very modest amount of money to several 'well connected' male elders to provide refreshments, a marquis and chairs, but the men disappeared with the money.[26] Second, despite our insistence that the meeting should be a good cross-section of genders, age groups and socio-economic groups from the KGR, only elite male community leaders showed up (Figure 10.5).

Despite our efforts, the top-down Fulani social system proved hard to circumvent (e.g. Riesman, 1977), as leaders continued to restrict information to the broader community. It also reflected the more 'traditional' structure of the remote KGR in comparison to other Fulani communities in Nigeria; for example, in neighbouring Plateau State where the ICONZ team operated a related research project on trypanosomiasis and tick-borne diseases, we found Fulani communities much more interested in research and less suspicious of outsiders (Majekodunmi *et al.*, 2014).[27] This questioned the commonly assumed narrative that 'working through' community

FIGURE 10.5 KGR community leaders and elites attending a sensitization workshop in 2011 (credit: Marie Ducrotoy)

leaders in global health offers a panacea for engaging what are clearly very heterogeneous local communities. As one KGR leader commented: 'We have leaders, and we must always obey and respect them; if you go through our leaders people will follow; there is no other way.'

Ultimately, however, the continuation of our work in the KGR was salvaged through a few respected community members, who took to spreading information about the project without any specific financial incentive. This included the local private medical doctor and the head of the dairy cooperative. Their commonsense suggestion to have community meetings with the Imams of the KGR proved invaluable. But over time, we also learned that our local (paid) facilitator had generated much of the initial community suspicions, due to his own misgivings about our sampling strategy. His young age (late twenties) also placed him in direct conflict with the authority of the KGR elders. Through being aligned with the project, his status increased overtime, which in turn increased his ability to influence and convince householders to cooperate with the research. Because of these factors, community compliance with subsequent activities improved. By our repeat June survey, the notion of 'random sampling' had become accepted, with people even using it in their daily conversations. During the human sampling survey of October 2011, 1000 randomly selected participants willingly gave blood while knowing that nothing was going to be given in return.[28]

Despite this, the movement from suspicion to trust was eventually broken by a sense of disappointment. As the results from the lengthy laboratory analysis (described earlier) became known, the ICONZ project explored ways to disseminate and discuss these with the wider KGR community, and design a different type of intervention to address some of the other systemic human and livestock diseases on the KGR. However, a series of devastating bombings in 2012 in neighbouring Jos ensured that the European researchers could not travel back to Nigeria – rumours continued to circulate about the terrorist organization Boko Haram taking up residence in the KGR into 2014. A booklet was prepared, translated and disseminated through local facilitators in the KGR, summarizing the major research findings and key facts, treatments and management methods for relevant livestock diseases. However, the intensifying conflict situation in Northern Nigeria meant that all activities stopped rather abruptly in 2012, as even the Nigerian partners stopped all 'non-essential' travel to the area.

Conclusions

The ICONZ case study in the KGR illustrates the complexities of operationalizing One Health in a development context; it is an evolving process, moulded by politics, history, trust, funding, actor-networks and differing stakeholder priorities. These factors define the problem and the process in many ways. In Nigeria, the decision to work on brucellosis in the KGR was largely pre-determined by the political and professional interests of the research team, re-packaged as scientific argument and supported by a donor project with pre-contracted deliverables. The project focused on bacterial zoonoses, which were not found to be widely prevalent on the KGR, nor considered a community priority. A key message was that it is not practicable to jointly screen and intervene for BTB and brucellosis in pastoralist systems. While brucellosis did appear to be a politically important disease for Nigerian policy-makers, its examination in a remote pastoralist setting was always going to generate uncertain political interest from federal policy-makers (see Okello *et al.*, 2014c). Hence the ultimate goal of ICONZ – to generate evidence of burden and of intervention in order to bridge the research–policy nexus – was always going to be difficult.

The context of division, flux, secrecy, suspicion and tradition that pervaded the KGR created more than a simple 'barrier' to scientific knowledge production (Biruk, 2012); it redefined the terms by which the KGR could be used as a 'living laboratory' (Tilley, 2011). The assumption that ICONZ could map, sample, cost and capture the brucellosis situation using a cross-sectional survey in what had been conceptualized as the 'closed system' of the KGR was turned on its head. The priorities that guided ICONZ – to generate objective and generalizable data in order to inform global and national health advocacy for the NZDs in Africa – invariably underwent a process of translation by the perceptions and interests of both the Nigerian research team and different social actors in the KGR. As a 'flagship' One Health project, it was nonetheless not enough to 'sell' the project to the Fulani, or to the Nigerian researchers for that matter, in the same way as the project was 'sold' to the EU or to other global health actors. Researchers, then, had to scramble to negotiate both science and the social relationships that were essential to co-creating it, shifting boundaries to a more viable research process that would maintain access to the KGR and achieve some of the pre-determined ICONZ project objectives.

The end result was a valuable lesson in 'doing' One Health; despite the attempts at trans-disciplinarity, biomedical research programmes all too often appear to 'tack-on' social research as an afterthought, rather than identifying when and where it is most appropriate (Bardosh, 2014). Indeed, there appeared to be a reticence from both the Nigerian and European epidemiologists to incorporate social science into the plans from the outset. This justified the application of standardized research methodologies for humans and livestock, and the 'hunt' for brucellosis. But the 'system' under study quickly became much more complex, and in flux, than originally assumed. Employing a more participatory approach from the start would have gone a long way in redefining the research agenda and facilitating more appropriate local access and relevance (Catley *et al.*, 2012).

The overall philosophy of One Health is to implement a systems-based approach that is invariably influenced by extrinsic factors; these must be identified and understood through a suite of complementary disciplines and methodologies. There is a need to look beyond individual infections to the bigger picture of social inequality and the unjust exercise of power that sustains it. At a broader political level, the disconnect between what the Fulani want and what the Nigerian government *assumes* they want poses interesting questions around motivators for change and the broader political conduits and barriers to moving forwards with One Health interventions (Okello *et al.*, 2014c). In order to 'do One Health', projects should aim to engage these questions from the outset. In this sense, 'EcoHealth' offers a much more appealing and helpful conceptual terrain than current incarnations of One Health, centred as it is on six 'pillars' (Charron, 2012): systems thinking; transdisciplinary research; community participation; sustainability; gender and social equity; and knowledge to action.

In the end, despite the production of rather novel brucellosis data, ICONZ raised a lot more questions than it answered in Nigeria. The natural next step would be to explore where human brucellosis cases are most prominent in Nigeria through a hospital-based surveillance study, and to test the hypothesis that while pastoralist herds appear at present to have a lower infection rate of brucellosis compared to intensive production systems, intensification and sedentarization of pastoralists are increasing the disease. Despite the overarching purpose of the case study to bridge this research–policy nexus in Nigeria, it became clear that prevailing donor goals of packing research into policy over a short five-year project cycle is tenuous at best. The fact that brucellosis emergence is not a political priority in the current climate of ethno-religious crises, competition for land use and growing wealth disparities in Nigeria should also be acknowledged as one of the major 'vectors' for the disease (rather than the Fulani!), and a barrier to mitigate its future spread. Such questions are intertwined with broader challenges for the future of Fulani pastoralism – questions that were unfortunately all too apparent during our time on the KGR.

Notes

1 The Fulani are the largest migratory ethnic group in the world, known by different names and found throughout West Africa. They were the first people group in West Africa to convert to Islam.
2 ICONZ stands for Integrated Control of Neglected Zoonoses (see www.iconzafrica.org).
3 The authors were part of ICONZ throughout the life of the project, acting as work package co-leaders on policy issues (AO) and social research (KB) as well as on bacterial zoonoses diagnostics and epidemiology (MD), including leading much of the Nigerian case study work. SW was the ICONZ coordinator.
4 In livestock, the disease causes abortion, infertility and reduced milk yields. In people, brucellosis causes a flu-like illness with fever, weakness, malaise, myalgia and weight loss. The disease is often chronic and insidious, resulting in significant disability and complications (e.g. endocarditis, musculoskeletal lesions, spondylitis and neurobrucellosis).
5 The total project budget was over €6 million, but also included contributions from partner institutions and other project funds.
6 See www.advanz.org, accessed 30 July 2015.
7 This included four disease clusters: bacterial (anthrax, bovine TB and brucellosis); pig-associated (cysticercosis and other soil-transmitted helminths); small ruminant/dog (rabies, leishmaniasis and echinococcosis); and vector-borne disease (animal and human trypanosomiasis and tick-borne cattle diseases).
8 Other case studies, such as in Zambia (pig cluster), Morocco (dog cluster) and Uganda (vector control cluster), were deemed to be more successful in this regard.
9 Despite this, several crossovers for integrating brucellosis and BTB in terms of diagnostic approaches (simultaneous sampling for both diseases was deemed to be feasible and cost-effective) and prevention (through education on risk factors) did result in BTB being addressed later on in the case study.
10 For example, the Nigerian coordinator had written a review on brucellosis in Nigeria in 1993.
11 As of 2011, the KGR was home to 777 Fulani agro-pastoralist households who all still practised both wet and dry season transhumance. The total population was roughly 10,000 people, 40,000 cattle, 10,000 sheep and 5000 goats. Formal education is poor, and although most people attend Koranic School, illiteracy is very high. The KGR spans around 33,500 hectares, lying north and west of major migration routes of transhumant Fulani based in the Kano and Bauchi areas. It is relatively flat and is covered with tree savannah and shrub, and is far away from the bustle of the nearby towns. Two roads link it to major traffic arteries running across the north–south divide in Nigeria, but these are in very poor condition, especially during the wet season when the reserve is effectively cut off for five months.
12 Although collective prevalence (percentage of herds with one or more positive animal(s)) is usually used to qualify scale of infection as high (5–10 per cent), moderate (2–5 per cent) or low (≤1 per cent), this information was unavailable for this pilot study. An 8 per cent individual prevalence can be considered to be moderately high compared to other studies undertaken in the extensive cattle production system, which have reported individual prevalence values ranging from 2 per cent to 15 per cent (Ducrotoy *et al.*, 2014).
13 The research protocol specified that both human and livestock samples had to be screened in the field 24 hours after the collection of blood so that the team could return to herds or households with positive cases to collect further biological samples for bacteriology and collect data on health-seeking costs of positive patients.
14 The choice of test is dictated by sensitivity (tendency for false negatives) and specificity (tendency for positive results in uninfected animals/people). In this regard, RBT performs as well as other tests (Greiner *et al.*, 2009). The test is simple to perform and requires only basic equipment and materials (white tile, micro-pipette, toothpick, etc.), useful for application in field conditions in Africa, while also being very cheap, costing 5 cents of a euro, compared to others (e.g. fluorescent polarization assay and indirect ELISA) that cost US$5–10 per sample.

15 Field screening with RBT showed an individual and herd-cattle prevalence of 0.6 per cent and 4.8 per cent, respectively for the March survey (*n* = 1724) and 0.5 per cent and 17.5 per cent, respectively, for the June survey. Of the 275 sheep screened with RBT in March, only one was found to be RBT positive; no sheep were seropositive in the June survey (*n* = 119) and two sheep out of 718 were found to be RBT positive in the October survey. No goats were found to be RBT positive either during the March survey (*n* = 79) or the October survey (*n* = 779).

16 Such as: manual, rather than centrifugal, separation of sera; inability to maintain cold-chain for storage of RBT antigens; poor operator timing of antigen–serum mixing; and testing outdoors in the daytime heat.

17 This was despite the provision of standard diagnostic kits and instructions for 1:1 protocols to be used by all ICONZ brucellosis case study countries to enable cross-comparison of results.

18 An increasing tendency in the developing country context is the reliance on technically appealing and expensive quantitative tests, such as ELISAs, in detriment of the simpler, cheaper and more robust RBT. Whereas it is well established that these do not have better sensitivity and specificity than RBT in the absence of vaccination (Greiner *et al.*, 2009), they need careful validation under local conditions so that cut-offs suggested by the makers in Europe/USA are unlikely to be adequate in Africa (Greiner and Gardner, 2000).

19 There are contrasting perspectives to consider, and some did not consider brucellosis a hazard in pastoralist herds. Esuruoso (1974) wrote:

> Cattle ... in nomadic herds ... on the move ... are not likely to accumulate infection or spread it from one animal to the other as in settled herds. This factor, and the intense heat of the sun in fairly open country (Sudan Savannah zone) will provide some of the reasons for the low infection rate ... in the northern herds. ... It would appear, therefore, that nomadic herding in Nigeria imposes a natural limit on the rate of brucellosis infection in cattle.

20 The disparity between our KGR results and those of Mai and colleagues (2012) is unclear, but may be due to differences in sampling approach, location, degree of nomadism in the Fulani study population and use of diagnostics. For the Mai *et al.* (2012) study, herd selection was based on proximity to a reliable laboratory and farmer cooperation, a potential source of bias. Increasing shifts from nomadism to a more sedentary and intensive mode of cattle rearing for the Fulani – on the increase since the 1990s due to increasing displacement from traditional grazing routes – are also very likely explanations. For example, Alausa (1979) provides evidence of this kind of transmission by describing a large outbreak of brucellosis in the 1970s in Ibapara, where the Sahelian drought prompted an influx and settling of nomadic herds.

21 This mode of administration reduces serological interference (the ability to differentiate between infected and vaccinated animals), which is a huge problem after implementation of a brucellosis vaccination campaign.

22 See: www.hrw.org/news/2011/05/16/nigeria-post-election-violence-killed-800, accessed 30 July 2015.

23 The Fulani social hierarchy is based on a chieftaincy system: a settled pastoral community will fall under one *Sarkin Fulbe*, elected by District Heads and legitimized in a ceremony performed by an Emir. The District Head is also responsible for the appointment of *Ardo'en* (Village Heads), representing the interests of particular clans. An *Ardo* can inherit title and position from his father. The *Sarkin Fulbe* typically meets with the *Ardo'en* to discuss concerns, such as ongoing disputes about the management and use of pastoral resources (Blench, 1996).

24 Participatory ranking, interviews, focus groups and questionnaire data all support this, placing brucellosis and BTB at the bottom of the list of cattle diseases. *Hanta*, a dual aetiology condition (liver fluke and black disease (*clostridrium novyi*)) and *samore* (trypanosomiasis) were the two priority cattle diseases. We also found that many households in

the KGR community spend more money on prophylactic treatment for cattle than they do on human health, revealing a harrowing gap in access to medical services, especially for children and women. *Bakale* matched our scientific understanding of brucellosis in cattle as confirmed through questionnaires and FGD, and most people had a good understanding of the disease, its transmission and its clinical signs in cattle, but were not aware that small ruminants can also suffer from the disease. Transmission to humans was also less well known, although *Bakale* in humans (especially as a cause of orchitis in men) was widely recognized.

25 We told them that the stones represented herds of different sizes. In order to find the stone (or herd) infected with brucellosis, we would have to randomly pick out a stone, because we do not know which stones (big or little) have the disease.

26 The money was given to an advisor to the District Head and KGR community member, in good faith, based on the recommendations of the Nigerian research team, who had solicited his input to assist with the setting up of a feed store in the reserve.

27 This included a BBSRC-funded project: Community-based Interventions Against Tsetse and Trypanosomiasis on the Jos Plateau, Nigeria (http://gtr.rcuk.ac.uk/project/626E5B46-5693-4603-B190-4CF03F74B2A3, accessed 30 July 2015).

28 The only segment of the KGR community which would not cooperate for the human sampling were members of the Yabaji clan, who have held on more to their traditional 'Bororo' nomadic cultural heritage and beliefs, and remain intensely suspicious of outsiders.

11

IMAGINED FUTURES

New directions for One Health

Kevin Bardosh

This book has emphasized the fact that zoonotic pathogens are deeply interwoven into the broader political economies that pervade our modern world. Dynamics of power and politics shape the origin, distribution and consequences of zoonotic infections, as well as the assemblages of research and policy processes that accompany them, in complex and context-specific ways. While these are often hidden from view, this book has sought to untangle these relationships, and reveal how understanding them is an essential step forward in envisioning and enabling more sustainable and equitable futures, both in Africa and elsewhere.

A series of diverse case studies have mapped out this conceptual terrain, exploring the interrelationships between human, animal and ecosystem health, and the systems of surveillance, preparedness, response and prevention that surround them. This included attention to the various narratives circulating around One Health in research and policy circles at the global level, the characteristics and evolution of Nipah virus scientific networks and the multiple science-policy controversies surrounding trypanosomiasis control. It involved the politics of brucellosis research among Fulani pastoralists in Northern Nigeria, as well as the relationships between endemic disease, health systems and biosecurity funding in remote research stations, like the 'Lassa lab' in post-conflict Sierra Leone. It has concentrated on how different narratives about disease dynamics, expertise and development shape zoonoses response pathways in Ghana and Zambia. And it has included delving into contested histories and institutional landscapes, where deep-seated inequalities and exclusions influence preparedness and response systems to epidemics of Rift Valley fever in Kenya and Ebola in West Africa.

In a field where critical social science analyses have been few and far between (Dry and Leach, 2010; Scoones, 2010; Craddock and Hinchliffe, 2015), this final chapter asks: what are the implications in moving an appreciation of power and politics to the forefront of current zoonosis research and policy approaches, and what does this mean for the 'operationalization' of One Health in Africa? Centred on collaboration and integration between disciplines and sectors, One Health has been presented as a 'renaissance movement' (Karesh and Stephen, 2014), redefining the contours of how zoonotic disease should be conceptualized and approached.[1] This book has questioned important aspects of these burgeoning rhetorical claims by providing contextualized knowledge about the particular, real-world challenges faced in Africa. This has allowed us to unpack the prevailing discourses surrounding One Health – discourses that are fast becoming accepted orthodoxies, and guiding significant research and policy agendas across the globe.

The case studies presented showed how zoonotic infections connect disparate domains – between culture, society, economy, infrastructure, technology, politics, biology and ecology – in ways that create particular conundrums for research and control. As assemblages that span the local and global, they relate different material, cognitive and biological worlds, from the 'risky practices' of remote rural villages to the variety of global resource flows and governance structures that have an impact on them (Collier and Ong, 2005). Zoonotic infections should not be viewed in isolation; rather, such connections link pathogens to a series of interrelated global challenges – from food insecurity, systemic poverty, climate change, environmental degradation and dysfunctional governance and political regimes. These not only influence epidemiological patterns, but also mediate the ability for different actors – from global agencies, states, civil society, the private sector, universities, local governments and communities – to understand and respond to them.

Without deeper consideration of the everyday connections and disconnections between social, political and ecological worlds, the risk is that One Health will perpetuate the current compartmentalization between science, health, development and politics. The expansive vision of 'One World, One Health' may, in turn, become 'side-tracked' and 'siloed' within new sets of expert-driven agendas, lofty rhetoric detached from local realities and priorities, and narrowed, technocratic interventions far removed from the social determinants of health.

This final chapter reflects on these crosscutting themes. It charts out new conceptual territory, delineating some of the ways in which socio-political analysis can assist in placing sustainability and social justice at the centre of current zoonosis research and policy landscapes. It asks: What is the value in moving power and politics to the heart of One Health, and how can this be done? What types of systems are needed to ground One Health in particular local contexts, and to address some of the systemic socio-political barriers involved? What new forms of knowledge and expertise are required? And how can governance and funding pathways be improved to facilitate this? Revisiting some of the prevailing tensions in global health and development outlined in the introduction of this book – the interactions between the global and local; the disjunctions between policy and practice; the trade-offs between technology and participation; and dynamics of knowledge and expertise – this chapter offers both theoretical and practical suggestions for how current programmes and policies can be improved by paying attention to power and politics, and what types of methodological innovations are needed to advance this agenda.

Shifting conceptual boundaries: from pathogens to politics

The case studies in this book have shown that conceptual standpoints matter; how we understand and approach the problem of zoonotic disease is important because it shapes the object of research and informs the logics of response, intervention and policy. Animal-borne infections are viewed differently by different social groups, and these divergent perceptions are influenced by issues of power, knowledge, interests and values (Keeley and Scoones, 2003). Different narratives about problems and solutions create incompatible priorities, as we have seen, between people, land, animals, economy and the environment that need to be appreciated and engaged with.

In this sense, the book has questioned the focus of much current zoonosis research and policy effort, and argued that the current movement towards interspecies and ecological health needs to include more explicit recognition of the complex, multi-scale dynamics between pathogens and their wider social, political and environmental contexts. Shifting the boundaries of the problem away from an emphasis on the *containment* of pathogens to the *configurations* that surround, perpetuate and sustain them is imperative to realizing a more holistic and accurate view (Rosenberg, 1992; Wilcox and Colwell, 2005). Wallace *et al.* (2015) have called this 'structural One Health' – locating the roots of zoonotic health ecologies in histories, shifting cultural boundaries and economic geographies, including a focus on markets, industries and governance regimes.

This book has offered a number of pertinent examples. Bardosh *et al.*, for example, showed the ways in which normative framings of the West African Ebola outbreak de-politicized the origins of the crisis, which was rather located in a series of systemic and historically embedded inequalities in income, health and political voice. Ducrotoy *et al.* discussed the roots of marginalization and stigmatization among Fulani pastoralists in Nigeria, and how this shaped the research process for brucellosis in the Kachia Grazing Reserve. Wilkinson highlighted how biosecurity funding, together with wider government policy neglect, sidelined field outreach activities and attention to wider questions of disease ecology for Lassa fever in Sierra Leone, including rodent dynamics, socio-economic status and the potential effects of international mining. In Zambia, Grant *et al.* revealed the ways in which trypanosomiasis is influenced by changes in markets and livelihoods, including the cotton industry, demand for charcoal from growing urban centres, trends in human migration and tourism.

While the importance of these wider political economies are increasingly being acknowledged, we have also seen how there remains a prevailing tendency for more narrow perspectives. The biosciences, in many cases, continue to view disease as a predominately pathophysiological process, detached from ecological and social realities (Baer *et al.*, 2003). Although One Health proponents emphasize the need to incorporate a social-ecological perspective into epidemiology and intervention (Zinsstag *et al.*, 2015b), these are also being used to support grand claims of 'predicting' disease emergence and 'preventing' future pandemics (Wolfe, 2005). New tools – immunological techniques, genomics, phylogenic analysis, and geospatial modelling – are being applied in the hopes of unravelling what are very complex spatial and temporal relationships. The goal is to model risk in order to inform public policy.

However, incredibly complex feedback-loops and non-linear relationships generate interpretative problems for causal analysis that need to be accounted for (Stirling and Scoones, 2009; Myers *et al.*, 2013; Lloyd-Smith *et al.*, 2015). In most cases, the quantitative, statistical and generalizable continue to reign supreme in zoonosis modelling and science, where risk is commonly assessed through 'science-based' models (Bickerstaff and Simmons, 2004; Leach and Scoones, 2013). However, as Stirling and Scoones (2009) argued in light of the avian influenza crisis, claims of 'rigorous science' are nonetheless supported by utilitarian assumptions, fragmented knowledge and methodological shortcomings.[2]

As these new zoonosis models try to influence policy, questions remain as to what the ultimate purpose and consequences will be. Too often the assumption is disease models will generate knowledge that leads to rational policy decisions and effective implementation. There can be a dangerous over-confidence in these models, where simplifications are hidden under the banner of 'sound science' (Stirling and Scoones, 2009). The result can be an erasure of the local and complex, and of ambiguities and uncertainties, making 'the messy world of public health … to look, here and there, like a bench science laboratory' (Adams, 2013, p65). This book has questioned this linear, de-politicized perspective, and highlighted alternative sources of knowledge that should now be considered. To avoid a narrowing of perspective and a disconnect between science and society, more attention needs to be given to the embedded human behaviours, cultural artefacts and systems of socio-political relationships involved in zoonotic disease transmission, and in the models that claim to represent them (Leach and Scoones, 2013). This has all become more apparent in policy circles due to the failures in the Ebola response in West Africa (Abramowitz *et al.*, 2015; Funk *et al.*, 2010). The burgeoning science of scenario planning offers one alternative attempt to get to grips with these uncertainties, helping us to identify a range of possible future disease scenarios and their related social and ecological dynamics.[3]

Shifting conceptual boundaries from pathogens to politics also re-directs attention to the root drivers of zoonotic disease, and who is ultimately responsible for addressing them. The focus on the biological and ecological has tended to perpetuate an overemphasis on 'bad' or 'risky' behaviours of often poor and marginalized people – as in wet market trading or bushmeat hunting – rather than the structural inequalities that generate risk (Singer, 2015). These discourses place the onus of improving biosecurity on local communities without appreciating the structural barriers involved. Placing structural inequalities and political ecologies at the forefront of our understanding of zoonotic disease renews our attention to the failures of development in Africa that generate disease risk and underpin local vulnerabilities – in livelihoods, ecologies and governance systems. For example, there is a need to consider how interrelationships between populations, and their biological and socio-political relationships, foster the clustering of co-infection and risk across the human–animal–ecosystem interface (Singer and Clair, 2003; Rock *et al.*, 2009). In this sense, discussions about 'hotspots' should also be discussions about 'non-state' regions – geographies where the state–citizen contract is severed or non-existent (Prince, 2014).

While this may all seem obvious, the consequences are not. Ultimately, our understanding and framing of these problems have far-reaching implications for how we prioritize funding and respond to zoonotic disease threats.

Science, technology, and participation

Viewing zoonotic diseases as assemblages of socio-political relationships draws attention to the importance of new modes and systems of action. What are the implications, and the possibilities for change? One Health is premised on a new ethos of *doing* health; however, the case studies of this book have questioned important aspects of current capacities and priorities in public health, veterinary, agriculture and conservation regimes in Africa to operationalize this lofty rhetoric. The issue is not only about getting different experts to work together on research questions and projects, but also about challenging entrenched norms around technology, poverty and citizen participation. As Scoones showed with trypanosomiasis, the tendency for quick techno-fixes leads to a narrowing of framings where technologies become tied to specific researcher interests, prestige, resources and institutional logics. The focus becomes about the next magic bullet and the perennial promise of 'big impact' just around the corner (Kelly and Beisel, 2011). But this discourse narrows the organizational and institutional relationships needed to enact more grassroots change. This is not to say that new technologies are not urgently needed, as a number of chapters in this book discussed. Millstone *et al.*, for example, showed how a new Rift Valley fever (RVF) vaccine could significantly improve RVF preparedness and response pathways. Wilkinson similarly discussed the benefits of new Lassa fever diagnostics in addressing knowledge gaps about incidence and epidemiology, which then helped drive greater policy attention. Rather, it is to realize that an over-emphasis on particular applications of science and technology hide important alternative pathways.

There are, after all, important trade-offs generated by competing perspectives and their accompanying priorities. Leach and Scoones (2006) discussed three framings of science and technology for development: the magic bullet, the technology transfer and the citizen engagement model. The latter was identified as the 'slow race' to making science and technology work for the poor, where magic bullets are replaced with a much more nuanced appreciation of people, places and the participatory process. As new sets of surveillance and response infrastructures and technologies (such as web-based surveillance and mobile technologies) and knowledge networks proliferate under the One Health banner, 'big data' and 'big systems' need to be accompanied with 'small data' and localized systems. But even where seemingly appropriate technologies do exist, challenges of implementation – in access, delivery, adoption and use – are often problematic and contingent. There is, for example, a so-called 'toolbox' of validated control options, grounded in decades of research findings, already in circulation for the neglected zoonotic diseases (NZDs), but major knowledge 'gaps' are still pervasive in how to move these interventions into different local contexts, scale them up and generate real, lasting impact (Molyneux et al., 2011).[4] Even 'basic' interventions – such as rabies vaccination, passive surveillance of animal deaths, mass treatment of livestock with veterinary drugs, stopping open defecation and improving slaughterhouse and wet market hygiene – often flounder (Bardosh et al., 2014b). There are reasons for this – but uncovering the multifaceted mosaic of factors involved is very often removed from the concerns of project logics and scientific concerns; despite its benefits, funding into the 'implementation gap' continues to receive relatively modest attention (Allotey et al., 2008).

The interface between technologies, delivery and use in Africa is one fraught with socio-political complexities. Biomedicine is not monolithic, but seen as somewhat unpredictable and fragmented in a pluralistic medical landscape where health systems are poor and politics pervasive (Prince, 2014). Attention to issues of access and use have become paramount in global health, but are compounded in the field of zoonoses through the need to consider wider system dynamics – livestock extension systems, crop and landscape changes, vector control, market systems and conservation, among others. One major consideration is the need to foster sustainable capacity within district and local outreach teams and to promote community-based surveillance, treatments, prevention and resilience. This book has shown the importance of addressing this gap. Millstone et al., for example, revealed how community-based animal health workers (CAHWs) and pastoralists could play significant roles in improving prediction, forecasting and early warning systems for RVF in Kenya. With Lassa fever, Wilkinson discussed the need for more innovative rodent trap techniques and community outreach. Similar examples were given with brucellosis in Nigeria, trypanosomiasis in Zambia and Ebola in West Africa.

It is here, in these local service delivery and citizen–state relationships, that lasting changes in resilience and sustainability for One Health will most likely be generated. Many of the 'implementation gaps' discussed in global policy circles are, in effect, the result of a lack of basic foresight, appropriate expertise and capacity. While no panacea, improvements can certainly be made by giving more attention to local needs and the process of implementation (Parker and Allen, 2013; Crawshaw et al., 2014; Coffin et al., 2015; Sripa et al., 2015). Sometimes rather small changes, implemented with attention to local contexts over time, can generate the most lasting impacts, even with relatively modest sums of funding (Bardosh, 2015).

Thinking critically about local systems, of technology and participation, also demands a more explicit engagement with the nuances of 'community' than is given in current One Health practice. A 'community' is not amorphous, and reifying them is counterproductive. Social differentiation across class, gender, ethnicity, religion, identity and livelihood activities is important (Scoones, 2009). Without delving into the complex textures of these local settings, in an attempt to 'ground One Health', simplistic assumptions will be glossed over, perpetuating divides between research and policy actors and the publics they seek to engage (Briggs, 2003).

Local people and field staff have to innovate, to understand the burden of zoonoses and to appreciate the social and environmental changes around them. As we saw with Ebola and RVF, local logics and incentives are often behind the drivers of 'resistance', and more attention to understanding the histories of, and incentives for, local involvement and change are urgently needed (Paul *et al.*, 2015). This includes the full spectrum of community participation, from compliance with passive reporting of animal deaths to broader citizen-driven change. What are the opportunities for behaviour and structural change, what mediation and facilitation is needed and what are the limitations? Greater attention to participatory approaches are certainly needed, helping to ground research questions and interventions more in local priorities, and assist in moving beyond pre-determined plans towards more iterative, long-term and adaptive approaches (Montavon *et al.*, 2013) – a theme much more emphasized in EcoHealth than in more mainstream One Health circles (Charron, 2012).

But considering community participation as an integral component of a One Health approach should not result in routinized lip-service, whereby participation is rendered technical, reinforcing established power dynamics and providing shallow interpretations of community dynamics (Cooke and Kothari, 2001). Learning from the wider debates within international development circles about 'participation' should help to avoid such practical and methodological shortcomings.

At the core of the One Health venture, then, should be an attempt to redefine researcher–community–policy relationships. If politics, and not necessarily pathogens, are the overarching focus, then the focus on *systems* becomes more about addressing biosocial relations, in context and as process, and tracing their relationships with zoonotic infections across local, national, regional and global scales.

Plural forms of knowledge and expertise

This book has also shown how disciplinary divides still run deep, how sectors remain siloed in important and long-standing ways and that divisions of power between different actors generate long-standing conflicts. Embedded interests run against generating trans-disciplinary knowledge, while relationships between researchers and policy-makers can be weak. Policy circles and professional incentives do not necessarily encourage working across divides, or fostering long-term community–researcher networks needed to enact these changes.

These are very real challenges. One Health advocates have strived to address them – through fostering partnerships, promoting new competences through trainings and aspiring towards a shared language emphasizing integrated thinking. This has increasingly occurred through new courses at universities, the establishment of centres of excellence and north–south exchanges, with many occurring in Africa (Travis *et al.*, 2014; Bonfoh *et al.*, 2015). Over time, there has also been more emphasis on longer-term capacity building documented in the literature. Regional networks have developed, funded by the major international donors: these include the Regional Network for Asian Schistosomiasis and Other Helminth Zoonoses, the Asia Partnership on Emerging Infectious Diseases Research (APEIR), the Afrique One consortium and OH-NextGen, to name but a few (Yang *et al.*, 2010; Travis *et al.*, 2014; Okello *et al.*, 2015). A number of country-specific research initiatives and government platforms have also proliferated, such as the Kenyan Zoonotic Disease Unit.[5] Their sustainability and impact are hard to gauge, however.

Nonetheless, much of the current fanfare continues to be about getting vets and medics together. For many zoonoses, especially those deemed emerging or 'pre-emerging', fundamental scientific questions, of biological transmission, ecology, infection, pathogenesis and treatment, remain tremendously important. More attention to these scientific questions and complexities are, in many cases, fundamental. But social science expertise is highly pertinent to all these issues. To date, however, social science has been marginal at best. Some efforts are underway to change this.[6] A number of current projects are, for example, emphasizing getting together other experts, including economists, ecologists, medical anthropologists, political scientists and wildlife experts.[7] Communities of practice, widely promoted in fostering the related EcoHealth movement, have been shown to be important avenues towards fostering multidisciplinary research groups, and can also help generate links between different research and policy networks (Stephen and Daibes, 2010; Bertone *et al.*, 2013; McKellar *et al.*, 2014). The recent Ebola Response Anthropology Platform is one step in the right direction, representative of contemporary attempts at developing transnational knowledge networks.[8]

Transdisciplinary research demands attention to re-framing the boundaries of problems, methodologies and collaborations (Wickson *et al.*, 2006). As the trumpet-call for interdisciplinary research and action continues under the One Health banner (Min *et al.*, 2013), this book has highlighted the need to reconsider the continued divides between the natural and social sciences (Rosenfield, 1992; Albert *et al.*, 2008, 2015) and the gaps between research and policy (Meagher *et al.*, 2008).

Integrating political economy and community-based participatory analysis, as well as other research methodologies, into the evolving practice of One Health will require learning and adaptation by research and practitioner networks (Rowe and Frewer, 2000; Draper *et al.*, 2010). A number of case studies in this book, for example, have highlighted the importance of trust, leadership, incentives and relationships to facilitating more holistic research and policy approaches. In order for plural forms of expertise and knowledge to be prioritized, new institutional linkages and policy–research networks are required. A critical praxis is important to maintain, guided by problem solving and acceptance of multiple forms of data and evidence.

Innovations in governance and policy pathways

The diffusion and evolution of a One Health approach to zoonotic disease will be especially shaped by different governance and policy regimes. This will require shifting prevailing institutional hierarchies, relationships and norms at multiple levels – from the global, regional, national and local – which are structured and maintained by broader systems of funding and patronage. Realigning bulky bureaucracies, shifting incentives for research, building capacities and multi-sectoral partnerships, prioritizing the needs of the poor and understanding context are not easy. This is especially the case when we consider the broader political economy of global health and development funding, dictated by fads, fashions and whims, and the tendencies to 'depoliticize' aid and interventions (Ferguson, 1994; Mosse, 2011).

This book has highlighted multiple, overlapping governance challenges. These include donor-driven and technocratic agendas, fragmented national policy systems, short-term grant cycles, elite capture, competing priorities between sectors, weak district capacities for implementation, poor communication between stakeholders and top-down consultations. We have seen how diseases like RVF are left to languish in neglect between inter-epidemic periods. Funding of the Lassa lab in Kenema, Sierra Leone raised questions about the prioritization of bench-science and defence priorities in comparison to other pathways. In Ghana, Waldman *et al.* report on the 'politics of precaution' that predominated around unknown bat-associated zoonotic threats in contrast to other risks and priorities. And we also saw in Nigeria how researcher interests and long-standing stigmatization of the Fulani led to inappropriate research aims to investigate brucellosis.

One Health advocates need to take a much more complex view of the policy process, away from linear models and towards consideration of narratives, actors, interests, governance arrangements, issues of resilience and questions of equity (Keeley and Scoones, 2003). Dominated by donor and biosecurity agendas, funding for zoonoses tends to be tied to specific policy narratives – around biosecurity, trade, conservation, technology or poverty alleviation. These lock-in around specific logics and pathways in ways that can severely limit the ability to adapt to emerging challenges and engage interlocking priorities and system dynamics. This critique has been most heavily voiced in relation to the top-down and 'one-size-fits-all' approach to avian influenza (e.g. Scoones, 2010; Mwacalimba, 2012; Okello *et al.*, 2014b). Moving funding and policy models away from the crisis and emergency mode, however, may prove to be rather difficult. Significant resources are mobilized around pandemic threats, and they offer a 'policy window' to propel zoonoses into the limelight. Some scholars have emphasized that this can be used to stretch across the emerging/endemic disease divide, and support improved systems for endemic diseases of the poor (Parkes *et al.*, 2005; Halliday *et al.*, 2012; Schwind *et al.*, 2014). But there remain real dangers with this 'piggy-backing' approach as it can lead to piecemeal application and cooptation.

One Health advocates are acutely aware of the need to mobilize resources from funding agencies and generate buy-in from funders, agencies, governments and others, something that underpins the interest in new metrics to reveal 'value-for-money' and 'win–win' scenarios. Some perils, of course, exist. One is the fact that focused disciplinary questions – around biological or ecological dynamics – and pilot studies of new technologies tend to garner the most support, where quantitative indicators, linear notions of causation and short-term impacts prevail. There is an inevitable politics attached to funding, given current resource-allocation regimes. These are difficult social arenas to operate in, and ones that generate tensions between different goals, disciplines and notions of impact. More holistic framings of problems – of the connectivities and conundrums discussed at length in this book – are key to advancing more interdisciplinary knowledge, as well as stronger knowledge-to-action initiatives with impact.

One Health must go beyond the rhetoric and develop practical field-based examples, especially those that directly engage with the complex world of political economy. There has been a vast proliferation in expert commissions and consultations on ecosystems and human health – the Millennium Ecosystem Assessment,[9] the Intergovernmental Panel on Climate Change,[10] and reports on Biodiversity and Human Health[11] and Planetary Health (Whitmee *et al.*, 2015). These all establish ambitious policy goals, but they may simply represent 'talking shops' unless such high-level discussions are followed by concerted efforts to address the systemic barriers to change. Tackling real-world One Health problems demands long-term investments. A good example of this has been with the International Development Research Center's (IDRC) investment in building the field of EcoHealth over nearly two decades (Charron, 2012). Other major funders – from the Bill & Melinda Gates Foundation, Wellcome Trust, Rockefeller Foundation, US National Institutes of Health (NIH), National Science Foundation (NSF), Department for International Development (DFID), United States Agency for International Development (USAID), the European Union and others – are also fostering One Health initiatives. Other efforts are involving the private sector, through public–private partnerships (PPPs) – for example for the long-term control of zoonotic sleeping sickness in Uganda (Welburn and Coleman, 2015). A central lesson from this book is that all these initiatives – if they are to live up to their claims of being holistic, cross-sectoral and transdisciplinary – must start to take social dimensions and political economy more seriously.

Conclusions

This book has revealed how emerging and endemic zoonotic diseases connect disparate social, political and biological domains, cutting across divides and demanding new perspectives and approaches. Tensions between different priorities and interests abound, and have major implications for the resilience of global surveillance, response, preparedness and prevention systems. This book has offered a fresh perspective from the social sciences on these debates, oriented around the burgeoning One Health movement that seeks to connect human, animal and ecosystem health. It has sought to unpack the lofty rhetoric – around collaboration and integration across disciplines and sectors – that promotes a particular type of globalism surrounding the research and control of zoonotic diseases. With a series of case studies from Africa, our aim has been to situate the rhetoric of One Health in the uncertain, real world – a world where divergences of power, knowledge construction, material resources, norms and values predominate.

Without a more concerted appreciation of One Health as a socio-political movement, the aspirations of researchers, practitioners and policy-makers in advancing a more holistic understanding and engagement with zoonotic diseases will fail to live up to expectations. One Health promises to break down divides and shift conceptual boundaries about disease, health and the environment. This is played out in particular settings – from boardrooms, field offices, rural villages and remote forests – and a better consideration of these social and political human worlds is paramount to re-thinking what the One Health approach means in practical terms.

Ultimately, as discussed throughout this book, it is counterproductive to separate One Health from larger questions of development in Africa. In order to support more resilient and equitable futures, new knowledge and forms of action for zoonotic disease research and policy are urgently needed. In this sense, advancing healthier people, animals and environments will require shifting away from narrow, technocratic research and policy agendas and towards greater attention to power, politics, participation, transdisciplinarity and systems thinking. Moving an appreciation of political economy to the forefront of the agenda is one important step forward.

Notes

1 The One Health movement has a number of contemporary parallels in EcoHealth (Charron, 2012) and Planetary Health (Whitmee et al., 2015) that also stress the relationships between ecology, health and systems thinking.
2 For an interesting and recent debate, see the scientific controversy surrounding the so-called 'worm wars' – mass drug administration for parasitic worms: www.buzzfeed.com/bengoldacre/deworming-trials, accessed 30 July 2015.
3 See: http://globalhealth.thelancet.com/2015/03/31/preparing-zoonotic-surprise and www.diseasescenarios.org, accessed 30 July 2015.
4 See www.who.int/neglected_diseases/intersectoral_collaboration_to_defeat_zoonoses/en, accessed 30 July 2015.
5 See: http://zdukenya.org, accessed 30 July 2015.
6 Rock et al. (2009) developed a schematic to explore the interrelationships between humans, animals, the physical environment and the socio-cultural environment. This included the spheres of: medicine, animal science, evolutionary and comparative medicine, environment, population health, agricultural science and public health, as well as gender studies, demographics, political economy, public policy, history, indigenous knowledge, communication studies, sociology, anthropology, economics and governance.
7 Some examples include: Emerging Pandemic Threats programme funded by USAID (www.usaid.gov/news-information/fact-sheets/emerging-pandemic-threats-program, accessed 30 July 2015); Bill & Melinda Gates Foundation (BMGF) One Health challenge call; UK Government Zoonoses and Emerging Livestock Systems (ZELS) Programme (see www.bbsrc.ac.uk/funding/opportunities/2012/zoonoses-emerging-livestock-systems);

the EU-funded Integrated Control of Neglected Zoonoses (ICONZ) project (www.iconzafrica.org); and the Dynamic Drivers of Disease in Africa Consortium (DDDAC) (http://steps-centre.org/project/drivers_of_disease), all accessed 30 July 2015.

8 See: www.ebola-anthropology.net, accessed 30 July 2015.
9 See: www.millenniumassessment.org/en/index.html, accessed 30 July 2015.
10 See: www.ipcc.ch, accessed 30 July 2015.
11 See: www.cbd.int/en/health, accessed 30 July 2015.

REFERENCES

Abramowitz, S. (2014) 'How the Liberian health sector became a vector for Ebola', *Cultural Anthropology Online*, 7 October, www.culanth.org/fieldsights/598-how-the-liberian-health-sector-became-a-vector-for-ebola, accessed 18 July 2015.

Abramowitz, S. A., McLean, K. E., McKune, S. L., Bardosh, K. L., Fallah, M., Monger, J., Tehoungue, K. and Omidian, P. A. (2015) 'Community-centered responses to Ebola in urban Liberia: The view from below', *PLoS Neglected Tropical Diseases* vol. 9, no. 4, doi: 10.1371/journal.pntd.0003706.

ACAPS (2015) 'Ebola outbreak in West Africa lessons learned from quarantine: Sierra Leone and Liberia', http://acaps.org/img/documents/t-acaps_thematic_note_ebola_west_africa_quarantine_sierra_leone_liberia_19_march_2015.pdf, accessed 13 June 2015.

Adams, J. D., Black, G. C., Clemmons, J. R. and Stephan, P. E. (2005) 'Scientific teams and institutional collaborations: Evidence from US universities, 1981–1999', *Research Policy*, vol. 34, no. 3, pp. 259–285.

Adams, V. (2013) 'Evidence-based global public health: Subjects, profits, erasures', in J. Biehl and A. Petryna (eds) *When People Come First: Critical Studies in Global Health*, Princeton University Press, Princeton, NJ.

Adamson, S., Marich, A. and Roth, I. (2011) 'One Health in NSW: Coordination of human and animal health sector management of zoonoses of public health significance', *NSW Public Health Bulletin*, vol. 22, no. 5–6, pp. 105–112.

Agidee, Y. (2011) *Forest Carbon in Ghana: Spotlight on Community Resource Management Areas*, Forest Trends, Washington, DC.

Aklilu, Y. and Catley, A. (2009) *Livestock Exports from the Horn of Africa: An Analysis of Benefits by Pastoralist Wealth Group and Policy Implications*, Report commissioned by the Food and Agriculture Organization (FAO) under the Livestock Policy Initiative of the Intergovernmental Authority on Development (IGAD).

Alausa, O. K. (1979) 'The investigation and control of a large-scale community outbreak of brucellosis in Nigeria', *Public Health*, vol. 93, no. 3, pp. 185–193.

Alausa, O. K. (1980) 'Brucellosis: socio-economic problems and control in various countries', *Tropical and Geographical Medicine*, vol. 32, no. 1, pp. 5–11.

Albert, M., Laberge, S., Hodges, B. D., Regehr, G. and Lingard, L. (2008) 'Biomedical scientists' perception of the social sciences in health research', *Social Science & Medicine*, vol. 66, no. 12, pp. 2520–2531.

Albert, M., Paradis, E. and Kuper, A. (2015) 'Interdisciplinary promises versus practices in medicine: The decoupled experiences of social sciences and humanities scholars', *Social Science & Medicine*, vol. 126, pp. 17–25.

Allotey, P., Reidpath, D. D., Ghalib, H., Pagnoni, F. and Skelly, W. C. (2008) 'Efficacious, effective, and embedded interventions: Implementation research in infectious disease control', *BMC Public Health*, vol. 8, no. 1, p. 343, doi: 10.1186/1471-2458-8-343.

Altizer, S., Bartel, R. and Han, B. A. (2011) 'Animal migration and infectious disease risk', *Science*, vol. 331, no. 6015, pp. 296–302.

Amwanyi, A. S., Gould, H. L., Sharif, S. K., Nguku, P. M., Omolo, J. O., Mutonga, D., Rao, C. Y., Lenderman, E. R., Schnabel, D., Paweska, J. T., Katz, M., Hightower, A., Kariuki Njenga, M., Feikin, D. R. and Breiman, R. F. (2010) 'Risk factors for severe Rift Valley fever infection in Kenya, 2007', *American Journal of Tropical Medicine and Hygiene*, vol. 83, no. 2, pp. 14–21.

Anderson, N. E., Mubanga, J., Fèvre, E. M., Picozzi, K., Eisler, M. C., Thomas, R. and Welburn, S. C. (2011) 'Characterisation of the wildlife reservoir community for human and animal trypanosomiasis in the Luangwa Valley, Zambia', *PLoS Neglected Tropical Diseases*, vol. 5, e1211, doi: 10.1371/journal.pntd.0001211v.

Anderson, N. E., Mubanga, J., Machila, N., Atkinson, P. M., Dzingirai, V. and Welburn, S. C. (2015) 'Sleeping sickness and its relationship with development and biodiversity conservation in the Luangwa Valley, Zambia', *Parasites & Vectors*, vol. 8, doi: 10.1186/s13071-015-0827-0.

Anholt, R. M., Stephen, C. and Copes, R. (2012) 'Strategies for collaboration in the interdisciplinary field of emerging zoonotic diseases', *Zoonoses and Public Health*, vol. 59, no. 4, pp. 229–240.

Anoko, J. N. (2014) 'Communication with rebellious communities during an outbreak of Ebola virus disease in Guinea: An anthropological approach', www.ebola-anthropology.net/case_studies/communication-with-rebellious-communities-during-an-outbreak-of-ebola-virus-disease-in-guinea-an-anthropological-approach, accessed 18 July 2015.

Anyamba, A., Linthicum, K. J., Small, J., Britch, S. C., Pak, E., de La Rocque, S., Formenty, P., Hightower, A. W., Breiman, R. F., Chretien, J.-P., Tucker, C. J., Schnabel, D., Sang, R., Haagsma, K., Latham, M., Lewandowski, H. B., Magdi, S. O., Mohamed, M. A., Nguku, P. M., Reynes, J.-M. and Swanepoel, R. (2010) 'Prediction, assessment of the Rift Valley fever activity in East and Southern Africa 2006–2008 and possible vector control strategies', *The American Journal of Tropical Medicine and Hygiene*, vol. 83, suppl. 2, pp. 43–51.

Appadurai, A. (1986) *The Social Life of Things: Commodities in Cultural Perspective*, Cambridge University Press, Cambridge.

Atlas, R. and Maloy, S. (2014) *One Health: People, Animals, and the Environment*, ASM Press, Washington, DC.

Axelsson, R. and Axelsson, S. B. (2006) 'Integration and collaboration in public health: A conceptual framework', *The International Journal of Health Planning and Management*, vol. 21, no. 1, pp. 75–88.

Azhar, E. I., El-Kafrawy, S. A., Farraj, S. A., Hassan, A. M., Al-Saeed, M. S., Hashem, A. M. and Madani, T. A. (2014) 'Evidence for camel-to-human transmission of MERS coronavirus', *New England Journal of Medicine*, vol. 370, no. 26, pp. 2499–2505.

Baer, H. A., Singer, M. and Susser, I. (2003) *Medical Anthropology and the World System*, Greenwood Publishing Group, Westport, CT.

Bandyopadhyay, S. and Tembo, G. (2009) *Household Welfare and Natural Resource Management around National Parks in Zambia*, Policy Research Working Paper 4932, World Bank, Washington, DC.

Banerjee, A. K. and Bhatty, M. A. (1970) 'A survey of bovine brucellosis in Northern Nigeria (a preliminary communication)', *Bulletin of Epizootic Diseases of Africa*, vol. 18, no. 4, pp. 333–338.

Barclay, H. and Vreysen, M. (2011) 'Conclusions from a dynamic population model for tsetse: Response to comments', *Population Ecology*, vol. 53, no. 2, pp. 417–420.

Bardosh, K. (2014) 'Global aspirations, local realities: The role of social science research in controlling neglected tropical diseases', *Infectious Diseases of Poverty*, vol. 3, no. 1, 35, doi: 10.1186/2049-9957-3-35.

Bardosh, K. (2015) 'Deadly flies, poor profits and veterinary pharmaceuticals: Sustaining the control of sleeping sickness in Uganda', *Medical Anthropology*, in press.

Bardosh, K., Waiswa, C. and Welburn, S. (2013) 'Conflict of interest: Use of pyrethroids and amidines against tsetse and ticks in zoonotic sleeping sickness endemic areas of Uganda', *Parasites and Vectors*, vol. 6, 204, doi:10.1186/1756-3305-6-204.

Bardosh, K., Inthavong, P., Xayaheuang, S. and Okello, A. L. (2014a) 'Controlling parasites, understanding practices: The biosocial complexity of a One Health intervention for neglected zoonotic helminths in northern Lao PDR', *Social Science & Medicine*, vol. 120, pp. 215–223.

Bardosh, K., Sambo, M., Sikana, L., Hampson, K. and Welburn, S. C. (2014b) 'Eliminating rabies in Tanzania? Local understandings and responses to mass dog vaccination in Kilombero and Ulanga districts', *PLoS Neglected Tropical Diseases*, vol. 8, no. 6, e2935.

Barrett, R. and Armelagos, G. (2013) *An Unnatural History of Emerging Infections*, Oxford University Press, Oxford.

Barrett, K. and Okali, C. (1998) 'Partnerships for tsetse control: Community participation and other options', *World Animal Review*, vol. 90, pp. 39–46.

Bausch, D. G. and Schwarz, L. (2014) 'Outbreak of Ebola virus disease in Guinea: Where ecology meets economy', *PLoS Neglected Tropical Diseases*, vol. 8, no. 7, e3056.

Bayart, J. (1993) *The State in Africa: The Politics of the Belly*, Longman, London.

Beinart, W. and Brown, K. (2013) *African Local Knowledge and Livestock Health: Diseases and Treatments in South Africa*, Boydell and Brewer Ltd, Woodbridge.

Bertone, M. P., Meessen, B., Clarysse, G., Hercot, D., Kelley, A., Kafando, Y., Lange, I., Pfaffmann, J., Ridde, V., Sieleunou, I. and Witter, S. (2013) 'Assessing communities of practice in health policy: A conceptual framework as a first step towards empirical research', *Health Research Policy and Systems*, vol. 11, no. 1, 39, doi: 10.1186/1478-4505-11-39.

Bett, B., Wanyoike, F., Sang, R., Bukachi, S., Wanyoike, S., Said, M., Ontiri, E., Kifugo, S., Otieno, T. F., Lutomiah, J., Njeru, I., Karanga, J. and Lindhal, J. (2014) 'Rift Valley fever (RVF) case study report', http://steps-centre.org/wp-content/uploads/DDDAC-Rift-Valley-Fever-Case-Study-update_April-2014.pdf, accessed 11 July 2015.

Bickerstaff, K. and Simmons, P. (2004) 'The right tool for the job? Modeling, spatial relationships, and styles of scientific practice in the UK foot and mouth crisis', *Environment and Planning D*, vol. 22, no. 3, pp. 393–412.

Biehl, J. and Petryna, A. (eds) (2013) *When People Come First: Critical Studies in Global Health*, Princeton University Press, Princeton, NJ.

Birmingham, K. and Kenyon, G. (2001) 'Lassa fever is unheralded problem in West Africa', *Nature Medicine*, vol. 7, p. 878.

Biruk, C. (2012) 'Seeing like a research project: Producing "high-quality data" in AIDS research in Malawi', *Medical Anthropology*, vol. 31, no. 4, pp. 347–366.

Blench, R. (1996) *Aspects of Resource Conflict in Semi-Arid Africa*, Overseas Development Institute, London.

Bogich, T. L., Chunara, R., Scales, D., Chan, E., Pinheiro, L. C., Chmura, A. A., Carroll, C., Daszak, P. and Brownstein, J. S. (2012) 'Preventing pandemics via international development: A systems approach', *PLoS Medicine*, vol. 9, no. 12, e1001354, doi:10.1371/journal.pmed.1001354.

Bonfoh, B., Schelling, E., Tanner, M. and Zinsstag, J. (2011) 'Proof of One Health concept: Towards capacity building and intersectoral interventions', *Ecohealth*, vol. 7, S117.

Bonfoh, B., Mahamat, M. B., Schelling, E., Ouattara, K., Cailleau, A., Haydon, D., Cleaveland, S., Zinsstag, J. and Tanner, M. (2015) 'Individual and institutional capacity building in global health research in Africa', in J. Zinsstag, E. Schelling, D. Waltner-Toews, M. Whittaker and M. Tanner (eds) *One Health: The Theory and Practice of Integrated Health Approaches*, CABI, Oxford.

Borio, L., Inglesby, T., Peters, C., Schmaljohn, A. L., Hughes, J. M., Jahrling, P. B., Ksiazek, T., Johnson, K. M., Meyerhoff, A. and O'Toole, T. (2002) 'Hemorrhagic fever viruses as biological weapons', *JAMA: The Journal of the American Medical Association*, vol. 287, no. 18, pp. 2391–2405.

Bouyer, J., Seck, M. and Sall, B. (2013) 'Letter to editor: Misleading guidance for decision making on tsetse eradication. Response to Shaw *et al.* (2013)', *Preventive Veterinary Medicine*, vol. 112, no. 3–4, pp. 443–446.

Branco, L., Grove, J., Boisen, M., Shaffer, J., Goba, A., Fullah, M., Momoh, M., Grant, D. and Garry, R. (2011) 'Emerging trends in Lassa fever: Redefining the role of immunoglobulin M and inflammation in diagnosing acute infection', *Virology Journal*, vol. 8, p. 478, doi: 10.1186/1743-422X-8-478.

Breiman, R. F., Minjauw, B., Sharif, S. K., Ithondeka, P. and Kariuki Njenga, M. (2010) 'Rift Valley fever: Scientific pathways toward public health prevention and response', *American Journal of Tropical Medicine and Hygiene*, vol. 83, no. 2, pp. 1–4.

Briggs, C. L. (2003) 'Why nation-states and journalists can't teach people to be healthy: Power and pragmatic miscalculation in public discourses on health', *Medical Anthropology Quarterly*, vol. 17, no. 3, pp. 287–321.

Briggs, C. L. and Mantini-Briggs, C. (2003) *Stories in the Time of Cholera: Racial Profiling During a Medical Nightmare*, University of California Press, Berkeley, CA.

Britch, S. C., Binepal, Y. S., Ruder, M. G., Kariithi, H. M., Linthicum, K. J., Anyamba, A., Small, J. L., Tucker, C. J., Ateya, L. O., Oriko, A. A., Gacheru, S. and Wilson, W. C. (2013) 'Rift Valley fever risk map model and seroprevalence in selected wild ungulates and camels from Kenya', *PLoS ONE*, vol. 8, no. 6, doi: 10.1371/journal.pone.0066626.

Budd, L. (1999) *Economic Analysis: Department for International Development (DFID)-funded Tsetse and Trypanosome Research and Development since 1980*, DFID, Livestock Production Programme, Animal Health Programme/Natural Resources Systems Programme, London.

Buntain, B., Allen-Scott, L., North, M., Rock, M. and Hatfield, J. (2015) 'Enabling academic One Health environments', in J. Zinsstag, E. Schelling, D. Waltner-Toews, M. Whittaker and M. Tanner (eds) *One Health: The Theory and Practice of Integrated Health Approaches*, CABI, Wallingford.

Burawoy, M. (2001) 'Manufacturing the global', *Ethnography*, vol. 2, pp. 147–159.

Burt, R. S. (2001) 'Structural holes versus network closure as social capital', in N. Lin, K. Cook and R. S. Burt (eds) *Social Capital: Theory and Research*, Transaction Publishers, New Brunswick, NJ.

Buse, K. and Harmer, A. M. (2007) 'Seven habits of highly effective global public–private health partnerships: Practice and potential', *Social Science & Medicine*, vol. 64, no. 2, pp. 259–271.

Butcher, N., Tan, M. and Sheikh, M. (2012) 'Rift Valley fever in the Horn of Africa: challenges and opportunities', *Journal of Public Health Africa*, vol. 3, no. 2, pp. 98–100.

Buyst, H. (1977) 'The epidemiology of sleeping sickness in the historical Luangwa Valley', *Annales de la Societe Belge de Medecine Tropicale*, vol. 57, no. 4–5, pp. 349–360.

Calain, P. (2007a) 'From the field side of the binoculars: A different view on global public health surveillance', *Health Policy and Planning*, vol. 22, no. 1, pp. 13–20.

Calain, P. (2007b) 'Exploring the international arena of global public health surveillance', *Health Policy and Planning*, vol. 22, no. 1, pp. 2–12.

Carson, R. (1962) *Silent Spring*, Houghton Mifflin, Boston, MA.

Cassidy, A. (2012) 'Vermin, victims and disease: UK framings of badgers in and beyond the bovine TB controversy', *Sociologia Ruralis*, vol. 52, no. 2, pp. 192–214.

Catley, A., Alders, R. G. and Wood, J. L. (2012) 'Participatory epidemiology: approaches, methods, experiences', *Veterinary Journal*, vol. 191, no. 2, pp. 151–160.

CDC (2003) 'Progress toward global eradication of dracunculiasis, January–June 2003', *Morbidity and Mortality Weekly Report*, vol. 52, no. 37, pp. 881–883.

CDC (2011a) *A CDC Framework for Preventing Infectious Diseases: Sustaining the Essentials and Innovating for the Future*, Centres for Disease Control and Prevention, Atlanta, GA, www.cdc.gov/oid/docs/ID-Framework.pdf, accessed 8 July 2015.

CDC (2011b) 'Report summary for June 201:. Country management and support visit to Ghana', *CDC's Country Management and Support Initiative*, www.cdc.gov/globalaids/publications/CMS-Summaries/Ghana-CMS-Summary_2-25-13.pdf, accessed 10 July 2015.

Charron, D. F. (2012) 'Ecohealth: origins and approach', in D. Charron (ed.) *Ecohealth Research in Practice*, Springer, New York, pp. 1–30.

Chien, Y. J. (2013) 'How did international agencies perceive the avian influenza problem? The adoption and manufacture of the "One World, One Health" framework', *Sociology of Health & Illness*, vol. 35, no. 2, pp. 213–226.

Chileshe, A. (2001) *A Brief on the Forestry Outlook Study*, Forestry Department, Ministry of Environment and Natural Resources, Lusaka, www.fao.org/3/a-ac428e.pdf, accessed 22 July 2015.

Chitanga, S., Marcotty, T., Namangala, B., van den Bossche, P., van den Abbeele, J. and Delespaux, V. (2011) 'High prevalence of drug resistance in animal trypanosomes without a history of drug exposure', *PLoS Neglected Tropical Diseases*, vol. 5, no. 12, e1454, doi:10.1371/journal.pntd.0001454.

Chivian, E. and Bernstein, A. (eds) (2008) *Sustaining Life: How Human Health Depends on Biodiversity*, Oxford University Press, Oxford.

Chua, K. B. (2003) 'Nipah virus outbreak in Malaysia', *Journal of Clinical Virology*, vol. 26, no. 3, pp. 265–275.

Clements, A. C. A., Pfeiffer, D. U., Martin, V. and Otte, M. J. (2007) 'A Rift Valley fever atlas for Africa', *Preventative Veterinary Medicine*, vol. 82, no. 1–2, pp. 72–82.

Coffin, J. L., Monje, F., Asiimwe-Karimu, G., Amuguni, H. J. and Odoch, T. (2015) 'A One Health, participatory epidemiology assessment of anthrax (*Bacillus anthracis*) management in Western Uganda', *Social Science & Medicine*, vol. 129, pp. 44–50.

Coker, R., Rushton, J., Mounier-Jack, S., Karimuribo, E., Lutumba, P., Kambarage, D., Pfeiffer, D. C., Stärk, K. and Rweyemamu, M. (2011) 'Towards a conceptual framework to support one-health research for policy on emerging zoonoses', *The Lancet: Infectious Diseases*, vol. 11, no. 4, pp. 326–331.

Collier, S. J. and Ong, A. (2005) 'Global assemblages, anthropological problems', in S. J. Collier and A. Ong (eds) *Global Assemblages: Technology, Politics and Ethics as Anthropological Problems*, Oxford and Carlton, Blackwell, Malden, MA.

Collier, S. J., Lakoff, A. and Rabinow, P. (2004) 'Biosecurity: Towards an anthropology of the contemporary', *Anthropology Today*, vol. 20, no. 5, pp. 3–7.

Conrad, P. A., Mazet, J. A., Clifford, D., Scott, C. and Wilkes, M. (2009) 'Evolution of a transdisciplinary "One Medicine–One Health" approach to global health education at the University of California, Davis', *Preventive Veterinary Medicine*, vol. 92, no. 4, pp. 268–274.

Conrad, P. A., Meek, L. A. and Dumit, J. (2013) 'Operationalizing a One Health approach to global health challenges', *Comparative Immunology, Microbiology and Infectious Diseases*, vol. 36, no. 3, pp. 211–216.

Conraths, F. J., Schwabenbauer, K., Vallat, B., Meslin, F. X., Füssel, A. E., Slingenbergh, J. and Mettenleiter, T. C. (2011) 'Animal health in the 21st century: A global challenge', *Preventive Veterinary Medicine*, vol. 102, no. 2, pp. 93–97.

Cook, R. A., Karesh, W. B. and Osofsky, S. A. (2004) *The Manhattan Principles on 'One World, One Health': Building Interdisciplinary Bridges to Health in a Globalized World*, Wildlife Conservation Society, New York.

Cooke, B. and Kothari, U. (eds) (2001) *Participation: The New Tyranny?* Zed Books, London.

Courtenay, M., Conrad, P., Wilkes, M., La Ragione, R. and Fitzpatrick, N. (2014) 'Interprofessional initiatives between the human health professions and veterinary medical students: A scoping review', *Journal of Interprofessional Care*, vol. 28, no. 4, pp. 323–330.

Craddock, S. and Hinchliffe, S. (2015) 'One World, One Health? Social science engagements with the one health agenda', *Social Science & Medicine*, vol. 129, pp. 1–4, doi: 10.1016/j.socscimed.2014.11.016.

Crane, J. T. (2013) *Scrambling for Africa: AIDS, Expertise, and the Rise of American Global Health Science*, Cornell University Press, Ithaca, NY.

Crawshaw, L., Fèvre, S., Kaesombath, L., Sivilai, B., Boulom, S. and Southammavong, F. (2014) 'Lessons from an integrated community health education initiative in rural Laos', *World Development*, vol. 64, pp. 487–502.

Cruzan Morton, C. (2013) 'The virus hunter', *Brandeis Magazine*, Spring, www.brandeis.edu/magazine/2013/spring/featured-stories/virus.html, accessed 2 January 2014.

Cummings, J. N. and Kiesler, S. (2005) 'Collaborative research across disciplinary and organizational boundaries', *Social Studies of Science*, vol. 35, pp. 703–722.

Dakubo, C. Y. (2010) *Ecosystems and Human Health: A Critical Approach to Ecohealth Research and Practice*, Springer Science & Business Media, New York.

Dantas-Torres, F., Chomel, B. B. and Otranto, D. (2012) 'Ticks and tick-borne diseases: A One Health perspective', *Trends in Parasitology*, vol. 28, no. 10, pp. 437–446.

Daszak, P., Cunningham, A. A. and Hyatt, A. D. (2001) 'Anthropogenic environmental change and the emergence of infectious diseases in wildlife', *Acta Tropica*, vol. 78, no. 2, pp. 103–116.

David-West, K. B. (1978) 'Dairy development in Nigeria: A review', in E. A. Olaloku and K. B. David-West (eds) *Developing A Nigerian Dairy Industry: Proceedings of the First National Seminar on Dairy Development, held in Vom, Nigeria, 10–13 July 1978*, Federal Livestock Department, Lagos.

Davies, S. E., Elbe, S., Howell, A. and McInnes, C. (2014) 'Global health in international relations: Editors' introduction', *Review of International Studies*, vol. 40, no. 5, pp. 825–834.

Day, M. J. (2011) 'One Health: The importance of companion animal vector-borne diseases', *Parasites and Vectors*, vol. 4, no. 49, doi:10.1186/1756-3305-4-49.

Dean, A. S., Crump, L., Greter, H., Schelling, E. and Zinsstag, J. (2012) 'Global burden of human brucellosis: A systematic review of disease frequency', *PLoS Neglected Tropical Diseases*, vol. 6, no. 10, e1865, doi:10.1371/journal.pntd.0001865.

Degeling, C. and Kerridge, I. (2013) 'Hendra in the news: Public policy meets public morality in times of zoonotic uncertainty', *Social Science & Medicine*, vol. 82, pp. 156–163.

Delespaux, V., Dinka, H., Masumu, J., van den Bossche, P. and Geerts, S. (2008) 'Five-fold increase in *Trypanosoma congolense* isolates resistant to diminazene aceturate over a seven-year period in Eastern Zambia', *Drug Resistance Updates*, vol. 11, no. 6, pp. 205–209.

Dijkman, J., Hall, A., Steglich, M., Sones, K., Keskin, E., Adwera, A. and Wakungu, J. (2010) *Innovation Response Capacity in Relation to Livestock-Related Emergencies in Africa*, IGAD LPI Working Paper 03-10, IGAD Livestock Policy Initiative, Addis Ababa, http://cgspace.cgiar.org/handle/10568/24986, accessed 11 July 2015.

Dingwall, R., Hoffman, L. M. and Staniland, K. (eds) (2013) *Pandemics and Emerging Infectious Diseases: The Sociological Agenda*, John Wiley & Sons, Chichester.

Donaldson, R. (2009) *The Lassa Ward: One Man's Fight Against One of the World's Deadliest Diseases*, Transworld Publishers, London.

Doucleff, M. (2013) 'Deadly Middle East coronavirus found in an Egyptian tomb bat', *SHOTS Health News from NPR*, www.npr.org/blogs/health/2013/08/21/214164172/deadly-middle-east-coronavirus-found-in-an-egyptian-tomb-bat, accessed 2 January 2014.

Douthwaite, R. and Tingle, C. (eds) (1994) *DDT in the Tropics: The Impact on Wildlife in Zimbabwe of Ground-Spraying for Tsetse Fly Control*, Natural Resources Institute, Chatham.

Downie, R. (2012) *The Road to Recovery: Rebuilding Liberia's Health System*, CSIS Global Health Policy Center, http://csis.org/files/publication/120822_Downie_RoadtoRecovery_web.pdf, accessed 18 July 2015.

Draper, A. K., Hewitt, G. and Rifkin, S. (2010) 'Chasing the dragon: Developing indicators for the assessment of community participation in health programmes', *Social Science & Medicine*, vol. 71, no. 6, pp. 1102–1109.

Dry, S. (2010) 'New rules for health? Epidemics and the international health regulations' in S. Dry and M. Leach (eds) *Epidemics: Science, Governance, and Social Justice*, Earthscan, London.

Dry, S. and Leach, M. (2010) *Epidemics: Science, Governance and Social Justice*, Earthscan, London.

Ducrotoy, M. J., Bertu, W. J., Ocholi, R. A., Gusi, A. M., Bryssinckx, W., Welburn, S. and Moriyon, I. (2014) 'Brucellosis as an emerging threat in developing economies: Lessons from Nigeria', *PLoS Neglected Tropical Diseases*, vol. 8, no. 7, e3008, doi:10.1371/journal.pntd.0003008.

Dudley, J. P. (2008) 'Public health and epidemiological considerations for avian influenza risk mapping and risk assessment', *Ecology and Society*, vol. 13, no. 2, art. 21.

Duncan, R. S. and Chapman, C. A. (1991) 'Seed dispersal and potential forest succession in abandoned agriculture in tropical Africa', *Ecological Applications*, vol. 9, no. 3, pp. 998–1008.

DVS (2014) *Standard Operating Procedure for Livestock Vaccination Against Rift Valley Fever (RVF)*, Directorate of Veterinary Services, Ministry of Agriculture, Livestock and Fisheries, Nairobi.

Elbe, S. (2010a) *Security and Global Health*, Polity Press, Cambridge.

Elbe, S. (2010b) 'Haggling over viruses: The downside risks of securitizing infectious disease', *Health Policy and Planning*, vol. 25, no. 6, pp. 476–485.

Epstein, J. H., Prakash, V., Smith, C. S., Daszak, P., Jakati, R. D., McLaughlin, A. B., Meehan, G., Field, H. E. and Cunningham, A. A. (2008) 'Evidence for Henipavirus infection in Indian *Pteropusgiganteus* (Chiroptera; Pteropodidae) fruit bats', *Emerging Infectious Diseases*, vol. 14, pp. 1309–1311, doi: 10.3201/eid1408.071492.

Erikson, S. L. (2012) 'Global health business: The production and performativity of statistics in Sierra Leone and Germany', *Medical Anthropology*, vol. 31, no. 4, pp. 367–384.

Esuruoso, G. O. (1974) 'Bovine brucellosis in Nigeria', *Veterinary Journal*, vol. 95, no. 1, pp. 54–58.

Fairhead, J. (2015) 'Understanding social resistance to Ebola response in Guinea', submitted: *African Studies Review*.

Fairhead, J. and Leach, M. (1996) *Misreading the African Landscape: Society and Ecology in a Forest–Savanna Mosaic*, Cambridge University Press, Cambridge.

Fairhead, J. and Leach, M. (1998) *Reframing Deforestation: Global Analyses and Local Realities: Studies in West Africa*, Routledge, London.

Fairhead, J., Leach, M. and Small, M. (2006) 'Where techno-science meets poverty: Medical research and the economy of blood in The Gambia, West Africa', *Social Science & Medicine*, vol. 63, no. 4, pp. 1109–1120.

Falola, T. and Heaton, M. (2008) *A History of Nigeria*, Cambridge University Press, Cambridge.

Fanthorpe, R. (2006) 'On the limits of liberal peace: Chiefs and democratic decentralization in post-war Sierra Leone', *African Affairs*, vol. 5, no. 418, pp. 27–49.

FAO (2002) *Preparation of Rift Valley Fever Contingency Plan*, Food and Agriculture Organization, Rome.

FAO (2011) *One Health Programme Strategic Framework for Eastern Africa, 2011–2015*, FAO-ECTAD, Nairobi.

FAO (2013a) *World Livestock 2013: Changing Disease Landscapes*, FAO Press, Rome.

FAO (2013b) *Lessons from HPAI: A Technical Stocktaking of Outputs, Outcomes, Best Practices and Lessons Learned from the Fight Against Highly Pathogenic Avian Influenza in Asia, 2005–2011*, FAO Press, Rome.

FAO and WHO (2009) *Rift Valley Fever Outbreaks Forecasting Models*, Joint FAO–WHO Experts' Consultation, 29 Setember to 1 October 2008, Global Alert and Response Report, WHO Document WHO/HSE/GAR/BDP/2009.2, Food and Agriculture Organization, Rome.

FAO, OIE, WHO, UNSIC, UNICEF and WB (2008) *Contributing to One World, One Health: A Strategic Framework for Reducing Risks of Infectious Diseases at the Animal–Human–Ecosystems Interface*, FAO, Rome.

FAO, OIE and WHO (2010) *Sharing Responsibilities and Coordinating Global Activities to Address Health Risks at the Animal–Human–Ecosystems Interfaces: A Tripartite Concept Note*, www.who.int/influenza/resources/documents/tripartite_concept_note_hanoi_042011_en.pdf, accessed 24 July 2015.

Farmer, P. (1997) 'Social scientists and the new tuberculosis', *Social Science & Medicine*, vol. 44, no. 3, pp. 347–358.

Farmer, P. (2004a) *Pathologies of Power: Health, Human Rights, and the New War on the Poor*, University of California Press, California.

Farmer, P. (2004b) 'An anthropology of structural violence', *Current Anthropology*, vol. 45, no. 3, pp. 305–325.

Farmer, P. (2005) *Pathologies of Power: Health, Human Right and the New War on the Poor*, University of California Press, Berkeley, CA.

Farmer, P. (2014) 'Diary', *London Review of Books*, October, www.lrb.co.uk/v36/n20/paul-farmer/diary, accessed 18 July 2015.

Fastring, D. R. and Griffith, J. A. (2009) 'Malaria incidence in Nairobi, Kenya and dekadal trends in NDVI and climatic variables', *Geocarto International*, vol. 24, no. 3, pp. 207–221.

Faye, S. (2014) 'How anthropologists help medics fight Ebola in Guinea', *SciDevNet*, www.scidev.net/global/cooperation/feature/anthropologists-medics-ebola-guinea.html, accessed 14 October 2014.

Feldmann, U. and Parker, A. (2010) 'Using a pest to attack itself: the role of the sterile insect technique (SIT) in tsetse control', *Public Health Journal*, vol. 21, pp. 38–42.

Ferguson, J. (1994) *The Anti-Politics Machine: Development, De-Politicisation and Bureaucratic Power in Lesotho*, University of Minneapolis Press, Minneapolis, MN.

Ferme, M. (2001) *The Underneath of Things: Violence, History, and the Everyday in Sierra Leone*, University of California Press, Berkeley, CA.

Fernandez, A., Richardson, R. B., Tschirley, D. L. and Tembo, G. (2010) *Wildlife Conservation in Zambia: Impacts on Rural Household Welfare*, Working Paper 40, Food Security Research Project, Lusaka.

Fèvre, E. M., Odiit, M., Coleman, P. G., Woolhouse, M. E. and Welburn, S. C. (2008) 'Estimating the burden of rhodesiense sleeping sickness during an outbreak in Serere, eastern Uganda', *BMC Public Health*, vol. 8, no. 1, doi: 10.1186/1471-2458-8-96.

Fichet-Calvet, E. and Rogers, D. J. (2009) 'Risk maps of Lassa fever in West Africa', *PLoS Neglected Tropical Diseases*, vol. 3, no. 3, doi: 10.1371/journal.pntd.0000388.

Figuié, M. (2014) 'Towards a global governance of risks: International health organisations and the surveillance of emerging infectious diseases', *Journal of Risk Research*, vol. 17, no. 4, pp. 469–483.

Ford, J. (1971) *The Role of the Trypanosomiases in African Ecology: A Study of the Tsetse Fly Problem*, Clarendon Press, Oxford.

Forster, P. (2012) *To Pandemic or Not? Reconfiguring Global Responses to Influenza*, STEPS Working Paper 51, STEPS Centre, Brighton.

Franco, A. O., Gomes, M. G. M., Rowland, M., Coleman, P. G. and Davies, C. R. (2014) 'Controlling malaria using livestock-based interventions: A One Health approach', *PLoS ONE*, vol. 9, no. 7, e101699.

Franco, C. (2009) 'Billions for biodefense: Federal agency biodefense funding, FY2009-FY2010', *Biosecurity and Bioterrorism: Biodefense Strategy, Practice, and Science*, vol. 7, no. 3, pp. 291–309.

Frazzoli, C., Mantovani, A. and Dragone, R. (2014) 'Local role of food producers' communities for a global One-Health framework: The experience of translational research in an Italian dairy chain', *Journal of Agricultural Chemistry and Environment*, vol. 3, no. 2, p. 14.

Frost, L. J. and Reich, M. R. (2008) *Access: How do Good Health Technologies Get to Poor People in Poor Countries?* Harvard Center for Population and Development Studies, Boston, MA.

Fuller, J. G. (1974) *Fever! The Hunt for a New Killer Virus*, Reader's Digest Press, New York.

Funk, S., Salathé, M. and Jansen, V. A. (2010) 'Modelling the influence of human behaviour on the spread of infectious diseases: A review', *Journal of the Royal Society Interface*, vol. 7, no. 50, pp. 1247–1256.

Fyfe, C. (1962) *A History of Sierra Leone*, Oxford University Press, Oxford.

Galaz, V. (2010) *Socio-Ecological Perspectives on Zoonotic Disease*, Background paper, Stockholm Resilience Centre, Kräftriket.

Galaz, V. (2014) *Global Environmental Governance, Technology and Politics: The Anthropocene Gap*, Edward Elgar, Cheltenham.

Gale, J. (2009) 'Virus hunters find Ebola, Marburg source in fruit bat (Update 1)', *Bloomberg News*, 2 October, www.bloomberg.com/apps/news?pid=newsarchive&sid=aCDY59ymDHII, accessed 2 January 2014.

Galtung, J. (1969) 'Violence, peace, and peace research', *Journal of Peace Research*, vol. 6, no. 3, pp. 167–191.

Gargano, L. M., Gallagher, P. F., Barrett, M., Howell, K., Wolfe, C., Woods, C. and Hughes, J. M. (2013) 'Issues in the development of a research and education framework for One Health', *Emerging Infectious Diseases*, vol. 19, no. 3, e121103, doi: 0.3201/eid1903.121103.

Garrett, L. (1994) *The Coming Plague: Newly Emerging Diseases in a World Out of Balance*, Farrar, Straus and Giroux, New York, NY.

Garry, R. (2004) 'Preclinical development of recombinant antigen Lassa fever diagnostics: Technical proposal', National Institutes of Health, Bethesda, MD.

Gberie, L. (2005) *A Dirty War in West Africa: The RUF and the Destruction of Sierra Leone*, Indiana University Press, Bloomington, IN.

Geerts, S. and Holmes, P. H. (1998) *Drug Management and Parasite Resistance in Bovine Trypanosomiasis in Africa*, FAO, Rome.

Geissler, P. W. (2005) ' "Kachinja are coming!" Encounters around medical research work in a Kenyan village', *Africa*, vol. 75, no. 2, pp. 173–202.

Geissler, P. W. (2013) 'Public secrets in public health: Knowing not to know while making scientific knowledge', *American Ethnologist*, vol. 40, no. 1, pp. 13–34.

Geissler, P. W. (2014) 'The archipelago of public health: Comments on the landscape of medical research in twenty-first-century Africa', in R. J. Prince and R. Marsland (eds) *Making and Unmaking Public Health in Africa: Ethnographic and Historical Perspectives*, Ohio University Press, Athens.

Gibbs, P. (2014) 'The evolution of One Health: A decade of progress and challenges for the future', *Veterinary Record*, vol. 174, no. 4, pp. 85–91, doi:10.1136/vr.g143.

Giles-Vernick, T., Owona-Ntsama, J., Landier, J. and Eyangoh, S. (2015) 'The puzzle of Buruli ulcer transmission, ethno-ecological history and the end of "love" in the Akonolinga district, Cameroon', *Social Science & Medicine*, vol. 129, pp. 20–27.

Gire, S. K., Stremlau, M., Andersen, K. G., Schaffner, S. F., Bjornson, Z., Rubins, K., Hensley, L., Mccormick, J. B., Lander, E. S. and Garry, R. F. (2012) 'Emerging disease or diagnosis?', *Science*, vol. 338, no. 6108, pp. 750–752.

Gire, S. K., Goba, A., Andersen, K. G., Sealfon, R. S., Park, D. J., Kanneh, L., Jalloh, S., Momoh, M., Fullah, M., Dudas, G., Wohl, S., Moses, L. M., Yozwiak, N. L., Winnicki, S., Matranga, C. B., Malboeuf, C. M., Qu, J., Gladden, A. D., Schaffner, S. F., Yang, X., Jiang, P. P., Nekoui, M., Colubri, A., Coomber, M. R., Fonnie, M., Moigboi, A., Gbakie, M., Kamara, F. K., Tucker, V., Konuwa, E., Saffa, S., Sellu, J., Jalloh, A. A., Kovoma, A., Koninga, J., Mustapha, I., Kargbo, K., Foday, M., Yillah, M., Kanneh, F., Robert, W., Massally, J. L., Chapman, S. B., Bochicchio, J., Murphy, C., Nusbaum, C., Young, S., Birren, B. W., Grant, D. S., Scheiffelin, J. S., Lander, E. S., Happi, C., Gevao, S. M., Gnirke, A., Rambaut, A., Garry, R. F., Khan, S. H., Sabeti, P. C. and Scheiffelin, J. S. (2014) 'Genomic surveillance elucidates Ebola virus origin and transmission during the 2014 outbreak', *Science*, vol. 345, no. 6202, pp. 1369–1372.

GNA (2006) 'Workshop on avian influenza held at Techiman', 20 January, www.ghanaweb.com/GhanaHomePage/NewsArchive/artikel.php?ID=97918, accessed 12 January 2014.

Godfroid, J., Al Dahouk, S., Pappas, G., Roth, F., Matope, G., Muma, J., Marcotty, T., Pfeiffer, D. and Skjerve, E. (2013) 'A "One Health" surveillance and control of brucellosis in developing countries: Moving away from improvisation', *Comparative Immunology, Microbiology and Infectious Diseases*, vol. 36, no. 3, pp. 241–248.

GoK (2010) *National Climate Change Response Strategy*, Government Press, Nairobi.

Goldberg, T. L., Paige, S. B. and Chapman, C. (2012) 'The Kibale EcoHealth project: Exploring connections among human health, animal health, and landscape dynamics in western Uganda', in A. Aguirre, R. Ostfeld and P. Daszak (eds) *New Directions in Conservation Medicine*, Oxford University Press, Oxford.

GOSL (2005) *Sierra Leone Poverty Reduction Strategy Paper*, Government of Sierra Leone, Freetown.

Gostin, L. and Friedman, E. (2014) 'Ebola: a crisis in global health leadership', *The Lancet*, vol. 384, no. 995, pp. 1323–1325.

Gould, J. (2010) *Left Behind: Rural Zambia in the Third Republic*, Lembani Trust, Lusaka.

Government of Zambia (2013) *Report of the Committee on Agriculture for the Second Session of the Eleventh National Assembly*, 27 September 2012, Government of Zambia, Lusaka, www.parliament.gov.zm/sites/default/files/documents/committee_reports/Agric%20 main%20Report%202013.pdf, accessed 22 July 2015.

Grace, D. (2014) 'The business case for One Health', *Onderstepoort Journal of Veterinary Research*, vol. 81, no. 2, art. 725.

Grace, D. and Bett, B. (2014) 'Zoonotic diseases and their drivers in Africa', in C. Butler (ed.) *Climate Change and Global Health*, CABI, Boston, MA, pp. 228–236.

Grace, D., Mutua, F., Ochungo, P., Kruska, R., Jones, K., Brierley, L., Lapar, M. L., Said, M., Herrero, M., Phuc, P. M., Thao, N. B., Akuku, I. and Ogutu, F. (2012a) *Mapping of Poverty and Likely Zoonoses Hotspots*, International Livestock Research Institute, Nairobi.

Grace, D., Gilbert, J., Randolph, T. and Kang'ethe, E. (2012b) 'The multiple burdens of zoonotic disease and an ecohealth approach to their assessment', *Tropical Animal Health and Production*, vol. 44, pp. 67–73.

Grace, D., Kang'ethe, E. and Waltner-Toews, D. (2012c) 'Participatory and integrative approaches to food safety in developing country cities', *Tropical Animal Health and Production*, vol. 44, no. 1 (Supp.), S1–2.

Grant, I. F. (2001) 'Insecticides for tsetse and trypanosomiasis control: Is the environmental risk acceptable?' *Trends in Parasitology*, vol. 17, no. 1, pp. 10–14.

Greiner, M. and Gardner, I. A. (2000) 'Epidemiologic issues in the validation of veterinary diagnostic tests', *Preventive Veterinary Medicine*, vol. 45, no. 1–2, pp. 3–22.

Greiner, M., Verloo, D. and De Massis, F. (2009) 'Meta-analytical equivalence studies on diagnostic tests for bovine brucellosis allowing assessment of a test against a group of comparative tests', *Preventive Veterinary Medicine*, vol. 92, no. 4, pp. 373–381.

Gronvall, G. K., Fitzgerald, J., Chamberlain, A., Inglesby, T. V. and O'Toole, T. (2007) 'High-containment biodefense research laboratories: Meeting report and center recommendations', *Biosecurity and Bioterrorism*, vol. 5, no. 1, pp. 75–85.

Gumbo, D. J., Moombe, K. B., Kandulu, M. M., Kabwe, G., Ojanen, M., Ndhlovu, E. and Sunderland, T. C. H. (2013) *Dynamics of the Charcoal and Indigenous Timber Trade in Zambia: A Scoping Study in Eastern, Northern and Northwestern Province*, Occasional Paper 86, CIFOR, Bogor, Indonesia.

Gurley, E. S., Montgomery, J. M., Jahangir Hossain, M., Rafiqul Islam, M., Abdur Rahim Molla, M., Shamsuzzaman, S. M., Akram, K., Zaman, K., Asgari, N., Comer, J. A., Azad, A. K., Rollin, P. E., Ksiazek, T. G. and Breiman, R. F. (2007a) 'Risk of nosocomial transmission of Nipah virus in a Bangladesh hospital', *Infection Control and Hospital Epidemiology*, vol. 28, no. 6, pp. 740–742.

Gurley, E. S., Montgomery, J. M., Hossain, M. J., Bell, M., Azad, A. K., Islam, M. R., Molla, M. A. R., Carroll, D. S., Ksiazek, T. G. and Rota, P. A. (2007b) 'Person-to-person transmission of Nipah virus in a Bangladeshi community', *Emerging Infectious Diseases*, vol. 13, no. 7, pp. 1031–1037.

Hacking, I. (2000) *The Social Construction of What?*, Harvard University Press, Cambridge, MA.

Hall, P. E. (1910) 'Notes on the movements of *Glossina morsitans* in the Lundazi district, North Eastern Rhodesia', *Bulletin of Entomological Research*, vol. 1, no. 3, pp. 183–184.

Halliday, J., Daborn, C., Auty, H., Mtema, Z., Lembo, T., Barend, M., Handel, I. Knobel, D., Hampson, K. and Cleaveland, S. (2012) 'Bringing together emerging and endemic zoonoses surveillance: Shared challenges and a common solution', *Philosophical Transactions of the Royal Society of London B: Biological Sciences*, vol. 367, no. 1604, pp. 2872–2880.

Hansen, M. C., Potapov, P. V., Moore, R., Hancher, M., Turubanova, S. A., Tyukavina, A., Thau, D., Stehman, S. V., Goetz, S. J., Loveland, T. R., Kommareddy, A., Egorov, A., Chini, L., Justice, C. O. and Townshend, J. R. G. (2013) 'High-resolution global maps of 21st-century forest cover change', *Science*, vol. 342, no. 6160, pp. 850–853.

Hargrove, J. W. (2003) *Tsetse Eradication: Sufficiency, Necessity and Desirability*, Report of meeting 9–10 September 2002 of DFID Animal Health Programme, Centre for Tropical Veterinary Medicine, University of Edinburgh, Edinburgh.

Hargrove, J. W. (2004) 'Tsetse population dynamics', in I. Maudlin, P. Holmes and M. Miles (eds), *Trypanosomiases*, CABI Publishing, Cambridge, pp. 113–137.

Hargrove, J. W., Torr, S. J. and Kindness, H. M. (2003) 'Insecticide-treated cattle against tsetse (Diptera: Glossinidae): What governs success?', *Bulletin of Entomological Research*, vol. 93, no. 3, pp. 203–217.

Hargrove, J. W., Torr, S. J. and Vale, G. A. (2011) 'Comment on Barclay and Vreysen: Published dynamic population model for tsetse cannot fit field data', *Population Ecology*, vol. 53, no. 2, pp. 413–415.

Hargrove, J. W., Ouifki, R., Kajunguri, D., Vale, G. A. and Torr, S. J. (2012) 'Modeling the control of trypanosomiasis using trypanocides or insecticide-treated livestock', *PLoS Neglected Tropical Diseases*, vol. 6, no. 5, doi: 10.1371/journal.pntd.0001615.

Häsler, B., Gilbert, W., Jones, B. A., Pfeiffer, D. U., Rushton, J. and Otte, M. J. (2013) 'The economic value of One Health in relation to the mitigation of zoonotic disease risks', in J. S. MacKenzie, M. Jeggo, P. S. Daszak and J. A. Richt (eds) *One Health: The Human–Animal–Environment Interfaces in Emerging Infectious Diseases*, Springer-Verlag Berlin, Heidelberg, pp. 127–151.

Häsler, B., Hiby, E., Gilbert, W., Obeyesekere, N., Bennani, H. and Rushton, J. (2014) 'A One Health framework for the evaluation of rabies control programmes: A case study from Colombo City, Sri Lanka', *PLoS Neglected Tropical Diseases*, vol. 8, no. 10, e3270.

Hayman, D. T. S., Suu-Ire, R., Breed, A. C., McEachern, J. A., Wang, L., Wood, J. L. N. and Cunningham, A. A. (2008a) 'Evidence of Henipavirus infection in West African fruit bats', *PLoS ONE*, vol. 3, no. 7, doi: 10.1371/journal.pone.0002739.

Hayman, D. T. S., Fooks, A. R., Horton, D., Suu-Ire, R., Breed, A. C., Cunningham, A. A. and Wood, J. L. N. (2008b) 'Antibodies against Lagos bat virus in megachiroptera from West Africa', *Emerging Infectious Diseases*, vol. 14, no. 6, pp. 926–928.

Hayman, D. T. S., Emmerich, P., Yu, M., Wang, L.-F., Suu-Ire, R., Cunningham, A. A. and Wood, J. L. N. (2010) 'Long-term survival of an urban fruit bat seropositive for Ebola and Lagos bat viruses', *PLoS ONE*, vol. 5, no. 8, doi: 10.1371/journal.pone.0011978.

Hayman, D. T. S., Yu, M., Crameri, G., Wang, L.-F., Suu-Ire, R., Wood, J. L. and Cunningham, A. A. (2012) 'Ebola virus antibodies in fruit bats, Ghana, West Africa', *Emerging Infectious Diseases*, vol. 18, no. 7, pp. 1207–1209, doi: 10.3201/eid1807.111654.

Herring, A. and Swedlund, A. (2010) *Plagues and Epidemics: Infected Spaces Past and Present*, Berg, Oxford.

Hewlett, B. and Hewlett, B. (2008) *Ebola, Culture and Politics: The Anthropology of an Emerging Disease*, Cengage Learning, Belmont, CA.

Hinchliffe, S. (2007) *Geographies of Nature: Societies, Environments, Ecologies*, Sage, London.

Hinchliffe, S. (2014) 'More than one world, more than one health: Re-configuring interspecies health', *Social Science & Medicine*, vol. 129, pp. 28–35.

Hislop, D. (2013) *Knowledge Management in Organizations: A Critical Introduction*, Oxford University Press, Oxford.

Hoffman, D. (2011) *The War Machines: Young Men and Violence in Sierra Leone and Liberia*, Duke University Press, Chapel Hill, NC.

Højbjerg, C. K., Knörr, J. and Schroven, A. (2013) *The Interaction of Global and Local Models of Governance: New Configurations of Power in Upper Guinea Coast Societies*. Max Planck Institute for Social Anthropology Working Paper 149, www.eth.mpg.de/pubs/wps/pdf/mpi-eth-working-paper-0149, accessed 18 July 2015.

Hossain, L., Karimi, F., Wigand, R. T. and Crawford, J. W. (2015) 'Evolutionary longitudinal network dynamics of global zoonotic research', *Scientometrics*, vol. 103, no. 2, pp. 337–353.

Hueston, W., Appert, J., Denny, T., King, L., Umber, J. and Valeri, L. (2013) 'Assessing global adoption of One Health approaches', *Ecohealth*, vol. 10, no. 3, pp. 228–233.

Iacono, G. L., Cunningham, A. A., Fichet-Calvet, E., Garry, R. F., Grant, D. S., Khan, S. H., Leach, M., Moses, L. M., Schieffelin, J. S., Shaffer, J. G., Webb, C. T. and Wood, J. L. (2015) 'Using modelling to disentangle the relative contributions of zoonotic and anthroponotic transmission: The case of Lassa fever', *PLoS Neglected Tropical Diseases*, vol. 9, no. 1, e3398, doi: 10.1371/journal.pntd.0003398.

IDMC (2009) 'Nigeria: No end to internal displacement. A profile of the internal displacement situation', Internal Displacement Monitoring Centre, Norwegian Refugee Council, Switzerland.

ILRAD (1991) *Annual Report of the International Laboratory for Research on Animal Diseases 1990*, ILRAD, Nairobi.

ILRI and DVS (2008) *Learning the Lessons of Rift Valley Fever: Improved Detection and Mitigation of Outbreaks – Participatory Assessment of Rift Valley Fever Surveillance and Rapid Response Activities*, ILRI and Kenyan Department of Veterinary Services, Nairobi.

ILRI and FAO (2009) *Decision-Support Tool for Prevention and Control of Rift Valley Fever Epizootics in the Greater Horn of Africa, Version 1*, Food and Agriculture Organization/International Livestock Research Institute, Nairobi/Rome.

ILRI and FAO (2014) *Risk-based Decision-Support Framework for Prevention and Control of Rift Valley Fever Epizootics in the Greater Horn of Africa, Version 4*, Food and Agriculture Organization/International Livestock Research Institute, Nairobi/Rome.

Institute for Health Metrics and Evaluation (2012) *Financing Global Health 2012: The End of the Golden Age?* IHME, Seattle, WA.

Institute of Medicine and National Research Council (2009) *Sustaining Global Surveillance and Response to Emerging Zoonotic Diseases*, National Academies Press, Washington, DC.

IRIN (2009a) 'Nigeria: Impunity for perpetrators of sectarian violence', *Humanitarian News and Analysis*, www.irinnews.org/report/84092/nigeria-impunity-for-perpetrators-of-sectarian-violence, accessed 30 July 2015.

IRIN (2009b) 'Nigeria: Government steps in to curb farmer–nomad clashes', *Humanitarian News and Analysis*, www.irinnews.org/report/86539/nigeria-government-steps-in-to-curb-far, accessed 30 July 2015.

IRIN (2010) 'Nigeria: Educating the nomads', *Humanitarian News and Analysis* www.irinnews.org/report/90353/nigeria-educating-the-nomads, accessed 30 July 2015.

Ishmael, H. (2005) 'Indigenous knowledge on bats and their implications on bat conservation at the Bouyem traditional area', BSc Thesis in Natural Resource Management, Kwame Nkrumah University of Science and Technology, Kumasi.

Iyengar, P., Kerber, K., Howe, C. J. and Dahn, B. (2014) 'Services for mothers and newborns during the Ebola outbreak in Liberia: The need for improvement in emergencies' *PLoS Currents Outbreaks*, 16 April, edition 1, doi: 10.1371/currents.outbreaks.4ba31830 8719ac86fbef91f8e56cb66f.

Jambai, A. and MacCormack, C. (1996) 'Maternal health, war, and religious tradition: Authoritative knowledge in Pujehun District, Sierra Leone', *Medical Anthropology Quarterly*, vol. 10, no. 2, pp. 270–286.

Jasanoff, S. (2005) *Designs on Nature: Science and Democracy in Europe and the United States*, Princeton University Press, Princeton, NJ.

Jayne, T. S., Govereh, J., Mwanaumo, A., Nyoro, J. and Chapoto, A. (2002) 'False promise or false premise? The experience of food and input market reform in eastern and southern Africa', *World Development*, vol. 30, no. 11, pp. 1967–1985.

Jephcott, F. (2013) 'Early detection of zoonotic spillover in West Africa: The implications of rural health-seeking behaviours and facility-level nosology', MPhil Thesis, University of Cambridge, Cambridge.

Jerolmack, C. (2013) 'Who's worried about turkeys? How 'organisational silos' impede zoonotic disease surveillance', *Sociology of Health & Illness*, vol. 35, no. 2, pp. 200–212.

Jones, B. (2009) *Beyond the State in Rural Uganda*, Edinburgh University Press, Edinburgh.

Jones, B., McKeever, D., Grace, D., Pfeiffer, D., Mutua, F., Njuki, J., McDermott, J., Rushton, J., Said, M., Ericksen, P., Kock, R. and Alonso, S. (2011) *Zoonoses (Project 1) Wildlife/Domestic Livestock Interactions*, Final Report, Department for International Development, London, ILRI, London, Royal Veterinary College, Nairobi.

Jones, B., Grace, D., Kock, R., Alonso, S., Rushton, J., Said, M. Y., McKeever, D. Mutuab, F., Young, J., McDermott, J. and Pfeiffer, D. U. (2013) 'Zoonosis emergence linked to agricultural intensification and environmental change', *Proceedings of the National Academy of Sciences*, vol. 110, no. 21, pp. 8399–8404.

Jones, K. E., Patel, N. G., Levy, M. A., Storeygard, A., Balk, D., Gittleman, J. L. and Daszak, P. (2008) 'Global trends in emerging infectious diseases', *Nature*, vol. 451, no. 7181, pp. 990–993.

Jost, C. C., Nzietchueng, S., Kihu, S., Bett, B., Njogu, G., Swai, E. S. and Mariner, J. C. (2010) 'Epidemiological assessment of the Rift Valley fever outbreak in Kenya and Tanzania in 2006 and 2007', *American Journal of Tropical Medicine and Hygiene*, vol. 83, no. 2, pp. 65–72.

Justice, J. (1986) *Policies, Plans and People: Culture and Health Development in Nepal*, California University Press, Berkeley, CA and London.

K'Oloo, T. O., Ilukor, J., Mockshell, J., Ilatsia, E. D. and Birner, R. (2015) 'Are government veterinary paraprofessionals serving the poor? The perceptions of smallholder livestock farmers in Western Kenya', *Tropical Animal Health and Production*, vol. 47, no. 1, pp. 243–245.

Kabayo, J. P. (2002) 'Aiming to eliminate tsetse from Africa', *Trends in Parasitology*, vol. 18, no. 11, pp. 473–475.

Kahn, R. E., Clouser, D. F. and Richt, J. A. (2009) 'Emerging infections: A tribute to the One Medicine, One Health concept', *Zoonoses and Public Health*, vol. 56, no. 6/7, pp. 407–428.

Kamins, A. O., Restif, O., Ntiamoa-Baidu, Y., Suu-Ire, R., Hayman, D. T. S., Cunningham, A. A., Wood, J. L. N. and Rowcliffe, J. M. (2011) 'Uncovering the fruit bat bushmeat commodity chain and the true extent of fruit bat hunting in Ghana, West Africa', *Biological Conservation*, vol. 144, no. 12, pp. 3000–3008.

Kaneene, J. B., Kaplan, B., Steele, J. H., and Thoen, C. O. (2014) 'One Health approach for preventing and controlling tuberculosis in animals and humans', in C. O. Thoan, J. H. Steele and J. B. Kaneene (eds) *Zoonotic Tuberculosis:* Mycobacterium Bovis *and Other Pathogenic Mycobacteria*, 3rd edition, Wiley Blackwell, Oxford.

Karesh, W. and Stephen, C. (2014) 'Introduction: Is One Health delivering results?', *Revue Scientifique et Technique*, vol. 33, no. 2, pp. 375–379.

Keeley, J. and Scoones, I. (2003) *Understanding Environmental Policy Processes: Cases from Africa*, Earthscan, London.

Kelly, A. H. and Beisel, U. (2011) 'Neglected malarias: The frontlines and back alleys of global health', *BioSocieties*, vol. 6, no. 1, pp. 71–87.

Keshavjee, S. (2014) *Blindspot: How Neoliberalism Infiltrated Global Health*, University of California Press, Berkeley, CA.

Kgori, P. M., Modo, S. and Torr, S. J. (2006) 'The use of aerial spraying to eliminate tsetse from the Okavango Delta of Botswana', *Acta Tropica*, vol. 99, no. 2–3, pp. 184–199.

Khan, S. H., Goba, A., Chu, M., Roth, C., Healing, T., Marx, A., Fair, J., Guttieri, M. C., Ferro, P. and Imes, T. (2008) 'New opportunities for field research on the pathogenesis and treatment of Lassa fever', *Antiviral Research*, vol. 78, no. 1, pp. 103–115.

Kim, J. Y., Shakow, A., Mate, K., Vanderwarker, C., Gupta, R. and Farmer, P. (2005) 'Limited good and limited vision: Multidrug-resistant tuberculosis and global health policy', *Social Science & Medicine*, vol. 61, no. 4, pp. 847–859.

Kinghorn, A., Yorke, W. and Lloyd, L. (1913) 'Final report of the Luangwa Sleeping Sickness Commission of the BSA Co 1911–1912', *Annals of Tropical Medicine and Parasitology*, vol. 7, pp. 183–283.

Kingsley, P. (2015) 'Inscrutable medicines and marginal markets: Tackling substandard veterinary drugs in Nigeria', *Pastoralism*, vol. 5, no. 2, doi: 10.1186/s13570-014-0021-6.

Kittayapong, P., Thongyuan, S., Olanratmanee, P., Aumchareoun, W., Koyadun, S., Kittayapong, R. and Butraporn, P. (2012) 'Application of eco-friendly tools and eco-biosocial strategies to control dengue vectors in urban and peri-urban settings in Thailand', *Pathogens and Global Health*, vol. 106, no. 8, pp. 446–454.

Kucharski, A. J., Camacho, A., Checchi, F., Waldman, R. J., Grais, R. F., Cabrol, J. C., Briand, S., Baguelin, M., Flasche, S., Funk, S. and Edmunds, W. J. (2015) 'Evaluation of the benefits and risks of introducing Ebola community care centers, Sierra Leone', *Emerging Infectious Diseases*, vol. 21, no. 3, doi: 10.3201/eid2103.141892.

Kunz, T. H., Braun de Torrez, E., Bauer, D., Lobova, T. and Fleming, T. H. (2011) 'Ecosystem services provided by bats', *Annals of the New York Academy of Sciences*, vol. 1223, no. 1, pp. 1–38.

LaBeaud, A. D., Ochiai, Y., Peters, C. J., Muchiri, E. M. and King, C. H. (2007) 'Spectrum of Rift Valley fever virus transmission in Kenya: Insights from three distinct regions', *American Journal of Tropical Medicine and Hygiene*, vol. 76, no. 5, pp. 795–800.

Lachenal, G. (2014) *Ebola 2014: Chronicle of a Well Prepared Disaster*, Somatosphere, http://somatosphere.net/2014/10/chronicle-of-a-well-prepared-disaster.html, accessed 22 July 2015.

Lakoff, A. (2010) 'Two regimes of global health', *Humanity*, vol. 1, no. 1, pp. 59–79.

Lakoff, A. and Collier, S. J. (2008) *Biosecurity Interventions: Global Health and Security in Question*, Columbia University Press, New York.

Lapinski, M. K., Funk, J. A. and Moccia, L. T. (2014) 'Recommendations for the role of social science research in One Health', *Social Science & Medicine* (ePub ahead of print), www.ncbi.nlm.nih.gov/pubmed/25311785, accessed 7 July 2015.

Latour, B. (2000) 'When things strike back: A possible contribution of "science studies" to the social sciences', *The British Journal of Sociology*, vol. 51, no. 1, pp. 107–123.

Launiala, A. (2009) 'How much can a KAP survey tell us about people's knowledge, attitudes and practices? Some observations from medical anthropology research on malaria in pregnancy in Malawi', *Anthropology Matters*, vol. 11, no. 1, www.anthropologymatters.com/index.php/anth_matters/article/view/31/53, accessed 31 July 2015.

Laveissiere, C. and Couret, D. (1981) 'Tests for riverine tsetse fly control with screens impregnated with insecticide', *Cahiers O.R.S.T.O.M. (Office de la Recherche Scientifique et*

Technique Outre-Mer) Serie Entomologie Medicale et Parasitologie, vol. 19, no. 4, pp. 271–284.

Leach, M. (2015) 'The Ebola crisis and post-2015 development', *Journal of International Development*, in press.

Leach, M. and Hewlett, B. S. (2010) 'Haemorrhagic fevers: Narratives, politics and pathways', in S. Dry and M. Leach (eds) *Epidemics: Science, Governance and Social Justice*, Earthscan, London.

Leach, M. and Scoones, I. (2006) *The Slow Race: Making Technology Work for the Poor*, Demos, London.

Leach, M. and Scoones, I. (2013) 'The social and political lives of zoonotic disease models: Narratives, science and policy', *Social Science & Medicine*, vol. 88, pp. 10–17.

Leach, M., Fairhead, J., Millimouno, D. and Diallo A. (2008) 'New therapeutic landscapes in Africa: Parental categories and practices in seeking infant health in the Republic of Guinea', *Social Science & Medicine*, vol. 66, no. 10, pp. 2157–2167.

Leach, M., Scoones, I. and Stirling, A. (2010a) *Dynamic Sustainabilities: Technology, Environment, Social Justice*, Earthscan/James & James, London.

Leach, M., Scoones, I. and Stirling, A. (2010b) 'Governing epidemics in an age of complexity: Narratives, politics and pathways to sustainability', *Global Environmental Change*, vol. 20, no. 3, pp. 369–377.

Leboeuf, A. (2011) *Making Sense of One Health: Cooperating at the Human–Animal–Ecosystem Health Interface*, IFRI Health and Environment Report 7, Institut Francais des Relations Internationals, Paris.

Lee, K. and Brumme, Z. L. (2013) 'Operationalizing the One Health approach: The global governance challenges', *Health Policy and Planning*, vol. 28, no. 7, pp. 778–785.

Lee, K., Buse, K. and Fustukian, S. (2003) *Health Policy in a Globalising World*, Cambridge University Press, Cambridge.

Lélé, S. and Norgaard, R. B. (2005) 'Practicing interdisciplinarity', *BioScience*, vol. 55, no. 11, pp. 967–975.

Leonard, D. (2000) *Africa's Changing Markets for Health and Veterinarian Services: The New Institutional Issues*, Macmillan Press, London.

Leonard, D., Brass, J. N., Nelson, M., Ear, S., Fahey, D., Fairfield, T., Gning, M. J., Halderman, M., McSherry, B., Moehler, D. C., Prichard, W., Turner, R., Vu, T. and Dijkman, J. (2010) 'Does patronage still drive politics for the rural poor in the developing world? A comparative perspective from the livestock sector', *Development and Change*, vol. 41, no. 3, pp. 475–494.

Leroy, E. M., Kumulungui, B., Pourrut, X., Rouquet, P., Hassanin, A., Yaba, P., Délicat, A., Paweska, J. T., Gonzalez, J.-P. and Swanepoel, R. (2005) 'Fruit bats as reservoirs of Ebola virus', *Nature*, vol. 438, no. 7068, pp. 575–576.

Leung, Z., Middleton, D. and Morrison, K. (2012) 'One Health and EcoHealth in Ontario: A qualitative study exploring how holistic and integrative approaches are shaping public health practice in Ontario', *BMC Public Health*, vol. 12, no. 358, doi: 10.1186/1471-2458-12-358.

Lewis, D. and Mosse, D. (2006) *Development Brokers and Translators: The Ethnography of Aid and Agencies*, Kumarian Press, Bloomfield.

Lewis, D., Kaweche, G. B. and Mwenya, A. (1990) 'Wildlife conservation outside protected areas: Lessons from an experiment in Zambia', *Conservation Biology*, vol. 4, no. 2, pp. 171–180.

Lindsey, P. A., Nyirenda, V. R., Barnes, J. I., Becker, M. S., McRobb, R., Tambling, C. J., Taylor, W. A., Watson, F. G. and t'Sas-Rolfes, M. (2014) 'Underperformance of African protected area networks and the case for new conservation models: Insights from Zambia', *PLoS ONE*, vol. 9, no. 5, e94109, doi: 10.1371/journal.pone.0094109.

Lloyd-Smith, J. O., Funk, S., McLean, A. R., Riley, S. and Wood, J. L. (2015) 'Nine challenges in modelling the emergence of novel pathogens', *Epidemics*, vol. 10, pp. 35–39.

Lorway, R. and Khan, S. (2014) 'Reassembling epidemiology: Mapping, monitoring and making-up people in the context of HIV prevention in India', *Social Science & Medicine*, vol. 112, pp. 51–62.

Lovemore, D. F. (1994) 'Overview of past and present tsetse distributions and control in Zimbabwe', Sacema Tsetse project reprint, Sacema, www.sacema.com/uploads/tsetse/tsetse-project/tsetse-project-reprint-1387.pdf, accessed 31 July 2015.

Luby, S. P. (2013) 'The pandemic potential of Nipah virus', *Antiviral Research*, vol. 199, no. 1, pp. 38–43.

Luby, S. P., Gurley, E. S. and Hossain, M. J. (2009) 'Transmission of human infection with Nipah virus', *Emerging Infections*, vol. 49, no. 11, pp. 1743–1748.

Maconachie, R. (2014) 'Dispossession, exploitation or employment? Youth livelihoods and extractive industry investment in Sierra Leone', *Futures*, vol. 62, pp. 75–82.

Mai, H. M., Irons, P. C., Kabir, J. and Thompson, P. N. (2012) 'A large seroprevalence survey of brucellosis in cattle herds under diverse production systems in Northern Nigeria', *BMC Veterinary Research*, vol. 8, no. 144, doi: 10.1186/1746-6148-8-144.

Majekodunmi, A. O., Fajinmi, A., Dongkum, C., Shaw, A. P. and Welburn, S. C. (2014) 'Pastoral livelihoods of the Fulani on the Jos Plateau of Nigeria', *Pastoralism*, vol. 4, no. 20, pp. 1–16, doi: 10.1186/s13570-014-0020-7.

Marcotty, T., Matthys, F., Godfroid, J., Rigouts, L., Ameni, G., Gey Van, P. N., Kazwala, R., Muma, J., Van Helden, P., Walravens, K., De Klerk, L. M., Geoghegan, C., Mbotha, D., Otte, M., Amenu, K., Abu, S. N., Botha, C., Ekron, M., Jenkins, A., Jori, F., Kriek, N., McCrindle, C., Michel, A., Morar, D., Roger, F., Thys, E. and Van Den Bossche, P. (2009) 'Zoonotic tuberculosis and brucellosis in Africa: Neglected zoonoses or minor public-health issues? The outcomes of a multi-disciplinary workshop', *Annals of Tropical Medicine and Parasitology*, vol. 103, no. 5, pp. 401–411.

Marmot, M., Friel, S., Bell, R., Houweling, T. A. and Taylor, S. (2008) 'Closing the gap in a generation: Health equity through action on the social determinants of health', *The Lancet*, vol. 372, no. 9650, pp. 1661–1669.

Maudlin, I. (2006) 'African trypanosomiasis', *Annals of Tropical Medicine and Parasitology*, vol. 100, no. 8, pp. 679–701.

Maudlin, I., Eisler, M. C. and Welburn, S. C. (2009) 'Neglected and endemic zoonoses', *Philosophical Transactions of the Royal Society B: Biological Sciences*, vol. 364, no. 1530, pp. 2777–2787.

Maudlin, I., Eisler, M. C. and Welburn, S. C. (2009) 'Neglected and endemic zoonoses', *Philosophical Transactions of the Royal Society B: Biological Sciences*, vol. 364, no. 1530, pp. 2777–2787.

Maurice, N. A., Wungak, S. Y., Gana, B. A., Nanven, M. B., Ngbede, E. O., Ibrahim, A., Aworh, M. K., Konzing, L., Hambolu, S. E. and Gugong, V. T. (2013) 'Seroprevalence of bovine brucellosis in northern Plateau State, North Central Nigeria', *Asian Pacific Journal of Tropical Disease*, vol. 3, no. 5, pp. 337–340.

Mazet, J. A., Clifford, D. L., Coppolillo, P. B., Deolalikar, A. B., Erickson, J. D. and Kazwala, R. R. (2009) 'A "one health" approach to address emerging zoonoses: the HALI project in Tanzania', *PLoS Medicine*, vol. 6, no. 12, e1000190.

McCormick, J. B., Fisher-Hoch, S. and Horvitz, L. A. (1999) *Level 4: Virus Hunters of the CDC*, Barnes and Noble, New York.

McDermott, J. J. and Arimi, S. M. (2002) 'Brucellosis in sub-Saharan Africa: Epidemiology, control and impact', *Veterinary Microbiology*, vol. 90, no. 1–4, pp. 111–134.

McGovern, M. (2012) *Unmasking the State: Making Guinea Modern*, Chicago University Press, Chicago.

McGranahan, G. and Satterthwaite, D. (2014) *Urbanisation Concepts and Trends*, IIED Working Paper, IIED, London.

McKellar, K. A., Pitzul, K. B., Juliana, Y. Y. and Cole, D. C. (2014) 'Evaluating communities of practice and knowledge networks: A systematic scoping review of evaluation frameworks', *EcoHealth*, vol. 11, no. 3, pp. 383–399.

McSherry, B., Brass, J. and Leonard, D. K. (2007) *The Political Economy of Pro-Poor Livestock Policy Reform in Kenya*, IGAD LPI Working Paper no. 03-08, Intergovernmental Authority of Development Livestock Policy Initiative, Djibouti.

Meagher, L., Lyall, C. and Nutley, S. (2008) 'Flows of knowledge, expertise and influence: A method for assessing policy and practice impacts from social science research', *Research Evaluation*, vol. 17, no. 3, pp. 163–173.

Mehta, L. (ed.) (2011) *The Limits to Scarcity*, Routledge, London.

Meltzer, M. I., Atkins, C. Y., Santibanez, S., Knust, B., Petersen, B. W., Ervin, E. D., Nichol, S. T., Damon, I. K. and Washington, M. L. (2014) 'Estimating the future number of cases in the Ebola epidemic: Liberia and Sierra Leone, 2014–2015', *Morbidity and Mortality Weekly Report*, vol. 63, no. 3, pp. 1–14.

Middleton, D., Pallister, J., Klein, R., Feng, Y. R., Haining, J., Arkinstall, R., Frazer, L., Huang, J.-A., Edwards, N., Wareing, M., Elhay, M., Hashmi, Z., Bingham, J., Yamada, M., Johnson, D., White, J., Foord, A., Heine, H. G., Marsh, G. A., Broder, C. C. and Wang, L.-F. (2014) 'Hendra virus vaccine, a One Health approach to protecting horse, human, and environmental health', *Emerging Infectious Diseases*, vol. 20, no. 3, http://dx.doi.org/10.3201/eid2003.131159.

Miller, J. M. and Griffin, P. M. (2012) 'One Health through the eyes of clinical and public health microbiology: Scientists from a variety of disciplines are needed to understand infectious diseases and prevent human infections', *Microbe*, vol. 7, no. 1, pp. 23–27.

Min, B., Allen-Scott, L. K. and Buntain, B. (2013) 'Transdisciplinary research for complex One Health issues: A scoping review of key concepts', *Preventive Veterinary Medicine*, vol. 112, no. 3, pp. 222–229.

MLD (2010) *Contingency Plan for Rift Valley Fever: Final Draft*, Ministry of Livestock Development, Nairobi.

Molyneux, D., Hallaj, Z., Keusch, G. T., McManus, D. P., Ngowi, H., Cleaveland, S., Ramos-Jimenez, P., Gotuzzo, E., Kar, K., Sanchez, A., Garba, A., Carabin, H., Bassili, A., Chaignat, C. L., Meslin, F.-Z., Abushama, H. M., Willingham, A. L. and Kioy, D. (2011) 'Zoonoses and marginalised infectious diseases of poverty: Where do we stand', *Parasites and Vectors*, vol. 4, no. 106, doi:10.1186/1756-3305-4-106.

Monath, T. P., Newhouse, V. F., Kemp, G. E., Setzer, H. W. and Cacciapuoti, A. (1974) 'Lassa virus isolation from *Mastomys natalensis* rodents during an epidemic in Sierra Leone', *Science*, vol. 185, no. 4147, pp. 263–265.

Montavon, A., Jean-Richard, V., Bechir, M., Daugla, D. M., Abdoulaye, M., Naré, R. N., Diguimbaye-Djaibé, C., Alfarouk, I. O., Schelling, E., Wyss, K., Tanner, M., and Zinsstag, J. (2013) 'Health of mobile pastoralists in the Sahel: Assessment of 15 years of research and development', *Tropical Medicine & International Health*, vol. 18, no. 9, pp. 1044–1052.

Montgomery, J. M., Hossain, M. J., Gurley, E., Carroll, D. S., Croisier, A., Bertherat, E., Asgari, N., Formenty, P., Keeler, N., Comer, J., Bell, M. R., Akram, K., Molla, A. R., Zaman, K., Islam, M. R., Wagoner, K., Mills, J. N., Rollin, P. E., Ksiazek, T. G. and Breiman, R. F. (2008) 'Risk factors for Nipah virus encephalitis in Bangladesh', *Emerging Infectious Diseases*, vol. 14, no. 10, pp. 1526–1532.

Moran, M. and Hoffman, D. (2014) 'Ebola in perspective', *Cultural Anthropology*, 7 October, www.culanth.org/fieldsights/585-ebola-in-perspective, accessed 18 July 2015.

Moses, L., Kamara, A., Gorgra, A. and Koroma, B. (2012) 'Lassa fever case study: Situation analysis', Dynamic Drivers of Disease in Africa Research Programme, STEPS Centre, Brighton.

Moses, L., Kargbo, K., Koninga, J., Adams, K., Kanneh, L., Veltus, E., Lewinski, J., Fonnie, R., Robert, W., Khan, S., Rogers, D. and Bausch, D. (manuscript in preparation) 'Predictors of natal *Mastomys* (*Mastomys natalensis*) infestation in Lassa fever-endemic villages of eastern Sierra Leone'.

Mosse, D. (2005) *Cultivating Development: An Ethnography of Aid Policy and Practice*, Pluto Press, London.

Mosse, D. (ed.) (2011) *Adventures in Aidland: The Anthropology of Professionals in International Development* (vol. 6), Berghahn Books, New York.

MSF (2015) *Pushed to the Limit and Beyond: A Year into the Largest Ever Ebola Outbreak*, www. msf.org/sites/msf.org/files/msf1yearebolareport_en_230315.pdf, accessed 18 July 2015.

Munang'andu, H. M., Siamudaala, V., Munyeme, M. and Nalubamba, K. S. (2012) 'A review of ecological factors associated with the epidemiology of wildlife trypanosomiasis in the Luangwa and Zambezi Valley ecosystems of Zambia', *Interdisciplinary Perspectives on Infectious Diseases*, 2012, http://dx.doi.org/10.1155/2012/372523, accessed 14 July 2015.

Munyua, P., Murithi, R. M., Wainwright, S., Githinji, J., Hightower, A., Mutonga, D., Macharia, J., Ithondeka, P. M., Musaa, J., Breiman, R. F., Bloland, P. and Njenga, M. K. (2010) 'Rift Valley fever outbreak in livestock in Kenya, 2006–2007', *American Journal of Tropical Medicine and Hygiene*, vol. 83, no. 2, pp. 58–64.

Murray, M., Trail, J. C. M., Davis, C. E. and Black, S. J. (1984) 'Genetic resistance to African trypanosomiasis', *Journal of Infectious Diseases*, vol. 149, no. 3, pp. 311–319.

Murray, M., Holmes, P., Wright, N., Jarrett, O., and Kennedy, P. (2014) 'History of One Health and One Medicine', *Veterinary Record*, vol. 174, no. 9, p. 227.

Mwacalimba, K. K. (2012) 'Globalised disease control and response distortion: A case study of avian influenza pandemic preparedness in Zambia', *Critical Public Health*, vol. 22, no. 4, pp. 391–405.

Mwanakasale, V. and Songolo, P. (2011) 'Disappearance of some human African trypanosomiasis transmission foci in Zambia in the absence of a tsetse fly and trypanosomiasis control program over a period of forty years', *Transactions of the Royal Society of Tropical Medicine and Hygiene*, vol. 105, no. 3, pp. 167–172.

Myers, S. S., Gaffikin, L., Golden, C. D., Ostfeld, R. S., Redford, K. H., Ricketts, T. H., Turner, W. and Osofsky, S. A. (2013) 'Human health impacts of ecosystem alteration', *Proceedings of the National Academy of Sciences*, vol. 110, no. 47, pp. 18753–18760.

Nading, A. M. (2013) 'Humans, animals, and health: From ecology to entanglement', *Environment and Society: Advances in Research*, vol. 4, no. 1, pp. 60–78.

Nading, A. M. (2014) *Mosquito Trails: Ecology, Health, and the Politics of Entanglement*, University of California Press, Berkeley, CA.

Nahapiet, J. and Ghoshal, S. (1998) 'Social capital, intellectual capital, and the organizational advantage', *Academy of Management Review*, vol. 23, no. 2, pp. 242–266.

Narrod, C., Zinsstag, J. and Tiongco, M. (2012) 'A One Health framework for estimating the economic costs of zoonotic diseases on society', *EcoHealth*, vol. 9, no. 2, pp. 150–162.

Ndeledje, N., Bouyer, J., Stachurski, F., Grimaud, P., Belem, A. M. G., Molélé Mbaïndingatoloum, F., Bengaly, Z., Oumar Alfaroukh, I., Cecchi, G. and Lancelot, R. (2013) 'Treating cattle to protect people? Impact of footbath insecticide treatment on tsetse density in Chad', *PLoS ONE*, vol. 8, no. 6, e67580, doi:10.1371/journal.pone.0067580.

Nguyen-Viet, H., Unger, F., Gilbert, J., McDermott, J., Lapar, L., Mehta-Bhatt, P., Duc Phuc, P., Xuan Sinh, D. and Grace, D. (2014) *One Health and Ecohealth in Southeast Asia: Highlights of Research by the International Livestock Research Institute and its Partners*, ILRI Research Brief 26, International Livestock Research Institute, Nairobi.

Nichter, M. (2008) *Global Health: Why Cultural Perceptions, Social Representations, and Biopolitics Matter*, University of Arizona Press, Tucson, AZ.

Nossiter, A. (2014) 'Ebola now preoccupies once-skeptical leader in Guinea', *New York Times*, www.nytimes.com/2014/12/01/world/africa/ebola-now-preoccupies-once-skeptical-leader-in-guinea.html, accessed 14 June 2015.

Nyirenda, V. R., Myburgh, W. J., Reilly, B. K., Phiri, A. I. and Chabwela, H. N. (2013) 'Wildlife crop damage valuation and conservation: Conflicting perception by local farmers in the Luangwa Valley, Eastern Zambia', *International Journal of Biodiversity and Conservation*, vol. 5, no. 11, pp. 741–750.

Odiit, M., Coleman, P. G., Liu, W. C., McDermott, J. J., Fèvre, E. M., Welburn, S. C. and Woolhouse, M. E. (2005) 'Quantifying the level of under-detection of trypanosoma brucei rhodesiense sleeping sickness cases', *Tropical Medicine and International Health*, vol. 10, no. 9, pp. 840–849.

Ogodo, O. (2007) 'The impact of Rift Valley fever in Kenya', *New Agriculturalist* March, www.new-ag.info/en/developments/devItem.php?a=35, accessed 31 July 2015.

OIE (2007) *Rift Valley Fever Control and Preventive Strategies, Regional Representations for the Middle East and Africa*, Report of Workshop, Cario, 13–15 July.

OIE (2013) 'Rift Valley Fever', in *Manual of Diagnostic Tests and Vaccines for Terrestrial Animals*, World Organisation for Animal Health, Paris.

Okello, A. L., Gibbs, E. P., Vandersmissen, A. and Welburn, S. C. (2011) 'One Health and the neglected zoonoses: Turning rhetoric into reality', *The Veterinary Record*, vol. 169, no. 11, pp. 281–285.

Okello, A. L., Bardosh, K., Smith, J. and Welburn, S. C. (2014a) 'One Health: Past successes and future challenges in three African contexts', *PLoS Neglected Tropical Diseases*, vol. 8, no. 5, e2884.

Okello, A. L., Welburn, S. and Smith, J. (2014b) 'Crossing institutional boundaries: Mapping the policy process for improved control of endemic and neglected zoonoses in sub-Saharan Africa', *Health Policy Plan*, vol. 30, no. 6, pp. 804–812.

Okello, A. L., Majekodunmi, A. O., Malala, A., Welburn, S. C. and Smith, J. (2014c) 'Identifying motivators for state–pastoralist dialogue: Exploring the relationships between livestock services, self-organisation and conflict in Nigeria's pastoralist Fulani', *Pastoralism*, vol. 4, no. 12, pp. 1–14.

Okello, A. L., Beange, I., Shaw, A., Moriyon, I., Gabriel, S., Bardosh, K., Johansen, M. V., Saarnak, C., Mukaratirwa, S., Berkvens, D. and Welburn, S. C. (2015) 'Raising the political profile of the neglected zoonotic diseases: Three complementary European commission-funded projects to streamline research, build capacity and advocate for control', *PLoS Neglected Tropical Diseases*, vol. 9, no. 3, e0003505.

Ollila, E. (2005) 'Global health priorities: Priorities of the wealthy?', *Globalization and Health*, vol. 1, no. 6, doi: 10.1186/1744-8603-1-6.

Oosterhoff, P., Wilkinson, A., and Yei-Mokuwa, E. (2015) *Policy Briefing on Community-based Ebola Care Centres*, Ebola Response Anthropology Platform, www.ebola-anthropology.net/wp-content/uploads/2015/03/Policy-briefing-ERAP-evaluation-CCC-Sierra-Leone-Oosterhoff-Wilkinson-Yei-Mokuwa.pdf, accessed 18 July 2015.

Ostfeld, R. S. (2009) 'Biodiversity loss and the rise of zoonotic pathogens', *Clinical Microbiology and Infection*, vol. 15, suppl. 1, pp. 40–43.

Oxby, C. (1984) 'Settlement schemes for herders in the subhumid tropics of West Africa:

Issues of land rights and ethnicity', *Development Policy Review*, vol. 2, no. 2, pp. 217–233.

Paige, S. B., Malavé, C., Mbabazi, E., Mayer, J. and Goldberg, T. L. (2015) 'Uncovering zoonoses awareness in an emerging disease "hotspot"', *Social Science & Medicine*, vol. 129, pp. 78–86.

Palatnik de Sousa, C. B. and Day, M. J. (2011) 'One Health: The global challenge of epidemic and endemic leishmaniasis', *Parasites & Vectors*, vol. 4, no. 1, pp. 1–10.

Pappas, G., Papadimitriou, P., Akritidis, N., Christou, L. and Tsianos, E. V. (2006) 'The new global map of human brucellosis', *Lancet Infectious Diseases*, vol. 6, no. 2, pp. 91–99.

Parker, M. and Allen, T. (2013) 'De-politicizing parasites: Reflections on attempts to control the control of neglected tropical diseases', *Medical Anthropology*, vol. 33, no. 3, pp. 223–239.

Parkes, M. W., Bienen, L., Breilh, J., Hsu, L. N., McDonald, M., Patz, J. A., Rosenthal, J. P., Sahani, M., Sleigh, A., Waltner-Toews, D. and Yassi, A. (2005) 'All hands on deck: Transdisciplinary approaches to emerging infectious disease', *EcoHealth*, vol. 2, no. 4, pp. 258–272.

Paul, M. C., Figuié, M., Kovitvadhi, A., Valeix, S., Wongnarkpet, S., Poolkhet, C., Kasemsuwane, S., Ducrotc, C., Roger, F. and Binot, A. (2015) 'Collective resistance to HPAI H5N1 surveillance in the Thai cockfighting community: Insights from a social anthropology study', *Preventive Veterinary Medicine*, vol. 120, no. 1, pp. 106–114.

Peel, A. J., Baker, K. S., Crameri, G., Barr, J. A., Hayman, D. T., Wright, E., Broder, C. C., Fernández-loras, A., Fooks, A. R. and Wang, L.-F. (2012) 'Henipavirus neutralising antibodies in an isolated island population of African fruit bats', *PloS ONE*, no. 7, e30346.

Petit, D., Sondorp, E., Mayhew, S., Roura, M. and Roberts, B. (2013) 'Implementing a basic package of health services in post-conflict Liberia: Perceptions of key stakeholders', *Social Science & Medicine*, vol. 78, pp. 42–49.

Pica-Ciamarra, U. and Otte, J. (2011) 'The "Livestock Revolution": Rhetoric and reality', *Outlook on Agriculture*, vol. 40, no. 1, pp. 7–19.

Pielke, R. A. (2007) *The Honest Broker: Making Sense of Science in Policy and Politics*, Cambridge University Press, Cambridge.

Prince, R.J. (2014) 'Situating health and the public in Africa: Historical and anthropological perspectives', in R. Marsland and J. Prince (eds) *Making and Unmaking Public Health in Africa: Ethnographic and Historical Perspectives*, Ohio University Press, Athens, GA.

Pulliam, J. R. (2008) 'Viral host jumps: Moving toward a predictive framework', *EcoHealth*, vol. 5, no. 1, pp. 80–91.

Rabinowitz, P. and Conti, L. (2013) 'Links among human health, animal health, and ecosystem health', *Annual Review of Public Health*, vol. 34, pp. 189–204.

Reagans, R. E. and Zuckerman, E. W. (2008) 'Why knowledge does not equal power: The network redundancy trade-off', *Industrial and Corporate Change*, vol. 17, pp. 903–944.

Reno, W. (1995) *Corruption and State Politics in Sierra Leone*, Cambridge University Press, Cambridge.

Reno, W. (1998) *Warlord Politics and African States*, Lynne Rienner, Boulder, CO.

Reusken, C. B., Messadi, L., Feyisa, A., Ularamu, H., Godeke, G. J., Danmarwa, A., Dawo, F., Jemli, M., Melaku, S., Shamaki, D., Woma, Y., Wungak, Y., Gebremedhin, E. Z., Zutt, I., Bosch, B.-J., Haagmans, B. L. and Koopmans, M. P. (2014) 'Geographic distribution of MERS coronavirus among dromedary camels, Africa', *Emerging Infectious Diseases*, vol. 20, no. 8, doi: 10.3201/eid2008.140590.

Rich, K. M. and Wanyoike, F. (2010) 'An assessment of the regional and national socioeconomic impacts of the 2007 Rift Valley fever outbreak in Kenya', *American Journal of Tropical Medicine and Hygiene*, vol. 83, no. 2, pp. 52–57.

Richards, P. (1996) *Fighting for the Rain Forest: War, Youth and Resources in Sierra Leone*, International African Institute, London.

Richards, P., Amara, J., Ferme, M. C., Kamara, P., Mokuwa, E., Sheriff, A. I., Suluku, R. and Voors, M. (2015) 'Social pathways for Ebola virus disease in rural Sierra Leone, and some implications for containment', *PLoS Neglected Tropical Diseases*, vol. 9, no. 4, doi: 10.1371/journal.pntd.0003567.

Richmond, J. K. and Baglole, D. J. (2003) 'Lassa fever: Epidemiology, clinical features, and social consequences', *British Medical Journal*, vol. 327, no. 7426, pp. 1271–1275.

Riesman, P. (1977) *Freedom in Fulani Social Life: An Introspective Ethnography*, University of Chicago Press, Chicago.

Rikin, E. U. (1988) 'Brucellosis of cattle in Nigeria: Proposals for a control program under intensive and extensive husbandry systems', *Acta Veterinaria Scandinavica*, vol. 84, pp. 94–97.

Roberts, C. J. and Gray, A. R. (1973) 'Studies on trypanosome resistant cattle: Part 2 the effect of trypanosomiasis on Ndama Muturu and Zebu cattle', *Tropical Animal Health and Production*, vol. 5, no. 4, pp. 220–233.

Robinson, T. P., Harris, R. S., Hopkins, J. S. and Williams, B. G. (2002) 'An example of decision support for trypanosomiasis control using a geographical information system in Eastern Zambia', *International Journal of Geographical Information Science*, vol. 16, no. 4, pp. 345–360.

Rock, M., Buntain, B. J., Hatfield, J. M. and Hallgrímsson, B. (2009) 'Animal–human connections, "one health", and the syndemic approach to prevention', *Social Science & Medicine*, vol. 68, no. 6, pp. 991–995.

Roe, E. M. (1991) 'Development narratives, or making the best of blueprint development', *World Development*, vol. 19, no. 4, pp. 287–300.

Roe, E. M. (1994) *Narrative Policy Analysis: Theory and Practice*, Duke University Press, Durham, NC.

Roe, E. and Schulman, P. (2008) *High Reliability Management*, Stanford Business, Palo Alto, CA.

Rogers, D. J. and Randolph, S. E. (1988) 'Tsetse flies in Africa: Bane or boon?', *Conservation Biology*, vol. 2, no. 1, pp. 57–65.

Rogers, D. J. and Randolph, S. E. (2002) 'A response to the aim of eradicating tsetse from Africa', *Trends in Parasitology*, vol. 18, no. 12, pp. 534–536.

Rosenberg, C. (1992) *Explaining Epidemics and Other Studies in the History of Medicine*, Cambridge University Press, Cambridge.

Rosenfield, P. L. (1992) 'The potential of transdisciplinary research for sustaining and extending linkages between the health and social sciences', *Social Science & Medicine*, vol. 35, no. 11, pp. 1343–1357.

Roth, F., Zinsstag, J., Orkhon, D., Chimed-Ochir, G., Hutton, G., Cosivi, O., Carrin, G. and Otte, J. (2003) 'Human health benefits from livestock vaccination for brucellosis: Case study', *Bulletin of the World Health Organization*, vol. 81, no. 12, pp. 867–876.

Rothstein, B. and Uslaner, E. M. (2005) 'All for all: Equality, corruption, and social trust', *World Politics*, vol. 58, pp. 41–72.

Rowe, G. and Frewer, L. J. (2000) 'Public participation methods: A framework for evaluation', *Science, Technology & Human Values*, vol. 25, no. 1, pp. 3–29.

Rubin, C., Myers, T., Stokes, W., Dunham, B., Harris, S., Lautner, B. and Annelli, J. (2013) 'Review of Institute of Medicine and National Research Council recommendations for One Health initiative', *Emerging Infectious Diseases*, vol. 19, no. 12, pp. 1913–1917.

Rushton, J., Häsler, B., de Haan, N. and Rushton, R. (2012) 'Economic benefits or drivers of a "One Health" approach: Why should anyone invest?', *Onderstepoort Journal of Veterinary Research*, vol. 79, no. 2, pp. 461.

Rutto. J. J., Osano, O., Thuranira, E. G., Kurgat, R. K. and Odenyo, V. A. O. (2013) 'Socio-economic and cultural determinants of human African trypanosomiasis at the Kenya–Uganda transboundary', *PLoS Neglected Tropical Diseases*, vol. 7, no. 4, e2186, doi: 10.1371/journal.pntd.0002186.

Rweyemamu, M., Kambarage, D., Karimuribo, E., Wambura, P., Matee, M., Kayembe, J. M., Mweene, A., Neves, L., Masumu, J., Kasanga, C., Hang'ombe, B., Kayunze, K., Misinzo, G., Simuunza, M. and Paweska, J. T. (2013) 'Development of a One Health national capacity in Africa: The Southern African Centre for Infectious Disease Surveillance (SACIDS) One Health virtual centre model', *Current Topics in Microbiology and Immunology*, vol. 336, pp. 73–94, doi: 10.1007/82_2012_244.

Ryan, S. J. and Walsh, P. D. (2011) 'Consequences of non-intervention for infectious disease in African great apes', *PLoS ONE*, vol. 6, no. 12, e29030, doi: 10.1371/journal.pone.0029030.

Saéz, A. M., Weiss, S., Nowak, K., Lapeyre, V., Zimmermann, F., Düx, A., Kühl, H. S., Kaba, M., Regnaut, S., Merkel, K., Sachse, A., Thiesen, U., Villányi, L., Boesch, C., Dabrowski, P. W., Radonić, A., Nitsche, A., Leendertz, S. A. J., Petterson, S., Becker, S., Krähling, V., Couacy-Hymann, E., Akoua-Koffi, C., Weber, N., Schaade, L., Fahr, J., Borchert, M., Gogarten, J. F., Calvignac-Spencer, S. and Leendertz, F. H. (2015) 'Investigating the zoonotic origin of the West African Ebola epidemic', *EMBO Molecular Medicine*, vol. 7, no. 1, pp. 17–23.

Safahieh, H., Sanni, S. and Zainab, A. (2012) 'International contribution to Nipah virus research 1999–2010', *Malaysian Journal of Library & Information Science*, vol. 17, no. 3, pp. 35–47.

Sawford, K., Vollman, A. R. and Stephen, C. (2012) 'A focused ethnographic study of Sri Lankan government field veterinarians' decision making about diagnostic laboratory submissions and perceptions of surveillance', *PLoS ONE*, vol. 7, no. 10, e48035, doi:10.1371/journal.pone.0048035.

Schelling, E. and Hattendorf, J. (2015) 'One Health study design', in J. Zinsstag, E. Schelling, D. Waltner-Toews, M. Whittaker and M. Tanner (eds) *One Health: The Theory and Practice of Integrated Health Approaches*, CABI International, Wallingford and Boston, MA.

Schelling, E., Wyss, K., Béchir, M., Moto, D. D. and Zinsstag, J. (2005) 'Synergy between public health and veterinary services to deliver human and animal health interventions in rural low income settings', *British Medical Journal (Clinical research ed.)*, vol. 331, no. 7527, pp. 1264–1267.

Schelling, E., Bechir, M., Ahmed, M. A., Wyss, K., Randolph, T. F. and Zinsstag, J. (2007) 'Human and animal vaccination delivery to remote nomadic families, Chad', *Emerging Infectious Diseases*, vol. 13, no. 3, pp. 373–379.

Scherr, S. J. (2000) 'A downward spiral? Research evidence on the relationship between poverty and natural resource degradation', *Food Policy*, vol. 25, no. 4, pp. 479–498.

Schmoch, U. and Schubert, T. (2008) 'Are international co-publications an indicator for quality of scientific research?', *Scientometric*, vol. 74, no. 3, pp. 361–377.

Schoepp, R. J., Rossi, C. A., Khan, S. H., Goba, A. and Fair, J. N. (2014) 'Undiagnosed acute viral febrile illnesses, Sierra Leone', *Emerging Infectious Diseases*, vol. 20, no. 7, p. 1176.

Schwind, J. S., Goldstein, T., Thomas, K., Mazet, J. A. and Smith, W. A. (2014) 'Capacity building efforts and perceptions for wildlife surveillance to detect zoonotic pathogens: Comparing stakeholder perspectives', *BMC Public Health*, vol. 14, no. 1, e684.

Scoones, I. (2009) 'Livelihoods perspectives and rural development', *The Journal of Peasant Studies*, vol. 36, no. 1, pp. 171–196.

Scoones, I. (2010) *Avian Influenza: Science, Policy and Politics*, Earthscan, London.

Scoones, I. and Wolmer, W. (2006) '*Livestock, Disease, Trade and Markets: Policy Choices for the Livestock Sector in Africa*', IDS Working Paper 269, Institute of Development Studies, Brighton.

Scott, J. C. (1990) *Domination and the Arts of Resistance: Hidden Transcripts*, Yale University Press, New Haven, CT.

Scott, J. C. (1999) *Seeing like a State: How Certain Schemes to Improve the Human Condition Have Failed*, Yale University Press, New Haven, CT.

Selby, R., Bardosh, K., Picozzi, K., Waiswa, C. and Welburn, S. C. (2013) 'Cattle movements and trypanosomes: Restocking efforts and the spread of *Trypanosoma brucei rhodesiense* sleeping sickness in post-conflict Uganda', *Parasites & Vectors*, vol. 6, no. 1, 281, doi:10.1186/1756-3305-6-281.

Sell, T. K. and Watson, M. (2013) 'Federal agency biodefense funding, FY2013–FY2014', *Biosecurity and Bioterrorism: Biodefense Strategy, Practice, and Science*, vol. 11, no. 3, pp. 196–216.

SEMG (1997) *Scientific Environmental Monitoring Group Activities October 1995–1997*, Final Report to the RTTCP (Regional Tsetse and Trypanosomiasis Control Programme) Harare, Zimbabwe.

Senior, K. (2009) 'Is the end in sight for sleeping sickness in Africa?' *Lancet Infectious Diseases*, vol. 9, no. 10, p. 595.

Shaw, A. P. M., Torr, S. J., Waiswa, C., Cecchi, G., Wint, W., Mattioli, R. C. and Robinson, T. P. (2013) 'Reply to the letter to the Editor by Bouyer *et al.* (2013)', *Preventive Veterinary Medicine*, vol. 112, no. 3–4, pp. 447–449.

Shaw, R. (2014) *Memories of the Slave Trade: Ritual and the Historical Imagination in Sierra Leone*, Chicago University Press, Chicago, IL.

Simarro, P. P., Cecchi, G., Paone, M., Franco, J. R., Diarra, A., Ruiz, J. A., Fèvre, E. M., Courtin, F., Mattioli, R. C. and Jannin, J. G. (2010) 'The atlas of human African trypanosomiasis: A contribution to global mapping of neglected tropical diseases', *International Journal of Health Geographics*, vol. 9, no. 57, doi:10.1186/1476-072X-9-57.

Simarro, P. P., Cecchi, G., Franco, J. R., Paone, M., Diarra, A., Ruiz-Postigo, J. A., Fèvre, E. M., Mattioli, R. C. and Jannin, J. G. (2012) 'Estimating and mapping the population at risk of sleeping sickness', *PLoS Neglected Tropical Diseases*, vol. 6, no. 10, e1859, doi:10.1371/journal.pntd.0001859.

Simukoko, H., Marcotty, T., Phiri, I., Geysen, D., Vercruysse, J. and van den Bossche, P. (2007) 'The comparative role of cattle, goats and pigs in the epidemiology of livestock trypanosomiasis on the plateau of Eastern Zambia', *Veterinary Parasitology*, vol. 147, no. 3–4, pp. 231–238.

Singer, M. (2015) *The Anthropology of Infectious Disease*, Left Coast Press, Walnut Creek, CA.

Singer, M. and Clair, S. (2003) 'Syndemics and public health: Reconceptualizing disease in bio-social context', *Medical Anthropology Quarterly*, vol. 17, no. 4, pp. 423–441.

Smith, J., Sones, K., Grace, D., MacMillan, S., Tarawali, S. and Herrero, M. (2013) 'Beyond milk, meat, and eggs: Role of livestock in food and nutrition security', *Animal Frontiers*, vol. 3, no. 1, pp. 6–13.

Smith, J., Taylor, E. M. and Kingsley, P. (2015) 'One World–One Health and neglected zoonotic disease: Elimination, emergence and emergency in Uganda', *Social Science & Medicine*, vol. 129, pp. 12–19.

Sogoba, N., Feldmann, H. and Safronetz, D. (2012) 'Lassa fever in West Africa: Evidence for an expanded region of endemicity', *Zoonoses and Public Health*, vol. 59, pp. 43–47.

Sripa, B., Tangkawattana, S., Laha, T., Kaewkes, S., Mallory, F. F., Smith, J. F. and Wilcox,

B. A. (2015) 'Toward integrated opisthorchiasis control in northeast Thailand: The Lawa project', *Acta Tropica*, vol. 141, pp. 361–367.

Ssenyonga, J. W., Mohamed-Ahmed, M. M. and Kiros, F. G. (1996) 'The development and validation of a model for community-managed tsetse trapping technology in Lambwe Valley, Kenya', Research Methodology Paper, no. 20, Social Sciences Department ICIPE, Nairobi.

Staples, A. (2006) *The Birth of Development: How the World Bank, Food and Agriculture Organization and the World Health Organization Changed the World, 1945–1965*, Kent State University Press, Kent, OH.

Stenning, D. J. (1957) 'Transhumance, migratory drift, migration: Patterns of pastoral Fulani nomadism', *Journal of the Royal Anthropological Institute of Great Britain and Ireland*, vol. 87, no. 1, pp. 57–73.

Stephen, C. and Daibes, I. (2010) 'Defining features of the practice of global health research: An examination of 14 global health research teams', *Global Health Action*, vol. 9, no. 3, doi: 10.3402/gha.v3i0.5188.

Stirling, A. C. and Scoones, I. (2009) 'From risk assessment to knowledge mapping: Science, precaution, and participation in disease ecology', *Ecology and Society*, vol. 14, no. 2, art. 14.

Swallow, B. M., Mulatu, W. and Leak, S. G. A. (1995) 'Potential demand for a mixed public–private animal health input: Evaluation of a pour-on insecticide for controlling tsetse-transmitted trypanosomiasis in Ethiopia', *Preventive Veterinary Medicine*, vol. 24, no. 4, pp. 265–275.

Swynnerton, C. F. M. (1933) 'Some traps for tsetse-flies', *Bulletin of Entomological Research*, vol. 24, no. 1, pp. 69–102.

Takahashi, S., Metcalf, C. J. E., Ferrari, M. J., Moss, W. J., Truelove, S. A., Tatem, A. J., Grenfell, B. T. and Lessler, J. (2015) 'Reduced vaccination and the risk of measles and other childhood infections post-Ebola', *Science*, vol. 347, no. 6227, pp. 1240–1242.

Thomas, C. D., Cameron, A., Green, R. E., Bakkenes, M., Beaumont, L. J., Collingham, Y. C., Erasmus, B. F. N., de Siqueira, M. F., Grainger, A., Hannah, L., Hughes, L., Huntley, B., van Jaarsveld, A. S., Midgley, G. F., Miles, L., Ortega-Huerta, M. A., Townsend Peterson, A., Phillips, O. L. and Williams, S. E. (2004) 'Extinction risk from climate change', *Nature*, vol. 427, no. 6970, pp. 145–148.

Thomas, M. R., Smith, G., Ferreira, F. H. G., Evans, D., Maliszewska, M., Cruz, M., Himelein, K. and Over, M. (2015) *The Economic Impact of Ebola on Sub-Saharan Africa: Updated Estimates for 2015*, World Bank, Washington, DC.

Thompson, R. C. (2013) 'Parasite zoonoses and wildlife: One Health, spillover and human activity', *International Journal for Parasitology*, vol. 43, no. 12, pp. 1079–1088.

Tilley, H. (2011) *Africa as a Living Laboratory: Empire, Development, and the Problem of Scientific Knowledge, 1870–1950*, University of Chicago Press, Chicago.

Tomley, F. M. and Shirley, M. W. (2009) 'Livestock infectious diseases and zoonoses', *Philosophical Transactions of the Royal Society of London B: Biological Sciences*, vol. 364, no. 1530, pp. 2637–2642.

Torr, S. J., Maudlin, I. and Vale, G. A. (2007) 'Less is more: Restricted application of insecticide to cattle to improve the cost and efficacy of tsetse control', *Medical and Veterinary Entomology*, vol. 21, no. 1, pp. 53–64.

Torr, S. J., Mangwiro, T. N. C. and Hall, D. R. (2011) 'Shoo fly, don't bother me! Efficacy of traditional methods of protecting cattle from tsetse', *Medical and Veterinary Entomology*, vol. 25, no. 2, pp. 192–201.

Travis, D., Chapman, D., Craft, M., Deen, J., Farnham, M. W., Garcia, C., Hueston, W. D., Kock, R., Mahero, M., Mugisha, L., Nzietchueng, S., Nutter, F. B., Olson, D.,

Pekol, A., Pelican, K. M., Robertson, C. and Rwego, I. B. (2014) 'One Health: Lessons learnt from East Africa', in R. Atlas and S. Maloy (ed.) *One Health: People, Animals, and the Environment*, ASM Press, Washington, DC.

Vail, L. (1977) 'Ecology and history: Example of Eastern Zambia', *Journal of Southern African Studies*, vol. 3, no. 2, pp. 129–155.

Vale, G. A. (1974) 'Responses of tsetse flies (Diptera, Glossinidae) to mobile and stationary baits', *Bulletin of Entomological Research*, vol. 64, no. 4, pp. 545–588.

Vale, G. A. and Torr, S. J. (2005) 'User-friendly models of the costs and efficacy of tsetse control: Application to sterilizing and insecticidal techniques', *Medical and Veterinary Entomology*, vol. 19, no. 3, pp. 293–305.

Vale, G. A., Lovemore, D. F., Flint, S. and Cockbill, G. F. (1988) 'Odour-baited targets to control tsetse flies, *Glossina* spp. (Diptera, Glossinidae), in Zimbabwe', *Bulletin of Entomological Research*, vol. 78, no. 1, pp. 31–49.

van den Bossche, P. (2001) 'Some general aspects of the distribution and epidemiology of bovine trypanosomosis in southern Africa', *International Journal for Parasitology*, vol. 31, no. 5–6, pp. 592–598.

van den Bossche, P., de la Rocque, S., Hendrickx, G. and Bouyer, J. (2010) 'A changing environment and the epidemiology of tsetse-transmitted livestock trypanosomiasis', *Trends in Parasitology*, vol. 26, no. 5, pp. 236–243.

van Gool, F. and Mattioli, R. (2010) 'Quality and good veterinary practices of trypanocidal drugs: Key factors for a sustainable and profitable livestock production in sub-Sahara Africa', *Journal of the Commonwealth Veterinary Association*, vol. 26, no. 1, pp. 18–22.

Vandersmissen, A. and Welburn, S. C. (2014) 'Current initiatives in One Health: Consolidating the One Health Global Network', *Revue Scientifique et Technique (International Office of Epizootics)*, vol. 33, no. 2, pp. 421–432.

Vinetz, J. M., Wilcox, B. A., Aguirre, A., Gollin, L. X., Katz, A. R., Fujioka, R. S., Maly, K., Horwitz, P. and Chang, H. (2005) 'Beyond disciplinary boundaries: Leptospirosis as a model of incorporating transdisciplinary approaches to understand infectious disease emergence', *EcoHealth*, vol. 2, no. 4, pp. 291–306.

Vogel, K. M. (2008) 'Biodefense: Considering the sociotechnical dimension' in A. Lakoff and S. Collier (eds) *Biosecurity Interventions: Global Health and Security in Question*, Columbia University Press, New York.

von Kaufmann, R. (1986) 'The expected impact and future of the ILCA Subhumid Zone Programme', in R. V. Kaufmann, S. Chater and R. Blench (eds) *Livestock Systems Research in Nigeria's Subhumid Zone: Proceedings of the Second ILCA/NAPRI Symposium*, Kaduna, Nigeria, 29 October–2 November, ILCA, Addis Ababa.

Vrbova, L., Stephen, C., Kasman, N., Boehnke, R., Doyle-Waters, M., Chablitt-Clark, A., Gibson, B., FitzGerald, M. and Patrick, D. M. (2010) 'Systematic review of surveillance systems for emerging zoonoses: Review of emerging zoonoses surveillance', *Transboundary and Emerging Diseases*, vol. 57, pp. 154–161.

Vreysen, M. J. B. (2001) 'Principles of area-wide integrated tsetse fly control using the sterile insect technique', *Médicine Tropicale*, vol. 61, no. 4–5, pp. 397–411.

Vreysen, M. J. B., Saleh, K. M., Ali, M. Y., Abdulla, A. M., Zhu, Z. R., Juma, K. G., Dyck, V. A., Msangi, A. R., Mkonyi, P. A. and Feldmann, H. U. (2000) '*Glossina austeni* (Diptera: Glossinidae) eradicated on the island of Unguja, Zanzibar, using the sterile insect technique', *Journal of Economic Entomology*, vol. 93, no. 1, pp. 123–135.

Wagner, C. S. and Leydesdorff, L. (2005) 'Network structure, self-organization, and the growth of international collaboration in science', *Research Policy*, vol. 34, no. 10, pp. 1608–1618.

Wald, P. (2008) *Contagious: Cultures, Carriers, and the Outbreak Narrative*, Duke University Press, Durham, NC.

Wallace, R. G., Bergmann, L., Kock, R., Gilbert, M., Hogerwerf, L., Wallace, R. and Holmberg, M. (2015) 'The dawn of Structural One Health: A new science tracking disease emergence along circuits of capital', *Social Science & Medicine*, vol. 129, pp. 68–77.

Waller, R. and Homewood, K. (1997) 'Elders and experts: Contesting veterinary knowledge in a pastoral community', in A. Cunningham and B. Andrews (eds) *Western Medicine as Contested Knowledge*, Manchester University Press, Manchester.

Waltner-Toews, D. (2001) 'An ecosystem approach to health and its applications to tropical and emerging diseases', *Cadernos de Saúde Pública*, vol. 17, pp. 7–36.

Welburn S. C. and Coleman, P. (2015) 'Human and animal african trypanosomiasis', in J. Zinsstag, E. Schelling, D. Waltner-Toews, M. Whittaker and M. Tanner (eds) *One Health: The Theory and Practice of Integrated Health Approaches*, CABI International, Wallingford and Boston, MA.

Welburn, S. C. and Maudlin, I. (2012) 'Priorities for the elimination of sleeping sickness', *Advances in Parasitology*, vol. 79, pp. 299–337.

Wendland, C. L. (2012) 'Moral maps and medical imaginaries: Clinical tourism at Malawi's College of Medicine', *American Anthropologist*, vol. 114, no. 1, pp. 108–122.

Wenger, E. (2000) 'Communities of practice and social learning systems', *Organization*, vol. 7, pp. 225–246.

Whiteford, L. M. and Manderson, L. (2000) *Global Health Policy, Local Realities: The Fallacy of the Level Playing Field*, Lynne Rienner Publishers, London.

Whitmee, S., Haines, A., Beyrer, C., Boltz, F., Capon, A., Dias, B., Ezeh, A., Frumkin, H., Gong, P., Head, P., Horton, R., Mace, G. M., Marten, R., Myers, S. S., Nishtar, S., Osofsky, S. A., Pattanayak, S. K., Pongsiri, M. J., Romanelli, C., Soucat, A., Vega, J. and Yach, D. (2015) 'Safeguarding human health in the Anthropocene epoch: Report of The Rockefeller Foundation–*Lancet* Commission on planetary health', *The Lancet*, www.thelancet.com/commissions/planetary-health, accessed 27 July 2015.

Whitty, C., Farrar, J., Ferguson, N., Edmunds, W. J., Piot, P., Leach, M. and Davies, S. (2014) 'Infectious disease: Tough choices to reduce Ebola transmission', *Nature*, vol. 515, no. 7526, pp. 92–194.

WHO (2005a) 'Update on Lassa fever in West Africa', *World Health Organisation, Weekly Epidemiological Record*, vol. 10, pp. 85–92.

WHO (2005b) *International Health Regulations (2005)*, 2nd edition, World Health Organization, Geneva.

WHO (2007) *Outbreaks of Rift Valley Fever in Kenya, Somalia and United Republic of Tanzania*, World Health Organization, Geneva.

WHO (2008) *Integrated Control of Neglected Zoonotic Diseases in Africa: Applying the 'One Health' Concept*, Report of a joint WHO/EU/ILRI/DBL/FAO/OIE/AU meeting, Nairobi, 13–15 November 2007, http://whqlibdoc.who.int/hq/2008/WHO_HTM_NTD_NZD_2008.1_eng.pdf, accessed 8 July 2015.

WHO (2009) *Rift Valley Fever Outbreaks Forecasting Models*, a Joint FAO–WHO experts' consultation, document: WHO/HSE/GAR/BDP/2009.2, World Health Organization, Geneva, http://whqlibdoc.who.int/hq/2009/WHO_HSE_GAR_BDP_2009.2_eng.pdf?ua=1, accessed 11 July 2015.

WHO (2010) *The Control of Neglected Zoonotic Diseases: Community Based Interventions for NZDs Prevention and Control*, report of the Third Conference organized with ICONZ, DFID-RiU, SOS, EU,TDR and FAO with the participation of ILRI and OIE, http://whqlibdoc.who.int/publications/2011/9789241502528_eng.pdf, accessed 11 July 2015.

WHO (2015a) *Ebola Interim Assessment Panel: Report by the Secretariat*, World Health Organization, Geneva, http://apps.who.int/gb/ebwha/pdf_files/WHA68/A68_25-en.pdf, accessed 18 July 2015.

WHO (2015b) 'Benin: WHO's medical detectives work with national health authorities to solve a mystery', www.who.int/features/2015/benin-lassa-fever/en, accessed 10 July 2015.

Wickson, F., Carew, A. L. and Russell, A. W. (2006) 'Transdisciplinary research: Characteristics, quandaries and quality', *Futures*, vol. 38, no. 9, pp. 1046–1059.

Wilcox, B. A. and Colwell, R. R. (2005) 'Emerging and reemerging infectious diseases: Biocomplexity as an interdisciplinary paradigm', *EcoHealth*, vol. 2, no. 4, pp. 244–257.

Wilkinson, A. (2013) *The Process and Practice of Diagnosis: Innovations in Diagnostics for Lassa fever in Sierra Leone*, University of Sussex, Brighton.

Wilkinson, A. and Leach, M. (2015) 'Briefing: Ebola – myths, realities, and structural violence', *African Affairs*, vol. 114, no. 454, pp. 136–148.

Wilkinson, R. and Pickett, K. (2009) *The Spirit Level: Why Equality is Better for Everyone*, Penguin, London.

Winer, J. N., Nakagawa, K., Conrad, P. A., Brown, L. and Wilkes, M. (2015) 'Evaluation of medical and veterinary students' attitudes toward a One Health interprofessional curricular exercise', *Journal of Interprofessional Care*, vol. 29, no. 1, pp. 49–54.

Wolfe, N. (2005) 'Bushmeat hunting, deforestation, and prediction of zoonotic disease emergence', *Emerging Infectious Diseases*, vol. 11, pp. 1822–1827.

Wolfe, N. (2011) *The Viral Storm: The Dawn of a New Pandemic Age*, Macmillan Press, London.

Wolfe, N., Daszak, P., Kilpatrick, A. M. and Burke, D. S. (2005) 'Bushmeat hunting, deforestation, and prediction of zoonotic disease', *Emerging Infectious Diseases*, vol. 11, no. 12, pp. 1822–1827.

Wood, J. L., Leach, M., Waldman, L., MacGregor, H., Fooks, A. R., Jones, K. E., Restif, O., Dechmann, D., Hayman, D. T., Baker, K. S., Peel, A. J., Kamins, A. O., Fahr, J., Ntiamoa-Baidu, Y., Suu-Ire, R., Breiman, R. F., Epstein, J. H., Field, H. E. and Cunningham, A. A. (2012) 'A framework for the study of zoonotic disease emergence and its drivers: Spillover of bat pathogens as a case study', *Philosophical Transactions of the Royal Society B: Biological Sciences*, vol. 367, no. 1604, pp. 2881–2892.

Woods, A. and Bresalier, M. (2014) 'One Health, many histories', *Veterinary Record*, vol. 174, no. 26, pp. 650–654.

Woolhouse, M. E. J. and Gowtage-Sequeria, S. (2005) 'Host range and emerging and reemerging pathogens', *Emerging Infectious Diseases*, vol. 11, pp. 1842–1847.

World Bank (2010) *People, Pathogens and Our Planet Volume 1: Towards a One Health Approach for Controlling Zoonotic Diseases*, World Bank, Washington, DC.

World Bank (2012) *People, Pathogens and Our Planet: The Economics of One Health*, World Bank, Washington, DC, https://openknowledge.worldbank.org/handle/10986/11892, accessed 27 July 2015.

Yang, G. J., Utzinger, J., Lv, S., Qian, Y. J., Li, S. Z., Wang, Q., Bergquist, R., Vounatsou, P., Li, W., Yang, K. and Zhou, X. N. (2010) 'The Regional Network for Asian Schistosomiasis and Other Helminth Zoonoses (RNAS+): Target diseases in face of climate change', *Advances in Parasitology*, vol. 73, pp. 101–113.

Zinsstag, J. (2012) 'Convergence of ecohealth and one health', *EcoHealth*, vol. 9, no. 4, pp. 371–373.

Zinsstag, J., Schelling, E., Wyss, K. and Mahamat, M. B. (2006) 'Potential of cooperation between human and animal health to strengthen health systems', *The Lancet*, vol. 366, no. 9503, pp. 2142–2145.

Zinsstag, J., Schelling, E., Roth, F., Bonfoh, B., de Savigny, D. and Tanner, M. (2007) 'Human benefits of animal interventions for zoonosis control', *Emerging Infectious Diseases*, vol. 13, no. 4, pp. 527–531.

Zinsstag, J., Mackenzie, J. S., Jeggo, M., Heymann, D. L., Patz, J. A. and Daszak, P. (2012) 'Mainstreaming One Health', *EcoHealth*, vol. 9, no. 2, pp. 107–110.

Zinsstag, J., Schelling, E., Waltner-Toews, D., Whittaker, M. and Tanner, M. (eds) (2015a) *One Health: The Theory and Practice of Integrated Health Approaches*, CABI International, Wallingford and Boston, MA.

Zinsstag, J., Fuhrimann, S., Hattendorf, J. and Chitnis, N. (2015b) 'Animal–human transmission models', in J. Zinsstag, E. Schelling, D. Waltner-Toews, M. Whittaker and M. Tanner (eds) *One Health: The Theory and Practice of Integrated Health Approaches*, CABI International, Wallingford and Boston, MA.

INDEX